The Poems of
John Keats

The Poems of
John Keats

❊

Introduction, Glossary and Notes by
PAUL WRIGHT

Wordsworth Poetry Library

This edition published 1994 by Wordsworth Editions Limited
8b East Street, Ware, Hertfordshire SG12 9HJ
Additional material incorporated 2001

Text copyright © Wordsworth Editions Limited 1994
Introduction, Glossary and Notes copyright © Paul Wright 2001

ISBN 1 85326 404 0

2 4 6 8 10 9 7 5 3 1

Typeset by Antony Gray
Printed and bound in Great Britain
by Mackays of Chatham plc, Chatham. Kent

INTRODUCTION

In March 1819, just when he was entering his most productive period, a then little known poet wrote to his brother: '[T]he fire is at its last click – I am sitting with my back to it with one foot askew upon the rug and the other with the heel a little elevated from the carpet . . . These are trifles – but . . . [c]ould I see the same thing done of any great Man long since dead it would be a great delight: as to know [in] what position Shakespeare sat when he began "To be or not to be" – such thing[s] become interesting from the distance of time and place.'[1] The statement is interesting in itself for its characteristic eye for the apparent 'trifles' of life, its sense of, and concern with, the literary past, and, not least, its faulty grammar. The writer was, of course, John Keats. He, too, is now 'long since dead'; and many of his most famous lines, from his poems and his letters, have achieved a near proverbial familiarity on a par with Hamlet's remark. From our own 'distance of time and place' it is tempting to label him as simply another dead poet, a 'great Man'. Despite his own doubt, which itself formed the subject matter of much of his poetry, this he is. Yet, it is important to remember that this greatness must not, and cannot, be separated from the apparent 'trifles' of a life. Indeed, the 'delight', if any, we take in the poems should derive as much from a sense of Keats 'with one foot askew upon the rug', grounded in what he elsewhere calls 'circumstances' not that dissimilar to our own, as it does from any view of him as a 'great Man'.

Paradoxically, from the first, the claims made for Keats's greatness as a poet depended on an overestimation of what one of his earliest champions, the liberal journalist and poet Leigh Hunt, called an 'origin . . . of the

---

1 *Letters*, 2:73. For full details of this and all other references turn to the Bibliography at the end of this Introduction. Keats's letters will be cited by volume and page number; critical and other material will be given by surname, if necessary date and volume, and page number, in parenthesis after the quotation.

humblest description' (see Gittings, p. 17). As a Romantic poet, writing in the shadow of Rousseau and Wordsworth and an apparent prioritising of the simple over the sophisticated, it is interesting to note that both his supporters and detractors, whilst he was alive and later, sought to turn him into something of a 'noble savage'. The truth of his origins and his life, in so far as it can be reclaimed, is rather different.

Keats was born on 31 October 1795 in London. He came from a comfortable trade background, what once might have been called the lower middle classes, a growing group in Regency England: his father, Thomas, was, before his death from a riding accident in 1804 which did reduce the family circumstances, manager of a livery stables; and his mother, Frances, whose own death from the 'family disease' tuberculosis, or consumption, in 1810 greatly influenced the young Keats who nursed her, came from the relatively prosperous Jennings family. On her remarriage she was involved in complex legal wrangles over the family fortune worthy of a Dickens novel. At a time when it was possible to live well off under £200 a year, Keats's grandmother settled about £9,000 on Keats and his two brothers and sister. Although it would have enabled him to indulge in the life of a poet, which he would later crave, Keats saw little of this money, and its true extent did not become clear until after his death. However, whatever his privations after 1804, Keats's background was in no sense one of absolute poverty.

Given his origins, it is not surprising that Keats and his brother George were sent to Enfield Academy, run by John Clarke, between 1803 and 1811. What is surprising is the extent to which he was held to be 'uneducated' by hostile reviewers during his lifetime, or to suffer from 'educational deficits' by more recent critics (Levinson, p. 7). This view is derived from an odd mix of the Romantic concern with 'natural' genius, which was inherited by the Victorians who did so much to create the 'myth of John Keats', and the Regency literary establishment's distrust of middle-class cultural aspirations. Whilst he was denied the university education of Shelley, say, and whilst it is important to remember a young Keats, always conscious of his diminutive stature, who was fond of cricket and fighting, such a view is simply misleading. Something of the depth of Keats's learning can be gleaned from the recollections of Charles Cowden Clarke, John Clarke's son and Keats's friend. He recalls:

> such was Keats's indefatigable energy for the last two or three successive half-years . . . that upon each occasion he took first prize by a considerable distance. He was at work before the first school hour began, and that was at seven . . . at his Latin or French translation . . .   [Clarke, p. 122]

Although often attacked for his lack of Greek, the mark of the truly educated at the turn of the nineteenth century, and for daring to rework the material of classical culture, Keats began his life-long interest in classical mythology under the guidance of the Clarkes, reading, most notably Lemprière's *Classical Dictionary*. Yet, more than actual work, or the vast amount of material that he read in the school library, including Spenser and probably Milton, as well as popular novels, histories and scientific works, it is perhaps to the Enfield Academy that Keats owes a great deal of the state of mind or attitude which explains so much of his poetry: Nicholas Roe characterises this as 'imaginative' yet 'practical', identifying in particular its bias towards observation and experimentation, and as 'reformist and republican' (Roe, 1997, pp. 28, 34–5). Indeed, it might be argued that his very recourse to the stuff of mythology, which is so evident and has been seen as a weakness, particularly in the early poetry, is itself part of a broader attempt to (mis)represent classical Greece as an ideal society in contrast to the oppressive regime of the British government around the time of the Napoleonic Wars, which also provide a backdrop to nearly all of Keats's poetic output (Butler, pp. 130–7).

Many of Keats's earliest poems might be said to share the liberal, reformist viewpoint of the Clarkes and others: 'On Peace', 'To Hope', 'To Kosciusko' (a Polish freedom fighter), 'Written on the Day that Mr Leigh Hunt left Prison' (marking Hunt's release after a two-year prison sentence for libelling the Prince Regent in his journal *The Examiner*, which Keats first got to know through the Clarkes and in which his first published poem, 'O Solitude', appeared in 1816), *Sleep and Poetry*, the very versification of which has been seen as a kind of political act (see Keach), and what one contemporary review called 'a jacobinical apostrophe' (Redpath, p. 68), suggesting a link to the French revolutionaries, or Jacobins, at the start of Book 3 of Keats's epic romance *Endymion*. Here, echoing the language to be found in Hunt's journalism, the poet berates those 'who lord it o'er their fellow-men/ With most prevailing tinsel . . . they still are dight/ By the blear-eyed nations in empurpled vests,/ And crowns and turbans' (*Endymion*, III, 1–12). This is all the more remarkable because the poem as a whole is often seen as representative of a Keatsian otherworldliness and disregard for political reality, or indeed any kind of reality.

Such views still persist due in no small part to the lack of interest, until very recently, in the next phase of Keats's life. On leaving school Keats began a five-year apothecary's apprenticeship; the exam which he passed in July 1816 would have enabled him to practice as something akin to a family doctor to the lower classes. The choice of profession was in part a sound career move for someone of Keats's background, and it might also be understood in terms of his experiences of nursing his dying mother, coupled with an earnest 'idea of doing some good for the world' (*Letters*, 2:271). He was, at least at the start, a good student, and his commitment to his career was such that in 1816 he began to study further to qualify as a surgeon. However, from the days of his apprenticeship, his career vied with poetry for his attention: he took to imitating the dress of Lord Byron, and to writing poetry during lectures!

The legacy of his professional training, and he never entirely abandoned thoughts of a medical career (*Letters*, 1:277; 2:70,114,121,125,298), can clearly be seen in his poems (in his use of imagery derived from contemporary medical theories and practice, for example in the odes 'On a Grecian Urn' and 'To Psyche'), and in the figure of Apollo, who, as Geoffrey Hartman remarks, 'haunts Keats early and late' (Hartman, p. 145), he found a god who was both doctor and poet, and through whom he could explore the idea of poetry as alternative therapy, as something which might, in some sense, be able 'to cure/ The languid sick' ('I stood tiptoe', ll. 222–3; see also *The Fall of Hyperion*, I, ll. 189–90). Beyond localised details and recurring motifs, however, the life of a medical student at the turn of the nineteenth century does much to qualify the view of Keats as a largely naïve figure who existed, for better or worse, in the world of the imagination. His surgical training involved not only lectures, but walking the wards and observing often crude operations amongst a crowd of rowdy students (some would even gamble and cook breakfast in the corner of the operating theatre), in the days before antiseptics and anaesthetics, and working under the incompetent surgeon William 'Mad Billy' Lucas. And, he would have found in the medical debates of the day a continuation of many of the ideas he encountered at the Enfield Academy. As G. S Rousseau suggests:

> It is probably true that the etiology of European Romanticism is located as much in the medical researches of the eighteenth century as in the disturbances of the sacred and the profane in the increasingly industrialised society.   [Rousseau, p. 130]

Thus, from his lecturers and his reading, Keats would have learned, amongst other things, to question the existence of God and the Soul, to trust knowledge gained only from experience and to believe that human bodies were simply material objects which underwent continual change. Many of these views resurface later in Keats's letters; and the medical context does much to ground them as more than the timeless statements of a great poet. As a good experimentalist he could believe that 'axioms . . . are not axioms until they are proved upon our pulses' (*Letters*, 1:279); and his famous views on the identity of the poet might be said to owe as much to his training, where he learnt '[o]ur bodies every seven years are completely fresh materialed' (*Letters*, 2:208), as they do to any personality traits. This is exemplified in the often quoted letter to his friend Woodhouse written in October 1818 –

> As to the poetical Character itself . . . it has no self . . . A Poet is the most unpoetical of anything in existence; because he has no Identity – he is continually inform[ing] – and filling some other body. [*Letters*, 1:386–7]

– and more generally in seeing Keats as the poet of what he called in another letter 'Negative Capability' (*Letters*, 1:193), which might be glossed as the ability to lose one's identity in something other than oneself.[2] Yet, if he had this ability, it led as much to anxiety as it did to a sense of transcendence. Prefiguring a more ambiguous sense of the fluidity of the self found in the twentieth century in, say, Ray Bradbury's *The Martian Chronicles*, but none the less current in the medical theory of Keats's day, the 'Poetical Character' letter continues:

> When I am in a room with People . . . the identity of everyone . . . begins to press upon me [so] that I am in a very little time annihilated.
>
> [*Letters*, 1:387]

It is arguably this tension between these two ways of understanding selflessness, as either self-transcendence or self-annihilation, which concerns much of Keats's poetry; many of the poems which might be seen as escapist romance fantasies, and are undeniably at one level a kind of Keatsian celebration, or perhaps a critique, of the erotic and the sensual (*Endymion*, *The Eve of St Agnes*, *Lamia*), are equally concerned with the vexed issue of the self and self-transcendence.

The precise impact of Keats's medical training, like so much about the details of a life, cannot be determined. However, his friend George Felton Mathew, to whom Keats addressed a poem, certainly saw him as part of some kind of youth- or class-based Regency movement. He saw him as:

> . . . of the sceptical and republican school. An advocate for the innovations which were making progress in his time. A fault finder with everything established.   [Rollins, 2, pp. 185–6]

---

2 A useful summary of the literature on 'Negative Capability' is provided in the note in *Letters*.

It was Keats the 'fault finder' who chose not to sit his surgical examinations in February 1817 in order to see through the press his first collection of poems, called *Poems*, which was published in March. Many of these were written whilst Keats was training to be a doctor, and they have often been seen, in their indulgence in classical mythology, erotic fantasy and a kind of technicolour natural world, as a naïve if necessary escape from Keats's daily experiences. They have also been seen as 'an ill-judged publication' (Barnard, p. 18), and we do well to remember that they are the work of a poet in his early twenties. However, this is true of all of Keats's writing, and having sketched some of his experiences to this point it is hard to accept the view of Keats which seeks to divide the poems up into early, middle and late, since there is only a gap of two years between this collection and his mature work. Whilst there clearly is development, there is also continuity and a degree of sophistication evident in these early pieces which form a continuum with, say, the great Odes.

This is seen clearly in what might otherwise be dismissed as something of a 'trifle', the opening dedication 'To Leigh Hunt Esq.'. The sonnet marks at one level Keats's sense of gratitude to Leigh Hunt, in whose circle, which included Wordsworth, Shelley and Hazlitt, Keats moved from 1816. Indeed, it was an association which enabled the literary establishment to label Keats as a member of Hunt's parvenu 'Cockney School' of poets, and which has coloured the appreciation of Keats ever since. However, more than this, it might be said to act as a key to the entire collection, if not to Keats's poetry as a whole, and to suggest that the poetry grows out of Keats's already significant intellectual experience, rather than simply being an escape from what he calls 'the agonies, the strife/ Of human hearts' (*Sleep and Poetry*, ll. 124–5), many of which he had already experienced by 1817. The sonnet opens with a characteristically Romantic note of regret as to the nature of the modern world:

> Glory and loveliness have pass'd away;
>> For if we wander out in early morn,
>> No wreathed incense do we see upborne
>
>> . . .
>
> No crowd of nymphs soft voic'd and young, and gay . . .
>
> [*Dedication*, ll. 1–5]

Rehearsing the idea of a naïve poet, Leigh Hunt said of Keats 'he never beheld an oak tree without seeing a Dryad' (Hunt, p. 283), a classical tree–spirit. However, he must have been a poor reader of dedicatory poems since what the poem tells us is that it is unable to make such an identification: 'we see . . . No crowd of Nymphs'! And it is this inability to access the mythic or the transcendent in any straightforward way which constitutes so much of Keats's poetry, from Apollo's fleeing chariot in *Sleep and Poetry* (l. 155) and Endymion's pursuit of his hard-to-pin-down goddess, through Lycius' ambiguous relationship with Lamia to the poet's hope that he might catch a glimpse of Ceres in 'To Autumn'.

Yet Keats is not claiming that the gods have no uses, or that they cannot be reclaimed in some way. The dedication continues:

> But there are left delights as high as these,
>   And I shall ever bless my destiny,
> That in a time, when under peasant trees
>   Pan is no longer sought, I feel a free,
> A leafy luxury, seeing I could please
>   With these poor offerings, a man like thee.
>
> [*Dedication*, ll. 9–14]

Martin Aske finds in this kind of sentiment what he calls 'a language of consolation' (Aske, p. 49) typical of Keats (see, for example, 'Ode on a Grecian Urn'). But, the consolation is of a particular kind, which is rather more complex than a simple desire to escape into the world of mythology: 'Pan is no longer sought' because that world, and perhaps the revolutionary ideal represented by fanciful reinventions of the cult of Pan, are no longer accessible; but in its place are 'poor offerings', the poems themselves.

Poetry is, then, a consolation of a kind. It is tempting to see in the phrase 'leafy luxury' both an indulgence in sensual experience which marks so much of Keats's poetry, and, for a poet who enjoyed puns, a play on the pages of a book. Already, in 1817, Keats is suggesting that the consolation of literature, as of art as a whole, might be scant compensation for what has been lost: but it is all there is. In this respect many of the poems of the 1817 volume share two traits, which anticipate the later poetry. First they are positioned within a protective and protected, but limited, space: 'the 'bowery green' of 'I stood tiptoe' (l. 84); the 'bowery shore' of 'Calidore' (l. 26); the 'flowery spot, sequester'd, wild, romantic' of 'To George Felton Mathew' (l. 37); the 'bowery nook' of *Sleep and Poetry* (l. 63). Each of these 'bowers' is a transposed environment, not a naïve celebration. Each is bounded and sustained, perhaps, by a book, a poem or even a single line. As the poet declares in 'I stood tiptoe', nature as consolation for the loss of belief systems, or simply as an antidote to harsh personal or political realities, is only a consolation to the extent that it has already entered the protective space of a poem:

> In the calm grandeur of a sober line,
> We see the waving of the mountain pine;
> And when a tale is beautifully staid,
> We feel the safety of a hawthorn glade . . .
>
> ['I stood tiptoe', ll. 127–30]

This observation leads to the second common feature. As Jackson Bate notes, many of Keats's poems are '[p]oetry about trying to write poetry' (Bate, p. 70), and poetry very conscious that it is simply recycling old stories. This sense, often called belatedness, is apparent in poems like 'On First Looking into Chapman's Homer', where the poet is conscious not only of reading Homer, but of necessarily reading him in translation, and in the invocation of the goddess Psyche, who would later form the subject of one of the odes, in 'I stood tiptoe':

> So felt he, who first told how Psyche went
> On the smooth wind to the realms of wonderment;
> What Psyche felt, and Love, when their full lips
> First touch'd; what amorous, and fondling nips
> They gave each other's cheeks . . .
>
> ['I stood tiptoe', ll. 141–5]

This passage is in some sense representative of *Poems* in that it is concerned with the reworking of the material of myth, and, not least, because the chosen myth, the meeting between Psyche and Eros (or Love), is, like so many of Keats's subjects, an 'amorous' encounter, recounted with a physicality which both contemporary reviewers and many modern readers and critics find awkward and dismiss as part of his 'Cockney' vulgarity or his immaturity.

Yet, more than this, the poem admits that it is recounting an old story which has already been 'told' (l. 141) by another poet. This kind of exposure occurs more harshly in Keats's later engagements with the world of legend (see *Endymion*, V, 770–9, and *The Eve of St Agnes*, st. 42). Here, in a world where Pan is no longer to be found, myths can only exist as stories. The gods may ascend to heaven (l. 149), but we are left on earth with a mixture of feelings climaxing in dread: 'The silver lamp, – the ravishment, – the wonder – / The darkness, – loneliness, – the fearful thunder' (ll. 147–8), which marks for the poet the inevitable conclusion of the encounter between Psyche and Eros.

Similarly, in *Sleep and Poetry*, a poem which might be taken as something of a Keatsian manifesto and which was completed around the same time as 'I stood tiptoe', towards the end of 1816, the poet is aware that he exists in a world inimical to myth, and perhaps even to the claims of the imagination. He exists in a world like the world of the dedication, in which 'visions all are fled . . . and in their stead/ A sense of real things comes doubly strong' (ll. 155–7). For Keats, we might remember, 'real things' are all too real: coupled with his own experiences as a medical student was an awareness of living in politically oppressive and increasingly utilitarian times. These he would later attack in Apollonius, the 'bald-headed philosopher' (*Lamia*, II, l. 245), and the materialism of the brothers in *Isabella*. And this doubt, already apparent in 1816, provides a useful corrective context for Keats's famous claim for the power of the imagination, which, perhaps more than anything, makes him a Romantic poet.

In November 1817, Keats wrote to a friend, Benjamin Bailey, the letters to whom contain many of Keats's 'axioms' about poetry: 'What the imagination seizes as Beauty must be truth – whether it existed before or not' (*Letters*, 1:184). This is often seen as a very confident or a very naïve statement. However, against the background of so many of the 1817 *Poems*, which mark in some sense the limitations of poetry, the key word 'must', here, might be seen to register hope rather than certainty. And, it is this hope which is recorded in *Sleep and Poetry*: in response to the departed chariot of Apollo, which represents all at once the curative possibilities of idealised medicine, the kind of imagination which can simply create beauty and guarantee truth, a political ideal and the mythic past, the poet declares:

> I will strive
> Against all doubtings, and will keep alive
> The thought of that same chariot, and the strange
> Journey it went.   [ll. 159–62]

This doubt, of course, is simply the doubt of a would-be poet; yet, it is also a more fundamental doubt as to the role of poetry itself in the modern world. And it is significant that this doubt, which many critics find only in Keats's poetry from 1819 onwards, coupled with a desire to 'strive' to 'keep' poetry 'alive', if only as secondary offerings, is already apparent in the 1817 *Poems*.

Keats made this choice clear in the very same month that he wrote to Bailey. His publisher, John Taylor, records a meeting between Keats and his guardian Richard Abbey:

[Abbey] communicated his plans to his ward, but his Surprise was not moderate to hear in Reply that he did not intend to be a Surgeon – Not intend to be a Surgeon, why what do you mean to be? I mean to rely on

my Abilities as a Poet – John . . . you are either Mad or a Fool to talk in
so Absurd a Manner.   [Rollins 1, pp. 307–8]

Again, such an exchange serves well to remind us that Keats's own journey
to poetic greatness was in no sense obvious or predetermined. Someone like
Keats might, indeed, be 'mad' to consider poetry as anything other than a
hobby. However, although he began to neglect his studies as early as the
middle of the previous year, it can be no coincidence that this definite stand
was made in the same month that he completed his most sustained effort,
the long poetic romance *Endymion*.

Endymion is in part another apprentice piece. In the shadow of Milton's
Paradise Lost, Keats, like many of his contemporaries, felt that he couldn't
really be a poet unless he composed a long poem. Recalling Cowden Clarke's
earnest schoolboy, he set himself 'a test, a trial' of completing a poem of
'4,000 lines' (*Letters*, 1:169) through the second half of 1817, some of the
summer of which he spent with Bailey in Oxford continuing his self-
education. *Endymion* clearly betrays this sense of a deliberate enterprise, both
its sheer size and its meandering subject-matter, again raiding the storehouse
of classical mythology, make it difficult for the modern reader. However, in
this we are not alone: Percy Shelley, with whom Keats felt a keen sense of
poetic friendship and competition, wrote in September that 'no person
should possibly get to the end of it', and more recent criticism has dismissed
it as 'an absurd rigmarole' and as 'rambling' (Jones, pp. 142, 128). Indeed,
Keats himself felt that it had 'not at all succeeded' (*Letters*, 2:65). Yet, at other
times he could provide useful clues as to how the poem should be read.
Continuing the 'bower' motif from the 1817 *Poems*, of which *Endymion* is in
some sense a part ('I stood tiptoe' is called 'Endymion' in the letters and in
many ways may be read as a false start to the later poem), Keats saw it as 'a
little Region to wander in' in which 'the images as so numerous that many are
forgotten' (*Letters*, 2:170). We are meant, then, perhaps, not to read it in one
go, nor to become overly concerned with its lack of plot, as many earlier
critics did by seeking to impose on it some overbearing consistent allegory.[3]
Jack Stillinger suggests, helpfully, that in reading *Endymion* 'we shall have to
relax on the question of coherence' (Stillinger, p. 26).

Be that as it may, Keats's doubts reflect more than a fair view of the
shortcomings of *Endymion* as a whole. In particular, here, his hero is unable
to choose between the mytho-erotic realm and the real world, and so the

---

3 For a summary of allegorical readings of *Endymion*, see C. Godfrey, '*Endymion*', in
   Reassessment, pp. 20–38.

narrative solves the problem by revealing that the real woman to whom Endymion is attracted is (luckily) his goddess in disguise. This dilemma is replayed in later poems, perhaps, more successfully precisely because it is not so cleanly resolved (see *The Eve of St Agnes*, *Lamia* and 'La Belle Dame sans Merci'). His doubts were also a response to yet more hostile reviews, which again chose to focus on what the literary establishment saw as vulgar eroticism. For example, the anonymous reviewer of *The British Critic* of June 1818 wrote:

> . . . not all the flimsy veil of words in which he would involve moral images can atone for their impurity; and we will not disgust our readers by retailing to them the artifices of vicious refinement, by which, under the semblance of 'slippery blisses, twinkling eyes, soft completion of faces, and smooth excesses of hands', [Keats] would palm upon the unsuspicious and innocent imaginations better adapted to the stews.
>
> (Mathews, p. 94)

It might be hoped that such an assessment would encourage the reading of the poem! *Endymion* is a poetic trial. It is a repository for Keatsian statements on beauty ('A thing of beauty is a joy forever') – which we might note are quickly qualified by an awareness of death and harsh realities – and the powers of the imagination, as exemplified in the famous 'fellowship with essence' passage (*Endymion*, I, 777ff). It is, in part, as we have seen, a political manifesto. It is also a poem about love: a quest for romance in which the shepherd-King Endymion goes in search of, and after many trials and encounters with other mythic figures, is united with, his lover, the Moon goddess Cynthia. As with the Psyche story from 'I stood tiptoe', these undoubtedly amorous encounters are described with an often frantic physicality. These might reflect Keats's own feelings about sex: he confessed to 'hav[ing] not the right feeling towards women' (*Letters*, 1:341), and created in Circe in Book III an anti-goddess who anticipates his Lamia and Belle Dame. Equally, they might reflect Endymion's role as, at this stage anyway, the disappointed lover. For example, recalling his very first meeting with Cynthia, Endymion declares, 'I e'en dar'd to press/ Her very cheek against my crowned lip' (*Endymion*, I, 661–2). Yet, just as with the Psyche story, such precarious physicality, apparent both in the need to 'press' the goddess, and in the fact that this act is some kind of 'dare', might also reveal an urgency behind the need to confirm her presence in a world suspicious of myths. This movement is seen most graphically in Endymion's encounter with the goddess in her earthly guise of the Indian maid of Book IV. At the moment of consummation:

He saw her body fading gaunt and spare
In the cold moonshine. Straight he seiz'd her wrist;
It melted from his grasp: her hand he kiss'd,
And, horror! kiss'd his own – he was alone.

[*Endymion*, IV, 507–10)

It was, perhaps, with passages like this in mind that Byron accused Keats of a kind of poetic masturbation: 'he is always f[ri]gg[in]g his Imagination'. Although meant, obviously, as a put down, yet another attempt to dismiss 'poor Keats', this remark is actually quite insightful. Like so much of Keats, the poem is, in a sense, about the limitations of the imagination. Endymion is alone, not only because realising love is difficult, but because grasping the mythic, or laying hold of the beautiful is next to impossible. Again, as with the Psyche story, there is a sense, here, of trying to work up excitement over what is recognised within the poem itself as an 'old tale' (*Endymion*, IV, 779 – see also the descriptions of the Latmians, I, 139ff, and the Glaucus story in Book III). However false or forced the ending, Endymion is united with his goddess, but only within the bounds, the 'little Region', of the poem. Prefiguring what happens at the end of *The Eve of St Agnes* when the intensity of the romance between Madeline and Porphyro is qualified by the realisation that, as figures from romance, 'they are gone . . . ages long ago' (st. 42), the poem ends not with the triumphant lovers, but with Endymion's sister, Peona, who wanders 'home through the gloomy wood in wonderment' (*Endymion*, IV, 1003).

Whatever his own sense of gloom as to the nature of and the prospects for his largest single poem by far, Keats allowed *Endymion* to be published with something of a disclaimer for a preface in April 1818. He himself had left London for Devon. In part, this was to prevent his ailing younger brother, Tom, whom Keats would soon nurse through the full symptoms of tuberculosis, just as he had his mother, from returning to the capital; and in part, to continue his own self-education (*Letters*, 1:271), to 'strengthen [his] reach as a poet' (*Letters*, 1:342) and to continue the wide reading, already being signalled in poems like 'On Sitting Down to read *King Lear* Once Again', 'Spenser! a jealous honourer of thine' and 'On Seeing a Lock of Milton's Hair'. In the summer he travelled to the Lake District, already, as the home of Wordsworth and Coleridge, something of a magnet for aspiring Romantic poets, and to Scotland, the home of Burns.

Keats cut short his tour due to his own ill health: a chronic sore throat, the first signs, though he would not know it, of his own tubercular infection. His older brother George was married and living in America (Keats's long journal letters to him are a valuable source for many of his ideas), and his younger brother Tom was becoming more and more ill. And he had to face the disapproval of the reviewers.

As 1818 wore on Tom became increasingly reliant upon Keats. By September, Keats recorded, in language which echoes his more frequently quoted pronouncements on selflessness, a sense of the suffocating proximity of his brother: 'His identity presses upon me all day that . . . I am obliged to write, and plunge into abstract images . . . so that I now live in continual fever' (*Letters*, 1:369). Interestingly here, in what, again, might seem a 'trifle', and clearly through a kind of empathetic association of ideas, in dealing with his brother's fever, Keats begins to think about his own writing not as a potentially curative act, but as 'continual fever'. His very language admits the fact that, for him, the apparently 'abstract' activity of writing, or, indeed, the production of any art form, only has meaning in so far as it is part of 'the fever and the fret' of the world ('To a Nightingale', III, 13). This is the realisation achieved in the Odes. Hartman calls them 'a feverish attempt to enter the life of the pictured scene, to be totally where the imagination is' (Hartman, p. 130), which they are, and which they know they are.

However, the Odes were still in the future for Keats in the winter of 1818–19. The 'abstract' writing he had in mind was his next attempt at reworking classical material: the unfinished epic *Hyperion*. Although it did receive some praise along with the title poems, marking an ultimately ironic turn in the general response to Keats, when it was published in 1820 in *Lamia, Isabella, The Eve of St Agnes and Other Poems*, critically the poem is often seen as a 'detour' (Dickstein, p. 185) or a 'lapse' (Levinson, p. 193), writing which, although in part about death, was produced to take Keats's mind off Tom. Tom's death in December 1819 is often seen as a watershed in Keats's development. Yet, without denying its obvious significance, we would do well to remember that Keats the medical student, who had nursed his own mother, was well aware of the harsh realities of life, which his brother's death simply confirmed. Similarly, *Hyperion* and its later reworking, the also unfinished *Fall of Hyperion*, rather than a 'detour', should be seen as a considered development of already existing themes and ideas. Keats had been thinking about the story of the fall of the Titans and their replacement by the Olympians since at least the previous winter: *Endymion* looks forward to it; Keats read Dante, in translation, on his summer tour to prepare him for his own 'grand attempt at Epic' (*Letter*, 1:331); and its 'naked and [G]recian Manner' was predicted in a letter written in January 1818 – though, much of its scenery is actually inspired by the landscapes Keats saw on his travels.

Hyperion continues Keats's fascination with the material of mythology. In, perhaps, its central passage the sea-god Oceanus, foreseeing the demise of his race and the coming of new gods, proffers a very Keatsian message:

> to bear the naked truths
> And to envisage circumstance, all calm,
> That is the top of sovereignty . . .
> . . . on our heels a fresh perfection treads,
> A power more strong in beauty, born of us
> And fated to excel us . . .
>
> [*Hyperion*, II, 203–14]

This can be read as a statement of faith in beauty: the replacement gods, exemplified by Apollo who will replace Hyperion as the sun god, are not only stronger, but stronger because they are more beautiful. The poem's dynastic struggle can also be read as a kind of psycho-drama: the young replacing the old, or more specifically the young poets (Keats) replacing the old (Wordsworth) (Sperry, p. 182). Recently, it has been viewed as an indication of Keats's 'liberal' faith in 'history as progressive enlightenment' (Roe, 1997, pp. 51–3). A letter written to George in September 1819, at a time when many other Romantic figures had begun to despair of human progress following the failure of the French Revolution, the Napoleonic Wars and increasing social unrest in England, gives some sense of this faith in progress. Keats writes:

> All civil[is]ed countries become gradually more enlighten'd and there should be continual change for the better.   [*Letters*, 2:193]

'There *should* be continual change.' 'First in beauty *should* be first in might'. These statements might equally be taken, again like so much of Keats, as a hope rather than a certainty. He could equally express doubts as to the likelihood of human improvement. For example, echoing Lear on the heath, he also wrote to George:

> Man is originally a poor forked creature . . . If he improves . . . at each stage, at each ascent, there are waiting for him a fresh set of annoyances . . . he is mortal and there is still a heaven above his head.
>
> [*Letters*, 2:101]

This might recall the inaccessibility of the mythic in earlier poems. It is also true to say that both *Hyperion*s are concerned more with the fallen lot of the deposed gods or the earthbound poet. They are named after the displaced god, after all. As with *Endymion*, there is a sense in both poems that 'heaven', whether it represents a personal, poetical or political ideal, is always 'above' our 'heads'. Like the schoolboy Keats, Apollo, the new god, seeks 'Knowledge enormous' (*Endymion*, Bk III, l. 113), but as soon as he is deified, perhaps, inevitably, the poem stops; and *The Fall*, similarly, breaks off with a fading glimpse of the departing god Hyperion as '[o]n he flared' (*Hyperion*, II, l. 61).

Whatever the fate of gods, Keats himself faced fresh annoyances as 1819 progressed. He wrote to Fanny Brawne, the daughter of a neighbour, to whom he had become secretly engaged in June 1819, and who is the subject of some tortured late poems ('Ode to Fanny', 'Lines to Fanny'):

> I have never known any unalloy'd happiness for many days together: the death or sickness of someone has always spoilt my hours. [*Letters*, 2:123]

Their engagement had to remain secret because of Keats's precarious financial situation. He was urged to call in his debts, and he considered a return to the medical profession or a career in journalism working for the liberal press. He even contemplated, however briefly, 'see[ing] what he could do without poetry' (*Letters*, 2:84). George's fortunes were on the wane, and he wrote to Keats asking for financial assistance. Both remained unaware of the true extent of their inheritance. And, after nursing Tom, Keats's own health was to deteriorate until by the end of the year he was exhibiting the full symptoms of tuberculosis himself.

However, rather than giving up poetry, it is to 1819, what Robert Gittings calls 'the living year', that we owe, perhaps, Keats's most significant achievement: the Odes. Although it is important to note that he himself did not seem to give them particular importance, burying them simply as 'other poems' in the 1820 volume, these are the poems on which his claims to be a 'great Man' always have been seen to rest. At their best they show a maturity of technique, though their language could still trouble readers then as it does now (see, for example, the dense imagery of st. 2 of 'Ode to a Nightingale' and the repetition of 'happy' in the 'Ode on a Grecian Urn'). Further, their strength lies in the very fact that, as his abortive attempts at epic and also drama suggest, Keats, like many Romantics, was perhaps best suited to relatively short reflective pieces. Yet, once again, it is important to stress that they form part of a continuum with much of the work that went before.

What are often called the Spring Odes (all those except 'To Autumn') were composed from mid-April to mid-May 1819 when, briefly, Keats enjoyed 'fine weather and health and books' (*Letters*, 2:56). In a concentrated form they exhibit many of the key Keatsian themes. The 'Ode to Psyche' revisits some of the material found in 'I stood tiptoe' and developed through the longer treatments of myth by suggesting that a 'bower' can be created for the goddess against the harness of an unbelieving world, but only as a precarious and, as yet, empty space in the poet's mind which waits to be filled. 'To a Nightingale' uses the familiar Romantic device of the nightingale to, again, explore the limitations of imaginative transcendence: as the bird flies away, it ends with a typical note of Keatsian doubt, 'Fled is that music . . . do I wake or sleep?' (VIII, 10). And, 'The Ode on a Grecian Urn' explores the familiar theme of the relationship between the timelessness of art and the world of 'human passion' (l. 28). Its (in)famous concluding aphorism, on which more has been written than on any other lines in Keats, suggests the triumph of art: '"Beauty is truth, truth beauty" − that is all/ Ye know on earth and all ye need to know' (ll. 49–50).[4] Yet, we would do well to remember that the poem suggests that this truth is only obtainable as a kind of ambivalent stasis (turned into art objects lovers cannot die, but they cannot kiss either), and that the urn itself would have been made to contain the ashes of the dead, reminding the reader of the very world of experience which it never completely overcomes, and in which, of course, it must exist if it is to make any sense.

If it is a misreading to suggest that 'On a Grecian Urn' argues for triumph of art over experience, then it is equally a misreading to suggest that Keats's last ode 'To Autumn', written in September 1819, is, in its calm acceptance (or, perhaps, even denial) of the inevitability of change, decay, death and at least seasonal rebirth, an evasion of harsh realities.[5] Indeed, much recent criticism has begun to suggest that the change it comments on in the autumn of 1819, when England was suffering food shortages and political upheaval, is precisely the necessary political change alluded to in Hyperion, which Keats was reworking at this time (Roe, 1997, pp. 254–67). Such readings are possible, and indeed they complement the more traditional view that the poem is simply about autumn and the relationship between art and human experience. As Helen Vendler reminds us, any poem, and, perhaps, particularly a poem by Keats, is concerned with 'inexpressibly complex articulations of language architectural in form' (Vendler, p. 10) as much as it is with the world of circumstance; a poem is both connected in some way to the world around it, and yet concerned also with its own largely self-contained aesthetic considerations. Which is to say that we must not lose sight of the poem as a poem, and the poet as a poet.

Like 'On a Grecian Urn', 'To Autumn' suggests that art, and great poetry,

---

4 For a discussion on some of the critical responses, see Stillinger, pp. 167–73.
5 For a reading which sees 'To Autumn' as an evasion of reality, see Hartman, pp. 124–46.

can create a near transcendent stasis. And, in some senses, it can be seen itself as an embodiment of the Keatsian dictum that 'a thing of beauty is a joy forever' (*Endymion*, I, l. 1). It is worth quoting at length:

> Season of mists and mellow fruitfulness,
>   Close bosom-friend of the maturing sun;
> Conspiring with him how to load and bless
>   With fruit the vines that round the thatch-eves run;
> To bend with apples the moss'd cottage-trees,
>   And fill all fruit with ripeness to the core;
>   . . . to set budding more,
> And still more, later flowers for the bees,
> Until they think warm days will never cease . . .
>
> Who hath not seen thee oft amid thy store?
>   . . .
>   Or by a cyder-press, with patient look,
>   Thou watchest the last oozings hours by hours.

The Autumn 'fruit' is filled 'with ripeness to the core' (line 6). In a finely chosen phrase in which the sound and the meaning work perfectly together, the 'last oozings' (line 22) of cider are slowed until they take 'hours', so that the reader, like the bees, is tricked into 'think[ing] warm days will never cease' (line 10). That it is a trick might be signalled by the slightly jarring rhyme of 'bees' with 'cease'. Yet, the suggestion is that ripe fruit is nearly over-ripe fruit, just as the 'full-grown lambs' (line 30) of the last verse are really sheep, and even drops that take hours are still trapped in time. The last verse opens: 'Where are the songs of Spring?' (line 23), and the reader is asked to collude in the fanciful perpetuation of autumn in the instruction, 'Think not of them' (line 24), as if art can postpone destructive thought, or the process of change itself. But, following such a plea, what else do we think of but spring? Similarly, the figure who might actually exist in a timeless realm, the goddess of autumn addressed in the second verse, like so many of Keats's mythical figures, is present, but only fleetingly so in the question: 'Who hath not seen thee oft . . . ?' (line 12).

As with all great art, like the *Mona Lisa*, say, it is virtually impossible to come to 'To Autumn' fresh, to read it without the burden of knowing it is a 'great' poem. It also presents to anyone seeking to reconstruct a version of Keats across 'the distance of time', just as he sought a sense of who Shakespeare was, the nearly irresistible sense of closure to the life. Some accounts almost give the impression that Keats placed the final full stop at the end of the poem, and then like Endymion and Cynthia, or Madeline and Porphyro, faded into history. He actually lived on for over a year, composed more poetry which, although of varying quality, and clearly affected by his failing health, has been seen by some critics to presage a potential 'new phase' (de Man, p. xxvii) in his writing. This, of course, was never realised. Yet, whatever we think of them, if nothing else, the poems to and about Fanny Brawne help to qualify the Romantic myth of Keats, as exemplified in this view of 'To Autumn', as a poet all too ready to accept death.

Keats died in Rome in February 1821, to where he had decamped, as was then common, in a misguided attempt to alleviate the symptoms of his tuberculosis or consumption. If anything the difficult journey to Rome probably hastened his inevitable demise. The house in which he died is now a museum in his memory, and he is buried in the city's Protestant graveyard; his gravestone bears his chosen epitaph: 'Here lies one whose name was writ in water.'

Yet even before his death, and Keats had a peculiarly perceptive sense of leading what he called 'a posthumous life' (Letters, 2:358) in Rome, the 'trifles', and not so trifling elements, of his life were being turned into something of a Romantic myth. He becomes '[l]ike a pale flower by some sad maiden cherished' (l. 48) in Shelley's poetic tribute Adonais, written in the year of his death. This kind of language, suggesting a natural feebleness, becomes a staple of accounts of Keats well into the twentieth century, as does the epithet 'poor Keats', as used for example by his contemporary and friend William Hazlitt, who was one of the first to begin the slightly absurd idea that Keats was somehow killed by adverse criticism. He wrote, a month before Keats's actual death, in his essay collection Table Talk:

> A crew of mischievous critics . . . fixed the epithet of the Cockney School to one or two writers . . . This epithet proved too much for one of the writers in question, and stuck like a barbed arrow in his heart. Poor Keats . . . unable to endure the miscreant cry and idiot laugh, withdrew to sigh his last breath in foreign climes.   (Howe, 8, p. 99)

Both 'mischievous' and sympathetic critics and readers of Keats had, and perhaps still have, an interest in perpetuating the myth of 'poor Keats'. To take just one more example, a poet much influenced by him, as were many nineteenth- and early-twentieth-century poets, W. B. Yeats wrote: 'I see a schoolboy when I think of him/ With his face and nose pressed to the sweetshop window' ('Ego Dominus Tuus'). Yet it is possible to overdo the sense of exclusion, be it social or intellectual. As the 'trifles' of his life suggest, the schoolboy Keats, like the man, did have access to many kinds of sweets and worked hard to taste others. Ultimately, as this collection attests, his story is one of inclusion not one of exclusion. Like Shakespeare, and other 'great' men and women 'long since dead', he achieved and, indeed, exceeded his ambition, expressed in one final extract from a letter to his brother George, written in October 1818: 'I think I shall be among the English Poets after my death' (*Letters*, 1:394).

DR PAUL WRIGHT
Trinity College, Carmarthen

Bibliography

For the letters of John Keats, see *Letters of John Keats*, 2 vols, edited by
  H. E Rollins, Harvard University Press, Cambridge, Mass. 1958

Studies on Romanticism and background material

Marylin Butler, *Romantics, Rebels and Reactionaries*, Oxford University
  Press, London and New York 1981

Stuart Curran (ed.), *The Cambridge Companion to British Romanticism*,
  Cambridge University Press, London and New York 1993

Charles Cowden Clarke, *Recollections of Writers* (1878), Fontwell,
  London 1969

P. P. Howe (ed.), *The Complete Works of William Hazlitt*, 21 vols, J. M Dent,
  London 1934

Leigh Hunt, *Imagination and Fancy*, Smith and Elder, London 1891

G. M. Matthews (ed.), *Keats: The Critical Heritage*, Routledge, London 1971

Theodore Redpath (ed.), *The Young Romantic and Critical Opinion 1807–24*,
  Harrap, London 1973

H. E. Rollins (ed.), *The Keats Circle*, 2 vols., Harvard University Press,
  Cambridge, Mass. 1948

G. S. Rousseau, 'Science and the Discovery of the Imagination', *Eighteenth-
  Century Studies*, Vol. 3, 1970, pp. 108–35

Biographies of Keats

W. Jackson Bate, *John Keats*, Harvard University Press, Cambridge, Mass.
  1963

Stephen Coote, *John Keats: A Life*, Hodder & Stoughton, London 1995

Robert Gittings, *John Keats*, Penguin, Harmonsworth 1968

Andrew Motion, *John Keats*, Faber and Faber, London 1998

Introductory critical studies

John Barnard, *John Keats*, Cambridge University Press, London and New
  York 1993

William Walsh, *Introduction to Keats*, Methuen, London and New York
  1981

Specialist studies

Hermione de Almeida, *Romantic Medicine and John Keats*, Oxford University Press, London and New York 1991

Martin Aske, *Keats and Hellenism*, Cambridge University Press, London and New York 1985

Andrew Bennett, *Keats, Narrative and Audience*, Cambridge University Press, London and New York 1994

Morris Dickstein, *Keats and His Poetry*, University of Chicago Press, Chicago 1971

Walter H. Evert, *Aesthetic and Myth in the Poetry of Keats*, Princeton University Press, Princeton, NJ 1965

Donald Gollnicht, *The Poet-Physician: Keats and Medical Science*, University of Pittsburg Press, Pittsburg 1984

Geoffrey Hartman, *The Fate of Reading*, Chicago University Press, Chicago 1975

Ian Jack, *Keats and the Mirror of Art*, Clarendon Press, Oxford 1967

John Jones, *John Keats: The Dream of Truth*, Chatto, London 1969

William Keach, 'Cockney Couplets: Keats and the Politics of Style', *Studies in Romanticism*, Vol. 25, Summer 1986

Majorie Levinson, *Keats's Life of Allegory*, Basil Blackwell, Oxford 1989

Paul de Man, Introduction to *Selected Poetry*, New American Library, New York and Toronto 1966

Kenneth Muir, *John Keats: A Reassessment*, Liverpool University Press, Liverpool 1959

Christopher Ricks, *Keats and Embarrassment,* Oxford University Press, Oxford and New York 1974

Nicholas Roe, *John Keats and the Culture of Dissent*, Clarendon Press, Oxford 1997

Nicholas Roe (ed.), *Keats and History*, Cambridge University Press, London and New York, 1995

Robert M. Ryan, *Keats and the Religious Sense*, Princeton University Press, Princeton, NJ 1976

Stuart Sperry, *Keats the Poet*, Princeton University Press, Princeton, NJ 1973

Jack Stillinger, *The Hoodwinking of Madeline and Other Essays on Keats's Poems*, University of Illinois Press, Chicago 1971

Helen Vendler, *The Odes of John Keats*, Harvard University Press,
   Cambridge, Mass. 1983

Useful websites

Many general Romantic links and links specific to Keats can be found on
'The Voice of the Shuttle', web pages: http://vos.ucsb.edu

   A number of links are also maintained at Malcolm Davidson's site 'John
Keats: a guide for readers' at http://members.ubs.net/homepage/m/a/d/
madavidson

   Discussion groups and other information on Keats and Romanticism in
general can be found at 'Romantic Circles': www.rc.umd.edu

CONTENTS

ENDYMION
A Poetic Romance

LAMIA, ISABELLA, THE EVE OF ST AGNES, etc.,

POSTHUMOUS AND FUGITIVE POEMS

POEMS WRITTEN LATE IN 1819

POEMS
published in 1817

Dedication

TO LEIGH HUNT Esq.

Glory and loveliness have pass'd away;
 For if we wander out in early morn,
 No wreathed incense do we see upborne
Into the east, to meet the smiling day:
No crowd of nymphs soft voic'd and young, and gay,
 In woven baskets bringing ears of corn,
 Roses, and pinks, and violets, to adorn
The shrine of Flora in her early May.
But there are left delights as high as these,
 And I shall ever bless my destiny,
That in a time, when under pleasant trees
 Pan is no longer sought, I feel a free,
A leafy luxury, seeing I could please
 With these poor offerings, a man like thee.

I stood tiptoe upon a little hill

Places of nestling green for Poets made.

Story of Rimini[1]

I stood tiptoe upon a little hill,
The air was cooling, and so very still,
That the sweet buds which with a modest pride
Pull droopingly, in slanting curve aside,
Their scantly leav'd, and finely tapering stems,
Had not yet lost those starry diadems
Caught from the early sobbing of the morn.
The clouds were pure and white as flocks new shorn,
And fresh from the clear brook; sweetly they slept
On the blue fields of heaven, and then there crept   10
A little noiseless noise among the leaves,
Born of the very sigh that silence heaves:
For not the faintest motion could be seen
Of all the shades that slanted o'er the green.
There was wide wand'ring for the greediest eye,
To peer about upon variety;
Far round the horizon's crystal air to skim,
And trace the dwindled edgings of its brim;
To picture out the quaint, and curious bending
Of a fresh woodland alley, never ending;   20
Or by the bowery clefts, and leafy shelves,
Guess where the jaunty streams refresh themselves.
I gazed awhile, and felt as light, and free
As though the fanning wings of Mercury
Had play'd upon my heels: I was light-hearted,
And many pleasures to my vision started;
So I straightway began to pluck a posey
Of luxuries bright, milky, soft and rosy.

A bush of May flowers with the bees about them;
Ah, sure no tasteful nook would be without them;   30
And let a lush labernum oversweep them,
And let long grass grow round the roots to keep them
Moist, cool and green; and shade the violets,

That they may bind the moss in leafy nets.
A filbert hedge with wild briar overtwined,
And clumps of woodbine taking the soft wind
Upon their summer thrones; there too should be
The frequent chequer of a youngling tree,
That with a score of light green brethren shoots
From the quaint mossiness of aged roots: 40
Round which is heard a spring-head of clear waters
Babbling so wildly of its lovely daughters
The spreading blue-bells: it may haply mourn
That such fair clusters should be rudely torn
From their fresh beds, and scattered thoughtlessly
By infant hands, left on the path to die.

Open afresh your round of starry folds,
Ye ardent marigolds!
Dry up the moisture from your golden lids,
For great Apollo bids   50
That in these days your praises should be sung
On many harps, which he has lately strung;
And when again your dewiness he kisses,
Tell him, I have you in my world of blisses:
So haply when I rove in some far vale,
His mighty voice may come upon the gale.

Here are sweet peas, on tip-toe for a flight:
With wings of gentle flush o'er delicate white,
And taper fingers catching at all things,
To bind them all about with tiny rings.   60

Linger awhile upon some bending planks
That lean against a streamlet's rushy banks,
And watch intently Nature's gentle doings:
They will be found softer than ring-dove's cooings.
How silent comes the water round that bend;
Not the minutest whisper does it send
To the o'erhanging sallows:[2] blades of grass
Slowly across the chequer'd shadows pass.
Why, you might read two sonnets, ere they reach
To where the hurrying freshnesses aye preach   70

A natural sermon o'er their pebbly beds;
Where swarms of minnows show their little heads,
Staying their wavy bodies 'gainst the streams,
To taste the luxury of sunny beams
Temper'd with coolness. How they ever wrestle
With their own sweet delight, and ever nestle
Their silver bellies on the pebbly sand.
If you but scantily hold out the hand,
That very instant not one will remain;
But turn your eye, and they are there again.   80
The ripples seem right glad to reach those cresses,
And cool themselves among the em'rald tresses;
The while they cool themselves, they freshness give,
And moisture, that the bowery green may live:
So keeping up an interchange of favours,
Like good men in the truth of their behaviours.
Sometimes goldfinches one by one will drop
From low hung branches; little space they stop;
But sip, and twitter, and their feathers sleek;
Then off at once, as in a wanton freak: 90
Or perhaps, to show their black, and golden wings,
Pausing upon their yellow flutterings.
Were I in such a place, I sure should pray
That naught less sweet, might call my thoughts away,
Than the soft rustle of a maiden's gown
Fanning away the dandelion's down;
Than the light music of her nimble toes
Patting against the sorrel as she goes.
How she would start, and blush, thus to be caught
Playing in all her innocence of thought.   100
O let me lead her gently o'er the brook,
Watch her half-smiling lips, and downward look;
O let me for one moment touch her wrist;
Let me one moment to her breathing list;
And as she leaves me may she often turn
Her fair eyes looking through her locks auburne.
What next? A tuft of evening primroses,
O'er which the mind may hover till it dozes;
O'er which it well might take a pleasant sleep,
But that 'tis ever startled by the leap   110

Of buds into ripe flowers; or by the flitting
Of diverse moths, that aye their rest are quitting;
Or by the moon[3] lifting her silver rim
Above a cloud, and with a gradual swim
Coming into the blue with all her light.
O Maker of sweet poets, dear delight
Of this fair world, and all its gentle livers;
Spangler of clouds, halo of crystal rivers,
Mingler with leaves, and dew and tumbling streams,
Closer of lovely eyes to lovely dreams,   120
Lover of loneliness, and wandering,
Of upcast eye, and tender pondering!
Thee must I praise above all other glories
That smile us on to tell delightful stories.
For what has made the sage or poet write
But the fair paradise of Nature's light?
In the calm grandeur of a sober line,
We see the waving of the mountain pine;
And when a tale is beautifully staid,
We feel the safety of a hawthorn glade: 130
When it is moving on luxurious wings,
The soul is lost in pleasant smotherings:
Fair dewy roses brush against our faces,
And flowering laurels spring from diamond vases;
O'er head we see the jasmine and sweet briar,
And bloomy grapes laughing from green attire;
While at our feet, the voice of crystal bubbles
Charms us at once away from all our troubles:
So that we feel uplifted from the world,
Walking upon the white clouds wreath'd and curl'd.   140
So felt he, who first told, how Psyche went
On the smooth wind to realms of wonderment;
What Psyche felt, and Love, when their full lips
First touch'd; what amorous, and fondling nips
They gave each other's cheeks; with all their sighs,
And how they kist each other's tremulous eyes:
The silver lamp, – the ravishment, – the wonder –
The darkness, – loneliness, – the fearful thunder;
Their woes gone by, and both to heaven upflown,
To bow for gratitude before Jove's throne.   150

So did he feel, who pull'd the boughs aside,
That we might look into a forest wide,
To catch a glimpse of Fauns, and Dryades
Coming with softest rustle through the trees;
And garlands woven of flowers wild, and sweet,
Upheld on ivory wrists, or sporting feet:
Telling us how fair, trembling Syrinx fled
Arcadian Pan, with such a fearful dread.
Poor nymph, – poor Pan, – how he did weep to find,
Nought but a lovely sighing of the wind   160
Along the reedy stream; a half-heard strain,
Full of sweet desolation – balmy pain.

What first inspired a bard of old to sing
Narcissus pining o'er the untainted spring?
In some delicious ramble, he had found
A little space, with boughs all woven round;
And in the midst of all, a clearer pool
Than e'er reflected in its pleasant cool,
The blue sky here, and there, serenely peeping
Through tendril wreaths fantastically creeping.   170
And on the bank a lonely flower he spied,
A meek and forlorn flower, with naught of pride,
Drooping its beauty o'er the watery clearness,
To woo its own sad image into nearness:
Deaf to light Zephyrus it would not move;
But still would seem to droop, to pine, to love.
So while the poet stood in this sweet spot,
Some fainter gleamings o'er his fancy shot;
Nor was it long ere he had told the tale
Of young Narcissus, and sad Echo's bale.   180

Where had he been, from whose warm head out-flew
That sweetest of all songs, that ever new,
That aye refreshing, pure deliciousness,
Coming ever to bless
The wanderer by moonlight? to him bringing
Shapes from the invisible world, unearthly singing
From out the middle air, from flowery nests,
And from the pillowy silkiness that rests

Full in the speculation of the stars.
Ah! surely he had burst our mortal bars;   190
Into some wond'rous region he had gone,
To search for thee, divine Endymion!

He was a Poet, sure a lover too,
Who stood on Latmus' top, what time there blew
Soft breezes from the myrtle vale below;
And brought in faintness solemn, sweet, and slow
A hymn from Dian's temple; while upswelling,
The incense went to her own starry dwelling.
But though her face was clear as infant's eyes,
Though she stood smiling o'er the sacrifice,   200
The Poet wept at her so piteous fate,
Wept that such beauty should be desolate:
So in fine wrath some golden sounds he won,
And gave meek Cynthia her Endymion.

Queen of the wide air; thou most lovely queen
Of all the brightness that mine eyes have seen!
As thou exceedest all things in thy shine,
So every tale, does this sweet tale of thine.
O for three words of honey, that I might
Tell but one wonder of thy bridal night!   210

Where distant ships do seem to show their keels,
Phoebus awhile delay'd his mighty wheels,
And turn'd to smile upon thy bashful eyes,
Ere he his unseen pomp would solemnise.
The evening weather was so bright, and clear,
That men of health were of unusual cheer;
Stepping like Homer at the trumpet's call,
Or young Apollo on the pedestal:
And lovely women were as fair and warm,
As Venus looking sideways in alarm.   220
The breezes were ethereal, and pure,
And crept through half-closed lattices to cure
The languid sick; it cool'd their fever'd sleep,
And soothed them into slumbers full and deep.
Soon they awoke clear eyed: nor burnt with thirsting,

Nor with hot fingers, nor with temples bursting:
And springing up, they met the wond'ring sight
Of their dear friends, nigh foolish with delight;
Who feel their arms, and breasts, and kiss and stare,
And on their placid foreheads part the hair.   230
Young men, and maidens at each other gaz'd
With hands held back, and motionless, amaz'd
To see the brightness in each other's eyes;
And so they stood, fill'd with a sweet surprise,
Until their tongues were loos'd in poesy.
Therefore no lover did of anguish die:
But the soft numbers, in that moment spoken,
Made silken ties, that never may be broken.
Cynthia! I cannot tell the greater blisses,
That follow'd thine, and thy dear shepherd's kisses: 240
Was there a poet born? – but now no more,
My wand'ring spirit must no further soar. –

Specimen of an Induction to a Poem

Lo! I must tell a tale of chivalry;
For large white plumes are dancing in mine eye.
Not like the formal crest of latter days:
But bending in a thousand graceful ways;
So graceful, that it seems no mortal hand,
Or e'en the touch of Archimago's wand,
Could charm them into such an attitude.
We must think rather, that in playful mood,
Some mountain breeze had turn'd its chief delight,
To show this wonder of its gentle might.   10
Lo! I must tell a tale of chivalry;
For while I muse, the lance points slantingly
Athwart the morning air: some lady sweet,
Who cannot feel for cold her tender feet,
From the worn top of some old battlement
Hails it with tears, her stout defender sent:
And from her own pure self no joy dissembling,
Wraps round her ample robe with happy trembling.
Sometimes, when the good Knight his rest would take,
It is reflected, clearly, in a lake,   20
With the young ashen boughs, 'gainst which it rests,
And th' half seen mossiness of linnets' nests.
Ah! shall I ever tell its cruelty,
When the fire flashes from a warrior's eye,
And his tremendous hand is grasping it,
And his dark brow for very wrath is knit?
Or when his spirit, with more calm intent,
Leaps to the honours of a tournament,
And makes the gazers round about the ring
Stare at the grandeur of the balancing?   30
No, no! this is far off: – then how shall I
Revive the dying tones of minstrelsy,
Which linger yet about long gothic arches
In dark green ivy, and among wild larches?
How sing the splendour of the revelries,
When butts of wine are drunk off to the lees?
And that bright lance, against the fretted wall,

Beneath the shade of stately banneral,
Is slung with shining cuirass, sword, and shield?
Where ye may see a spur in bloody field.   40
Light-footed damsels move with gentle paces
Round the wide hall, and show their happy faces;
Or stand in courtly talk by fives and sevens:
Like those fair stars that twinkle in the heavens.
Yet must I tell a tale of chivalry:
Or wherefore comes that steed so proudly by?
Wherefore more proudly does the gentle knight,
Rein in the swelling of his ample might?
Spenser! thy brows are arched, open, kind,
And come like a clear sunrise to my mind;   50
And always does my heart with pleasure dance,
When I think on thy noble countenance:
Where never yet was aught more earthly seen
Than the pure freshness of thy laurels green.
Therefore, great bard, I not so fearfully
Call on thy gentle spirit to hover nigh
My daring steps: or if thy tender care,
Thus startled unaware,
Be jealous that the foot of other wight
Should madly follow that bright path of light   60
Trac'd by thy lov'd Libertas; he will speak.
And tell thee that my prayer is very meek;
That I will follow with due reverence,
And start with awe at mine own strange pretence.
Him thou wilt hear; so I will rest in hope
To see wide plains, fair trees and lawny slope:
The morn, the eve, the light, the shade, the flowers;
Clear streams, smooth lakes, and overlooking towers.

Calidore

A Fragment

Young Calidore is paddling o'er the lake;
His healthful spirit eager and awake
To feel the beauty of a silent eve,
Which seem'd full loth this happy world to leave;
The light dwelt o'er the scene so lingeringly.
He bares his forehead to the cool blue sky,
And smiles at the far clearness all around,
Until his heart is well nigh overwound,
And turns for calmness to the pleasant green
Of easy slopes, and shadowy trees that lean   10
So elegantly o'er the waters' brim
And show their blossoms trim.
Scarce can his clear and nimble eyesight follow
The freaks, and dartings of the black-wing'd swallow,
Delighting much, to see it half at rest,
Dip so refreshingly its wings, and breast
'Gainst the smooth surface, and to mark anon,
The widening circles into nothing gone.

  And now the sharp keel of his little boat
Comes up with ripple, and with easy float,   20
And glides into a bed of water lilies:
Broad leav'd are they and their white canopies
Are upward turn'd to catch the heavens' dew.
Near to a little island's point they grew;
Whence Calidore might have the goodliest view
Of this sweet spot of earth. The bowery shore
Went off in gentle windings to the hoar
And light blue mountains: but no breathing man
With a warm heart, and eye prepared to scan
Nature's clear beauty, could pass lightly by   30
Objects that look'd out so invitingly
On either side. These, gentle Calidore
Greeted, as he had known them long before.

The sidelong view of swelling leafiness,
Which the glad setting sun, in gold doth dress;
Whence ever, and anon the jay outsprings,
And scales upon the beauty of its wings.
The lonely turret, shatter'd, and outworn,
Stands venerably proud; too proud to mourn
Its long lost grandeur: fir trees grow around,   40
Aye dropping their hard fruit upon the ground.
The little chapel[1] with the cross above
Upholding wreaths of ivy; the white dove,
That on the window spreads his feathers light,
And seems from purple clouds to wing its flight.

Green tufted islands casting their soft shades
Across the lake; sequester'd leafy glades,
That through the dimness of their twilight show
Large dock leaves, spiral foxgloves, or the glow
Of the wild cat's eyes,[2] or the silvery stems   50
Of delicate birch trees, or long grass which hems
A little brook. The youth had long been viewing
These pleasant things, and heaven was bedewing
The mountain flowers, when his glad senses caught
A trumpet's silver voice. Ah! it was fraught
With many joys for him: the warder's ken
Had found white coursers prancing in the glen:
Friends very dear to him he soon will see;
So pushes off his boat most eagerly,
And soon upon the lake he skims along,   60
Deaf to the nightingale's first under-song;
Nor minds he the white swans that dream so sweetly:
His spirit flies before him so completely.
And now he turns a jutting point of land,
Whence may be seen the castle gloomy, and grand:
Nor will a bee buzz round two swelling peaches,
Before the point of his light shallop reaches
Those marble steps that through the water dip:
Now over them he goes with hasty trip,
And scarcely stays to ope the folding doors: 70
Anon he leaps along the oaken floors
Of halls and corridors.

Delicious sounds! those little bright-eyed things
That float about the air on azure wings,
Had been less heartfelt by him than the clang
Of clattering hoofs; into the court he sprang,
Just as two noble steeds, and palfreys twain,
Were slanting out their necks with loosened rein;
While from beneath the threat'ning portcullis
They brought their happy burthens. What a kiss,   80
What gentle squeeze he gave each lady's hand!
How tremblingly their delicate ankles spann'd!
Into how sweet a trance his soul was gone,
While whisperings of affection
Made him delay to let their tender feet
Come to the earth; with an incline so sweet
From their low palfreys o'er his neck they bent:
And whether there were tears of languishment,
Or that the evening dew had pearl'd their tresses
He feels a moisture on his cheek, and blesses   90
With lips that tremble, and with glistening eye,
All the soft luxury
That nestled in his arms. A dimpled hand,
Fair as some wonder out of fairy land,
Hung from his shoulder like the drooping flowers
Of whitest Cassia, fresh from summer showers:
And this he fondled with his happy cheek
As if for joy he would no further seek;
When the kind voice of good Sir Clerimond[3]
Came to his ear, like something from beyond   100
His present being; so he gently drew
His warm arms, thrilling now with pulses new,
From their sweet thrall, and forward meekly bending,
Thank'd heaven that his joy was never ending;
While 'gainst his forehead he devoutly press'd
A hand heaven made to succour the distress'd;
A hand that from the world's bleak promontory
Had lifted Calidore for deeds of Glory.

Amid the pages, and the torches' glare,
There stood a knight, patting the flowing hair   110
Of his proud horse's mane: he was withal

A man of elegance, and stature tall:
So that the waving of his plumes would be
High as the berries of a wild ash tree,
Or as the winged cap of Mercury.
His armour was so dexterously wrought
In shape, that sure no living man had thought
It hard, and heavy steel: but that indeed
It was some glorious form, some splendid weed,
In which a spirit new come from the skies   120
Might live, and show itself to human eyes.
'Tis the far-fam'd, the brave Sir Gondibert,[4]
Said the good man to Calidore alert;
While the young warrior with a step of grace
Came up, – a courtly smile upon his face,
And mailed hand held out, ready to greet
The large-eyed wonder, and ambitious heat
Of the aspiring boy; who as he led
Those smiling ladies, often turn'd his head
To admire the visor arch'd so gracefully   130
Over a knightly brow; while they went by
The lamps that from the high roof'd hall were pendent,
And gave the steel a shining quite transcendent.

Soon in a pleasant chamber they are seated;
The sweet-lipp'd ladies have already greeted
All the green leaves that round the window clamber,
To show their purple stars, and bells of amber.
Sir Gondibert has doff'd his shining steel,
Gladdening in the free, and airy feel
Of a light mantle; and while Clerimond   140
Is looking round about him with a fond,
And placid eye, young Calidore is burning
To hear of knightly deeds, and gallant spurning
Of all unworthiness; and how the strong of arm
Kept off dismay, and terror, and alarm
From lovely woman: while brimful of this,
He gave each damsel's hand so warm a kiss,
And had such manly ardour in his eye,
That each at other look'd half staringly;
And then their features started into smiles

Sweet as blue heavens o'er enchanted isles.
Softly the breezes from the forest came,
Softly they blew aside the taper's flame;
Clear was the song from Philomel's far bower;
Grateful the incense from the lime-tree flower;
Mysterious, wild, the far heard trumpet's tone;
Lovely the moon in ether, all alone:
Sweet too the converse of these happy mortals,
As that of busy spirits when the portals
Are closing in the west; or that soft humming   160
We hear around when Hesperus is coming.
Sweet be their sleep.

To Some Ladies

What though while the wonders of nature exploring,
    I cannot your light, mazy footsteps attend;
Nor listen to accents, that almost adoring,
    Bless Cynthia's face, the enthusiast's friend:

Yet over the steep, whence the mountain stream rushes,
    With you, kindest friends, in idea I muse;
Mark the clear tumbling crystal, its passionate gushes,
    In spray that the wild flower kindly bedews.

Why linger you so, the wild labyrinth strolling?
    Why breathless, unable your bliss to declare?   10
Ah! you list to the nightingale's tender condoling,
    Responsive to sylphs, in the moonbeamy air.

'Tis morn, and the flowers with dew are yet drooping,
    I see you are treading the verge of the sea:
And now! ah, I see it – you just now are stooping
    To pick up the keepsake intended for me.

If a cherub, on pinions of silver descending,
    Had brought me a gem from the fretwork of heaven;
And smiles, with his star-cheering voice sweetly blending,
    The blessings of Tighe had melodiously given;   20

It had not created a warmer emotion
    Than the present, fair nymphs, I was blest with from you,
Than the shell, from the bright golden sands of the ocean
    Which the emerald waves at your feet gladly threw.

For, indeed, 'tis a sweet and peculiar pleasure
    (And blissful is he who such happiness finds),
To possess but a span of the hour of leisure,
    In elegant, pure, and aerial minds.

On Receiving a Curious Shell, and a
Copy of Verses from the Same Ladies

Hast thou from the caves of Golconda,[1] a gem
  Pure as the ice-drop that froze on the mountain?
Bright as the hummingbird's green diadem,
  When it flutters in sunbeams that shine through a fountain?

Hast thou a goblet for dark sparkling wine?
  That goblet right heavy, and massy, and gold?
And splendidly mark'd with the story divine
  Of Armida the fair, and Rinaldo the bold?[2]

Hast thou a steed with a mane richly flowing?
  Hast thou a sword that thine enemy's smart is?   10
Hast thou a trumpet rich melodies blowing?
  And wear'st thou the shield of the fam'd Britomartis?

What is it that hangs from thy shoulder, so brave,
  Embroider'd with many a spring peering flower?
 Is it a scarf that thy fair lady gave?
  And hastest thou now to that fair lady's bower?

Ah! courteous Sir Knight, with large joy thou art crown'd;
  Full many the glories that brighten thy youth!
I will tell thee my blisses, which richly abound
  In magical powers to bless, and to sooth.   20

On this scroll thou seest written in characters fair
  A sunbeamy tale of a wreath, and a chain;
And, warrior, it nurtures the property rare
  Of charming my mind from the trammels of pain.

This canopy mark: 'tis the work of a fay;
  Beneath its rich shade did King Oberon languish,
When lovely Titania was far, far away,
  And cruelly left him to sorrow, and anguish.

There, oft would he bring from his soft sighing lute
   Wild strains to which, spellbound, the nightingales
                           listen'd;   30
The wondering spirits of heaven were mute,
   And tears 'mong the dewdrops of morning oft glisten'd.

In this little dome, all those melodies strange,
   Soft, plaintive, and melting, for ever will sigh;
Nor e'er will the notes from their tenderness change;
   Nor e'er will the music of Oberon die.

So, when I am in a voluptuous vein,
   I pillow my head on the sweets of the rose,
And list to the tale of the wreath, and the chain,
   Till its echoes depart; then I sink to repose.   40

Adieu, valiant Eric! with joy thou art crown'd;
   Full many the glories that brighten thy youth,
I too have my blisses, which richly abound
   In magical powers, to bless and to sooth.

To —

[Georgiana Augusta Wylie,
afterwards Mrs George Keats]

Hast thou liv'd in days of old,
O what wonders had been told
Of thy lively countenance,
And thy humid eyes that dance
In the midst of their own brightness;
In the very fane of lightness.
Over which thine eyebrows, leaning,
Picture out each lovely meaning:
In a dainty bend they lie,
Like to streaks across the sky,   10
Or the feathers from a crow,
Fallen on a bed of snow.
Of thy dark hair that extends
Into many graceful bends:
As the leaves of Hellebore
Turn to whence they sprung before
And behind each ample curl
Peeps the richness of a pearl.
Downward too flows many a tress
With a glossy waviness;   20
Full, and round like globes that rise
From the censer to the skies
Through sunny air. Add too, the sweetness
Of thy honey'd voice; the neatness
Of thine ankle lightly turn'd;
With those beauties, scarce discern'd,
Kept with such sweet privacy,
That they seldom meet the eye
Of the little loves that fly
Round about with eager pry.   30
Saving when, with freshening lave,
Thou dipp'st them in the taintless wave;
Like twin water lilies, born
In the coolness of the morn.

O, if thou hadst breathed then,
Now the Muses had been ten.
Couldst thou wish for lineage higher
Than twin sister of Thalia?
At least for ever, evermore,
Will I call the Graces four.   40

   Hadst thou liv'd when chivalry
Lifted up her lance on high,
Tell me what thou wouldst have been?
Ah! I see the silver sheen
Of thy broider'd, floating vest
Cov'ring half thine ivory breast;
Which, O heavens! I should see,
But that cruel destiny
Has placed a golden cuirass there;
Keeping secret what is fair.   50
Like sunbeams in a cloudlet nested
Thy locks in knightly casque are rested:
O'er which bend four milky plumes
Like the gentle lily's blooms
Springing from a costly vase.
See with what a stately pace
Comes thine alabaster[1] steed;
Servant of heroic deed!
O'er his loins, his trappings glow
Like the northern lights on snow.   60
Mount his back! thy sword unsheath!
Sign of the enchanter's death;
Bane of every wicked spell;
Silencer of dragon's yell.
Alas! thou this wilt never do:
Thou art an enchantress too,
And wilt surely never spill
Blood of those whose eyes can kill.

To Hope

When by my solitary hearth I sit,
  And hateful thoughts enwrap my soul in gloom;
When no fair dreams before my 'mind's eye'[1] flit.
  And the bare heath of life presents no bloom:
    Sweet Hope, ethereal balm upon me shed,
    And wave thy silver pinions o'er my head.

Whene'er I wander, at the fall of night,
  Where woven boughs shut out the moon's bright ray,
Should sad Despondency my musings fright,
  And frown, to drive fair Cheerfulness away,   10
    Peep with the moonbeams through the leafy roof,
    And keep that fiend Despondence far aloof.

Should Disappointment, parent of Despair,
  Strive for her son to seize my careless heart;
When, like a cloud, he sits upon the air,
  Preparing on his spellbound prey to dart:
    Chase him away, sweet Hope, with visage bright,
    And fright him as the morning frightens night!

Whene'er the fate of those I hold most dear
  Tells to my fearful breast a tale of sorrow,   20
O bright-eyed Hope, my morbid fancy cheer;
  Let me awhile thy sweetest comforts borrow:
    Thy heaven-born radiance around me shed.
    And wave thy silver pinions o'er my head!

Should e'er unhappy love my bosom pain,
  From cruel parents, or relentless fair;
O let me think it is not quite in vain
  To sigh out sonnets to the midnight air!
    Sweet Hope, ethereal balm upon me shed,
    And wave thy silver pinions o'er my head!   30

In the long vista of the years to roll,
   Let me not see our country's honour fade:
O let me see our land retain her soul,
    Her pride, her freedom; and not freedom's shade.
      From thy bright eyes unusual brightness shed –
      Beneath thy pinions canopy my head!

Let me not see the patriot's high bequest,
   Great liberty! how great in plain attire!
With the base purple of a court oppress'd,
    Bowing her head, and ready to expire: 40
      But let me see thee stoop from heaven on wings
      That fill the skies with silver glitterings!

And as, in sparkling majesty, a star
   Gilds the bright summit of some gloomy cloud;
Brightening the half veil'd face of heaven afar:
    So, when dark thoughts my boding spirit shroud,
      Sweet Hope, celestial influence round me shed,
      Waving thy silver pinions o'er my head.

February 1815

Imitation of Spenser

   Now Morning from her orient chamber came,
   And her first footsteps touch'd a verdant hill;
   Crowning its lawny crest with amber flame,
   Silv'ring the untainted gushes of its rill;
   Which, pure from mossy beds, did down distill,
   And after parting beds of simple flowers,
   By many streams a little lake did fill,
   Which round its marge reflected woven bowers,
And, in its middle space, a sky that never lowers.

There the kingfisher saw his plumage bright   10
Vieing with fish of brilliant dye below;
Whose silken fins, and golden scales' light
Cast upward, through the waves, a ruby glow:
There saw the swan his neck of arched snow,
And oar'd himself along with majesty;
Sparkled his jetty eyes; his feet did show
Beneath the waves like Afric's ebony,
And on his back a fay reclined voluptuously.

Ah! could I tell the wonders of an isle
That in that fairest lake had placed been,   20
I could e'en Dido of her grief beguile;
Or rob from aged Lear[1] his bitter teen:[2]
For sure so fair a place was never seen,
Of all that ever charm'd romantic eye:
It seem'd an emerald in the silver sheen
Of the bright waters; or as when on high,
Through clouds of fleecy white, laughs the coerulean[3] sky.

And all around it dipp'd luxuriously
Slopings of verdure through the glossy tide,
Which, as it were in gentle amity,   30
Rippled delighted up the flowery side;
As if to glean the ruddy tears, it tried,
Which fell profusely from the rose-tree stem!
Haply it was the workings of its pride,
In strife to throw upon the shore a gem
Outvieing all the buds in Flora's diadem.

[Edmonton]

THREE SONNETS TO WOMAN

I

Woman![1] when I behold thee flippant, vain,
    Inconstant, childish, proud, and full of fancies;
    Without that modest softening that enhances
The downcast eye, repentant of the pain
That its mild light creates to heal again:
    E'en then, elate, my spirit leaps, and prances,
    E'en then my soul with exultation dances
For[1] that to love, so long, I've dormant lain:
But when I see thee meek, and kind, and tender,
    Heavens! how desperately do I adore   10
Thy winning graces; – to be thy defender
    I hotly burn – to be a Calidore –
A very Red Cross Knight – a stout Leander –
    Might I be loved by thee like these of yore.

II

Light feet, dark violet eyes, and parted hair;
Soft dimpled hands, white neck, and creamy breast,
Are things on which the dazzled senses rest
Till the fond, fixed eyes, forget they stare.
From such fine pictures, heavens! I cannot dare
To turn my admiration, though unpossess'd
They be of what is worthy, – though not drest
In lovely modesty, and virtues rare.
Yet these I leave as thoughtless as a lark;
These lures I straight forget, – e'en ere I dine,   10
Or thrice my palate moisten: but when I mark
Such charms with mild intelligences shine,
My ear is open like a greedy shark,
To catch the tunings of a voice divine.

III

Ah! who can e'er forget so fair a being?
Who can forget her half retiring sweets?
God! she is like a milk-white lamb that bleats
For man's protection. Surely the All-seeing,
Who joys to see us with his gifts agreeing,
Will never give him pinions, who intreats
Such innocence to ruin, – who vilely cheats
A dove-like bosom. In truth there is no freeing
One's thoughts from such a beauty; when I hear
A lay that once I saw her hand awake,   10
Her form seems floating palpable, and near;
Had I e'er seen her from an arbour take
A dewy flower, oft would that hand appear,
And o'er my eyes the trembling moisture shake.

EPISTLES

To George Felton Mathew

Sweet are the pleasures that to verse belong,
And doubly sweet a brotherhood in song;
Nor can remembrance, Mathew! bring to view
A fate more pleasing, a delight more true
Than that in which the brother poets[1] joy'd,
Who with combined powers, their wit employ'd
To raise a trophy to the drama's muses.
The thought of this great partnership diffuses
Over the genius loving heart, a feeling
Of all that's high, and great, and good, and healing.   10

Too partial friend! fain would I follow thee
Past each horizon of fine poesy;
Fain would I echo back each pleasant note
As o'er Sicilian seas, clear anthems float
'Mong the light skimming gondolas far parted,
Just when the sun his farewell beam has darted:
But 'tis impossible; far different cares
Beckon me sternly from soft 'Lydian airs',
And hold my faculties so long in thrall,
That I am oft in doubt whether at all   20
I shall again see Phoebus in the morning:
Or flush'd Aurora in the roseate dawning!
Or a white Naiad in a rippling stream;
Or a rapt seraph in a moonlight beam;
Or again witness what with thee I've seen,
The dew by fairy feet swept from the green,
After a night of some quaint jubilee
Which every elf and fay had come to see:
When bright processions took their airy march
Beneath the curved moon's triumphal arch.   30

But might I now each passing moment give
To the coy muse, with me she would not live

In this dark city, nor would condescend
'Mid contradictions her delights to lend.
Should e'er the fine-eyed maid to me be kind,
Ah! surely it must be whene'er I find
Some flowery spot, sequester'd, wild, romantic,
That often must have seen a poet frantic;
Where oaks, that erst the Druid[2] knew, are growing,
And flowers, the glory of one day, are blowing;   40
Where the dark-leav'd laburnum's drooping clusters
Reflect athwart the stream their yellow lustres,
And intertwined the cassia's arms unite,
With its own drooping buds, but very white.
Where on one side are covert branches hung,
'Mong which the nightingales have always sung
In leafy quiet: where to pry, aloof,
Atween the pillars of the sylvan roof,
Would be to find where violet beds were nestling,
And where the bee with cowslip bells was wrestling.   50
There must be too a ruin dark, and gloomy,
To say 'joy not too much in all that's bloomy.'

Yet this is vain – O Mathew lend thy aid
To find a place where I may greet the maid –
Where we may soft humanity put on,
And sit, and rhyme and think on Chatterton;
And that warm-hearted Shakespeare sent to meet him
Four laurell'd spirits, heaven-ward to intreat him.   60
With reverence would we speak of all the sages
Who have left streaks of light athwart their ages:
And thou shouldst moralise on Milton's blindness,
And mourn the fearful dearth of human kindness
To those who strove with the bright golden wing
Of genius, to flap away each sting
Thrown by the pitiless world. We next could tell
Of those who in the cause of freedom fell;
Of our own Alfred, of Helvetian Tell;[3]
Of him whose name to ev'ry heart's a solace,
High-minded and unbending William Wallace.[4]
While to the rugged north our musing turns   70
We well might drop a tear for him, and Burns.

Felton! without incitements such as these,
How vain for me the niggard Muse to tease:
For thee, she will thy every dwelling grace,
And make 'a sunshine in a shady place':
For thou wast once a flowret blooming wild,
Close to the source, bright, pure, and undefil'd,
Whence gush the streams of song: in happy hour
Came chaste Diana from her shady bower,
Just as the sun was from the east uprising;   80
And, as for him some gift she was devising,
Beheld thee, pluck'd thee, cast thee in the stream
To meet her glorious brother's greeting beam.
I marvel much that thou hast never told
How, from a flower, into a fish of gold
Apollo chang'd thee; hòw thou next didst seem
A black-eyed swan upon the widening stream;
And when thou first didst in that mirror trace
The placid features of a human face:
That thou hast never told thy travels strange,   90
And all the wonders of the mazy range
O'er pebbly crystal, and o'er golden sands;
Kissing thy daily food from Naiad's pearly hands.

November 1815

To My Brother George

Full many a dreary hour have I past,
My brain bewilder'd, and my mind o'ercast
With heaviness; in seasons when I've thought
No spherey strains[1] by me could e'er be caught
From the blue dome, though I to dimness gaze
On the far depth where sheeted lightning plays;
Or, on the wavy grass outstretch'd supinely,
Pry 'mong the stars, to strive to think divinely:
That I should never hear Apollo's song,
Though feathery clouds were floating all along   10
The purple west, and, two bright streaks between,
The golden lyre itself were dimly seen:
That the still murmur of the honey bee
Would never teach a rural song to me:
That the bright glance from beauty's eyelids slanting
Would never make a lay of mine enchanting,
Or warm my breast with ardour to unfold
Some tale of love and arms in time of old.

But there are times, when those that love the bay,
Fly from all sorrowing far, far away;   20
A sudden glow comes on them, naught they see
In water, earth, or air, but poesy.
It has been said, dear George, and true I hold it,
(For knightly Spenser to Libertas told it,)
That when a Poet is in such a trance,
In air he sees white coursers paw, and prance,
Bestridden of gay knights, in gay apparel,
Who at each other tilt in playful quarrel,
And what we, ignorantly, sheet lightning call,
Is the swift opening of their wide portal,   30
When the bright warder blows his trumpet clear,
Whose tones reach naught on earth but Poet's ear
When these enchanted portals open wide,
And through the light the horsemen swiftly glide,
The Poet's eye can reach those golden halls,
And view the glory of their festivals:

Their ladies fair, that in the distance seem
Fit for the silv'ring of a seraph's dream;
Their rich brimm'd goblets, that incessant run
Like the bright spots that move about the sun; 40
And, when upheld, the wine from each bright jar
Pours with the lustre of a falling star.
Yet further off, are dimly seen their bowers,
Of which, no mortal eye can reach the flowers;
And 'tis right just, for well Apollo knows
'Twould make the Poet quarrel with the rose.
All that's reveal'd from that far seat of blisses,
Is, the clear fountains' interchanging kisses,
As gracefully descending, light and thin,
Like silver streaks across a dolphin's fin, 50
When he upswimmeth from the coral caves,
And sports with half his tail above the waves.

These wonders strange he sees, and many more,
Whose head is pregnant with poetic lore.
Should he upon an evening ramble fare
With forehead to the soothing breezes bare,
Would he naught see but the dark, silent blue
With all its diamonds trembling through and through?
Or the coy moon, when in the waviness
Of whitest clouds she does her beauty dress, 60
And staidly paces higher up, and higher,
Like a sweet nun in holy day attire?
Ah, yes! much more would start into his sight –
The revelries, and mysteries of night:
And should I ever see them, I will tell you
Such tales as needs must with amazement spell[2] you.

These are the living pleasures of the bard:
But richer far posterity's award.
What does he murmur with his latest breath,
While his proud eye looks through the film of death? 70
'What though I leave this dull, and earthly mould,
Yet shall my spirit lofty converse hold
With after times. – The patriot shall feel
My stern alarum, and unsheath his steel;

Or, in the senate thunder out my numbers
To startle princes from their easy slumbers.
The sage will mingle with each moral theme
My happy thoughts sententious; he will teem
With lofty periods when my verses fire him,
And then I'll stoop from heaven to inspire him.   80
Lays have I left of such a dear delight
That maids will sing them on their bridal night.
Gay villagers, upon a morn of May,
When they have tired their gentle limbs with play,
And form'd a snowy circle on the grass,
And plac'd in midst of all that lovely lass
Who chosen is their queen, – with her fine head
Crowned with flowers purple, white, and red:
For there the lily, and the musk-rose, sighing,
Are emblems true of hapless lovers dying: 90
Between her breasts, that never yet felt trouble,
A bunch of violets full blown, and double,
Serenely sleep: – she from a casket takes
A little book, – and then a joy awakes
About each youthful heart, – with stifled cries,
And rubbing of white hands, and sparkling eyes:
For she's to read a tale of hopes, and fears;
One that I foster'd in my youthful years:
The pearls, that on each glist'ning circlet sleep,
Gush ever and anon with silent creep,   100
Lured by the innocent dimples. To sweet rest
Shall the dear babe, upon its mother's breast,
Be lull'd with songs of mine. Fair world, adieu!
Thy dales, and hills, are fading from my view:
Swiftly I mount, upon wide spreading pinions,
Far from the narrow bounds of thy dominions.
Full joy I feel, while thus I cleave the air,
That my soft verse will charm thy daughters fair,
And warm thy sons!' Ah, my dear friend and brother,
Could I, at once, my mad ambition smother,   110
For tasting joys like these, sure I should be
Happier, and dearer to society.
At times, 'tis true, I've felt relief from pain
When some bright thought has darted through my brain:

Through all that day I've felt a greater pleasure
Than if I'd brought to light a hidden treasure.
As to my sonnets, though none else should heed them,
I feel delighted, still, that you should read them.
Of late, too, I have had much calm enjoyment,
Stretch'd on the grass at my best lov'd employment   120
Of scribbling lines for you. These things I thought
While, in my face, the freshest breeze I caught.
E'en now I'm pillow'd on a bed of flowers
That crowns a lofty clift, which proudly towers
Above the ocean waves. The stalks, and blades,
Chequer my tablet with their quivering shades.
On one side is a field of drooping oats,
Through which the poppies show their scarlet coats;[3]
So pert and useless, that they bring to mind
The scarlet coats that pester humankind.   130
And on the other side, outspread, is seen
Ocean's blue mantle streak'd with purple, and green.
Now 'tis I see a canvass'd ship, and now
Mark the bright silver curling round her prow.
I see the lark down-dropping to his nest,
And the broad winged seagull never at rest;
For when no more he spreads his feathers free,
His breast is dancing on the restless sea.
Now I direct my eyes into the west,
Which at this moment is in sunbeams drest: 140
Why westward turn? 'Twas but to say adieu!
'Twas but to kiss my hand, dear George, to you!

Margate, August 1816

To Charles Cowden Clarke[1]

Oft have you seen a swan superbly frowning,
And with proud breast his own white shadow crowning;
He slants his neck beneath the waters bright
So silently, it seems a beam of light
Come from the galaxy: anon he sports, –
With outspread wings the Naiad Zephyr courts,
Or ruffles all the surface of the lake
In striving from its crystal face to take
Some diamond water drops, and them to treasure
In milky nest, and sip them off at leisure.   10
But not a moment can he there ensure them,
Nor to such downy rest can he allure them;
For down they rush as though they would be free,
And drop like hours into eternity.
Just like that bird am I in loss of time,
Whene'er I venture on the stream of rhyme;
With shatter'd boat, oar snapt, and canvas rent
I slowly sail, scarce knowing my intent;
Still scooping up the water with my fingers,
In which a trembling diamond never lingers.   20

   By this, friend Charles, you may full plainly see
Why I have never penn'd a line to thee:
Because my thoughts were never free, and clear,
And little fit to please a classic ear;
Because my wine was of too poor a savour
For one whose palate gladdens in the flavour
Of sparkling Helicon: – small good it were
To take him to a desert rude, and bare,
Who had on Baiae's shore reclin'd at ease,
While Tasso's page was floating in a breeze   30
That gave soft music from Armida's[2] bowers,
Mingled with fragrance from her rarest flowers:
Small good to one who had by Mulla's stream[3]
Fondled the maidens with the breasts of cream;
Who had beheld Belphoebe in a brook,
And lovely Una in a leafy nook,

And Archimago leaning o'er his book:
Who had of all that's sweet tasted, and seen,
From silv'ry ripple, up to beauty's queen;
From the sequester'd haunts of gay Titania,   40
To the blue dwelling of divine Urania:
One, who, of late, had ta'en sweet forest walks
With him who elegantly chats, and talks –
The wrong'd Libertas, – who has told you stories
Of laurel chaplets, and Apollo's glories;
Of troops chivalrous prancing through a city,
And tearful ladies made for love, and pity:
With many else which I have never known.
Thus have I thought; and days on days have flown
Slowly, or rapidly – unwilling still   50
For you to try my dull, unlearned quill.
Nor should I now, but that I've known you long;
That you first taught me all the sweets of song:
The grand, the sweet, the terse, the free, the fine;
What swell'd with pathos, and what right divine:
Spenserian vowels that elope with ease,
And float along like birds o'er summer seas;
Miltonian storms, and more, Miltonian tenderness;
Michael in arms, and more, meek Eve's[4] fair slenderness.
Who read for me the sonnet swelling loudly   60
Up to its climax and then dying proudly?
Who found for me the grandeur of the ode,
Growing, like Atlas, stronger from its load?
Who let me taste that more than cordial dram,
The sharp, the rapier-pointed epigram?
Show'd me that epic was of all the king,
Round, vast, and spanning all like Saturn's ring?
You too upheld the veil from Clio's beauty,
And pointed out the patriot's stern duty;
The might of Alfred, and the shaft of Tell;   70
The hand of Brutus,[5] that so grandly fell
Upon a tyrant's head. Ah! had I never seen,
Or known your kindness, what might I have been?
What my enjoyments in my youthful years,
Bereft of all that now my life endears?
And can I e'er these benefits forget?

And can I e'er repay the friendly debt?
No, doubly no; – yet should these rhymings please,
I shall roll on the grass with twofold ease:
For I have long time been my fancy feeding   80
With hopes that you would one day think the reading
Of my rough verses not an hour misspent;
Should it e'er be so, what a rich content!
Some weeks have pass'd since last I saw the spires
In lucent Thames reflected: – warm desires
To see the sun o'erpeep the eastern dimness,
And morning shadows streaking into slimness
Across the lawny fields, and pebbly water;
To mark the time as they grow broad, and shorter;
To feel the air that plays about the hills,   90
And sips its freshness from the little rills;
To see high, golden corn wave in the light
When Cynthia smiles upon a summer's night,
And peers among the cloudlets jet and white,
As though she were reclining in a bed
Of bean blossoms, in heaven freshly shed.
No sooner had I stepp'd into these pleasures
Than I began to think of rhymes and measures:
The air that floated by me seem'd to say
'Write! thou wilt never have a better day.'   100
And so I did. When many lines I'd written,
Though with their grace I was not oversmitten,
Yet, as my hand was warm, I thought I'd better
Trust to my feelings, and write you a letter.
Such an attempt required an inspiration
Of a peculiar sort, – a consummation; –
Which, had I felt, these scribblings might have been
Verses from which the soul would never wean:
But many days have passed since last my heart
Was warm'd luxuriously by divine Mozart;   110
By Arne delighted, or by Handel[6] madden'd;
Or by the song of Erin[7] pierc'd and sadden'd:
What time you were before the music[8] sitting,
And the rich notes to each sensation fitting.
Since I have walk'd with you through shady lanes
That freshly terminate in open plains,

And revel'd in a chat that ceased not
When at nightfall among your books we got:
No, nor when supper came, nor after that, –
Nor when reluctantly I took my hat;   120
No, nor till cordially you shook my hand
Midway between our homes: – your accents bland
Still sounded in my ears, when I no more
Could hear your footsteps touch the grav'ly floor.
Sometimes I lost them, and then found again;
You chang'd the footpath for the grassy plain.
In those still moments I have wish'd you joys
That well you know to honour: 'Life's very toys
With him,' said I, 'will take a pleasant charm;
It cannot be that aught will work him harm.'   130
These thoughts now come o'er me with all their might: –
Again I shake your hand, – friend Charles, good night.

September 1816

SONNETS

I

To My Brother George

Many the wonders I this day have seen:
   The sun, when first he kist away the tears
   That fill'd the eyes of morn; – the laurell'd peers
Who from the feathery gold of evening lean; –
The ocean with its vastness, its blue green,
   Its ships, its rocks, its caves, its hopes, its fears, –
   Its voice mysterious, which whoso hears
Must think on what will be, and what has been.
E'en now, dear George, while this for you I write,
   Cynthia is from her silken curtains peeping 10
So scantly, that it seems her bridal night,
   And she her half-discover'd revels keeping.
But what, without the social thought of thee,
Would be the wonders of the sky and sea?

II

To —

Had I a man's fair form, then might my sighs
   Be echoed swiftly through that ivory shell
   Thine ear, and find thy gentle heart; so well
Would passion arm me for the enterprise:
But ah! I am no knight whose foeman dies;
   No cuirass glistens on my bosom's swell;
   I am no happy shepherd of the dell
Whose lips have trembled with a maiden's eyes.
Yet must I dote upon thee, – call thee sweet,
   Sweeter by far than Hybla's honied roses 10
     When steep'd in dew rich to intoxication.
Ah! I will taste that dew, for me 'tis meet,
   And when the moon her pallid face discloses,
     I'll gather some by spells, and incantation.

III

Written on the Day that Mr Leigh Hunt Left prison[1]

What though, for showing truth to flatter'd state,
    Kind Hunt was shut in prison, yet has he,
    In his immortal spirit, been as free
As the sky-searching lark, and as elate.
Minion of grandeur! think you he did wait?
    Think you he naught but prison walls did see,
    Till, so unwilling, thou unturn'dst the key?
Ah, no! far happier, nobler was his fate!
In Spenser's halls he stray'd, and bowers fair,
    Culling enchanted flowers; and he flew   10
With daring Milton through the fields of air:
    To regions of his own his genius true
Took happy flights. Who shall his fame impair
    When thou art dead, and all thy wretched crew?

IV

How many bards gild the lapses of time!
    A few of them have ever been the food
    Of my delighted fancy, – I could brood
Over their beauties, earthly, or sublime:
And often, when I sit me down to rhyme,
    These will in throngs before my mind intrude:
    But no confusion, no disturbance rude
Do they occasion; 'tis a pleasing chime.   10
So the unnumber'd sounds that evening store;
The songs of birds – the whisp'ring of the leaves –
    The voice of waters – the great bell that heaves
With solemn sound, – and thousand others more,
    That distance of recognisance bereaves,
Make pleasing music, and not wild uproar.

V

To a Friend Who Sent Me Some Roses

As late I rambled in the happy fields,
   What time the skylark shakes the tremulous dew
   From his lush clover covert; – when anew
Adventurous knights take up their dinted shields:
I saw the sweetest flower wild nature yields,
   A fresh-blown musk-rose; 'twas the first that threw
   Its sweets upon the summer: graceful it grew
As is the wand that queen Titania wields.
And, as I feasted on its fragrancy,
   I thought the garden-rose it far excell'd: 10
But when, O Wells![1] thy roses came to me
   My sense with their deliciousness was spell'd:[2]
Soft voices had they, that with tender plea
   Whisper'd of peace, and truth, and friendliness unquell'd.

29 June 1816

VI

To G. A. W.

[Georgiana Augusta Wylie]

Nymph of the downward smile and sidelong glance,
   In what diviner moments of the day
   Art thou most lovely? – when gone far astray
Into the labyrinths of sweet utterance,
Or when serenely wand'ring in a trance
   Of sober thought? – or when starting away
   With careless robe to meet the morning ray
Thou spar'st the flowers in thy mazy dance?
Haply 'tis when thy ruby lips part sweetly,
   And so remain, because thou listenest: 10
But thou to please wert nurtured so completely
   That I can never tell what mood is best.
I shall as soon pronounce which Grace more neatly
   Trips it before Apollo than the rest.

VII

O Solitude! if I must with thee dwell,
  Let it not be among the jumbled heap
  Of murky buildings; climb with me the steep, –
Nature's observatory – whence the dell,
Its flowery slopes, its river's crystal swell,
  May seem a span; let me thy vigils keep
  'Mongst boughs pavillion'd, where the deer's swift leap
Startles the wild bee from the foxglove bell.
But though I'll gladly trace these scenes with thee,
  Yet the sweet converse of an innocent mind,   10
  Whose words are images of thoughts refin'd,
Is my soul's pleasure; and it sure must be
  Almost the highest bliss of humankind,
When to thy haunts two kindred spirits flee.

VIII

To My Brothers

Small, busy flames play through the fresh laid coals,
  And their faint cracklings o'er our silence creep
  Like whispers of the household gods[1] that keep
A gentle empire o'er fraternal souls.
And while, for rhymes, I search around the poles,
  Your eyes are fix'd, as in poetic sleep,
  Upon the lore so voluble and deep,
That aye at fall of night our care condoles.
This is your birthday Tom, and I rejoice
  That thus it passes smoothly, quietly.   10
Many such eves of gently whisp'ring noise
  May we together pass, and calmly try
What are this world's true joys, – ere the great voice,
  From its fair face, shall bid our spirits fly.

18 November 1816

IX

Keen, fitful gusts are whisp'ring here and there
    Among the bushes half leafless, and dry;
    The stars look very cold about the sky,
And I have many miles on foot to fare.
Yet feel I little of the cool bleak air,
    Or of the dead leaves rustling drearily,
    Or of those silver lamps that burn on high.
Or of the distance from home's pleasant lair:
For I am brimful of the friendliness
    That in a little cottage I have found;   10
Of fair-hair'd Milton's eloquent distress,
    And all his love for gentle Lycid drown'd;
Of lovely Laura[1] in her light green dress,
    And faithful Petrarch gloriously crown'd.

X

To one who has been long in city pent,
    'Tis very sweet to look into the fair
    And open face of heaven, – to breathe a prayer
Full in the smile of the blue firmament.
Who is more happy, when, with heart's content,
    Fatigued he sinks into some pleasant lair
    Of wavy grass, and reads a debonair[1]
And gentle tale of love and languishment?
Returning home at evening, with an ear
    Catching the notes of Philomel, – an eye   10
Watching the sailing cloudlet's bright career,
    He mourns that day so soon has glided by:
E'en like the passage of an angel's tear
    That falls through the clear ether silently.

XI

On First Looking into Chapman's Homer

Much have I travell'd in the realms of gold,[1]
   And many goodly states and kingdoms seen;
   Round many western islands have I been
Which bards in fealty to Apollo hold.
Oft of one wide expanse had I been told
   That deep-brow'd Homer ruled as his demesne;
   Yet did I never breathe its pure serene
Till I heard Chapman speak out loud and bold:
Then felt I like some watcher of the skies
   When a new planet swims into his ken;   10
Or like stout Cortez[2] when with eagle eyes
   He star'd at the Pacific – and all his men
Look'd at each other with a wild surmise –
   Silent, upon a peak in Darien.[3]

XII

On Leaving Some Friends at an Early Hour

Give me a golden pen, and let me lean
   On heap'd up flowers, in regions clear, and far;
   Bring me a tablet whiter than a star,
Or hand of hymning angel, when 'tis seen
The silver strings of heavenly harp atween:
   And let there glide by many a pearly car,
   Pink robes, and wavy hair, and diamond jar,
And half discovered wings, and glances keen.
The while let music wander round my ears,
   And as it reaches each delicious ending,   10
     Let me write down a line of glorious tone,
And full of many wonders of the spheres:
   For what a height my spirit is contending!
     'Tis not content so soon to be alone.

XIII

Addressed to Haydon

Highmindedness, a jealousy for good,
   A loving-kindness for the great man's fame,
   Dwells here and there with people of no name,
In noisome alley, and in pathless wood:
And where we think the truth least understood,
   Oft may be found a 'singleness of aim',[1]
   That ought to frighten into hooded shame
A money-mong'ring, pitiable brood.
How glorious this affection for the cause
   Of steadfast genius, toiling gallantly!   10
What when a stout unbending champion awes
   Envy, and Malice to their native sty?
Unnumber'd souls breathe out a still applause,
   Proud to behold him in his country's eye.

XIV

Addressed to the same

Great spirits[1] now on earth are sojourning;
   He of the cloud, the cataract, the lake,
   Who on Helvellyn's[2] summit, wide awake,
Catches his freshness from Archangel's wing:
He of the rose, the violet, the spring,
   The social smile, the chain for Freedom's sake:
   And lo! – whose stedfastness would never take
A meaner sound than Raphael's whispering.
And other spirits there are standing apart
   Upon the forehead of the age to come;   10
These, these will give the world another heart,
   And other pulses. Hear ye not the hum
Of mighty workings? –
   Listen awhile ye nations, and be dumb.

XV

On the Grasshopper and Cricket

The poetry of earth is never dead:
　　When all the birds are faint with the hot sun,
　　And hide in cooling trees, a voice will run
From hedge to hedge about the new-mown mead;
That is the Grasshopper's – he takes the lead
　　In summer luxury, – he has never done
　　With his delights; for when tired out with fun
He rests at ease beneath some pleasant weed.
The poetry of earth is ceasing never:
　　On a lone winter evening, when the frost　　　　10
　　　　Has wrought a silence, from the stove there shrills
The Cricket's song, in warmth increasing ever,
　　And seems to one in drowsiness half lost,
　　　　The Grasshopper's among some grassy hills.

30 December 1816

XVI

To Kosciusko

Good Kosciusko, thy great name alone
　　Is a full harvest whence to reap high feeling;
　　It comes upon us like the glorious pealing
Of the wide spheres – an everlasting tone.
And now it tells me, that in worlds unknown,
　　The names of heroes, burst from clouds concealing,
　　And change to harmonies, for ever stealing
Through cloudless blue, and round each silver throne.
It tells me too, that on a happy day,
　　When some good spirit walks upon the earth,　　　10
　　　　Thy name with Alfred's, and the great of yore
　　Gently commingling, gives tremendous birth
To a loud hymn, that sounds far, far away
　　To where the great God lives for evermore.

December 1816

XVII

Happy is England! I could be content
  To see no other verdure than its own;
  To feel no other breezes than are blown
Through its tall woods with high romances blent:
Yet do I sometimes feel a languishment
  For skies Italian, and an inward groan
  To sit upon an Alp as on a throne,
And half forget what world or worldling meant.
Happy is England, sweet her artless daughters;
  Enough their simple loveliness for me, 10
    Enough their whitest arms in silence clinging:
  Yet do I often warmly burn to see
    Beauties of deeper glance, and hear their singing,
And float with them about the summer waters.

Sleep and Poetry

As I lay in my bed slepe full unmete
Was unto me, but why that I ne might
Rest I ne wist, for there n'as erthly wight
[As I suppose] had more of hertis ese
Than I, for I n'ad sicknesse nor disese.[1]

Chaucer

What is more gentle than a wind in summer?
What is more soothing than the pretty hummer
That stays one moment in an open flower,
And buzzes cheerily from bower to bower?
What is more tranquil than a musk-rose blowing
In a green island, far from all men's knowing?
More healthful than the leafiness of dales?
More secret than a nest of nightingales?
More serene than Cordelia's countenance?
More full of visions than a high romance?   10
What, but thee Sleep? Soft closer of our eyes!
Low murmurer of tender Jullabies!
Light hoverer around our happy pillows!
Wreather of poppy buds, and weeping willows!
Silent entangler of a beauty's tresses!
Most happy listener! when the morning blesses
Thee for enlivening all the cheerful eyes
That glance so brightly at the new sun-rise.

But what is higher beyond thought than thee?
Fresher than berries of a mountain tree?   20
More strange, more beautiful, more smooth, more regal,
Than wings of swans, than doves, than dim-seen eagle?
What is it? And to what shall I compare it?
It has a glory, and naught else can share it:
The thought thereof is awful, sweet, and holy,
Chasing away all worldliness and folly;
Coming sometimes like fearful claps of thunder,
Or the low rumblings earth's regions under;
And sometimes like a gentle whispering
Of all the secrets of some wond'rous thing

That breathes about us in the vacant air;
So that we look around with prying stare,
Perhaps to see shapes of light, aerial limning,
And catch soft floatings from a faint-heard hymning;
To see the laurel wreath, on high suspended,
That is to crown our name when life is ended.
Sometimes it gives a glory to the voice,
And from the heart up-springs, rejoice! rejoice!
Sounds which will reach the Framer of all things,
And die away in ardent mutterings.   40

No one who once the glorious sun has seen,
And all the clouds, and felt his bosom clean
For his great Maker's presence, but must know
What 'tis I mean, and feel his being glow:
Therefore no insult will I give his spirit,
By telling what he sees from native merit.

O Poesy! for thee I hold my pen
That am not yet a glorious denizen[2]
Of thy wide heaven – Should I rather kneel
Upon some mountain-top until I feel   50
A glowing splendour round about me hung,
And echo back the voice of thine own tongue?
O Poesy! for thee I grasp my pen
That am not yet a glorious denizen
Of thy wide heaven; yet, to my ardent prayer,
Yield from thy sanctuary some clear air,
Smooth'd for intoxication by the breath
Of flowering bays, that I may die a death
Of luxury, and my young spirit follow
The morning sunbeams to the great Apollo   60
Like a fresh sacrifice; or, if I can bear
The o'erwhelming sweets, 'twill bring to me the fair
Visions of all places: a bowery nook
Will be elysium – an eternal book
Whence I may copy many a lovely saying
About the leaves, and flowers – about the playing
Of nymphs in woods, and fountains; and the shade
Keeping a silence round a sleeping maid;

And many a verse from so strange influence
That we must ever wonder how, and whence   70
It came. Also imaginings will hover
Round my fireside, and haply there discover
Vistas of solemn beauty, where I'd wander
In happy silence, like the clear Meander
Through its lone vales; and where I found a spot
Of awfuller shade, or an enchanted grot,
Or a green hill o'erspread with chequer'd dress
Of flowers, and fearful from its loveliness,
Write on my tablets all that was permitted,
All that was for our human senses fitted.   80
Then the events of this wide world I'd seize
Like a strong giant, and my spirit tease
Till at its shoulders it should proudly see
Wings to find out an immortality.

 Stop and consider! life is but a day;
A fragile dewdrop on its perilous way
From a tree's summit; a poor Indian's sleep
While his boat hastens to the monstrous steep
Of Montmorenci. Why so sad a moan?
Life is the rose's hope while yet unblown;   90
The reading of an ever-changing tale;
The light uplifting of a maiden's veil;
A pigeon tumbling in clear summer air;
A laughing schoolboy, without grief or care,
Riding the springy branches of an elm.

 O for ten years, that I may overwhelm
Myself in poesy; so I may do the deed
That my own soul has to itself decreed.
Then will I pass the countries that I see
In long perspective, and continually   100
Taste their pure fountains. First the realm I'll pass
Of Flora, and old Pan: sleep in the grass,
Feed upon apples red, and strawberries,
And choose each pleasure that my fancy sees;
Catch the white-handed nymphs in shady places,
To woo sweet kisses from averted faces, –

Play with their fingers, touch their shoulders white
Into a pretty shrinking with a bite
As hard as lips can make it: till agreed,
A lovely tale of human life we'll read.   110
And one will teach a tame dove how it best
May fan the cool air gently o'er my rest;
Another, bending o'er her nimble tread,
Will set a green robe floating round her head,
And still will dance with ever varied ease,
Smiling upon the flowers and the trees:
Another will entice me on, and on
Through almond blossoms and rich cinnamon;
Till in the bosom of a leafy world
We rest in silence, like two gems upcurl'd   120
In the recesses of a pearly shell.

     And can I ever bid these joys farewell?
Yes, I must pass them for a nobler life,
Where I may find the agonies, the strife
Of human hearts: for lo! I see afar,
O'ersailing the blue cragginess, a car
And steeds with streamy manes – the charioteer[3]
Looks out upon the winds with glorious fear:
And now the numerous tramplings quiver lightly
Along a huge cloud's ridge; and now with sprightly   130
Wheel downward come they into fresher skies,
Tipt round with silver from the sun's bright eyes.
Still downward with capacious whirl they glide;
And now I see them on the greenhill's side
In breezy rest among the nodding stalks.[4]
The charioteer with wond'rous gesture talks
To the trees and mountains; and there soon appear
Shapes of delight, of mystery, and fear,
Passing along before a dusky space
Made by some mighty oaks: as they would chase   140
Some ever-fleeting music on they sweep.
Lo! how they murmur, laugh, and smile, and weep:
Some with upholden hand and mouth severe;
Some with their faces muffled to the ear
Between their arms; some, clear in youthful bloom,

Go glad and smilingly athwart the gloom;
Some looking back, and some with upward gaze;
Yes, thousands in a thousand different ways
Flit onward – now a lovely wreath of girls
Dancing their sleek hair into tangled curls;   150
And now broad wings. Most awfully intent
The driver of those steeds is forward bent,
And seems to listen: O that I might know
All that he writes with such a hurrying glow.

The visions all are fled – the car is fled
Into the light of heaven, and in their stead
A sense of real things comes doubly strong,
And, like a muddy stream, would bear along
My soul to nothingness: but I will strive
Against all doubtings, and will keep alive   160
The thought of that same chariot, and the strange
Journey it went.
             Is there so small a range
In the present strength of manhood, that the high
Imagination cannot freely fly
As she was wont of old? prepare her steeds,
Paw up against the light, and do strange deeds
Upon the clouds? Has she not shown us all?
From the clear space of ether,[5] to the small
Breath of new buds unfolding? From the meaning
Of Jove's large eyebrow, to the tender greening   170
Of April meadows? Here her altar shone,
E'en in this isle; and who could paragon[6]
The fervid choir that lifted up a noise
Of harmony, to where it aye will poise
Its mighty self of convoluting sound,
Huge as a planet,[7] and like that roll round,
Eternally around a dizzy void?
Ay, in those days the Muses were nigh cloy'd
With honours; nor had any other care
Than to sing out and sooth their wavy hair.   180

Could all this be forgotten? Yes, a schism[8]
Nurtured by foppery and barbarism,

Made great Apollo blush for this his land.
Men were thought wise who could not understand
His glories: with a puling infant's force
They sway'd about upon a rocking horse,
And thought it Pegasus. Ah dismal soul'd!
The winds of heaven blew, the ocean roll'd
Its gathering waves – ye felt it not. The blue
Bared its eternal bosom, and the dew   190
Of summer nights collected still to make
The morning precious: beauty was awake!
Why were ye not awake? But ye were dead
To things ye knew not of, – were closely wed
To musty laws lined out with wretched rule
And compass vile: so that ye taught a school
Of dolts to smooth, inlay, and clip, and fit,
Till, like the certain wands of Jacob's wit,[9]
Their verses tallied. Easy was the task:
A thousand handicraftsmen wore the mask   200
Of Poesy. Ill-fated, impious race!
That blasphemed the bright Lyrist[10] to his face,
And did not know it, – no, they went about,
Holding a poor, decrepid standard out
Mark'd with most flimsy mottos, and in large
The name of one Boileau!
                                        O ye whose charge
It is to hover round our pleasant hills!
Whose congregated majesty so fills
My boundly reverence, that I cannot trace
Your hallowed names, in this unholy place,   210
So near those common folk; did not their shames
Affright you? Did our old lamenting Thames
Delight you? Did ye never cluster round
Delicious Avon,[11] with a mournful sound,
And weep? Or did ye wholly bid adieu
To regions where no more the laurel grew?
Or did ye stay to give a welcoming
To some lone spirits who could proudly sing
Their youth away, and die? 'Twas even so:
But let me think away those times of woe: 220
Now 'tis a fairer season; ye have breathed

Rich benedictions o'er us; ye have wreathed
Fresh garlands: for sweet music has been heard
In many places; – some has been upstirr'd
From out its crystal dwelling in a lake,
By a swan's ebon bill;[12] from a thick brake,
Nested and quiet in a valley mild,
Bubbles a pipe;[13] fine sounds are floating wild
About the earth: happy are ye and glad.

These things are doubtless: yet in truth we've had   230
Strange thunders from the potency of song;
Mingled indeed with what is sweet and strong,
From majesty: but in clear truth the themes
Are ugly clubs, the Poets' Polyphemes[14]
Disturbing the grand sea. A drainless shower
Of light is poesy; 'tis the supreme of power;
'Tis might half slumb'ring on its own right arm.
The very archings of her eyelids charm
A thousand willing agents to obey,
And still she governs with the mildest sway: 240
But strength alone though of the Muses born
Is like a fallen angel: trees uptorn,
Darkness, and worms, and shrouds, and sepulchres
Delight it; for it feeds upon the burrs,
And thorns of life; forgetting the great end
Of poesy, that it should be a friend
To sooth the cares, and lift the thoughts of man.

Yet I rejoice: a myrtle fairer than
E'er grew in Paphos, from the bitter weeds
Lifts its sweet head into the air, and feeds   250
A silent space with ever sprouting green.
All tenderest birds there find a pleasant screen,
Creep through the shade with jaunty fluttering,
Nibble the little cupped flowers and sing.
Then let us clear away the choking thorns
From round its gentle stem; let the young fawns,
Yeaned[15] in after times, when we are flown,
Find a fresh sward beneath it, overgrown
With simple flowers: let there nothing be

More boisterous than a lover's bended knee;   260
Nought more ungentle than the placid look
Of one who leans upon a closed book;
Nought more untranquil than the grassy slopes
Between two hills. All hail delightful hopes!
As she was wont, th' imagination
Into most lovely labyrinths will be gone,
And they shall be accounted poet kings
Who simply tell the most heart-easing things.
O may these joys be ripe before I die.

Will not some say that I presumptuously   270
Have spoken? that from hastening disgrace
'Twere better far to hide my foolish face?
That whining boyhood should with reverence bow
Ere the dread thunderbolt could reach? How!
If I do hide myself, it sure shall be
In the very fane, the light of Poesy:
If I do fall, at least I will be laid
Beneath the silence of a poplar shade;
And over me the grass shall be smooth shaven;
And there shall be a kind memorial graven.   280
But off Despondence! miserable bane!
They should not know thee, who athirst to gain
A noble end, are thirsty every hour.
What though I am not wealthy in the dower
Of spanning wisdom; though I do not know
The shiftings of the mighty winds that blow
Hither and thither all the changing thoughts
Of man: though no great minist'ring reason sorts
Out the dark mysteries of human souls
To clear conceiving: yet there ever rolls   290
A vast idea before me, and I glean
Therefrom my liberty; thence too I've seen
The end and aim of Poesy. 'Tis clear
As anything most true; as that the year
Is made of the four seasons – manifest
As a large cross, some old cathedral's crest,
Lifted to the white clouds. Therefore should I
Be but the essence of deformity,

A coward, did my very eyelids wink
At speaking out what I have dared to think. 300
Ah! rather let me like a madman run
Over some precipice; let the hot sun
Melt my Dedalian wings,[16] and drive me down
Convuls'd and headlong! Stay! an inward frown
Of conscience bids me be more calm awhile.
An ocean dim, sprinkled with many an isle,
Spreads awfully before me. How much toil!
How many days! what desperate turmoil!
Ere I can have explored its widenesses.
Ah, what a task! upon my bended knees, 310
I could unsay those – no, impossible!
Impossible!
        For sweet relief I'll dwell
On humbler thoughts, and let this strange assay[17]
Begun in gentleness die so away.
E'en now all tumult from my bosom fades:
I turn full hearted to the friendly aids
That smooth the path of honour; brotherhood,
And friendliness the nurse of mutual good.
The hearty grasp that sends a pleasant sonnet
Into the brain ere one can think upon it; 320
The silence when some rhymes are coming out;
And when they're come, the very pleasant rout:
The message certain to be done tomorrow.
'Tis perhaps as well that it should be to borrow
Some precious book from out its snug retreat,
To cluster round it when we next shall meet.
Scarce can I scribble on; for lovely airs
Are fluttering round the room like doves in pairs;
Many delights of that glad day recalling,
When first my senses caught their tender falling. 330
And with these airs come forms of elegance
Stooping their shoulders o'er a horse's prance,
Careless, and grand – fingers soft and round
Parting luxuriant curls; – and the swift bound
Of Bacchus from his chariot, when his eye
Made Ariadne's cheek look blushingly.
Thus I remember all the pleasant flow

Of words at opening a portfolio.

Things such as these are ever harbingers
To trains of peaceful images: the stirs   340
Of a swan's neck unseen among the rushes:
A linnet starting all about the bushes:
A butterfly, with golden wings broad parted,
Nestling a rose, convuls'd as though it smarted
With over pleasure – many, many more,
Might I indulge at large in all my store
Of luxuries: yet I must not forget
Sleep, quiet with his poppy coronet:
For what there may be worthy in these rhymes
I partly owe to him: and thus, the chimes   350
Of friendly voices had just given place
To as sweet a silence, when I 'gan retrace
The pleasant day, upon a couch at ease.
It was a poet's house[18] who keeps the keys
Of pleasure's temple. Round about were hung
The glorious features of the bards who sung
In other ages – cold and sacred busts
Smiled at each other. Happy he who trusts
To clear Futurity his darling fame!
Then there were fauns and satyrs taking aim   360
At swelling apples with a frisky leap
And reaching fingers, 'mid a luscious heap
Of vine-leaves. Then there rose to view a fane
Of liny marble, and thereto a train
Of nymphs approaching fairly o'er the sward:
One, loveliest, holding her white hand toward
The dazzling sunrise: two sisters sweet
Bending their graceful figures till they meet
Over the trippings of a little child:
And some are hearing, eagerly, the wild   370
Thrilling liquidity of dewy piping.
See, in another picture, nymphs are wiping
Cherishingly Diana's timorous limbs; –
A fold of lawny mantle dabbling swims
At the bath's edge, and keeps a gentle motion
With the subsiding crystal: as when ocean

Heaves calmly its broad swelling smoothness o'er
Its rocky marge, and balances once more
The patient weeds; that now unshent by foam
Feel all about their undulating home.   380

   Sappho's meek head was there half smiling down
At nothing; just as though the earnest frown
Of over thinking had that moment gone
From off her brow, and left her all alone.

   Great Alfred's too, with anxious, pitying eyes,
As if he always listened to the sighs
Of the goaded world; and Kosciusko's worn
By horrid suffrance – mightily forlorn.
Petrarch, outstepping from the shady green,
Starts at the sight of Laura; nor can wean   390
His eyes from her sweet face. Most happy they!
For over them was seen a free display
Of out-spread wings, and from between them shone
The face of Poesy: from off her throne
She overlook'd things that I scarce could tell.
The very sense of where I was might well
Keep Sleep aloof: but more than that there came
Thought after thought to nourish up the flame
Within my breast; so that the morning light
Surprised me even from a sleepless night;   400
And up I rose refresh'd, and glad, and gay,
Resolving to begin that very day
These lines; and howsoever they be done,
I leave them as a father does his son.

ENDYMION

A Poetic Romance

Inscribed to the Memory of

THOMAS CHATTERTON

1818

Preface

Knowing within myself the manner in which this Poem has been produced, it is not without a feeling of regret that I make it public.

What manner I mean, will be quite clear to the reader, who must soon perceive great inexperience, immaturity, and every error denoting a feverish attempt, rather than a deed accomplished. The two first books, and indeed the two last, I feel sensible are not of such completion as to warrant their passing the press; nor should they if I thought a year's castigation would do them any good; – it will not: the foundations are too sandy. It is just that this youngster should die away: a sad thought for me, if I had not some hope that while it is dwindling I may be plotting, and fitting myself for verses fit to live.

This may be speaking too presumptuously, and may deserve a punishment: but no feeling man will be forward to inflict it: he will leave me alone, with the conviction that there is not a fiercer hell than the failure in a great object. This is not written with the least atom of purpose to forestall criticisms of course, but from the desire I have to conciliate men who are competent to look, and who do look with a zealous eye, to the honour of English literature.

The imagination of a boy is healthy, and the mature imagination of a man is healthy; but there is a space of life between, in which the soul is in a ferment, the character undecided, the way of life uncertain, the ambition thick-sighted: thence proceeds mawkishness, and all the thousand bitters which those men I speak of must necessarily taste in going over the following pages.

I hope I have not in too late a day touched the beautiful mythology of Greece, and dulled its brightness: for I wish to try once more, before I bid it farewell.

Teignmouth, 10 April 1818

Book I

A Thing of beauty is a joy for ever:
Its loveliness increases; it will never
Pass into nothingness; but still will keep
A bower quiet for us, and a sleep
Full of sweet dreams, and health, and quiet breathing.
Therefore, on every morrow, are we wreathing
A flowery band to bind us to the earth,
Spite of despondence, of the inhuman dearth
Of noble natures, of the gloomy days,
Of all the unhealthy and o'er-darkened ways   10
Made for our searching: yes, in spite of all,
Some shape of beauty moves away the pall
From our dark spirits. Such the sun, the moon,
Trees old, and young, sprouting a shady boon
For simple sheep; and such are daffodils
With the green world they live in; and clear rills
That for themselves a cooling covert make
'Gainst the hot season; the mid forest brake,
Rich with a sprinkling of fair musk-rose blooms:
And such too is the grandeur of the dooms   20
We have imagined for the mighty dead;
All lovely tales that we have heard or read:
An endless fountain of immortal drink,
Pouring unto us from the heaven's brink.

Nor do we merely feel these essences
For one short hour; no, even as the trees
That whisper round a temple become soon
Dear as the temple's self, so does the moon,
The passion poesy, glories infinite,
Haunt us till they become a cheering light   30
Unto our souls, and bound to us so fast,
That, whether there be shine, or gloom o'ercast,
They always must be with us, or we die.

Therefore, 'tis with full happiness that I
Will trace the story of Endymion.

The very music of the name has gone
Into my being, and each pleasant scene
Is growing fresh before me as the green
Of our own valleys: so I will begin
Now while I cannot hear the city's din;   40
Now while the early budders are just new,
And run in mazes of the youngest hue
About old forests; while the willow trails
Its delicate amber; and the dairy pails
Bring home increase of milk. And, as the year
Grows lush in juicy stalks, I'll smoothly steer
My little boat, for many quiet hours,
With streams that deepen freshly into bowers.
Many and many a verse I hope to write,
Before the daisies, vermeil rimm'd and white,   50
Hide in deep herbage; and ere yet the bees
Hum about globes of clover and sweet peas,
I must be near the middle of my story.
O may no wintry season, bare and hoary,
See it half finish'd: but let Autumn bold,
With universal tinge of sober gold,
Be all about me when I make an end.
And now at once, adventuresome, I send
My herald thought into a wilderness:
There let its trumpet blow, and quickly dress   60
My uncertain path with green, that I may speed
Easily onward, thorough flowers and weed.

   Upon the sides of Latmos was outspread
A mighty forest; for the moist earth fed
So plenteously all weed-hidden roots
Into o'er-hanging boughs, and precious fruits.
And it had gloomy shades, sequestered deep,
Where no man went; and if from shepherd's keep
A lamb stray'd far a-down those inmost glens,
Never again saw he the happy pens   70
Whither his brethren, bleating with content,
Over the hills at every nightfall went.
Among the shepherds, 'twas believed ever,
That not one fleecy lamb which thus did sever

From the white flock, but pass'd unworried
By angry wolf, or pard with prying head,
Until it came to some unfooted plains
Where fed the herds of Pan: aye great his gains
Who thus one lamb did lose. Paths there were many,
Winding through palmy fern, and rushes fenny,   80
And ivy banks; all leading pleasantly
To a wide lawn, whence one could only see
Stems thronging all around between the swell
Of turf and slanting branches: who could tell
The freshness of the space of heaven above,
Edg'd round with dark tree tops? through which a dove
Would often beat its wings, and often too
A little cloud would move across the blue.

    Full in the middle of this pleasantness
There stood a marble altar, with a tress   90
Of flowers budded newly; and the dew
Had taken fairy phantasies to strew
Daisies upon the sacred sward last eve,
And so the dawned light in pomp receive.
For 'twas the morn: Apollo's upward fire
Made every eastern cloud a silvery pyre
Of brightness so unsullied, that therein
A melancholy spirit well might win
Oblivion, and melt out his essence fine
Into the winds: rain-scented eglantine   100
Gave temperate sweets to that well-wooing sun;
The lark was lost in him; cold springs had run
To warm their chilliest bubbles in the grass;
Man's voice was on the mountains; and the mass
Of nature's lives and wonders puls'd tenfold,
To feel this sun-rise and its glories old.

    Now while the silent workings of the dawn
Were busiest, into that self-same lawn
All suddenly, with joyful cries, there sped
A troop of little children garlanded;   110
Who gathering round the altar, seem'd to pry
Earnestly round as wishing to espy

Some folk of holiday: nor had they waited
For many moments, ere their ears were sated[1]
With a faint breath of music, which ev'n then
Fill'd out its voice, and died away again.
Within a little space again it gave
Its airy swellings, with a gentle wave,
To light-hung leaves, in smoothest echoes breaking
Through copse-clad valleys, – ere their death, o'ertaking 120
The surgy murmurs of the lonely sea.

   And now, as deep into the wood as we
Might mark a lynx's eye, there glimmered light
Fair faces and a rush of garments white,
Plainer and plainer showing, till at last
Into the widest alley they all past,
Making directly for the woodland altar.
O kindly muse! let not my weak tongue falter
In telling of this goodly company,
Of their old piety, and of their glee: 130
But let a portion of ethereal dew
Fall on my head, and presently unmew[2]
My soul; that I may dare, in wayfaring,
To stammer where old Chaucer us'd to sing.

   Leading the way, young damsels danced along,
Bearing the burden of a shepherd song;
Each having a white wicker[3] over brimm'd
With April's tender younglings:[4] next, well trimm'd,
A crowd of shepherds with as sunburnt looks
As may be read of in Arcadian books;   140
Such as sat listening round Apollo's pipe,
When the great deity, for earth too ripe,
Let his divinity o'erflowing die
In music, through the vales of Thessaly:[5]
Some idly trail'd their sheep-hooks on the ground,
And some kept up a shrilly mellow sound
With ebon-tipped flutes: close after these,
Now coming from beneath the forest trees,
A venerable priest full soberly,
Begirt with ministring[6] looks: alway his eye   150

Steadfast upon the matted turf he kept,
And after him his sacred vestments swept.
From his right hand there swung a vase, milk-white,
Of mingled wine, out-sparkling generous light;
And in his left he held a basket full
Of all sweet herbs that searching eye could cull:
Wild thyme, and valley-lilies whiter still
Than Leda's love, and cresses from the rill.
His aged head, crowned with beechen wreath,
Seem'd like a poll[7] of ivy in the teeth   160
Of winter hoar. Then came another crowd
Of shepherds, lifting in due time aloud
Their share of the ditty. After them appear'd,
Up-followed by a multitude that rear'd
Their voices to the clouds, a fair wrought car,[8]
Easily rolling so as scarce to mar
The freedom of three steeds of dapple brown:
Who stood therein did seem of great renown
Among the throng. His youth was fully blown,
Showing like Ganymede to manhood grown;   170
And, for those simple times, his garments were
A chieftain king's: beneath his breast, half bare,
Was hung a silver bugle, and between
His nervy[9] knees there lay a boar-spear keen.
A smile was on his countenance; he seem'd,
To common lookers on, like one who dream'd
Of idleness in groves Elysian:
But there were some who feelingly could scan
A lurking trouble in his nether lip,
And see that oftentimes the reins would slip   180
Through his forgotten hands: then would they sigh,
And think of yellow leaves, of owlets' cry,
Of logs piled solemnly. – Ah, well-a-day,
Why should our young Endymion pine away

    Soon the assembly, in a circle rang'd,
Stood silent round the shrine: each look was chang'd
To sudden veneration: women meek
Beckon'd their sons to silence; while each cheek
Of virgin bloom paled gently for slight fear.

Endymion too, without a forest peer,
Stood, wan, and pale, and with an awed face,
Among his brothers of the mountain chase.
In midst of all, the venerable priest
Eyed them with joy from greatest to the least,
And, after lifting up his aged hands,
Thus spake he: 'Men of Latmos! shepherd bands!
Whose care it is to guard a thousand flocks:
Whether descended from beneath the rocks
That overtop your mountains; whether come
From valleys where the pipe is never dumb;   200
Or from your swelling downs, where sweet air stirs
Blue harebells lightly, and where prickly furze
Buds lavish gold; or ye, whose precious charge
Nibble their fill at ocean's very marge,
Whose mellow reeds are touch'd with sounds forlorn
By the dim echoes of old Triton's horn:
Mothers and wives! who day by day prepare
The scrip, with needments,[10] for the mountain air;
And all ye gentle girls who foster up
Udderless lambs, and in a little cup   210
Will put choice honey for a favoured youth:
Yea, every one attend! for in good truth
Our vows are wanting to our great god Pan.
Are not our lowing heifers sleeker than
Night-swollen mushrooms? Are not our wide plains
Speckled with countless fleeces? Have not rains
Green'd over April's lap? No howling sad
Sickens our fearful ewes; and we have had
Great bounty from Endymion our lord.
The earth is glad: the merry lark has pour'd   220
His early song against yon breezy sky,
That spreads so clear o'er our solemnity.'

Thus ending, on the shrine he heap'd a spire
Of teeming sweets, enkindling sacred fire;
Anon he stain'd the thick and spongy sod
With wine, in honour of the shepherd-god.
Now while the earth was drinking it, and while
Bay leaves were crackling in the fragrant pile,

And gummy frankincense was sparkling bright
'Neath smothering parsley, and a hazy light   230
Spread greyly eastward, thus a chorus sang:

  'O Thou, whose mighty palace roof doth hang
From jagged trunks, and overshadoweth
Eternal whispers, glooms, the birth, life, death
Of unseen flowers in heavy peacefulness;
Who lov'st to see the hamadryads dress
Their ruffled locks where meeting hazels darken;
And through whole solemn hours dost sit, and hearken
The dreary melody of bedded reeds –
In desolate places, where dank moisture breeds   240
The pipy hemlock[11] to strange overgrowth;
Bethinking thee, how melancholy loth
Thou wast to lose fair Syrinx – do thou now,
By thy love's milky brow!
By all the trembling mazes that she ran,
Hear us, great Pan!

  'O thou, for whose soul-soothing quiet, turtles[12]
Passion their voices cooingly 'mong myrtles,
What time thou wanderest at eventide
Through sunny meadows, that outskirt the side   250
Of thine enmossed realms: O thou, to whom
Broad leaved fig trees even now foredoom
Their ripen'd fruitage; yellow girted bees
Their golden honeycombs; our village leas
Their fairest blossom'd beans and poppied corn;
The chuckling linnet its five young unborn,
To sing for thee; low creeping strawberries
Their summer coolness; pent up butterflies
Their freckled wings; yea, the fresh budding year
All its completions – be quickly near,   260
By every wind that nods the mountain pine,
O forester divine!

  'Thou, to whom every faun and satyr flies
For willing service; whether to surprise
The squatted hare while in half sleeping fit;

Or upward ragged precipices flit
To save poor lambkins from the eagle's maw;
Or by mysterious enticement draw
Bewildered shepherds to their path again;
Or to tread breathless round the frothy main,   270
And gather up all fancifullest shells
For thee to tumble into Naiads' cells,
And, being hidden, laugh at their out-peeping;
Or to delight thee with fantastic leaping,
The while they pelt each other on the crown
With silvery oak apples, and fir cones brown –
By all the echoes that about thee ring,
Hear us, O satyr king!

    'O Hearkener to the loud clapping shears
While ever and anon to his shorn peers   280
A ram goes bleating: Winder of the horn,
When snouted wild-boars routing tender corn
Anger our huntsmen: Breather round our farms,
To keep off mildews, and all weather harms:
Strange ministrant of undescribed sounds,
That come a swooning over hollow grounds,
And wither drearily on barren moors:
Dread opener of the mysterious doors
Leading to universal knowledge[13] – see,
Great son of Dryope,   290
The many that are come to pay their vows
With leaves about their brows!

    'Be still the unimaginable lodge
For solitary thinkings; such as dodge
Conception to the very bourne of heaven,
Then leave the naked brain: be still the leaven,
That spreading in this dull and clodded earth
Gives it a touch ethereal – a new birth:
Be still a symbol of immensity;
A firmament reflected in a sea;   300
An element filling the space between;
An unknown – but no more: we humbly screen
With uplift hands our foreheads, lowly bending,

And giving out a shout most heaven rending,
Conjure thee to receive our humble Paean,
Upon thy Mount Lycean!'

Even while they brought the burden to a close,
A shout from the whole multitude arose,
That lingered in the air like dying rolls
Of abrupt thunder, when Ionian shoals   310
Of dolphins bob their noses through the brine.
Meantime, on shady levels, mossy fine,
Young companies nimbly began dancing
To the swift treble pipe, and humming string.
Aye, those fair living forms swam heavenly
To tunes forgotten – out of memory:
Fair creatures! whose young children's children bred
Thermopylae[14] its heroes – not yet dead,
But in old marbles ever beautiful.
High genitors,[15] unconscious did they cull   320
Time's sweet first-fruits – they danc'd to weariness,
And then in quiet circles did they press
The hillock turf, and caught the latter end
Of some strange history, potent to send
A young mind from its bodily tenement.
Or they might watch the quoit-pitchers, intent
On either side; pitying the sad death
Of Hyacinthus, when the cruel breath
Of Zephyr slew him, – Zephyr penitent,
Who now, ere Phoebus mounts the firmament,   330
Fondles the flower amid the sobbing rain.
The archers too, upon a wider plain,
Beside the feathery whizzing of the shaft,
And the dull twanging bowstring, and the raft
Branch down sweeping from a tall ash top,
Call'd up a thousand thoughts to envelope
Those who would watch. Perhaps, the trembling knee
And frantic gape of lonely Niobe,
Poor, lonely Niobe! when her lovely young
Were dead and gone, and her caressing tongue   340
Lay a lost thing upon her paly lip,
And very, very deadliness did nip

Her motherly cheeks. Arous'd from this sad mood
By one, who at a distance loud halloo'd,
Uplifting his strong bow into the air,
Many might after brighter visions stare:
After the Argonauts, in blind amaze
Tossing about on Neptune's restless ways,
Until, from the horizon's vaulted side,
There shot a golden splendour far and wide,   350
Spangling those million poutings of the brine
With quivering ore: 'twas even an awful shine
From the exaltation of Apollo's bow;
A heavenly beacon in their dreary woe.
Who thus were ripe for high contemplating,
Might turn their steps towards the sober ring
Where sat Endymion and the aged priest
'Mong shepherds gone in eld, whose looks increas'd
The silvery setting of their mortal star.
There they discours'd upon the fragile bar   360
That keeps us from our homes ethereal;
And what our duties there: to nightly call
Vesper, the beauty-crest of summer weather;
To summon all the downiest clouds together
For the sun's purple couch; to emulate
In ministring the potent rule of fate
With speed of fire-tail'd exhalations;[16]
To tint her pallid cheek with bloom, who cons
Sweet poesy by moonlight: besides these,
A world of other unguess'd offices.   370
Anon they wander'd, by divine converse,
Into Elysium; vieing to rehearse
Each one his own anticipated bliss.
One felt heart-certain that he could not miss
His quick gone love, among fair blossom'd boughs,
Where every zephyr-sigh pouts, and endows
Her lips with music for the welcoming.
Another wish'd, mid that eternal spring,
To meet his rosy child, with feathery sails,[17]
Sweeping, eye-earnestly, through almond vales: 380
Who, suddenly, should stoop through the smooth wind,
And with the balmiest leaves his temples bind;

And, ever after, through those regions be
His messenger, his little Mercury.
Some were athirst in soul to see again
Their fellow huntsmen o'er the wide champaign
In times long past; to sit with them, and talk
Of all the chances in their earthly walk;
Comparing, joyfully, their plenteous stores
Of happiness, to when upon the moors,   390
Benighted, close they huddled from the cold,
And shar'd their famish'd scrips. Thus all out-told
Their fond imaginations, – saving him
Whose eyelids curtain'd up their jewels dim,
Endymion: yet hourly had he striven
To hide the cankering venom, that had riven
His fainting recollections. Now indeed
His senses had swoon'd off: he did not heed
The sudden silence, or the whispers low,
Or the old eyes dissolving at his woe,   400
Or anxious calls, or close of trembling palms,
Or maiden's sigh, that grief itself embalms:
But in the self-same fixed trance he kept,
Like one who on the earth had never stept.
Aye, even as dead still as a marble man,
Frozen in that old tale Arabian.[18]

Who whispers him so pantingly and close?
Peona, his sweet sister: of all those,
His friends, the dearest. Hushing signs she made,
And breath'd a sister's sorrow to persuade   410
A yielding up, a cradling on her care.
Her eloquence did breathe away the curse:
She led him, like some midnight spirit nurse
Of happy changes in emphatic dreams,
Along a path between two little streams, –
Guarding his forehead, with her round elbow,
From low-grown branches, and his footsteps slow
From stumbling over stumps and hillocks small;
Until they came to where these streamlets fall,
With mingled bubblings and a gentle rush,   420
Into a river, clear, brimful, and flush

With crystal mocking[19] of the trees and sky.
A little shallop, floating there hard by,
Pointed its beak over the fringed bank;
And soon it lightly dipt, and rose, and sank,
And dipt again, with the young couple's weight, –
Peona guiding, through the water straight,
Towards a bowery island opposite;
Which gaining presently, she steered light
Into a shady, fresh, and ripply cove,   430
Where nested was an arbour, overwove
By many a summer's silent fingering;
To whose cool bosom she was used to bring
Her playmates, with their needle broidery,
And minstrel memories of times gone by.

So she was gently glad to see him laid
Under her favourite bower's quiet shade,
On her own couch, new made of flower leaves,
Dried carefully on the cooler side of sheaves
When last the sun his autumn tresses shook,   440
And the tann'd harvesters rich armfuls took.
Soon was he quieted to slumbrous rest:
But, ere it crept upon him, he had prest
Peona's busy hand against his lips,
And still, a sleeping, held her finger-tips
In tender pressure. And as a willow keeps
A patient watch over the stream that creeps
Windingly by it, so the quiet maid
Held her in peace: so that a whispering blade
Of grass, a wailful gnat, a bee bustling   450
Down in the bluebells, or a wren light rustling
Among sere[20] leaves and twigs, might all be heard.

O magic sleep! O comfortable bird,
That broodest o'er the troubled sea of the mind
Till it is hush'd and smooth! O unconfin'd
Restraint! imprisoned liberty! great key
To golden palaces, strange minstrelsy,
Fountains grotesque, new trees, bespangled caves,
Echoing grottos, full of tumbling waves

And moonlight; aye, to all the mazy world   460
Of silvery enchantment! – who, upfurl'd
Beneath thy drowsy wing a triple hour,
But renovates and lives? – Thus, in the bower,
Endymion was calm'd to life again.
Opening his eyelids with a healthier brain,
He said: 'I feel this thine endearing love
All through my bosom: thou art as a dove
Trembling its closed eyes and sleeked wings
About me; and the pearliest dew not brings
Such morning incense from the fields of May,   470
As do those brighter drops that twinkling stray
From those kind eyes, – the very home and haunt
Of sisterly affection. Can I want
Aught else, aught nearer heaven, than such tears?
Yet dry them up, in bidding hence all fears
That, any longer, I will pass my days
Alone and sad. No, I will once more raise
My voice upon the mountain-heights; once more
Make my horn parley from their foreheads hoar:
Again my trooping hounds their tongues shall loll   480
Around the breathed boar: again I'll poll
The fair-grown yew tree, for a chosen bow:
And, when the pleasant sun is getting low,
Again I'll linger in a sloping mead
To hear the speckled thrushes, and see feed
Our idle sheep. So be thou cheered sweet,
And, if thy lute is here, softly entreat
My soul to keep in its resolved course.'

Hereat Peona, in their silver source,
Shut her pure sorrow drops with glad exclaim,   490
And took a lute, from which there pulsing came
A lively prelude, fashioning the way
In which her voice should wander. 'Twas a lay
More subtle cadenced, more forest wild
Than Dryope's lone lulling of her child;
And nothing since has floated in the air
So mournful strange. Surely some influence rare
Went, spiritual, through the damsel's hand;

For still, with Delphic[21] emphasis, she spann'd
The quick invisible strings, even though she saw   500
Endymion's spirit melt away and thaw
Before the deep intoxication.
But soon she came, with sudden burst, upon
Her self-possession – swung the lute aside,
And earnestly said: 'Brother, 'tis vain to hide
That thou dost know of things mysterious,
Immortal, starry; such alone could thus
Weigh down thy nature. Hast thou sinn'd in aught
Offensive to the heavenly powers? Caught
A Paphian dove upon a message sent?   510
Thy deathful bow against some deer-herd bent
Sacred to Dian? Haply, thou hast seen
Her naked limbs among the alders green;
And that, alas! is death. No, I can trace
Something more high perplexing in thy face!'

    Endymion look'd at her, and press'd her hand,
And said, 'Art thou so pale, who wast so bland
And merry in our meadows? How is this?
Tell me thine ailment: tell me all amiss! –
Ah! thou hast been unhappy at the change   520
Wrought suddenly in me. What indeed more strange?
Or more complete to overwhelm surmise?
Ambition is so sluggard: 'tis no prize,
That toiling years would put within my grasp,
That I have sighed for: with so deadly gasp
No man e'er panted for a mortal love.
So all have set my heavier grief above
These things which happen. Rightly have they done:
I, who still saw the horizontal sun
Heave his broad shoulder o'er the edge of the world,   530
Out-facing Lucifer, and then had hurl'd
My spear aloft, as signal for the chase –
I, who, for very sport of heart, would race
With my own steed from Araby; pluck down
A vulture from his towery perching; frown
A lion into growling, loth retire –
To lose, at once, all my toil-breeding fire,

And sink thus low! but I will ease my breast
Of secret grief, here in this bowery nest.

'This river does not see the naked sky,   540
Till it begins to progress silverly
Around the western border of the wood,
Whence, from a certain spot, its winding flood
Seems at the distance like a crescent moon:
And in that nook, the very pride of June,
Had I been used to pass my weary eves;
The rather for the sun unwilling leaves
So dear a picture of his sovereign power,
And I could witness his most kingly hour,
When he doth tighten up the golden reins,   550
And paces leisurely down amber plains
His snorting four.[22] Now when his chariot last
Its beams against the zodiac-lion[23] cast,
There blossom'd suddenly a magic bed
Of sacred ditamy, and poppies red:
At which I wondered greatly, knowing well
That but one night had wrought this flowery spell;
And, sitting down close by, began to muse
What it might mean. Perhaps, thought I, Morpheus,
In passing here, his owlet pinions shook;   560
Or, it may be, ere matron Night uptook
Her ebon urn, young Mercury, by stealth,
Had dipt his rod[24] in it: such garland wealth
Came not by common growth. Thus on I thought,
Until my head was dizzy and distraught.
Moreover, through the dancing poppies stole
A breeze, most softly lulling to my soul;
And shaping visions all about my sight
Of colours, wings, and bursts of spangly light;
The which became more strange, and strange, and dim, 570
And then were gulf'd in a tumultuous swim:
And then I fell asleep. Ah, can I tell
The enchantment that afterwards befell?
Yet it was but a dream: yet such a dream
That never tongue, although it overteem
With mellow utterance, like a cavern spring,

Could figure out and to conception bring
All I beheld and felt. Methought I lay
Watching the zenith, where the milky way
Among the stars in virgin splendour pours;   580
And travelling my eye, until the doors
Of heaven appear'd to open for my flight,
I became loth and fearful to alight
From such high soaring by a downward glance:
So kept me steadfast in that airy trance,
Spreading imaginary pinions wide.
When, presently, the stars began to glide,
And faint away, before my eager view:
At which I sigh'd that I could not pursue,
And dropt my vision to the horizon's verge;   590
And lo! from opening clouds, I saw emerge
The loveliest moon, that ever silver'd o'er
A shell for Neptune's goblet: she did soar
So passionately bright, my dazzled soul
Commingling with her argent spheres did roll
Through clear and cloudy, even when she went
At last into a dark and vapoury tent –
Whereat, methought, the lidless-eyed train
Of planets all were in the blue again.
To commune with those orbs, once more I rais'd   600
My sight right upward: but it was quite dazed
By a bright something, sailing down apace,
Making me quickly veil my eyes and face:
Again I look'd, and, O ye deities,
Who from Olympus watch our destinies!
Whence that completed form of all completeness?
Whence came that high perfection of all sweetness?
Speak, stubborn earth, and tell me where, O where
Hast thou a symbol of her golden hair?
Not oat-sheaves drooping in the western sun;   610
Not – thy soft hand, fair sister! let me shun
Such follying before thee – yet she had,
Indeed, locks bright enough to make me mad;
And they were simply gordian'd[25] up and braided.
Leaving, in naked comeliness, unshaded,
Her pearl round ears, white neck, and orbed brow;

The which were blended in, I know not how,
With such a paradise of lips and eyes,
Blush-tinted cheeks, half smiles, and faintest sighs
That, when I think thereon, my spirit clings   620
And plays about its fancy, till the stings
Of human neighbourhood envenom all.
Unto what awful power shall I call?
To what high fane? – Ah! see her hovering feet,
More bluely vein'd, more soft, more whitely sweet
Than those of sea-born Venus, when she rose
From out her cradle shell. The wind out-blows
Her scarf into a fluttering pavillion;
'Tis blue, and over-spangled with a million
Of little eyes, as though thou wert to shed,   630
Over the darkest, lushest bluebell bed,
Handfuls of daisies.' – 'Endymion, how strange!
Dream within dream!' – 'She took an airy range,
And then, towards me, like a very maid,
Came blushing, waning, willing, and afraid,
And press'd me by the hand: Ah! 'twas too much;
Methought I fainted at the charmed touch,
Yet held my recollection, even as one
Who dives three fathoms where the waters run
Gurgling in beds of coral: for anon,   640
I felt upmounted in that region
Where falling stars dart their artillery forth,
And eagles struggle with the buffeting north
That ballances the heavy meteor-stone; –
Felt too, I was not fearful, nor alone,
But lapp'd and lull'd along the dangerous sky.
Soon, as it seem'd, we left our journeying high,
And straightway into frightful eddies swoop'd;
Such as aye muster where grey time has scoop'd
Huge dens and caverns in a mountain's side: 650
There hollow sounds arous'd me, and I sigh'd
To faint once more by looking on my bliss –
I was distracted; madly did I kiss
The wooing arms which held me, and did give
My eyes at once to death: but 'twas to live,
To take in draughts of life from the gold fount

Of kind and passionate looks; to count, and count
The moments, by some greedy help that seem'd
A second self, that each might be redeem'd
And plunder'd of its load of blessedness.   660
Ah, desperate mortal! I e'en dar'd to press
Her very cheek against my crowned lip,
And, at that moment, felt my body dip
Into a warmer air: a moment more,
Our feet were soft in flowers. There was store
Of newest joys upon that alp. Sometimes
A scent of violets, and blossoming limes,
Loiter'd around us; then of honey cells,
Made delicate from all white-flower bells;
And once, above the edges of our nest,   670
An arch face peep'd, – an Oread as I guess'd.

    'Why did I dream that sleep o'er-power'd me
In midst of all this heaven? Why not see,
Far off, the shadows of his pinions dark,
And stare them from me? But no, like a spark
That needs must die, although its little beam
Reflects upon a diamond, my sweet dream
Fell into nothing – into stupid sleep.
And so it was, until a gentle creep,
A careful moving caught my waking ears,   680
And up I started: Ah! my sighs, my tears,
My clenched hands; – for lo! the poppies hung
Dew-dabbled on their stalks, the ouzel[26] sung
A heavy ditty, and the sullen day
Had chidden herald Hesperus away,
With leaden looks: the solitary breeze
Bluster'd, and slept, and its wild self did tease
With wayward melancholy; and I thought,
Mark me, Peona! that sometimes it brought
Faint fare-thee-wells, and sigh-shrilled adieus! –   690
Away. I wander'd – all the pleasant hues
Of heaven and earth had faded: deepest shades
Were deepest dungeons; heaths and sunny glades
Were full of pestilent light; our taintless rills
Seem'd sooty, and o'er-spread with upturn'd gills

Of dying fish; the vermeil rose had blown
In frightful scarlet, and its thorns out-grown
Like spiked aloe. If an innocent bird
Before my heedless footsteps stirr'd, and stirr'd
In little journeys, I beheld in it   700
A disguis'd demon, missioned to knit
My soul with under darkness; to entice
My stumblings down some monstrous precipice:
Therefore I eager followed, and did curse
The disappointment. Time, that aged nurse,
Rock'd me to patience. Now, thank gentle heaven!
These things, with all their comfortings, are given
To my down-sunken hours, and with thee,
Sweet sister, help to stem the ebbing sea
Of weary life.'
            Thus ended he, and both   710
Sat silent: for the maid was very loth
To answer; feeling well that breathed words
Would all be lost, unheard, and vain as swords
Against the enchased crocodile, or leaps
Of grasshoppers against the sun. She weeps,
And wonders; struggles to devise some blame;
To put on such a look as would say, *Shame
On this poor weakness!* but, for all her strife,
She could as soon have crush'd away the life
From a sick dove. At length, to break the pause,   720
She said with trembling chance: 'Is this the cause?
This all? Yet it is strange, and sad, alas!
That one who through this middle earth[27] should pass
Most like a sojourning demi-god, and leave
His name upon the harp-string, should achieve
No higher bard than simple maidenhood,
Singing alone, and fearfully, – how the blood
Left his young cheek; and how he used to stray
He knew not where; and how he would say, *nay*,
If any said 'twas love: and yet 'twas love;   730
What could it be but love? How a ring-dove
Let fall a sprig of yew tree in his path;
And how he died: and then, that love doth scathe,
The gentle heart, as northern blasts do roses;

And then the ballad of his sad life closes
With sighs, and an alas! – Endymion!
Be rather in the trumpet's mouth, – anon
Among the winds at large – that all may hearken!
Although, before the crystal heavens darken,
I watch and dote upon the silver lakes   740
Pictur'd in western cloudiness, that takes
The semblance of gold rocks and bright gold sands,
Islands, and creeks, and amber-fretted strands
With horses prancing o'er them, palaces
And towers of amethyst, – would I so tease
My pleasant days, because I could not mount
Into those regions? The Morphean fount
Of that fine element that visions, dreams,
And fitful whims of sleep are made of, streams
Into its airy channels with so subtle,   750
So thin a breathing, not the spider's shuttle,
Circled a million times within the space
Of a swallow's nest-door, could delay a trace,
A tinting of its quality: how light
Must dreams themselves be; seeing they're more slight
Than the mere nothing that engenders them!
Then wherefore sully the entrusted gem
Of high and noble life with thoughts so sick?
Why pierce high-fronted[28] honour to the quick
For nothing but a dream?' Hereat the youth   760
Look'd up: a conflicting of shame and ruth
Was in his plaited brow: yet, his eyelids
Widened a little, as when Zephyr bids
A little breeze to creep between the fans
Of careless butterflies: amid his pains
He seem'd to taste a drop of manna-dew,
Full palatable; and a colour grew
Upon his cheek, while thus he lifeful spake.

     'Peona! ever have I long'd to slake
My thirst for the world's praises: nothing base,   770
No merely slumberous phantasm, could unlace
The stubborn canvas for my voyage prepar'd –
Though now 'tis tatter'd; leaving my bark bar'd

And sullenly drifting: yet my higher hope
Is of too wide, too rainbow-large a scope,
To fret at myriads of earthly wrecks.
Wherein lies happiness? In that which becks
Our ready minds to fellowship divine,
A fellowship with essence; till we shine,
Full alchemis'd,[29] and free of space. Behold   780
The clear religion of heaven! Fold
A rose leaf round thy finger's taperness,
And soothe thy lips: hist, when the airy stress
Of music's kiss impregnates the free winds,
And with a sympathetic touch unbinds
Aeolian magic from their lucid[30] wombs:
Then old songs waken from enclouded tombs;
Old ditties sigh above their father's grave;
Ghosts of melodious prophecyings rave
Round every spot where trod Apollo's foot;   790
Bronze clarions awake, and faintly bruit,[31]
Where long ago a giant battle was;
And, from the turf, a lullaby doth pass
In every place where infant Orpheus slept.
Feel we these things? – that moment have we stept
Into a sort of oneness, and our state
Is like a floating spirit's. But there are
Richer entanglements, enthralments far
More self-destroying, leading, by degrees,
To the chief intensity: the crown of these   800
Is made of love and friendship, and sits high
Upon the forehead of humanity.
All its more ponderous and bulky worth
Is friendship, whence there ever issues forth
A steady splendour; but at the tip-top,
There hangs by unseen film, an orbed drop
Of light, and that is love: its influence,
Thrown in our eyes, genders a novel sense,
At which we start and fret; till in the end,
Melting into its radiance, we blend,   810
Mingle, and so become a part of it, –
Nor with aught else can our souls interknit
So wingedly: when we combine therewith,

Life's self is nourish'd by its proper pith,
And we are nurtured like a pelican brood.[32]
Aye, so delicious is the unsating food,
That men, who might have tower'd in the van
Of all the congregated world, to fan
And winnow from the coming step of time
All chaff of custom, wipe away all slime   820
Left by men-slugs and human serpentry,
Have been content to let occasion die,
Whilst they did sleep in love's elysium.
And, truly, I would rather be struck dumb,
Than speak against this ardent listlessness:
For I have ever thought that it might bless
The world with benefits unknowingly;
As does the nightingale, upperched high,
And cloister'd among cool and bunched leaves –
She sings but to her love, nor e'er conceives   830
How tiptoe Night holds back her dark-grey hood.
Just so may love, although 'tis understood
The mere commingling[33] of passionate breath,
Produce more than our searching witnesseth:
What I know not: but who, of men, can tell
That flowers would bloom, or that green fruit would swell
To melting pulp, that fish would have bright mail,
The earth its dower of river, wood, and vale,
The meadows runnels, runnels pebble-stones,
The seed its harvest, or the lute its tones,   840
Tones ravishment, or ravishment its sweet
If human souls did never kiss and greet?

'Now, if this earthly love has power to make
Men's being mortal, immortal; to shake
Ambition from their memories, and brim
Their measure of content: what merest whim,
Seems all this poor endeavour after fame,
To one, who keeps within his steadfast aim
A love immortal, an immortal too.
Look not so wilder'd;[34] for these things are true,   850
And never can be born of atomies[35]
That buzz about our slumbers, like brain-flies,

Leaving us fancy-sick. No, no, I'm sure,
My restless spirit never could endure
To brood so long upon one luxury,
Unless it did, though fearfully, espy
A hope beyond the shadow of a dream.
My sayings will the less obscured seem,
When I have told thee how my waking sight
Has made me scruple whether that same night   860
Was pass'd in dreaming. Hearken, sweet Peona!
Beyond the matron-temple[36] of Latona,
Which we should see but for these darkening boughs,
Lies a deep hollow, from whose ragged brows
Bushes and trees do lean all round athwart
And meet so nearly, that with wings outraught,
And spreaded tail, a vulture could not glide
Past them, but he must brush on every side.
Some moulder'd steps lead into this cool cell,
Far as the slabbed margin of a well,   870
Whose patient level peeps its crystal eye
Right upward, through the bushes, to the sky.
Oft have I brought thee flowers, on their stalks set
Like vestal primroses, but dark velvet
Edges them round, and they have golden pits:
'Twas there I got them, from the gaps and slits
In a mossy stone, that sometimes was my seat,
When all above was faint with midday heat.
And there in strife no burning thoughts to heed,
I'd bubble up the water through a reed;   880
So reaching back to boyhood: make me ships
Of moulted feathers, touchwood, alder chips,
With leaves stuck in them; and the Neptune be
Of their petty ocean. Oftener, heavily,
When lovelorn hours had left me less a child,
I sat contemplating the figures wild
Of o'erhead clouds melting the mirror[37] through.
Upon a day, while thus I watch'd, by flew
A cloudy Cupid, with his bow and quiver;
So plainly character'd,[38] no breeze would shiver   890
The happy chance: so happy, I was fain
To follow it upon the open plain,

And, therefore, was just going; when, behold!
A wonder, fair as any I have told –
The same bright face I tasted in my sleep,
Smiling in the clear well. My heart did leap
Through the cool depth. – It moved as if to flee –
I started up, when lo! refreshfully,
There came upon my face in plenteous showers
Dewdrops, and dewy buds, and leaves, and flowers,　　900
Wrapping all objects from my smothered sight,
Bathing my spirit in a new delight.
Aye, such a breathless honey-feel of bliss
Alone preserved me from the drear abyss
Of death, for the fair form had gone again.
Pleasure is oft a visitant; but pain
Clings cruelly to us, like the gnawing sloth[39]
On the deer's tender haunches: late, and loth,
'Tis scar'd away by slow returning pleasure.
How sickening, how dark the dreadful leisure　　910
Of weary days, made deeper exquisite,
By a fore-knowledge of unslumbrous night!
Like sorrow came upon me, heavier still,
Than when I wander'd from the poppy hill:
And a whole age of lingering moments crept
Sluggishly by, ere more contentment swept
Away at once the deadly yellow spleen.
Yes, thrice have I this fair enchantment seen;
Once more been tortured with renewed life.
When last the wintry gusts gave over strife　　920
With the conquering sun of spring, and left the skies
Warm and serene, but yet with moistened eyes
In pity of the shatter'd infant buds, –
That time thou didst adorn, with amber studs,
My hunting cap, because I laugh'd and smil'd,
Chatted with thee, and many days exil'd
All torment from my breast; – 'twas even then,
Straying about, yet, coop'd up in the den
Of helpless discontent, – hurling my lance
From place to place, and following at chance,　　930
At last, by hap,[40] through some young trees it struck,
And, plashing among bedded pebbles, stuck

In the middle of a brook, – whose silver ramble
Down twenty little falls, through reeds and bramble,
Tracing along, it brought me to a cave,
Whence it ran brightly forth, and white did lave[41]
The nether sides of mossy stones and rock, –
'Mong which it gurgled blythe adieus, to mock
Its own sweet grief at parting. Overhead,
Hung a lush screen of drooping weeds, and spread   940
Thick, as to curtain up some wood-nymph's home.
"Ah! impious mortal, whither do I roam?"
Said I, low voic'd: "Ah, whither! 'Tis the grot
Of Proserpine, when Hell, obscure and hot,
Doth her resign; and where her tender hands
She dabbles, on the cool and sluicy sands:
Or 'tis the cell of Echo, where she sits,
And babbles thorough silence, till her wits
Are gone in tender madness, and anon,
Faints into sleep, with many a dying tone   950
Of sadness. O that she would take my vows,
And breathe them sighingly among the boughs,
To sue her gentle ears for whose fair head,
Daily, I pluck sweet flowerets from their bed,
And weave them dyingly – send honey-whispers
Round every leaf, that all those gentle lispers
May sigh my love unto her pitying!
O charitable Echo! hear, and sing
This ditty to her! – tell her" – so I stay'd
My foolish tongue, and listening, half afraid,   960
Stood stupefied with my own empty folly,
And blushing for the freaks[42] of melancholy.
Salt tears were coming, when I heard my name
Most fondly lipp'd, and then these accents came:
"Endymion! the cave is secreter
Than the isle of Delos. Echo hence shall stir
No sighs but sigh-warm kisses, or light noise
Of thy combing hand, the while it travelling cloys
And trembles through my labyrinthine hair."
At that oppress'd I hurried in. – Ah! Where   970
Are those swift moments? Whither are they fled?
I'll smile no more, Peona; nor will wed

Sorrow the way to death; but patiently
Bear up against it: so farewell, sad sigh;
And come instead demurest meditation,
To occupy me wholly, and to fashion
My pilgrimage for the world's dusky brink.
No more will I count over, link by link,
My chain of grief: no longer strive to find
A half-forgetfulness in mountain wind   980
Blustering about my ears: aye, thou shalt see,
Dearest of sisters, what my life shall be;
What a calm round of hours shall make my days.
There is a paly flame of hope that plays
Where'er I look: but yet, I'll say 'tis naught –
And here I bid it die. Have not I caught,
Already, a more healthy countenance?
By this the sun is setting; we may chance
Meet some of our near-dwellers with my car.'
This said, he rose, faint-smiling like a star   990
Through autumn mists, and took Peona's hand:
They stept into the boat, and launch'd from land.

Book II

O sovereign power of love! O grief! O balm!
All records, saving thine, come cool, and calm,
And shadowy, through the mist of passed years:
For others, good or bad, hatred and tears
Have become indolent; but touching thine,
One sigh doth echo, one poor sob doth pine,
One kiss brings honey-dew from buried days.
The woes of Troy, towers smothering o'er their blaze,
Stiff-holden shields, far-piercing spears, keen blades,
Struggling, and blood, and shrieks – all dimly fades   10
Into some backward corner of the brain;
Yet, in our very souls, we feel amain
The close of Troilus and Cressid sweet.
Hence, pageant history! hence, gilded cheat!
Swart planet in the universe of deeds!
Wide sea, that one continuous murmur breeds
Along the pebbled shore of memory!
Many old rotten-timber'd boats there be
Upon thy vaporous bosom, magnified
To goodly vessels; many a sail of pride,   20
And golden keel'd, is left unlaunch'd and dry.
But wherefore this? What care, though owl did fly
About the great Athenian admiral's mast?[1]
What care, though striding Alexander past
The Indus with his Macedonian numbers?
Though old Ulysses tortured from his slumbers
The glutted Cyclops, what care? – Juliet[2] leaning
Amid her window-flowers, – sighing, – weaning
Tenderly her fancy from its maiden snow,
Doth more avail than these: the silver flow   30
Of Hero's tears, the swoon of Imogen,[3]
Fair Pastorella in the bandit's den,[4]
Are things to brood on with more ardency
Than the death-day of empires. Fearfully
Must such conviction come upon his head,
Who, thus far, discontent, has dared to tread,
Without one muse's smile, or kind behest,

The path of love and poesy. But rest,
In chaffing restlessness, is yet more drear
Than to be crush'd, in striving to uprear   40
Love's standard on the battlements of song.
So once more days and nights aid me along,
Like legion'd soldiers.
      Brain-sick shepherd prince,
What promise hast thou faithful guarded since
The day of sacrifice? Or, have new sorrows
Come with the constant dawn upon thy morrows?
Alas! 'tis his old grief. For many days,
Has he been wandering in uncertain ways:
Through wilderness, and woods of mossed oaks;
Counting his woe-worn minutes, by the strokes   50
Of the lone woodcutter; and listening still,
Hour after hour, to each lush-leav'd rill.
Now he is sitting by a shady spring,
And elbow-deep with feverous fingering
Stems the upbursting cold: a wild rose tree
Pavilions him in bloom, and he doth see
A bud which snares his fancy: lo! but now
He plucks it, dips its stalk in the water: how!
It swells, it buds, it flowers beneath his sight;
And, in the middle, there is softly pight   60
A golden butterfly; upon whose wings
There must be surely character'd strange things,
For with wide eye he wonders, and smiles oft.

  Lightly this little herald flew aloft,
Follow'd by glad Endymion's clasped hands:
Onward it flies. From languor's sullen bands
His limbs are loos'd, and eager, on he hies
Dazzled to trace it in the sunny skies.
It seem'd he flew, the way so easy was;
And like a new-born spirit did he pass   70
Through the green evening quiet in the sun,
O'er many a heath, through many a woodland dun,
Through buried paths, where sleepy twilight dreams
The summer time away. One track unseams
A wooded cleft, and, far away, the blue

Of ocean fades upon him; then, anew,
He sinks adown a solitary glen,
Where there was never sound of mortal men,
Saving, perhaps, some snow-light cadences
Melting to silence, when upon the breeze   80
Some holy bark let forth an anthem sweet,
To cheer itself to Delphi. Still his feet
Went swift beneath the merry-winged guide,
Until it reach'd a splashing fountain's side
That, near a cavern's mouth, for ever pour'd
Unto the temperate air: then high it soar'd,
And, downward, suddenly began to dip,
As if, athirst with so much toil, 'twould sip
The crystal spout-head: so it did, with touch
Most delicate, as though afraid to smutch[5]   90
Even with mealy[6] gold the waters clear.
But, at that very touch, to disappear
So fairy-quick, was strange! Bewildered,
Endymion sought around, and shook each bed
Of covert flowers in vain; and then he flung
Himself along the grass. What gentle tongue,
What whisperer disturb'd his gloomy rest?
It was a nymph uprisen to the breast
In the fountain's pebbly margin, and she stood
'Mong lilies, like the youngest of the brood.   100
To him her dripping hand she softly kist,
And anxiously began to plait and twist
Her ringlets round her fingers, saying: 'Youth!
Too long, alas, hast thou starv'd on the ruth,
The bitterness of love: too long indeed,
Seeing thou art so gentle. Could I weed
Thy soul of care, by heavens, I would offer
All the bright riches of my crystal coffer
To Amphitrite; all my clear-eyed fish,
Golden, or rainbow-sided, or purplish,   110
Vermilion-tail'd, or finn'd with silvery gauze;
Yea, or my veined pebble-floor, that draws
A virgin light to the deep; my grotto-sands
Tawny and gold, ooz'd slowly from far lands
By my diligent springs; my level lilies, shells,

My charming rod, my potent river spells;
Yes, every thing, even to the pearly cup
Meander gave me, – for I bubbled up
To fainting creatures in a desert wild.
But woe is me, I am but as a child   120
To gladden thee; and all I dare to say,
Is, that I pity thee; that on this day
I've been thy guide; that thou must wander far
In other regions, past the scanty bar
To mortal steps, before thou cans't be ta'en
From every wasting sigh, from every pain,
Into the gentle bosom of thy love.
Why it is thus, one knows in heaven above:
But, a poor Naiad, I guess not. Farewell!
I have a ditty for my hollow cell.'   130

   Hereat, she vanished from Endymion's gaze,
Who brooded o'er the water in amaze:
The dashing fount pour'd on, and where its pool
Lay, half asleep, in grass and rushes cool,
Quick waterflies and gnats were sporting still,
And fish were dimpling, as if good nor ill
Had fallen out that hour. The wanderer,
Holding his forehead, to keep off the burr[7]
Of smothering fancies, patiently sat down;
And, while beneath the evening's sleepy frown   140
Glow-worms began to trim their starry lamps,
Thus breath'd he to himself: 'Whoso encamps
To take a fancied city of delight,
O what a wretch is he! and when 'tis his,
After long toil and travelling, to miss
The kernel of his hopes, how more than vile:
Yet, for him there's refreshment even in toil;
Another city doth he set about,
Free from the smallest pebble-bead of doubt
That he will seize on trickling honeycombs: 150
Alas, he finds them dry; and then he foams,
And onward to another city speeds.
But this is human life: the war, the deeds,
The disappointment, the anxiety,

Imagination's struggles, far and nigh,
All human; bearing in themselves this good,
That they are still the air, the subtle food,
To make us feel existence, and to show
How quiet death is. Where soil is men grow,
Whether to weeds or flowers; but for me,   160
There is no depth to strike in: I can see
Naught earthly worth my compassing; so stand
Upon a misty, jutting head of land –
Alone? No, no; and by the Orphean lute,
When mad Eurydice is listening to't;
I'd rather stand upon this misty peak,
With not a thing to sigh for, or to seek,
But the soft shadow of my thrice-seen love,
Than be – I care not what. O meekest dove
Of heaven! O Cynthia, ten-times bright and fair!   170
From thy blue throne, now filling all the air,
Glance but one little beam of temper'd light
Into my bosom, that the dreadful might
And tyranny of love be somewhat scar'd!
Yet do not so, sweet queen; one torment spar'd,
Would give a pang to jealous misery,
Worse than the torment's self: but rather tie
Large wings upon my shoulders, and point out
My love's far dwelling. Though the playful rout
Of Cupids shun thee, too divine art thou,   180
Too keen in beauty, for thy silver prow
Not to have dipp'd in love's most gentle stream.
O be propitious, nor severely deem
My madness impious; for, by all the stars
That tend thy bidding, I do think the bars
That kept my spirit in are burst – that I
Am sailing with thee through the dizzy sky!
How beautiful thou art! The world how deep!
How tremulous-dazzlingly the wheels sweep
Around their axle! Then these gleaming reins,   190
How lithe! When this thy chariot attains
Its airy goal, haply some bower veils
Those twilight eyes? Those eyes! – my spirit fails –
Dear goddess, help! or the wide-gaping air

Will gulf me – help!' – At this with madden'd stare,
And lifted hands, and trembling lips he stood;
Like old Deucalion mountain'd o'er the flood,
Or blind Orion hungry for the morn.
And, but from the deep cavern there was borne
A voice, he had been froze to senseless stone;   200
Nor sigh of his, nor plaint, nor passion'd[8] moan
Had more been heard. Thus swell'd it forth: 'Descend,
Young mountaineer! descend where alleys bend
Into the sparry[9] hollows of the world!
Oft hast thou seen bolts of the thunder hurl'd
As from thy threshold; day by day hast been
A little lower than the chilly sheen
Of icy pinnacles, and dipp'dst thine arms
Into the deadening ether that still charms
Their marble being: now, as deep profound   210
As those are high, descend! He ne'er is crown'd
With immortality, who fears to follow
Where airy voices lead: so through the hollow,
The silent mysteries of earth, descend!'

He heard but the last words, nor could contend
One moment in reflection: for he fled
Into the fearful deep, to hide his head
From the clear moon, the trees, and coming madness.

'Twas far too strange, and wonderful for sadness;
Sharpening, by degrees, his appetite   220
To dive into the deepest. Dark, nor light,
The region; nor bright, nor sombre wholly,
But mingled up; a gleaming melancholy;
A dusky empire and its diadems;
One faint eternal eventide of gems.
Aye, millions sparkled on a vein of gold,
Along whose track the prince quick footsteps told,
With all its lines abrupt and angular:
Out-shooting sometimes, like a meteor-star,
Through a vast antre;[10] then the metal woof,   230
Like Vulcan's rainbow, with some monstrous roof
Curves hugely: now, far in the deep abyss,

It seems an angry lightning, and doth hiss
Fancy into belief: anon it leads
Through winding passages, where sameness breeds
Vexing conceptions of some sudden change;
Whether to silver grots, or giant range
Of sapphire columns, or fantastic bridge
Athwart a flood of crystal. On a ridge
Now fareth he, that o'er the vast beneath   240
Towers like an ocean-cliff, and whence he seeth
A hundred waterfalls, whose voices come
But as the murmuring surge. Chilly and numb
His bosom grew, when first he, far away
Descried[11] an orbed diamond, set to fray[12]
Old darkness from his throne: 'twas like the sun
Uprisen o'er chaos: and with such a stun
Came the amazement, that, absorb'd in it,
He saw not fiercer wonders – past the wit
Of any spirit to tell, but one of those   250
Who, when this planet's sphering time doth close,
Will be its high remembrancers: who they?
The mighty ones[13] who have made eternal day
For Greece and England. While astonishment
With deep-drawn sighs was quieting, he went
Into a marble gallery, passing through
A mimic temple, so complete and true
In sacred custom, that he well nigh fear'd
To search it inwards; whence far off appear'd,
Through a long pillar'd vista, a fair shrine,   260
And just beyond, on light tiptoe divine,
A quiver'd Dian.[14] Stepping awfully,
The youth approach'd; oft turning his veil'd eye
Down sidelong aisles, and into niches old.
And when, more near against the marble cold
He had touch'd his forehead, he began to thread
All courts and passages, where silence dead
Rous'd by his whispering footsteps murmured faint:
And long he travers'd to and fro, to acquaint
Himself with every mystery, and awe;   270
Till, weary, he sat down before the maw
Of a wide outlet, fathomless and dim,

To wild uncertainty and shadows grim.
There, when new wonders ceas'd to float before,
And thoughts of self came on, how crude and sore
The journey homeward to habitual self!
A mad-pursuing of the fog-born elf,[15]
Whose flitting lantern, through rude nettle-briar,
Cheats us into a swamp, into a fire,
Into the bosom of a hated thing.   280

    What misery most drowningly doth sing
In lone Endymion's ear, now he has raught
The goal of consciousness? Ah, 'tis the thought,
The deadly feel of solitude: for lo!
He cannot see the heavens, nor the flow
Of rivers, nor hill-flowers running wild
In pink and purple chequer, nor, up-pil'd,
The cloudy rack slow journeying in the west,
Like herded elephants; nor felt, nor prest
Cool grass, nor tasted the fresh slumberous air;   290
But far from such companionship to wear
An unknown time, surcharg'd[16] with grief, away,
Was now his lot. And must he patient stay,
Tracing fantastic figures with his spear?
'No!' exclaim'd he, 'why should I tarry here?'
No! loudly echoed times innumerable.
At which he straightway started, and 'gan tell
His paces back into the temple's chief;[17]
Warming and glowing strong in the belief
Of help from Dian: so that when again   300
He caught her airy form, thus did he plain,[18]
Moving more near the while: 'O Haunter chaste
Of river sides, and woods, and heathy waste,
Where with thy silver bow and arrows keen
Art thou now forested? O woodland Queen,
What smoothest air thy smoother forehead woos?
Where dost thou listen to the wide halloos
Of thy disparted[19] nymphs? Through what dark tree
Glimmers thy crescent? Wheresoe'er it be,
'Tis in the breath of heaven: thou dost taste   310
Freedom as none can taste it, nor dost waste

Thy loveliness in dismal elements;
But, finding in our green earth sweet contents,
There livest blissfully. Ah, if to thee
It feels Elysian, how rich to me,
An exil'd mortal, sounds its pleasant name!
Within my breast there lives a choking flame –
O let me cool't the zephyr-boughs[20] among!
A homeward fever parches up my tongue –
O let me slake it at the running springs!   320
Upon my ear a noisy nothing rings –
O let me once more hear the linnet's note!
Before mine eyes thick films and shadows float –
O let me 'noint them with the heaven's light!
Dost thou now lave thy feet and ankles white?
O think how sweet to me the freshening sluice!
Dost thou now please thy thirst with berry-juice?
O think how this dry palate would rejoice!
If in soft slumber thou dost hear my voice,
O think how I should love a bed of flowers! –   330
Young goddess! let me see my native bowers!
Deliver me from this rapacious deep!'

    Thus ending loudly, as he would o'erleap
His destiny, alert he stood: but when
Obstinate silence came heavily again,
Feeling about for its old couch of space
And airy cradle, lowly bow'd his face
Desponding, o'er the marble floor's cold thrill.
But 'twas not long; for, sweeter than the rill
To its old channel, or a swollen tide   340
To margin sallows, were the leaves he spied,
And flowers, and wreaths, and ready myrtle crowns
Up heaping through the slab: refreshment drowns
Itself, and strives its own delights to hide –
Nor in one spot alone; the floral pride
In a long whispering birth enchanted grew
Before his footsteps; as when heav'd anew
Old ocean rolls a lengthened wave to the shore,
Down whose green back the short-liv'd foam, all hoar,
Bursts gradual, with a wayward indolence.   350

Increasing still in heart, and pleasant sense,
Upon his fairy journey on he hastes;
So anxious for the end, he scarcely wastes
One moment with his hand among the sweets:
Onward he goes – he stops – his bosom beats
As plainly in his ear, as the faint charm
Of which the throbs were born. This still alarm,
This sleepy music, forc'd him walk tiptoe:
For it came more softly than the east could blow
Arion's magic to the Atlantic isles;   360
Or than the west, made jealous by the smiles
Of thron'd Apollo, could breathe back the lyre
To seas Ionian and Tyrian.

O did he ever live, that lonely man,
Who lov'd – and music slew not? 'Tis the pest
Of love, that fairest joys give most unrest;
That things of delicate and tenderest worth
Are swallow'd all, and made a seared dearth,
By one consuming flame: it doth immerse
And suffocate true blessings in a curse.   370
Half-happy, by comparison of bliss,
Is miserable. 'Twas even so with this
Dew-dropping melody, in the Carian's ear;[21]
First heaven, then hell, and then forgotten clear,
Vanish'd in elemental passion.

And down some swart abysm[22] he had gone,
Had not a heavenly guide benignant led
To where thick myrtle branches, 'gainst his head
Brushing, awakened: then the sounds again
Went noiseless as a passing noontide rain   380
Over a bower, where little space he stood;
For as the sunset peeps into a wood
So saw he panting light, and towards it went
Through winding alleys; and lo, wonderment!
Upon soft verdure saw, one here, one there,
Cupids a slumbering on their pinions fair.

After a thousand mazes overgone,
At last, with sudden step, he came upon
A chamber, myrtle wall'd, embowered high,
Full of light, incense, tender minstrelsy,   390
And more of beautiful and strange beside:
For on a silken couch of rosy pride,
In midst of all, there lay a sleeping youth[23]
Of fondest beauty; fonder, in fair sooth,
Than sighs could fathom, or contentment reach:
And coverlids gold-tinted like the peach,
Or ripe October's faded marigolds,
Fell sleek about him in a thousand folds –
Not hiding up an Apollonian curve
Of neck and shoulder, nor the tenting swerve   400
Of knee from knee, nor ankles pointing light;
But rather, giving them to the filled sight
Officiously. Sideway his face repos'd
On one white arm, and tenderly unclos'd,
By tenderest pressure, a faint damask mouth
To slumbery pout; just as the morning south
Disparts a dew-lipp'd rose. Above his head,
Four lily stalks did their white honours wed
To make a coronal; and round him grew
All tendrils green, of every bloom and hue,   410
Together intertwin'd and trammel'd fresh:
The vine of glossy sprout; the ivy mesh,
Shading its Ethiop[24] berries; and woodbine,
Of velvet leaves and bugle-blooms[25] divine;
Convolvulus in streaked vases flush;
The creeper, mellowing for an autumn blush;
And virgin's bower,[26] trailing airily;
With others of the sisterhood. Hard by,
Stood serene Cupids watching silently.
One, kneeling to a lyre, touch'd the strings,   420
Muffling to death the pathos[27] with his wings;
And, ever and anon, uprose to look
At the youth's slumber; while another took
A willow-bough, distilling odorous dew,
And shook it on his hair; another flew
In through the woven roof, and fluttering-wise

Rain'd violets upon his sleeping eyes.

At these enchantments, and yet many more,
The breathless Latmian wonder'd o'er and o'er;
Until, impatient in embarrassment,　　　　　　　　430
He forthright pass'd, and lightly treading went
To that same feather'd lyrist, who straightway,
Smiling, thus whisper'd: 'Though from upper day
Thou art a wanderer, and thy presence here
Might seem unholy, be of happy cheer!
For 'tis the nicest touch of human honour,
When some ethereal and high-favouring donor
Presents immortal bowers to mortal sense;
As now 'tis done to thee, Endymion. Hence
Was I in no wise startled. So recline　　　　　　　440
Upon these living flowers. Here is wine,
Alive with sparkles – never, I aver,
Since Ariadne was a vintager,
So cool a purple: taste these juicy pears,
Sent me by sad Vertumnus, when his fears
Were high about Pomona: here is cream,
Deepening to richness from a snowy gleam;
Sweeter than that nurse Amalthea skimm'd
For the boy Jupiter: and here, undimm'd
By any touch, a bunch of blooming plums　　　　450
Ready to melt between an infant's gums:
And here is manna pick'd from Syrian trees,
In starlight, by the three Hesperides.
Feast on, and meanwhile I will let thee know
Of all these things around us.'[28] He did so,
Still brooding o'er the cadence of his lyre;
And thus: 'I need not any hearing tire
By telling how the sea-born goddess pin'd
For a mortal youth, and how she strove to bind
Him all in all unto her doting self.　　　　　　　460
Who would not be so prison'd? but, fond elf,[29]
He was content to let her amorous plea
Faint through his careless arms; content to see
An unseiz'd heaven dying at his feet;
Content, O fool! to make a cold retreat,

When on the pleasant grass such love, lovelorn,
Lay sorrowing; when every tear was born
Of diverse passion; when her lips and eyes
Were clos'd in sullen moisture, and quick sighs
Came vex'd and pettish through her nostrils small.   470
Hush! no exclaim – yet, justly mightst thou call
Curses upon his head. – I was half glad,
But my poor mistress went distract and mad,
When the boar tusk'd him: so away she flew
To Jove's high throne, and by her plainings drew
Immortal tear-drops down the thunderer's beard;
Whereòn, it was decreed he should be rear'd
Each summer time to life. Lo! this is he,
That same Adonis, safe in the privacy
Of this still region all his winter-sleep.   480
Aye, sleep; for when our love-sick queen did weep
Over his waned corse, the tremulous shower
Heal'd up the wound, and, with a balmy power,
Medicined death to a lengthened drowsiness:
The which she fills with visions, and doth dress
In all this quiet luxury; and hath set
Us young immortals, without any let,
To watch his slumber through. 'Tis well nigh pass'd,
Even to a moment's filling up, and fast
She scuds with summer breezes, to pant through   490
The first long kiss, warm firstling, to renew
Embower'd sports in Cytherea's isle.
Look! how those winged listeners all this while
Stand anxious: see! behold!' – This claimant word
Broke through the careful silence; for they heard
A rustling noise of leaves, and out there flutter'd
Pigeons and doves: Adonis something mutter'd
The while one hand, that erst upon his thigh
Lay dormant, mov'd convuls'd and gradually
Up to his forehead. Then there was a hum   500
Of sudden voices, echoing, 'Come! come!
Arise! awake! Clear summer has forth walk'd
Unto the clover-sward, and she has talk'd
Full soothingly to every nested finch:
Rise, Cupids! or we'll give the bluebell pinch

To your dimpled arms. Once more sweet life begin!'
At this, from every side they hurried in,
Rubbing their sleepy eyes with lazy wrists,
And doubling over head their little fists
In backward yawns. But all were soon alive: 510
For as delicious wine doth, sparkling, dive
In nectar'd clouds and curls through water fair,
So from the arbour roof down swell'd an air
Odorous and enlivening; making all
To laugh, and play, and sing, and loudly call
For their sweet queen: when lo! the wreathed green
Disparted, and far upward could be seen
Blue heaven, and a silver car, air-borne,
Whose silent wheels, fresh wet from clouds of morn,
Spun off a drizzling dew, – which falling chill   520
On soft Adonis' shoulders, made him still
Nestle and turn uneasily about.
Soon were the white doves plain, with neck stretch'd out,
And silken traces lighten'd in descent;
And soon, returning from love's banishment,
Queen Venus leaning downward open arm'd:
Her shadow fell upon his breast, and charm'd
A tumult to his heart, and a new life
Into his eyes. Ah, miserable strife,
But for her comforting! unhappy sight,   530
But meeting her blue orbs! Who, who can write
Of these first minutes? The unchariest muse
To embracements warm as theirs makes coy excuse.

　　O it has ruffled every spirit there,
Saving Love's self, who stands superb to share
The general gladness: awfully he stands;
A sovereign quell is in his waving hands;
No sight can bear the lightning of his bow;
His quiver is mysterious, none can know
What themselves think of it; from forth his eyes   540
There darts strange light of varied hues and dies:
A scowl is sometimes on his brow, but who
Look full upon it feel anon the blue
Of his fair eyes run liquid through their souls.

Endymion feels it, and no more controls
The burning prayer within him; so, bent low,
He had begun a plaining of his woe.
But Venus, bending forward, said: 'My child,
Favour this gentle youth; his days are wild
With love – he – but alas! too well I see   550
Thou know'st the deepness of his misery.
Ah, smile not so, my son: I tell thee true,
That when through heavy hours I used to rue
The endless sleep of this new born Adon',
This stranger aye I pitied. For upon
A dreary morning once I fled away
Into the breezy clouds, to weep and pray
For this my love: for vexing Mars[30] had teas'd
Me even to tears: thence, when a little eas'd,
Down-looking, vacant, through a hazy wood,   560
I saw this youth as he despairing stood:
Those same dark curls blown vagrant in the wind;
Those same full fringed lids a constant blind
Over his sullen eyes: I saw him throw
Himself on wither'd leaves, even as though
Death had come sudden; for no jot he mov'd,
Yet mutter'd wildly. I could hear he lov'd
Some fair immortal, and that his embrace
Had zoned[31] her through the night. There is no trace
Of this in heaven: I have mark'd each cheek,   570
And find it is the vainest thing to seek;
And that of all things 'tis kept secretest.
Endymion! one day thou wilt be blest:
So still obey the guiding hand that fends
Thee safely through these wonders for sweet ends.
'Tis a concealment needful in extreme;
And if I guess'd not so, the sunny beam
Thou shouldst mount up to with me. Now adieu!
Here must we leave thee.' – At these words upflew
The impatient doves, uprose the floating car,   580
Up went the hum celestial. High afar
The Latmian saw them minish[32] into naught;
And, when all were clear vanish'd, still he caught
A vivid lightning from that dreadful bow.

When all was darkened, with Aetnean throe[33]
The earth clos'd – gave a solitary moan –
And left him once again in twilight lone.

   He did not rave, he did not stare aghast,
For all those visions were o'ergone, and past,
And he in loneliness: he felt assur'd   590
Of happy times, when all he had endur'd
Would seem a feather to the mighty prize.
So, with unusual gladness, on he hies
Through caves, and palaces of mottled ore,
Gold dome, and crystal wall, and turquois floor,
Black polish'd porticos of awful shade,
And, at the last, a diamond balustrade,
Leading afar past wild magnificence,
Spiral through ruggedest loopholes, and thence
Stretching across a void, then guiding o'er   600
Enormous chasms, where, all foam and roar,
Streams subterranean tease their granite beds;
Then heighten'd just above the silvery heads
Of a thousand fountains, so that he could dash
The waters with his spear; but at the splash,
Done heedlessly, those spouting columns rose
Sudden a poplar's height, and 'gan to enclose
His diamond path with fretwork, streaming round
Alive, and dazzling cool, and with a sound,
Haply, like dolphin tumults, when sweet shells   610
Welcome the float of Thetis. Long he dwells
On this delight; for, every minute's space,
The streams with changed magic interlace:
Sometimes like delicatest lattices,
Cover'd with crystal vines; then weeping trees.
Moving about as in a gentle wind,
Which, in a wink, to watery gauze refin'd,
Pour'd into shapes of curtain'd canopies,
Spangled, and rich with liquid broideries
Of flowers, peacocks, swans, and naiads fair.   620
Swifter than lightning went these wonders rare;
And then the water, into stubborn streams
Collecting, mimick'd the wrought oaken beams,

Pillars, and frieze, and high fantastic roof,
Of those dusk places in times far aloof
Cathedrals call'd. He bade a loth farewell
To these founts Protean,[34] passing gulf, and dell,
And torrent, and ten thousand jutting shapes,
Half seen through deepest gloom, and grisly gapes,
Blackening on every side, and overhead   630
A vaulted dome like Heaven's, far bespread
With starlight gems: aye, all so huge and strange,
The solitary felt a hurried change
Working within him into something dreary, –
Vex'd like a morning eagle, lost, and weary,
And purblind amid foggy, midnight wolds.
But he revives at once: for who beholds
New sudden things, nor casts his mental slough?
Forth from a rugged arch, in the dusk below,
Came mother Cybele! alone – alone –   640
In sombre chariot; dark foldings thrown
About her majesty, and front death-pale,
With turrets crown'd. Four maned lions hale
The sluggish wheels; solemn their toothed maws,
Their surly eyes brow-hidden, heavy paws
Uplifted drowsily, and nervy tails
Cowering their tawny brushes. Silent sails
This shadowy queen athwart, and faints away
In another gloomy arch.
                                    Wherefore delay,
Young traveller, in such a mournful place?   650
Art thou wayworn, or canst not further trace
The diamond path? And does it indeed end
Abrupt in middle air? Yet earthward bend
Thy forehead, and to Jupiter cloud-borne
Call ardently! He was indeed wayworn;
Abrupt, in middle air, his way was lost;
To cloud-borne Jove he bowed, and there crost
Towards him a large eagle, 'twixt whose wings,
Without one impious word, himself he flings,
Committed to the darkness and the gloom: 660
Down, down, uncertain to what pleasant doom,
Swift as a fathoming plummet[35] down he fell

Through unknown things; till exhaled asphodel,
And rose, with spicy fannings interbreath'd,
Came swelling forth where little caves were wreath'd
So thick with leaves and mosses, that they seem'd
Large honeycombs of green, and freshly teem'd
With airs delicious. In the greenest nook
The eagle landed him, and farewell took.

It was a jasmine bower, all bestrown   670
With golden moss. His every sense had grown
Ethereal for pleasure; 'bove his head
Flew a delight half-graspable: his tread
Was Hesperean;[36] to his capable ears
Silence was music from the holy spheres;
A dewy luxury was in his eyes;
The little flowers felt his pleasant sighs
And stirr'd them faintly. Verdant cave and cell
He wander'd through, oft wondering at such swell
Of sudden exaltation: but, 'Alas!'   680
Said he, 'will all this gush of feeling pass
Away in solitude? And must they wane,
Like melodies upon a sandy plain,
Without an echo? Then shall I be left
So sad, so melancholy, so bereft!
Yet still I feel immortal! O my love,
My breath of life, where art thou? High above,
Dancing before the morning gates of heaven?
Or keeping watch among those starry seven,[37]
Old Atlas' children? Art a maid of the waters,   690
One of shell-winding Triton's bright-hair'd daughters?
Or art, impossible! a nymph of Dian's,
Weaving a coronal of tender scions
For very idleness? Where'er thou art,
Methinks it now is at my will to start
Into thine arms; to scare Aurora's train,
And snatch thee from the morning; o'er the main
To scud like a wild bird, and take thee off
From thy sea-foamy cradle; or to doff
Thy shepherd vest, and woo thee mid fresh leaves.   700
No, no, too eagerly my soul deceives

Its powerless self: I know this cannot be.
O let me then by some sweet dreaming flee
To her entrancements: hither sleep awhile!
Hither most gentle sleep! and soothing foil
For some few hours the coming solitude.'

   Thus spake he, and that moment felt endued
With power to dream deliciously; so wound
Through a dim passage, searching till he found
The smoothest mossy bed and deepest, where   710
He threw himself, and just into the air
Stretching his indolent arms, he took, O bliss!
A naked waist: 'Fair Cupid, whence is this?'
A well-known voice sigh'd, 'Sweetest, here am I!'
At which soft ravishment, with doting cry
They trembled to each other. – Helicon!
O fountain'd hill! Old Homer's Helicon!
That thou wouldst spout a little streamlet o'er
These sorry pages; then the verse would soar
And sing above this gentle pair, like lark   720
Over his nested young: but all is dark
Around thine aged top, and thy clear fount
Exhales in mists to heaven. Aye, the count
Of mighty Poets is made up;[38] the scroll
Is folded by the Muses; the bright roll
Is in Apollo's hand: our dazed eyes
Have seen a new tinge in the western skies:
The world has done its duty. Yet, oh yet,
Although the sun of poesy is set,
These lovers did embrace, and we must weep   730
That there is no old power left to steep
A quill immortal in their joyous tears.
Long time ere silence did their anxious fears
Question that thus it was; long time they lay
Fondling and kissing every doubt away;
Long time ere soft caressing sobs began
To mellow into words, and then there ran
Two bubbling springs of talk from their sweet lips.
'O known Unknown! from whom my being sips
Such darling essence, wherefore may I not   740

Be ever in these arms? in this sweet spot
Pillow my chin for ever? ever press
These toying hands and kiss their smooth excess?
Why not for ever and for ever feel
That breath about my eyes? Ah, thou wilt steal
Away from me again, indeed, indeed –
Thou wilt be gone away, and wilt not heed
My lonely madness. Speak, delicious fair!
Is – is it to be so? No! Who will dare
To pluck thee from me? And, of thine own will,   750
Full well I feel thou wouldst not leave me. Still
Let me entwine thee surer, surer – now
How can we part? Elysium! who art thou?
Who, that thou canst not be for ever here,
Or lift me with thee to some starry sphere?
Enchantress! tell me by this soft embrace,
By the most soft complexion of thy face,
Those lips, O slippery blisses, twinkling eyes,
And by these tenderest, milky sovereignties –
These tenderest, and by the nectar-wine,   760
The passion' – 'O dov'd Ida[39] the divine!
Endymion! dearest! Ah, unhappy me!
His soul will 'scape us – O felicity!
How he does love me! His poor temples beat
To the very tune of love – how sweet, sweet, sweet.
Revive, dear youth, or I shall faint and die;
Revive, or these soft hours will hurry by
In tranced dulness; speak, and let that spell
Affright this lethargy! I cannot quell
Its heavy pressure, and will press at least   770
My lips to thine, that they may richly feast
Until we taste the life of love again.
What! dost thou move? dost kiss? O bliss! O pain!
I love thee, youth, more than I can conceive;
And so long absence from thee doth bereave
My soul of any rest: yet must I hence:
Yet, can I not to starry eminence
Uplift thee: nor for very shame can own
Myself to thee: Ah, dearest, do not groan
Or thou wilt force me from this secrecy,   780

And I must blush in heaven. O that I
Had done 't already; that the dreadful smiles
At my lost brightness, my impassion'd wiles,
Had waned from Olympus' solemn height,
And from all serious Gods; that our delight
Was quite forgotten, save of us alone!
And wherefore so ashamed? 'Tis but to atone
For endless pleasure, by some coward blushes:
Yet must I be a coward! – Horror rushes
Too palpable before me – the sad look   790
Of Jove – Minerva's start – no bosom shook
With awe of purity – no Cupid pinion
In reverence veiled – my crystalline dominion
Half lost, and all old hymns made nullity![40]
But what is this to love? O I could fly
With thee into the ken of heavenly powers,
So thou wouldst thus, for many sequent hours,
Press me so sweetly. Now I swear at once
That I am wise, that Pallas is a dunce –
Perhaps her love like mine is but unknown –   800
O I do think that I have been alone
In chastity: yes, Pallas has been sighing,
While every eve saw me my hair uptying
With fingers cool as aspen leaves. Sweet love,
I was as vague as solitary dove,
Nor knew that nests were built. Now a soft kiss –
Aye, by that kiss, I vow an endless bliss,
An immortality of passion's thine:
Ere long I will exalt thee to the shine
Of heaven ambrosial;[41] and we will shade   810
Ourselves whole summers by a river glade;
And I will tell thee stories of the sky,
And breathe thee whispers of its minstrelsy.
My happy love will overwing all bounds!
O let me melt into thee; let the sounds
Of our close voices marry at their birth;
Let us entwine hoveringly – O dearth
Of human words! roughness of mortal speech!
Lispings[42] empyrean will I sometime teach
Thine honied tongue – lute-breathings, which I gasp   820

To have thee understand, now while I clasp
Thee thus, and weep for fondness – I am pain'd,
Endymion: woe! woe! is grief contain'd
In the very deeps of pleasure, my sole life?' –
Hereat, with many sobs, her gentle strife
Melted into a languor. He return'd
Entranced vows and tears.
                              Ye who have yearn'd
With too much passion, will here stay and pity,
For the mere sake of truth; as 'tis a ditty
Not of these days, but long ago 'twas told   830
By a cavern wind unto a forest old;
And then the forest told it in a dream
To a sleeping lake, whose cool and level gleam
A poet caught as he was journeying
To Phoebus' shrine; and in it he did fling
His weary limbs, bathing an hour's space,
And after, straight in that inspired place
He sang the story up into the air,
Giving it universal freedom. There
Has it been ever sounding for those ears   840
Whose tips are glowing hot. The legend cheers
Yon sentinel[43] stars; and he who listens to it
Must surely be self-doom'd or he will rue it:
For quenchless burnings come upon the heart,
Made fiercer by a fear lest any part
Should be engulfed in the eddying wind.
As much as here is penn'd doth always find
A resting place, thus much comes clear and plain;
Anon the strange voice is upon the wane –
And 'tis but echo'd from departing sound,   850
That the fair visitant at last unwound
Her gentle limbs, and left the youth asleep. –
Thus the tradition of the gusty deep.

Now turn we to our former chroniclers. –
Endymion awoke, that grief of hers
Sweet paining on his ear: he sickly guess'd
How lone he was once more, and sadly press'd
His empty arms together, hung his head,

And most forlorn upon that widow'd bed
Sat silently. Love's madness he had known: 860
Often with more than tortured lion's groan
Moanings had burst from him; but now that rage
Had pass'd away: no longer did he wage
A rough-voic'd war against the dooming stars.
No, he had felt too much for such harsh jars:
The lyre of his soul Aeolian tun'd
Forgot all violence, and but commun'd
With melancholy thought: O he had swoon'd
Drunken from pleasure's nipple! and his love
Henceforth was dove-like. – Loth was he to move   870
From the imprinted couch, and when he did,
'Twas with slow, languid paces, and face hid
In muffling hands. So temper'd, out he stray'd
Half seeing visions that might have dismay'd
Alecto's[44] serpents; ravishments more keen
Than Hermes' pipe, when anxious he did lean
Over eclipsing eyes: and at the last
It was a sounding grotto, vaulted, vast,
O'er studded with a thousand, thousand pearls,
And crimson mouthed shells with stubborn curls,   880
Of every shape and size, even to the bulk
In which whales arbour[45] close, to brood and sulk
Against an endless storm. Moreover too,
Fish-semblances, of green and azure hue,
Ready to snort their streams. In this cool wonder
Endymion sat down, and 'gan to ponder
On all his life: his youth, up to the day
When 'mid acclaim, and feasts, and garlands gay,
He stept upon his shepherd throne: the look
Of his white palace in wild forest nook,   890
And all the revels he had lorded there:
Each tender maiden whom he once thought fair,
With every friend and fellow-woodlander –
Pass'd like a dream before him. Then the spur
Of the old bards to mighty deeds: his plans
To nurse the golden age 'mong shepherd clans:
That wondrous night: the great Pan-festival:
His sister's sorrow; and his wanderings all,

Until into the earth's deep maw he rush'd:
Then all its buried magic, till it flush'd
High with excessive love. 'And now,' thought he,
'How long must I remain in jeopardy
Of blank amazements that amaze no more?
Now I have tasted her sweet soul to the core,
All other depths are shallow: essences,
Once spiritual, are like muddy lees,
Meant but to fertilise my earthly root,
And make my branches lift a golden fruit
Into the bloom of heaven: other light,
Though it be quick and sharp enough to blight   910
The Olympian eagle's vision,[46] is dark,
Dark as the parentage of chaos. Hark!
My silent thoughts are echoing from these shells;
Or they are but the ghosts, the dying swells
Of noises far away? – list!' – Hereupon
He kept an anxious ear. The humming tone
Came louder, and behold, there as he lay,
On either side outgush'd, with misty spray,
A copious spring; and both together dash'd
Swift, mad, fantastic round the rocks, and lash'd   920
Among the conchs and shells of the lofty grot,
Leaving a trickling dew. At last they shot
Down from the ceiling's height, pouring a noise
As of some breathless racers whose hopes poise
Upon the last few steps, and with spent force
Along the ground they took a winding course.
Endymion follow'd – for it seem'd that one
Ever pursued; the other strove to shun –
Follow'd their languid mazes, till well nigh
He had left thinking of the mystery, –   930
And was now rapt in tender hoverings
Over the vanish'd bliss. Ah! what is it sings
His dream away? What melodies are these?
They sound as through the whispering of trees,
Not native in such barren vaults. Give ear!

'O Arethusa,[47] peerless nymph! why fear
Such tenderness as mine? Great Dian, why,

Why didst thou hear her prayer? O that I
Were rippling round her dainty fairness now,
Circling about her waist, and striving how   940
To entice her to a dive! then stealing in
Between her luscious lips and eyelids thin.
O that her shining hair was in the sun,
And I distilling from it thence to run
In amorous rillets down her shrinking form!
To linger on her lily shoulders, warm
Between her kissing breasts, and every charm
Touch raptur'd! – See how painfully I flow:
Fair maid, be pitiful to my great woe.
Stay, stay thy weary course, and let me lead,   950
A happy wooer, to the flowery mead
Where all that beauty snar'd me.' – 'Cruel god,
Desist! or my offended mistress' nod
Will stagnate all thy fountains: – tease me not
With syren words[48] – Ah, have I really got
Such power to madden thee? And is it true –
Away, away, or I shall dearly rue
My very thoughts: in mercy then away,
Kindest Alpheus, for should I obey
My own dear will, 'twould be a deadly bane.   960
O, Oread-Queen![49] would that thou hadst a pain
Like this of mine, then would I fearless turn
And be a criminal.[50] Alas, I burn,
I shudder – gentle river, get thee hence.
Alpheus! thou enchanter! every sense
Of mine was once made perfect in these woods.
Fresh breezes, bowery lawns, and innocent floods,
Ripe fruits, and lonely couch, contentment gave;
But ever since I heedlessly did lave
In thy deceitful stream, a panting glow   970
Grew strong within me: wherefore serve me so,
And call it love? Alas, 'twas cruelty.
Not once more did I close my happy eye
Amid the thrushes' song. Away! Avaunt!
O 'twas a cruel thing.' – 'Now thou dost taunt
So softly, Arethusa, that I think
If thou wast playing on my shady brink,

Thou wouldst bathe once again. Innocent maid!
Stifle thine heart no more; nor be afraid
Of angry powers: there are deities   980
Will shade us with their wings. Those fitful sighs
'Tis almost death to hear: O let me pour
A dewy balm upon them! – fear no more,
Sweet Arethusa! Dian's self must feel
Sometime these very pangs. Dear maiden, steal
Blushing into my soul, and let us fly
These dreary caverns for the open sky.
I will delight thee all my winding course,
From the green sea up to my hidden source
About Arcadian forests; and will show   990
The channels where my coolest waters flow
Through mossy rocks; where, 'mid exuberant green,
I roam in pleasant darkness, more unseen
Than Saturn in his exile; where I brim
Round flowery islands, and take thence a skim
Of mealy sweets,[51] which myriads of bees
Buzz from their honey'd wings: and thou shouldst please
Thyself to choose the richest, where we might
Be incense-pillow'd every summer night.
Doff all sad fears, thou white deliciousness,   1000
And let us be thus comforted; unless
Thou couldst rejoice to see my hopeless stream
Hurry distracted from Sol's temperate beam,
And pour to death along some hungry sands.' –
'What can I do, Alpheus? Dian stands
Severe before me: persecuting fate!
Unhappy Arethusa! thou wast late
A huntress free in' – At this, sudden fell
Those two sad streams adown a fearful dell.
The Latmian listen'd, but he heard no more,   1010
Save echo, faint repeating o'er and o'er
The name of Arethusa. On the verge
Of that dark gulf he wept, and said: 'I urge
Thee, gentle Goddess of my pilgrimage,
By our eternal hopes, to soothe, to assuage,
If thou art powerful, these lovers' pains;
And make them happy in some happy plains.'

He turn'd – there was a whelming sound[52] – he stept,
There was a cooler light; and so he kept
Towards it by a sandy path, and lo!   1020
More suddenly than doth a moment go,
The visions of the earth were gone and fled –
He saw the giant sea above his head.

Book III

There are who lord it o'er their fellow-men
With most prevailing tinsel: who unpen
Their baaing vanities, to browse away
The comfortable green and juicy hay
From human pastures; or, O torturing fact!
Who, through an idiot blink, will see unpack'd
Fire-branded foxes[1] to sear up and singe
Our gold and ripe-ear'd hopes. With not one tinge
Of sanctuary splendour, not a sight
Able to face an owl's, they still are dight[2]   10
By the blear-eyed nations in empurpled vests,[3]
And crowns, and turbans. With unladen breasts,
Save of blown self-applause, they proudly mount
To their spirit's perch, their being's high account,
Their tiptop nothings, their dull skies, their thrones –
Amid the fierce intoxicating tones
Of trumpets, shoutings, and belabour'd drums,
And sudden cannon. Ah! how all this hums,
In wakeful ears, like uproar past and gone –
Like thunder clouds[4] that spake to Babylon,   20
And set those old Chaldeans to their tasks. –
Are then regalities all gilded masks?
No, there are throned seats unscalable
But by a patient wing, a constant spell,
Or by ethereal things that, unconfin'd,
Can make a ladder of the eternal wind,
And poise about in cloudy thunder-tents
To watch the abysm-birth of elements.
Aye, 'bove the withering of old-lipp'd Fate
A thousand Powers keep religious state,   30
In water, fiery realm, and airy bourne;[5]
And, silent as a consecrated urn,
Hold sphery sessions for a season due.
Yet few of these far majesties, ah, few!
Have bared their operations to this globe –
Few, who with gorgeous pageantry enrobe
Our piece of heaven – whose benevolence

Shakes hand with our own Ceres; every sense
Filling with spiritual sweets to plenitude,
As bees gorge full their cells. And, by the feud   40
'Twixt Nothing and Creation, I here swear,
Eterne Apollo! that thy Sister fair
Is of all these the gentlier-mightiest.
When thy gold breath is misting in the west,
She unobserved steals unto her throne,
And there she sits most meek and most alone;
As if she had not pomp subservient;
As if thine eye, high Poet! was not bent
Towards her with the Muses in thine heart;
As if the ministring stars kept not apart,   50
Waiting for silver-footed messages.
O Moon! the oldest shades 'mong oldest trees
Feel palpitations when thou lookest in:
O Moon! old boughs lisp forth a holier din
The while they feel thine airy fellowship.
Thou dost bless every where, with silver lip
Kissing dead things to life. The sleeping kine,[6]
Couch'd in thy brightness, dream of fields divine:
Innumerable mountains rise, and rise,
Ambitious for the hallowing of thine eyes;   60
And yet thy benediction passeth not
One obscure hiding-place, one little spot
Where pleasure may be sent: the nested wren
Has thy fair face within its tranquil ken,
And from beneath a sheltering ivy leaf
Takes glimpses of thee; thou art a relief
To the poor patient oyster, where it sleeps
Within its pearly house. – The mighty deeps,
The monstrous sea is thine – the myriad sea!
O Moon! far-spooming[7] Ocean bows to thee,   70
And Tellus feels his forehead's cumbrous load.

    Cynthia! where art thou now? What far abode
Of green or silvery bower doth enshrine
Such utmost beauty? Alas, thou dost pine
For one as sorrowful: thy cheek is pale
For one whose cheek is pale: thou dost bewail

His tears, who weeps for thee. Where dost thou sigh?
Ah! surely that light peeps from Vesper's eye,
Or what a thing is love! 'Tis She, but lo!
How chang'd, how full of ache, how gone in woe!   80
She dies at the thinnest cloud; her loveliness
Is wan on Neptune's blue: yet there's a stress
Of love-spangles,[8] just off yon cape of trees,
Dancing upon the waves, as if to please
The curly foam with amorous influence.
O, not so idle: for down-glancing thence
She fathoms eddies, and runs wild about
O'erwhelming water-courses; scaring out
The thorny sharks from hiding-holes, and fright'ning
Their savage eyes with unaccustom'd lightning.   90
Where will the splendour be content to reach?
O love! how potent hast thou been to teach
Strange journeyings! Wherever beauty dwells,
In gulf or aerie, mountains or deep dells,
In light, in gloom, in star or blazing sun,
Thou pointest out the way, and straight 'tis won.
Amid his toil thou gav'st Leander breath;
Thou leddest Orpheus through the gleams of death;
Thou madest Pluto bear thin element;
And now, O winged Chieftain! [9]thou hast sent   100
A moonbeam to the deep, deep water-world,
To find Endymion.

                    On gold sand impearl'd
With lily shells, and pebbles milky white,
Poor Cynthia greeted him, and sooth'd her light
Against his pallid face: he felt the charm
To breathlessness, and suddenly a warm
Of his heart's blood: 'twas very sweet; he stay'd
His wandering steps, and half-entranced laid
His head upon a tuft of straggling weeds,
To taste the gentle moon, and freshening beads,   110
Lash'd from the crystal roof by fishes' tails.
And so he kept, until the rosy veils
Mantling the east, by Aurora's peering hand
Were lifted from the water's breast, and fann'd

Into sweet air; and sober'd morning came
Meekly through billows: – when like taper-flame
Left sudden by a dallying breath of air,
He rose in silence, and once more 'gan fare
Along his fated way.

                    Far had he roam'd,
With nothing save the hollow vast,[10] that foam'd,   120
Above, around, and at his feet; save things
More dead than Morpheus' imaginings:
Old rusted anchors, helmets, breast-plates large
Of gone sea-warriors; brazen beaks and targe;[11]
Rudders that for a hundred years had lost
The sway of human hand; gold vase emboss'd
With long-forgotten story, and wherein
No reveller had ever dipp'd a chin
But those of Saturn's vintage; mouldering scrolls,
Writ in the tongue of heaven, by those souls   130
Who first were on the earth; and sculptures rude
In ponderous stone, developing the mood
Of ancient Nox; – then skeletons of man,
Of beast, behemoth, and leviathan,[12]
And elephant, and eagle, and huge jaw
Of nameless monster. A cold leaden awe
These secrets struck into him; and unless
Dian had chased away that heaviness,
He might have died: but now, with cheered feel,
He onward kept; wooing these thoughts to steal   140
About the labyrinth in his soul of love.

   'What is there in thee, Moon! that thou shouldst move
My heart so potently? When yet a child
I oft have dried my tears when thou hast smil'd.
Thou seem'dst my sister: hand in hand we went
From eve to morn across the firmament.
No apples would I gather from the tree,
Till thou hadst cool'd their cheeks deliciously:
No tumbling water ever spake romance,
But when my eyes with thine thereon could dance: 150
No woods were green enough, no bower divine,

Until thou liftedst up thine eyelids fine:
In sowing time ne'er would I dibble take,
Or drop a seed, till thou wast wide awake;
And, in the summer tide of blossoming,
No one but thee hath heard me blythly sing
And mesh[13] my dewy flowers all the night.
No melody was like a passing spright
If it went not to solemnise thy reign.
Yes, in my boyhood, every joy and pain   160
By thee were fashion'd to the self-same end;
And as I grew in years, still didst thou blend
With all my ardours: thou wast the deep glen;
Thou wast the mountain-top – the sage's pen –
The poet's harp – the voice of friends – the sun;
Thou wast the river – thou wast glory won;
Thou wast my clarion's blast – thou wast my steed –
My goblet full of wine – my topmost deed: –
Thou wast the charm of women, lovely Moon!
O what a wild and harmonised tune   170
My spirit struck from all the beautiful!
On some bright essence could I lean, and lull
Myself to immortality: I prest
Nature's soft pillow in a wakeful rest.
But, gentle Orb! there came a nearer bliss –
My strange love came[14] – Felicity's abyss!
She came, and thou didst fade, and fade away –
Yet not entirely; no, thy starry sway
Has been an under-passion to this hour.
Now I begin to feel thine orby power   180
Is coming fresh upon me: O be kind,
Keep back thine influence, and do not blind
My sovereign vision. – Dearest love, forgive
That I can think away from thee and live! –
Pardon me, airy planet, that I prize
One thought beyond thine argent luxuries!
How far beyond!' At this a surpris'd start
Frosted the springing verdure of his heart;
For as he lifted up his eyes to swear
How his own goddess was past all things fair,   190
He saw far in the concave green of the sea

An old man sitting calm and peacefully.
Upon a weeded rock this old man sat,
And his white hair was awful, and a mat
Of weeds were cold beneath his cold thin feet;
And, ample as the largest winding-sheet,
A cloak of blue wrapp'd up his aged bones,
O'erwrought with symbols by the deepest groans
Of ambitious magic: every ocean-form
Was woven in with black distinctness; storm,   200
And calm, and whispering, and hideous roar,
Quicksand, and whirlpool, and deserted shore,
Were emblem'd in the woof; with every shape
That skims, or dives, or sleeps, 'twixt cape and cape.
The gulphing whale was like a dot in the spell,
Yet look upon it, and 'twould size and swell
To its huge self; and the minutest fish
Would pass the very hardest gazer's wish,
And show his little eye's anatomy.
Then there was pictur'd the regality   210
Of Neptune; and the sea nymphs round his state,
In beauteous vassage, look up and wait.
Beside this old man lay a pearly wand,
And in his lap a book, the which he conn'd[15]
So steadfastly, that the new denizen[16]
Had time to keep him in amazed ken,
To mark these shadowings, and stand in awe.

   The old man rais'd his hoary head and saw
The wilder'd stranger[17] – seeming not to see,
His features were so lifeless. Suddenly   220
He woke as from a trance; his snow-white brows
Went arching up, and like two magic ploughs
Furrow'd deep wrinkles in his forehead large,
Which kept as fixedly as rocky marge,
Till round his wither'd lips had gone a smile.
Then up he rose, like one whose tedious toil
Had watch'd for years in forlorn hermitage,
Who had not from mid-life to utmost age
Eas'd in one accent his o'er-burden'd soul,
Even to the trees. He rose: he grasp'd his stole,   230

With convuls'd clenches waving it abroad,
And in a voice of solemn joy, that aw'd
Echo into oblivion, he said: –

    'Thou art the man! Now shall I lay my head
In peace upon my watery pillow: now
Sleep will come smoothly to my weary brow.
O Jove! I shall be young again, be young!
O shell-borne Neptune, I am pierc'd and stung
With new-born life! What shall I do? Where go,
When I have cast this serpent-skin of woe? –   240
I'll swim to the syrens, and one moment listen
Their melodies, and see their long hair glisten;
Anon upon that giant's arm[18] I'll be,
That writhes about the roots of Sicily:
To northern seas I'll in a twinkling sail,
And mount upon the snortings of a whale
To some black cloud; thence down I'll madly sweep
On forked lightning, to the deepest deep,
Where through some sucking pool I will be hurl'd
With rapture to the other side of the world!   250
O, I am full of gladness! Sisters three,[19]
I bow full hearted to your old decree!
Yes, every god be thank'd, and power benign,
For I no more shall wither, droop, and pine.
Thou art the man!' Endymion started back
Dismay'd; and, like a wretch from whom the rack
Tortures hot breath, and speech of agony,
Mutter'd: 'What lonely death am I to die
In this cold region? Will he let me freeze,
And float my brittle limbs o'er polar seas?   260
Or will he touch me with his searing hand,
And leave a black memorial on the sand?
Or tear me piece-meal with a bony saw,
And keep me as a chosen food to draw
His magian fish through hated fire and flame?
O misery of hell! resistless, tame,
Am I to be burnt up? No, I will shout,
Until the gods through heaven's blue look out! –
O Tartarus! but some few days agone

Her soft arms were entwining me, and on   270
Her voice I hung like fruit among green leaves:
Her lips were all my own, and – ah, ripe sheaves
Of happiness! ye on the stubble droop,
But never may be garner'd. I must stoop
My head, and kiss death's foot. Love! love, farewell!
Is there no hope from thee? This horrid spell
Would melt at thy sweet breath. – By Dian's hind
Feeding from her white fingers, on the wind
I see thy streaming hair! and now, by Pan,
I care not for this old mysterious man!'   280

    He spake, and walking to that aged form,
Look'd high defiance. Lo! his heart 'gan warm
With pity, for the grey-hair'd creature wept.
Had he then wrong'd a heart where sorrow kept?
Had he, though blindly contumelious,[20] brought
Rheum to kind eyes, a sting to humane thought,
Convulsion to a mouth of many years?
He had in truth; and he was ripe for tears.
The penitent shower fell, as down he knelt
Before that care-worn sage, who trembling felt   290
About his large dark locks, and faltering spake:

    'Arise, good youth, for sacred Phoebus' sake!
I know thine inmost bosom, and I feel
A very brother's yearning for thee steal
Into mine own: for why? thou openest
The prison gates that have so long opprest
My weary watching. Though thou know'st it not,
Thou art commission'd to this fated spot
For great enfranchisement. O weep no more;
I am a friend to love, to loves of yore: 300
Aye, hadst thou never lov'd an unknown power
I had been grieving at this joyous hour.
But even now most miserable old,
I saw thee, and my blood no longer cold
Gave mighty pulses: in this tottering case
Grew a new heart, which at this moment plays
As dancingly as thine. Be not afraid,

For thou shalt hear this secret all display'd,
Now as we speed towards our joyous task.'

So saying, this young soul in age's mask   310
Went forward with the Carian side by side:
Resuming quickly thus; while ocean's tide
Hung swollen at their backs, and jewel'd sands
Took silently their footprints.
                                          'My soul stands[21]
Now past the midway from mortality,
And so I can prepare without a sigh
To tell thee briefly all my joy and pain.
I was a fisher once, upon this main,
And my boat danc'd in every creek and bay;
Rough billows were my home by night and day, –   320
The seagulls not more constant; for I had
No housing from the storm and tempests mad,
But hollow rocks, – and they were palaces
Of silent happiness, of slumberous ease:
Long years of misery have told me so.
Aye, thus it was one thousand years ago.
One thousand years! – Is it then possible
To look so plainly through them? to dispel
A thousand years with backward glance sublime?
To breathe away as 'twere all scummy slime   330
From off a crystal pool, to see its deep,
And one's own image from the bottom peep?
Yes: now I am no longer wretched thrall,[22]
My long captivity and moanings all
Are but a slime, a thin-pervading scum,
The which I breathe away, and thronging come
Like things of yesterday my youthful pleasures.

'I touch'd no lute, I sang not, trod no measures:
I was a lonely youth on desert shores.
My sports were lonely, mid continuous roars,   340
And craggy isles, and sea-mew's plaintive cry
Plaining discrepant between sea and sky.
Dolphins were still my playmates; shapes unseen
Would let me feel their scales of gold and green,

Nor be my desolation; and, full oft,
When a dread waterspout had rear'd aloft
Its hungry hugeness, seeming ready ripe
To burst with hoarsest thunderings, and wipe
My life away like a vast sponge of fate,
Some friendly monster, pitying my sad state,   350
Has dived to its foundations, gulf'd it down,
And left me tossing safely. But the crown
Of all my life was utmost quietude:
More did I love to lie in cavern rude,
Keeping in wait whole days for Neptune's voice,
And if it came at last, hark, and rejoice!
There blush'd no summer eve but I would steer
My skiff along green shelving coasts, to hear
The shepherd's pipe come clear from aery steep,
Mingled with ceaseless bleatings of his sheep: 360
And never was a day of summer shine,
But I beheld its birth upon the brine:
For I would watch all night to see unfold
Heaven's gates, and Aethon snort his morning gold
Wide o'er the swelling streams: and constantly
At brim of day-tide, on some grassy lea,
My nets would be spread out, and I at rest.
The poor folk of the sea-country I blest
With daily boon of fish most delicate:
They knew not whence this bounty, and elate   370
Would strew sweet flowers on a sterile beach.

  'Why was I not contented? Wherefore reach
At things which, but for thee, O Latmian!
Had been my dreary death? Fool! I began
To feel distemper'd[23] longings: to desire
The utmost privilege that ocean's sire
Could grant in benediction: to be free
Of all his kingdom. Long in misery
I wasted, ere in one extremest fit
I plung'd for life or death. To interknit   380
One's senses with so dense a breathing stuff
Might seem a work of pain; so not enough
Can I admire how crystal-smooth it felt,

And buoyant round my limbs. At first I dwelt
Whole days and days in sheer astonishment;
Forgetful utterly of self-intent;
Moving but with the mighty ebb and flow.
Then, like a new fledg'd bird that first doth show
His spreaded feathers to the morrow chill,
I tried in fear the pinions of my will.   390
'Twas freedom! and at once I visited
The ceaseless wonders of this ocean-bed.
No eed to tell thee of them, for I see
That thou hast been a witness – it must be –
For these I know thou canst not feel a drouth,
By the melancholy corners of that mouth.
So I will in my story straightway pass
To more immediate matter. Woe, alas!
That love should be my bane! Ah, Scylla fair!
Why did poor Glaucus ever – ever dare   400
To sue thee to his heart? Kind stranger-youth!
I lov'd her to the very white[24] of truth,
And she would not conceive it. Timid thing!
She fled me swift as sea-bird on the wing,
Round every isle, and point, and promontory,
From where large Hercules wound up his story
Far as Egyptian Nile. My passion grew
The more, the more I saw her dainty hue
Gleam delicately through the azure clear:
Until 'twas too fierce agony to bear;   410
And in that agony, across my grief
It flash'd, that Circe might find some relief –
Cruel enchantress! So above the water
I rear'd my head, and look'd for Phoebus' daughter.
Aeaea's isle was wondering at the moon: –
It seem'd to whirl around me, and a swoon
Left me dead-drifting to that fatal power.

  'When I awoke, 'twas in a twilight bower;
Just when the light of morn, with hum of bees,
Stole through its verdurous matting of fresh trees.   420
How sweet, and sweeter! for I heard a lyre,
And over it a sighing voice expire.

It ceased I caught light footsteps; and anon
The fairest face that morn e'er look'd upon
Push'd through a screen of roses. Starry Jove!
With tears, and smiles, and honey-words she wove
A net whose thraldom was more bliss than all
The range of flower'd Elysium. Thus did fall
The dew of her rich speech: "Ah! Art awake?
O let me hear thee speak, for Cupid's sake!   430
I am so oppress'd with joy! Why, I have shed
An urn of tears, as though thou wert cold dead;
And now I find thee living, I will pour
From these devoted eyes their silver store,
Until exhausted of the latest drop,
So it will pleasure thee, and force thee stop
Here, that I too may live: but if beyond
Such cool and sorrowful offerings, thou art fond
Of soothing warmth, of dalliance supreme;
If thou art ripe to taste a long love dream;   440
If smiles, if dimples, tongues for ardour mute,
Hang in thy vision like a tempting fruit,
O let me pluck it for thee." Thus she link'd
Her charming syllables, till indistinct
Their music came to my o'er-sweeten'd soul;
And then she hover'd over me, and stole
So near, that if no nearer it had been
This furrow'd visage thou hadst never seen.

'Young man of Latmos! thus particular
Am I, that thou may'st plainly see how far   450
This fierce temptation went: and thou may'st not
Exclaim, How then, was Scylla quite forgot?

'Who could resist? Who in this universe?
She did so breathe ambrosia; so immerse
My fine existence in a golden clime.
She took me like a child of suckling time,
And cradled me in roses. Thus condemn'd,
The current of my former life was stemm'd,
And to this arbitrary queen of sense
I bow'd a tranced vassal: nor would thence   460

Have mov'd, even though Amphion's harp had woo'd
Me back to Scylla o'er the billows rude.
For as Apollo each eve doth devise
A new appareling for western skies;
So every eve, nay every spendthrift hour
Shed balmy consciousness within that bower.
And I was free of haunts umbrageous;[25]
Could wander in the mazy forest-house
Of squirrels, foxes shy, and antler'd deer,
And birds from coverts innermost and drear   470
Warbling for very joy mellifluous sorrow –
To me new born delights!
                   'Now let me borrow,
For moments few, a temperament as stern
As Pluto's sceptre, that my words not burn
These uttering lips, while I in calm speech tell
How specious heaven was changed to real hell.

  'One morn she left me sleeping: half awake
I sought for her smooth arms and lips, to slake
My greedy thirst with nectarous camel-draughts;
But she was gone. Whereat the barbed shafts   480
Of disappointment stuck in me so sore,
That out I ran and search'd the forest o'er.
Wandering about in pine and cedar gloom
Damp awe assail'd me; for there 'gan to boom
A sound of moan, an agony of sound,
Sepulchral from the distance all around.
Then came a conquering earth-thunder; and rumbled
That fierce complain[26] to silence: while I stumbled
Down a precipitous path, as if impell'd.
I came to a dark valley. – Groanings swell'd   490
Poisonous about my ears, and louder grew,
The nearer I approach'd a flame's gaunt blue,
That glar'd before me through a thorny brake.
This fire, like the eye of gordian[27] snake,
Bewitch'd me towards; and I soon was near
A sight too fearful for the feel of fear:
In thicket hid I curs'd the haggard scene –
The banquet of my arms, my arbour queen,

Seated upon an uptorn forest root;
And all around her shapes, wizard and brute,   500
Laughing, and wailing, groveling, serpenting,
Showing tooth, tusk, and venom-bag, and sting!
O such deformities! Old Charon's self,
Should he give up awhile his penny pelf,[28]
And take a dream 'mong rushes Stygian,[29]
It could not be so fantasied. Fierce, wan,
And tyrannising was the lady's look,
As over them a gnarled staff she shook.
Oft-times upon the sudden she laugh'd out,
And from a basket emptied to the rout   510
Clusters of grapes, the which they raven'd quick
And roar'd for more; with many a hungry lick
About their shaggy jaws. Avenging, slow,
Anon she took a branch of mistletoe,
And emptied on't a black dull-gurgling phial:
Groan'd one and all, as if some piercing trial
Was sharpening for their pitiable bones.
She lifted up the charm: appealing groans
From their poor breasts went sueing to her ear
In vain; remorseless as an infant's bier   520
She whisk'd against their eyes the sooty oil.
Whereat was heard a noise of painful toil,
Increasing gradual to a tempest rage,
Shrieks, yells, and groans of torture pilgrimage;
Until their grieved bodies 'gan to bloat
And puff from the tail's end to stifled throat:
Then was appalling silence: then a sight
More wildering than all that hoarse affright;
For the whole herd, as by a whirlwind writhen,[30]
Went through the dismal air like one huge Python   530
Antagonising Boreas, – and so vanish'd.
Yet there was not a breath of wind: she banish'd
These phantoms with a nod. Lo! from the dark
Came waggish fauns, and nymphs, and satyrs stark,
With dancing and loud revelry, – and went
Swifter than centaurs after rapine bent. –
Sighing an elephant appear'd and bow'd
Before the fierce witch, speaking thus aloud

In human accent: "Potent goddess! chief
Of pains resistless! make my being brief,   540
Or let me from this heavy prison fly:
Or give me to the air, or let me die!
I sue not for my happy crown again;
I sue not for my phalanx[31] on the plain;
I sue not for my lone, my widow'd wife;
I sue not for my ruddy drops of life,
My children fair, my lovely girls and boys!
 I will forget them; I will pass these joys;
Ask nought so heavenward, so too – too high:
Only I pray, as fairest boon, to die,   550
Or be deliver'd from this cumbrous flesh,
From this gross, detestable, filthy mesh,
And merely given to the cold bleak air.
Have mercy, Goddess! Circe, feel my prayer!"

'That curst magician's name fell icy numb
Upon my wild conjecturing: truth had come
Naked and sabre-like against my heart.
I saw a fury whetting a death-dart;
And my slain spirit, overwrought with fright,
Fainted away in that dark lair of night.   560
Think, my deliverer, how desolate
My waking must have been! disgust, and hate,
And terrors manifold divided me
A spoil amongst them. I prepar'd to flee
Into the dungeon core of that wild wood:
I fled three days – when lo! before me stood
Glaring the angry witch. O Dis, even now,
A clammy dew is beading on my brow,
At mere remembering her pale laugh, and curse.
"Ha! ha! Sir Dainty! there must be a nurse   570
Made of rose leaves and thistledown, express,
To cradle thee my sweet, and lull thee: yes,
I am too flinty-hard for thy nice touch:
My tenderest squeeze is but a giant's clutch.
So, fairy-thing, it shall have lullabies
Unheard of yet: and it shall still its cries
Upon some breast more lily-feminine.

Oh, no – it shall not pine, and pine, and pine
More than one pretty, trifling thousand years;
And then 'twere pity, but fate's gentle shears[32]   580
Cut short its immortality. Sea-flirt!
Young dove of the waters! truly I'll not hurt
One hair of thine: see how I weep and sigh,
That our heart-broken parting is so nigh.
And must we part? Ah, yes, it must be so.
Yet ere thou leavest me in utter woe,
Let me sob over thee my last adieus,
And speak a blessing: Mark me! Thou hast thews[33]
Immortal, for thou art of heavenly race:
But such a love is mine, that here I chase   590
Eternally away from thee all bloom
Of youth, and destine thee towards a tomb.
Hence shalt thou quickly to the watery vast;
And there, ere many days be overpast,
Disabled age shall seize thee; and even then
Thou shalt not go the way of aged men;
But live and wither, cripple and still breathe
Ten hundred years: which gone, I then bequeath
Thy fragile bones to unknown burial.
Adieu, sweet love, adieu! – As shot stars fall,   600
She fled ere I could groan for mercy. Stung
And poison'd was my spirit: despair sung
A war-song of defiance 'gainst all hell.
A hand was at my shoulder to compel
My sullen steps; another 'fore my eyes
Moved on with pointed finger. In this guise
Enforced, at the last by ocean's foam
I found me; by my fresh, my native home.
Its tempering coolness, to my life akin,
Came salutary as I waded in;   610
And, with a blind voluptuous rage, I gave
Battle to the swollen billow-ridge, and drave[34]
Large froth before me, while there yet remain'd
Hale strength, nor from my bones all marrow drain'd.

'Young lover, I must weep – such hellish spite
With dry cheek who can tell? While thus my might

Proving upon this element, dismay'd,
Upon a dead thing's face my hand I laid;
I look'd – 'twas Scylla! Cursed, cursed Circe!
O vulture-witch, hast never heard of mercy?   620
Could not thy harshest vengeance be content,
But thou must nip this tender innocent
Because I lov'd her? – Cold, O cold indeed
Were her fair limbs, and like a common weed
The sea-swell took her hair. Dead as she was
I clung about her waist, nor ceas'd to pass
Fleet as an arrow through unfathom'd brine.
Until there shone a fabric crystalline,
Ribb'd and inlaid with coral, pebble, and pearl.
Headlong I darted; at one eager swirl   630
Gain'd its bright portal, enter'd, and behold!
'Twas vast, and desolate, and icy-cold;
And all around – But wherefore this to thee
Who in few minutes more thyself shalt see? –
I left poor Scylla in a niche and fled.
My fever'd parchings up, my seathing dread
Met palsy half way: soon these limbs became
Gaunt, wither'd, sapless, feeble, cramp'd, and lame.

 'Now let me pass a cruel, cruel space,
Without one hope, without one faintest trace   640
Of mitigation, or redeeming bubble
Of colour'd fantasy; for I fear 'Twould trouble
Thy brain to loss of reason: and next tell
How a restoring chance came down to quell
One half of the witch in me.

                              'On a day,
Sitting upon a rock above the spray,
I saw grow up from the horizon's brink
A gallant vessel: soon she seem'd to sink
Away from me again, as though her course
Had been resum'd in spite of hindering force –   650
So vanish'd: and not long, before arose
Dark clouds, and muttering of winds morose.
Old Aeolus would stifle his mad spleen,

But could not: therefore all the billows green
Toss'd up the silver spume against the clouds.
The tempest came: I saw that vessel's shrouds
In perilous bustle; while upon the deck
Stood trembling creatures. I beheld the wreck;
The final gulfing; the poor struggling souls:
I heard their cries amid loud thunder-rolls.   660
O they had all been sav'd but crazed eld
Annull'd my vigorous cravings: and thus quell'd
And curb'd, think on't, O Latmian! did I sit
Writhing with pity, and a cursing fit
Against that hell-born Circe. The crew had gone,
By one and one, to pale oblivion;
And I was gazing on the surges prone,
With many a scalding tear and many a groan,
When at my feet emerg'd an old man's hand,
Grasping this scroll, and this same slender wand.   670
I knelt with pain – reach'd out my hand – had grasp'd
These treasures – touch'd the knuckles – they unclasp'd –
I caught a finger: but the downward weight
O'erpowered me – it sank. Then 'gan abate
The storm, and through chill aguish[35] gloom outburst
The comfortable sun. I was athirst
To search the book, and in the warming air
Parted its dripping leaves with eager care.
Strange matters did it treat of, and drew on
My soul page after page, till well-nigh won   680
Into forgetfulness; when, stupefied,
I read these words, and read again, and tried
My eyes against the heavens, and read again.
O what a load of misery and pain
Each Atlas-line[36] bore off! – a shine of hope
Came gold around me, cheering me to cope
Strenuous with hellish tyranny. Attend!
For thou hast brought their promise to an end.

'In the wide sea there lives a forlorn wretch,
Doom'd with enfeebled carcase to outstretch   690
His loath'd existence through ten centuries,
And then to die alone. Who can devise

A total opposition? No one. So
One million times ocean must ebb and flow,
And he oppressed. Yet he shall not die,
These things accomplish'd: – If he utterly
Scans all the depths of magic, and expounds
The meanings of all motions, shapes and sounds;
If he explores all forms and substances
Straight homeward to their symbol-essences;   700
He shall not die. Moreover, and in chief,
He must pursue this task of joy and grief
Most piously; – all lovers tempest-tost,
And in the savage overwhelming lost,
He shall deposit side by side, until
Time's creeping shall the dreary space fulfil:
Which done, and all these labours ripened,
A youth, by heavenly power lov'd and led,
Shall stand before him; whom he shall direct
How to consummate all. The youth elect   710
Must do the thing, or both will be destroy'd.' –

'Then,' cried the young Endymion, overjoy'd,
'We are twin brothers in this destiny!
Say, I entreat thee, what achievement high
Is, in this restless world, for me reserv'd.
What! if from thee my wandering feet had swerv'd,
Had we both perish'd?' – 'Look!' the sage replied,
'Dost thou not mark a gleaming through the tide,
Of diverse brilliances? 'tis the edifice
I told thee of, where lovely Scylla lies;   720
And where I have enshrined piously
All lovers, whom fell storms have doom'd to die
Throughout my bondage.' Thus discoursing, on
They went till unobscur'd the porches shone;
Which hurryingly they gain'd, and enter'd straight.
Sure never since king Neptune held his state
Was seen such wonder underneath the stars.
Turn to some level plain where haughty Mars
Has legion'd all his battle; and behold
How every soldier, with firm foot, doth hold   730
His even breast: see, many steeled squares,

And rigid ranks of iron – whence who dares
One step? Imagine further, line by line,
These warrior thousands on the field supine: –
So in that crystal place, in silent rows,
Poor lovers lay at rest from joys and woes. –
The stranger from the mountains, breathless, trac'd
Such thousands of shut eyes in order plac'd;
Such ranges of white feet, and patient lips
All ruddy, – for here death no blossom nips.   740
He mark'd their brows and foreheads; saw their hair
Put sleekly on one side with nicest care;
And each one's gentle wrists, with reverence,
Put cross-wise to its heart.
       'Let us commence,'
Whisper'd the guide, stuttering with joy, 'even now.'
He spake, and, trembling like an aspen-bough,
Began to tear his scroll in pieces small,
Uttering the while some mumblings funeral.
He tore it into pieces small as snow
That drifts unfeather'd when bleak northerns blow;   750
And having done it, took his dark blue cloak
And bound it round Endymion: then struck
His wand against the empty air times nine. –
'What more there is to do, young man, is thine:
But first a little patience; first undo
This tangled thread, and wind it to a clue.[37]
Ah, gentle! 'tis as weak as spider's skein;
And shouldst thou break it – What, is it done so clean?
A power overshadows thee! O, brave!
The spite of hell is tumbling to its grave.   760
Here is a shell; 'tis pearly blank to me,
Nor mark'd with any sign or charactery –
Canst thou read aught? O read for pity's sake!
Olympus! we are safe! Now, Carian, break
This wand against yon lyre on the pedestal.'

 'Twas done: and straight with sudden swell and fall
Sweet music breath'd her soul away, and sigh'd
A lullaby to silence. – 'Youth! now strew
These minced leaves on me, and passing through

Those files of dead, scatter the same around,   770
And thou wilt see the issue.' – Mid the sound
Of flutes and viols, ravishing his heart,
Endymion from Glaucus stood apart,
And scatter'd in his face some fragments light.
How lightning-swift the change! a youthful wight
Smiling beneath a coral diadem,
Out-sparkling sudden like an upturn'd gem,
Appear'd and, stepping to a beauteous corse,[38]
Kneel'd down beside it, and with tenderest force
Press'd its cold hand, and wept, – and Scylla sigh'd!   780
Endymion, with quick hand, the charm applied –
The nymph arose: he left them to their joy,
And onward went upon his high employ,
Showering those powerful fragments on the dead.
And, as he pass'd, each lifted up his head,
As doth a flower at Apollo's touch.
Death felt it to his inwards: 'twas too much:
Death fell a weeping in his charnel-house.
The Latmian persever'd along, and thus
All were re-animated.[39] There arose   790
A noise of harmony, pulses and throes
Of gladness in the air – while many, who
Had died in mutual arms devout and true,
Sprang to each other madly; and the rest
Felt a high certainty of being blest.
They gaz'd upon Endymion. Enchantment
Grew drunken, and would have its head and bent.
Delicious symphonies, like airy flowers,
Budded, and swell'd, and, full-blown, shed full showers
Of light, soft, unseen leaves of sounds divine.   800
The two deliverers tasted a pure wine
Of happiness, from fairy-press ooz'd out.
Speechless they eyed each other, and about
The fair assembly wander'd to and fro,
Distracted with the richest overflow
Of joy that ever pour'd from heaven.
                                        – 'Away!'
Shouted the new born god; 'Follow, and pay
Our piety to Neptunus supreme!' –

Then Scylla, blushing sweetly from her dream,
They led on first, bent to her meek surprise,   810
Through portal columns of a giant size,
Into the vaulted, boundless emerald.[40]
Joyous all follow'd as the leader call'd,
Down marble steps; pouring as easily
As hour-glass sand, – and fast, as you might see
Swallows obeying the south summer's call,
Or swans upon a gentle waterfall.

Thus went that beautiful multitude, nor far,
Ere from among some rocks of glittering spar.
Just within ken, they saw descending thick   820
Another multitude. Whereat more quick
Moved either host. On a wide sand they met,
And of those numbers every eye was wet;
For each their old love found. A murmuring rose,
Like what was never heard in all the throes
Of wind and waters: 'tis past human wit
To tell; 'tis dizziness to think of it.

This mighty consummation made, the host
Mov'd on for many a league; and gain'd, and lost
Huge sea-marks; vanward swelling in array,   830
And from the rear diminishing away, –
Till a faint dawn surpris'd them. Glaucus cried,
'Behold! behold, the palace of his pride!
God Neptune's palaces!' With noise increas'd,
They shoulder'd on towards that brightening east.
At every onward step proud domes arose
In prospect, – diamond gleams, and golden glows
Of amber 'gainst their faces levelling.
Joyous, and many as the leaves in spring,
Still onward; still the splendour gradual swell'd.   840
Rich opal domes were seen, on high upheld
By jasper pillars, letting through their shafts
A blush of coral. Copious wonder-draughts
Each gazer drank; and deeper drank more near.
For what poor mortals fragment up, as mere

As marble was there lavish, to the vast
Of one fair palace, that far far surpass'd,
Even for common bulk, those olden three,
Memphis, and Babylon, and Nineveh.[41]

    As large, as bright, as colour'd as the bow   850
Of Iris, when unfading it doth show
Beyond a silvery shower, was the arch
Through which this Paphian army[42] took its march,
Into the outer courts of Neptune's state:
Whence could be seen, direct, a golden gate,
To which the leaders sped; but not half raught
Ere it burst open swift as fairy thought,
And made those dazzled thousands veil their eyes
Like callow eagles at the first sunrise.
Soon with an eagle nativeness their gaze   860
Ripe from hue-golden swoons took all the blaze,
And then, behold! large Neptune on his throne
Of emerald deep: yet not exalt alone;
At his right hand stood winged Love, and on
His left sat smiling Beauty's paragon.[43]

    Far as the mariner on highest mast
Can see all round upon the calmed vast,
So wide was Neptune's hall: and as the blue
Doth vault the waters, so the waters drew
Their doming curtains, high, magnificent,   870
Aw'd from the throne aloof; – and when storm-rent
Disclos'd the thunder-gloomings in Jove's air;
But sooth'd as now, flash'd sudden everywhere,
Noiseless, submarine cloudlets, glittering
Death to a human eye: for there did spring
From natural west, and east, and south, and north,
A light as of four sunsets, blazing forth
A gold-green zenith 'bove the Sea-God's head.
Of lucid depth the floor, and far outspread
As breezeless lake, on which the slim canoe   880
Of feather'd Indian darts about, as through
The delicatest air: air verily,
But for the portraiture of clouds and sky:

This palace floor breath-air, – but for the amaze
Of deep-seen wonders motionless, – and blaze
Of the dome pomp, reflected in extremes,
Globing a golden sphere.

                They stood in dreams
Till Triton blew his horn. The palace rang;
The Nereids danc'd; the Syrens faintly sang;
And the great Sea-King bow'd his dripping head.   890
Then Love took wing, and from his pinions shed
On all the multitude a nectarous dew.
The ooze-born Goddess[44] beckoned and drew
Fair Scylla and her guides to conference;
And when they reach'd the throned eminence
She kist the sea-nymph's cheek, – who sat her down
A toying with the doves. Then, – 'Mighty crown
And sceptre of this kingdom!' Venus said,
'Thy vows were on a time to Nais paid:
Behold!' – Two copious tear-drops instant fell   900
From the God's large eyes; he smil'd delectable,
And over Glaucus held his blessing hands. –
'Endymion! Ah! still wandering in the bands
Of love? Now this is cruel. Since the hour
I met thee in earth's bosom, all my power
Have I put forth to serve thee. What, not yet
Escap'd from dull mortality's harsh net?
A little patience, youth! 'twill not be long,
Or I am skilless quite: an idle tongue,
A humid eye, and steps luxurious,   910
Where these are new and strange, are ominous.
Aye, I have seen these signs in one of heaven,
When others were all blind: and were I given
To utter secrets, haply I might say
Some pleasant words: – but Love will have his day.
So wait awhile expectant. Pr'ythee soon,
Even in the passing of thine honeymoon,
Visit thou my Cythera: thou wilt find
Cupid well-natured, my Adonis kind;
And pray persuade with thee – Ah, I have done,   920
All blisses be upon thee, my sweet son!' –

Thus the fair goddess: While Endymion
Knelt to receive those accents halcyon.

   Meantime a glorious revelry began
Before the Water-Monarch. Nectar ran
In courteous fountains to all cups outreach'd;
And plunder'd vines, teeming exhaustless, pleach'd[45]
New growth about each shell and pendent lyre;
The which, in disentangling for their fire,
Pull'd down fresh foliage and coverture   930
For dainty toying. Cupid, empire-sure,
Flutter'd and laugh'd, and oft-times through the throng
Made a delighted way. Then dance, and song,
And garlanding grew wild; and pleasure reign'd.
In harmless tendril they each other chain'd,
And strove who should be smother'd deepest in
Fresh crush of leaves.
               O 'tis a very sin
For one so weak to venture his poor verse
In such a place as this. O do not curse,
High Muses! let him hurry to the ending.   940

   All suddenly were silent. A soft blending
Of dulcet instruments came charmingly;
And then a hymn.
              'King of the stormy sea!
Brother of Jove, and co-inheritor[46]
Of elements! Eternally before
Thee the waves awful bow. Fast, stubborn rock,
At thy fear'd trident shrinking, doth unlock
Its deep foundations, hissing into foam.
All mountain-rivers, lost in the wide home
Of thy capacious bosom, ever flow.   950
Thou frownest, and old Aeolus thy foe
Skulks to his cavern, 'mid the gruff complaint
Of all his rebel tempests. Dark clouds faint
When, from thy diadem, a silver gleam
Slants over blue dominion. Thy bright team
Gulphs[47] in the morning light, and scuds along
To bring thee nearer to that golden song
Apollo singeth, while his chariot

Waits at the doors of heaven. Thou art not
For scenes like this: an empire stern hast thou;   960
And it hath furrow'd that large front: yet now,
As newly come of heaven, dost thou sit
To blend and interknit
Subdued majesty with this glad time.
O shell-borne King sublime!
We lay our hearts before thee evermore –
We sing, and we adore!

         'Breathe softly, flutes;
Be tender of your strings, ye soothing lutes;
Nor be the trumpet heard! O vain, O vain;   970
Not flowers budding in an April rain,
Nor breath of sleeping dove, nor river's flow, –
No, nor the Aeolian twang of Love's own bow,
Can mingle music fit for the soft ear
Of goddess Cytherea!
Yet deign, white Queen of Beauty, thy fair eyes
On our souls' sacrifice.

         'Bright-winged Child![48]
Who has another care when thou hast smil'd?
Unfortunates on earth, we see at last   980
All death-shadows, and glooms that overcast
Our spirits, fann'd away by thy light pinions.
O sweetest essence! sweetest of all minions!
God of warm pulses, and dishevell'd hair,
And panting bosoms bare!
Dear unseen light in darkness! eclipser
Of light in light! delicious poisoner!
Thy venom'd goblet will we quaff until
We fill – we fill!
And by thy Mother's lips – '

         Was heard no more   990
For clamour, when the golden palace door
Opened again, and from without, in shone
A new magnificence. On oozy throne
Smooth-moving came Oceanus the old,
To take a latest glimpse at his sheep-fold,

Before he went into his quiet cave
To muse for ever – Then a lucid wave,
Scoop'd from its trembling sisters of mid-sea,
Afloat, and pillowing up the majesty
Of Doris, and the Aegean seer, her spouse[49] –   1000
Next, on a dolphin, clad in laurel boughs,
Theban Amphion leaning on his lute:
His fingers went across it – All were mute
To gaze on Amphitrite, queen of pearls,
And Thetis pearly too. –

                                        The palace whirls
Around giddy Endymion; seeing he
Was there far strayed from mortality.
He could not bear it – shut his eyes in vain;
Imagination gave a dizzier pain.
'O I shall die! sweet Venus, be my stay!   1010
Where is my lovely mistress? Well-away!
I die – I hear her voice – I feel my wing – '
At Neptune's feet he sank. A sudden ring
Of Nereids were about him, in kind strife
To usher back his spirit into life:
But still he slept. At last they interwove
Their cradling arms, and purpos'd to convey
Towards a crystal bower far away.

   Lo! while slow carried through the pitying crowd,
To his inward senses these words spake aloud;   1020
Written in star-light on the dark above:
Dearest Endymion! my entire love!
How have I dwelt in fear of fate: 'tis done –
Immortal bliss for me too hast thou won
Arise then! for the hen-dove shall not hatch
Her ready eggs, before I'll kissing snatch
Thee into endless heaven. Awake! Awake!'

   The youth at once arose: a placid lake
Came quiet to his eyes; and forest green,
Cooler than all the wonders he had seen.   1030
Lull'd with its simple song his fluttering breast.
How happy once again in grassy nest!

Book IV

Muse of my native land![1] loftiest Muse!
O first-born on the mountains! by the hues
Of heaven on the spiritual air begot:
Long didst thou sit alone in northern grot,
While yet our England was a wolfish den;
Before our forests heard the talk of men;
Before the first of Druids was a child; –
Long didst thou sit amid our regions wild
Rapt in a deep prophetic solitude.
There came an eastern[2] voice of solemn mood: –   10
Yet wast thou patient. Then sang forth the Nine,[3]
Apollo's garland: – yet didst thou divine
Such home-bred glory, that they cry'd in vain,
'Come hither, Sister of the Island!' Plain
Spake fair Ausonia;[4] and once more she spake
A higher summons: – still didst thou betake
Thee to thy native hopes. O thou hast won
A full accomplishment! The thing is done,
Which undone, these our latter days had risen
On barren souls. Great Muse, thou know'st what prison. 20
Of flesh and bone, curbs, and confines, and frets
Our spirit's wings: despondency besets
Our pillows; and the fresh tomorrow morn
Seems to give forth its light in very scorn
Of our dull, uninspired, snail-paced lives.
Long have I said, how happy he who shrives
To thee! But then I thought on poets gone,
And could not pray: – nor can I now – so on
I move to the end in lowliness of heart. –

'Ah, woe is me! that I should fondly part   30
From my dear native land! Ah, foolish maid!
Glad was the hour, when, with thee, myriads bade
Adieu to Ganges[5] and their pleasant fields!
To one so friendless the clear freshet yields
A bitter coolness; the ripe grape is sour:
Yet I would have, great gods! but one short hour

Of native air – let me but die at home.'

   Endymion to heaven's airy dome
Was offering up a hecatomb of vows,
When these words reach'd him. Whereupon he bows   40
His head through thorny-green entanglement
Of underwood, and to the sound is bent,
Anxious as hind towards her hidden fawn.

   'Is no one near to help me? No fair dawn
Of life from charitable voice? No sweet saying
To set my dull and sadden'd spirit playing?
No hand to toy with mine? No lips so sweet
That I may worship them? No eyelids meet
To twinkle on my bosom? No one dies
Before me, till from these enslaving eyes   50
Redemption sparkles! – I am sad and lost.'
Thou, Carian lord, hadst better have been tost
Into a whirlpool. Vanish into air,
Warm mountaineer! for canst thou only bear
A woman's sigh alone and in distress?
See not her charms! Is Phoebe passionless?
Phoebe is fairer far – O gaze no more: –
Yet if thou wilt behold all beauty's store,
Behold her panting in the forest grass!
Do not those curls of glossy jet surpass   60
For tenderness the arms so idly lain
Amongst them? Feelest not a kindred pain.
To see such lovely eyes in swimming search
After some warm delight, that seems to perch
Dovelike in the dim cell lying beyond
Their upper lids? – Hist!

                      'O for Hermes' wand,
To touch this flower into human shape!
That woodland Hyacinthus could escape
From his green prison, and here kneeling down
Call me his queen, his second life's fair crown!   70
Ah me, how I could love! – My soul doth melt
For the unhappy youth – Love! I have felt

So faint a kindness, such a meek surrender
To what my own full thoughts had made too tender,
That but for tears my life had fled away! –
Ye deaf and senseless minutes of the day,
And thou, old forest, hold ye this for true,
There is no lightning, no authentic dew
But in the eye of love: there's not a sound,
Melodious howsoever, can confound   80
The heavens and earth in one to such a death
As doth the voice of love: there's not a breath
Will mingle kindly with the meadow air,
Till it has panted round, and stolen a share
Of passion from the heart!' –

                              Upon a bough
He leant, wretched. He surely cannot now
Thirst for another love: O impious,
That he can ever dream upon it thus! –
Thought he, 'Why am I not as are the dead,
Since to a woe like this I have been led   90
Through the dark earth, and through the wondrous sea?
Goddess! I love thee not the less: from thee
By Juno's smile I turn not – no, no, no –
While the great waters are at ebb and flow. –
I have a triple soul! O fond pretence –
For both, for both[6] my love is so immense,
I feel my heart is cut for them in twain.'

    And so he groan'd, as one by beauty slain.
The lady's heart beat quick, and he could see
Her gentle bosom heave tumultuously.   ·   100
He sprang from his green covert: there she lay,
Sweet as a musk rose upon new-made hay;
With all her limbs on tremble, and her eyes
Shut softly up alive. To speak he tries.
'Fair damsel, pity me! forgive that I
Thus violate thy bower's sanctity!
O pardon me, for I am full of grief –
Grief born of thee, young angel! fairest thief!
Who stolen hast away the wings wherewith

I was to top the heavens. Dear maid, sith[7]   110
Thou art my executioner, and I feel
Loving and hatred, misery and weal,[8]
Will in a few short hours be nothing to me,
And all my story that much passion slew me;
Do smile upon the evening of my days:
And, for my tortur'd brain begins to craze,
Be thou my nurse; and let me understand
How dying I shall kiss that lily hand. –
Dost weep for me? Then should I be content.
Scowl on, ye fates! until the firmament   120
Outblackens Erebus, and the full-cavern'd earth
Crumbles into itself. By the cloud girth
Of Jove, those tears have given me a thirst
To meet oblivion.' – As her heart would burst
The maiden sobb'd awhile, and then replied:
'Why must such desolation betide
As that thou speak'st of? Are not these green nooks
Empty of all misfortune? Do the brooks
Utter a gorgon voice? Does yonder thrush,
Schooling its half-fledg'd little ones to brush   130
About the dewy forest, whisper tales? –
Speak not of grief, young stranger, or cold snails
Will slime the rose to night. Though if thou wilt,
Methinks 'twould be a guilt – a very guilt –
Not to companion thee, and sigh away
The light – the dusk – the dark – till break of day!'
'Dear lady,' said Endymion, ''tis past:
I love thee! and my days can never last.
That I may pass in patience still speak:
Let me have music dying, and I seek   140
No more delight – I bid adieu to all.
Didst thou not after other climates call,
And murmur about Indian streams?' – Then she,
Sitting beneath the midmost forest tree,
For pity sang this roundelay –

            'O Sorrow,
            Why dost borrow
The natural hue of health, from vermeil lips? –

To give maiden blushes
To the white rose bushes? 150
Or is't thy dewy hand the daisy tips?

'O Sorrow,
Why dost borrow
The lustrous passion from a falcon-eye? –
To give the glow-worm light?
Or, on a moonless night,
To tinge, on syren shores, the salt sea-spry?[9]

'O Sorrow,
Why dost borrow
The mellow ditties from a mourning tongue? – 160
To give at evening pale
Unto the nightingale,
That thou mayst listen the cold dews among?

'O Sorrow,
Why dost borrow
Heart's lightness from the merriment of May? –
A lover would not tread
A cowslip on the head,
Though he should dance from eve till peep of day –
Nor any drooping flower 170
Held sacred for thy bower,
Wherever he may sport himself and play.

'To Sorrow,
I bade good morrow,
And thought to leave her far away behind;
But cheerly, cheerly,
She loves me dearly;
She is so constant to me, and so kind:
I would deceive her
And so leave her, 180
But ah! she is so constant and so kind.

'Beneath my palm trees, by the river side,
I sat a-weeping: in the whole world wide
There was no one to ask me why I wept, –
And so I kept

Brimming the water-lily cups with tears
    Cold as my fears.

'Beneath my palm trees, by the river side,
I sat a weeping: what enamour'd bride,
Cheated by shadowy wooer from the clouds,   190
    But hides and shrouds
Beneath dark palm trees by a river side?

'And as I sat, over the light blue hills
There came a noise of revellers: the rills
Into the wide stream came of purple hue –
    'Twas Bacchus and his crew!
The earnest trumpet spake, and silver thrills
From kissing cymbals made a merry din –
    'Twas Bacchus and his kin![10]
Like to a moving vintage down they came,   200
Crown'd with green leaves, and faces all on flame;
All madly dancing through the pleasant valley,
    To scare thee, Melancholy![11]
O then, O then, thou wast a simple name!
And I forgot thee, as the berried holly
By shepherds is forgotten, when, in June,
Tall chesnuts keep away the sun and moon: –
    I rush'd into the folly!

'Within his car, aloft, young Bacchus stood,
Trifling his ivy-dart, in dancing mood,   210
    With sidelong laughing;
And little rills of crimson wine imbrued
His plump white arms, and shoulders, enough white
    For Venus' pearly bite:
And near him rode Silenus on his ass,
Pelted with flowers as he on did pass
    Tipsily quaffing.

'Whence came ye, merry Damsels! whence came ye!
So many, and so many, and such glee?
Why have ye left your bowers desolate,   220
    Your lutes, and gentler fate? –
"We follow Bacchus! Bacchus on the wing,
    A-conquering!

Bacchus, young Bacchus! good or ill betide,
We dance before him thorough[12] kingdoms wide: –
Come hither, lady fair, and joined be
      To our wild minstrelsy!"

'Whence came ye, jolly Satyrs! whence came ye!
So many, and so many, and such glee?
Why have ye left your forest haunts, why left   230
      Your nuts in oak-tree cleft? –
"For wine, for wine we left our kernel tree;
For wine we left our heath, and yellow brooms,
      And cold mushrooms;
For wine we follow Bacchus through the earth;
Great God of breathless cups and chirping mirth! –
Come hither, lady fair, and joined be
      To our mad minstrelsy!"

'Over wide streams and mountains great we went,
And, save when Bacchus kept his ivy tent,   240
Onward the tiger and the leopard pants,
      With Asian elephants:
Onward these myriads – with song and dance,
With zebras striped, and sleek Arabians' prance,
Web-footed alligators, crocodiles,
Bearing upon their scaly backs, in files,
Plump infant laughers mimicking the coil[13]
Of seamen, and stout galley-rowers' toil:
With toying oars and silken sails they glide,
      Nor care for wind and tide.   250

'Mounted on panthers' furs and lions' manes,
From rear to van they scour about the plains;
A three days' journey in a moment done:
And always, at the rising of the sun,
About the wilds they hunt with spear and horn,
      On spleenful unicorn.[14]

'I saw Osirian Egypt kneel adown
      Before the vine-wreath crown!
I saw parch'd Abyssinia[15] rouse and sing
      To the silver cymbals' ring!   260
I saw the whelming vintage hotly pierce

Old Tartary[16] the fierce!
The kings of Inde their jewel-sceptres vail,
And from their treasures scatter pearled hail;
Great Brahma from his mystic heaven groans,
            And all his priesthood moans;
Before young Bacchus' eye-wink turning pale. –
Into these regions came I following him,
Sick hearted, weary – so I took a whim
To stray away into these forests drear   270
            Alone, without a peer:
And I have told thee all thou mayest hear.

            'Young stranger!
            I've been a ranger
In search of pleasure throughout every clime:
            Alas, 'tis not for me!
            Bewitch'd I sure must be,
To lose in grieving all my maiden prime.

            'Come then, Sorrow!
            Sweetest Sorrow!   280
Like an own babe I nurse thee on my breast:
            I thought to leave thee
            And deceive thee,
But now of all the world I love thee best.

            'There is not one,
            No, no, not one
But thee to comfort a poor lonely maid;
            Thou art her mother,
            And her brother,
Her playmate, and her wooer in the shade.'

                                                          290

  O what a sigh she gave in finishing,
And look, quite dead to every worldly thing!
Endymion could not speak, but gazed on her;
And listened to the wind that now did stir
About the crisped oaks full drearily,
Yet with as sweet a softness as might be
Remember'd from its velvet summer song.
At last he said: 'Poor lady, how thus long

Have I been able to endure that voice?
Fair Melody! kind Syren! I've no choice;   300
I must be thy sad servant evermore:
I cannot choose but kneel here and adore.
Alas, I must not think – by Phoebe, no!
Let me not think, soft Angel! shall it be so?
Say, beautifullest, shall I never think?
O thou could'st foster me beyond the brink
Of recollection! make my watchful care
Close up its bloodshot eyes, nor see despair!
Do gently murder half my soul, and I
Shall feel the other half so utterly! –   310
I'm giddy at that cheek so fair and smooth;
O let it blush so ever! let it soothe
My madness! let it mantle rosy-warm
With the tinge of love, panting in safe alarm. –
This cannot be thy hand, and yet it is;
And this is sure thine other softling – this
Thine own fair bosom, and I am so near!
Wilt fall asleep? O let me sip that tear!
And whisper one sweet word that I may know
This is this world – sweet dewy blossom!' – *Woe*!   320
Woe! Woe to that Endymion! Where is he? –
Even these words went echoing dismally
Through the wide forest – a most fearful tone,
Like one repenting in his latest moan;
And while it died away a shade pass'd by,
As of a thunder cloud. When arrows fly
Through the thick branches, poor ring-doves sleek forth
Their timid necks and tremble; so these both
Leant to each other trembling, and sat so
Waiting for some destruction – when lo,   330
Foot-feather'd Mercury appear'd sublime
Beyond the tall tree tops; and in less time
Than shoots the slanted hail-storm, down he dropt
Towards the ground: but rested not, nor stopt
One moment from his home: only the sward
He with his wand light touch'd, and heavenward
Swifter than sight was gone – even before
The teeming earth a sudden witness bore

Of his swift magic. Diving swans appear
Above the crystal circlings white and clear;   340
And catch the cheated eye in wide surprise,
How they can dive in sight and unseen rise –
So from the turf outsprang two steeds jet-black,
Each with large dark blue wings upon his back.
The youth of Caria plac'd the lovely dame
On one, and felt himself in spleen[17] to tame
The other's fierceness. Through the air they flew,
High as the eagles. Like two drops of dew
Exhal'd to Phoebus' lips, away they are gone,
Far from the earth away – unseen, alone,   350
Among cool clouds and winds, but that the free,
The buoyant life of song can floating be
Above their heads, and follow them untir'd. –
Muse of my native land, am I inspir'd?
This is the giddy air; and I must spread
Wide pinions to keep here; nor do I dread
Or height, or depth, or width, or any chance
Precipitous: I have beneath my glance
Those towering horses and their mournful freight.
Could I thus sail, and see, and thus await   360
Fearless for power of thought, without thine aid? –
There is a sleepy dusk, an odorous shade
From some approaching wonder, and behold
Those winged steeds, with snorting nostrils bold
Snuff at its faint extreme, and seem to tire,
Dying to embers from their native fire!

There curl'd a purple mist around them; soon,
It seem'd as when around the pale new moon
Sad Zephyr droops the clouds like weeping willow:
'Twas Sleep slow journeying with head on pillow.   370
For the first time, since he came nigh dead born
From the old womb of night, his cave forlorn
Had he left more forlorn; for the first time,
He felt aloof the day and morning's prime –
Because into his depth Cimmerian[18]
There came a dream, showing how a young man,
Ere a lean bat could plump its wintery skin,

Would at high Jove's empyreal footstool win
An immortality, and how espouse
Jove's daughter, and be reckon'd of his house.   380
Now was he slumbering towards heaven's gate,
That he might at the threshold one hour wait
To hear the marriage melodies, and then
Sink downward to his dusky cave again.
His litter of smooth semilucent mist,
Diversely ting'd with rose and amethyst,
Puzzled those eyes that for the centre sought;
And scarcely for one moment could be caught
His sluggish form reposing motionless.
Those two on winged steeds, with all the stress   390
Of vision search'd for him, as one would look
Athwart the sallows of a river nook
To catch a glance at silver-throated eels. –
Or from old Skiddaw's top,[19] when fog conceals
His rugged forehead in a mantle pale,
With an eye-guess towards some pleasant vale
Descry a favourite hamlet faint and far.

    These raven horses, though they foster'd are
Of earth's splenetic fire, dully drop
Their full-vein'd ears, nostrils blood wide, and stop;   400
Upon the spiritless mist have they outspread
Their ample feathers, are in slumber dead, –
And on those pinions, level in mid air,
Endymion sleepeth and the lady fair.
Slowly they sail, slowly as icy isle
Upon a calm sea drifting: and meanwhile
The mournful wanderer dreams. Behold! he walks
On heaven's pavement; brotherly he talks
To divine powers: from his hand full fain
Juno's proud birds[20] are pecking pearly grain: 410
He tries the nerve of Phoebus' golden bow,
And asketh where the golden apples grow:
Upon his arm he braces Pallas' shield,
And strives in vain to unsettle and wield
A Jovian thunderbolt: arch Hebe brings
A full-brimm'd goblet, dances lightly, sings

And tantalizes long; at last he drinks,
And lost in pleasure at her feet he sinks,
Touching with dazzled lips her starlight hand.
He blows a bugle, – an ethereal band   420
Are visible above: the Seasons four, –
Green-kyrtled[21]Spring, flush Summer, golden store
In Autumn's sickle, Winter frosty hoar,
Join dance with shadowy Hours; while still the blast,
In swells unmitigated, still doth last
To sway their floating morris.[22] 'Whose is this?
Whose bugle?' he inquires; they smile – 'O Dis!
Why is this mortal here? Dost thou not know
Its mistress' lips? Not thou? – 'Tis Dian's: lo!
She rises crescented!' He looks, 'tis she,   430
His very goddess: goodbye earth, and sea,
And air, and pains, and care, and suffering;
Goodbye to all but love! Then doth he spring
Towards her, and awakes – and, strange, o'erhead,
Of those same fragrant exhalations bred,
Beheld awake his very dream: the gods
Stood smiling; merry Hebe laughs and nods;
And Phoebe bends towards him crescented.
O state perplexing! On the pinion bed,
Too well awake, he feels the panting side   440
Of his delicious lady. He who died
For soaring[23] too audacious in the sun,
When that same treacherous wax began to run,
Felt not more tongue-tied than Endymion.
His heart leapt up as to its rightful throne,
To that fair shadow'd passion puls'd its way –
Ah, what perplexity! Ah, well a day!
So fond, so beauteous was his bedfellow,
He could not help but kiss her: then he grew
Awhile forgetful of all beauty save   450
Young Phoebe's, golden hair'd; and so 'gan crave
Forgiveness: yet he turn'd once more to look
At the sweet sleeper, – all his soul was shook, –
She press'd his hand in slumber; so once more
He could not help but kiss her and adore.
At this the shadow wept, melting away.

That Latmian started up: 'Bright goddess, stay!
Search my most hidden breast! By truth's own tongue,
I have no daedale[24] heart: why is it wrung
To desperation? Is there nought for me,   460
Upon the bourne of bliss, but misery?'

　　These words awoke the stranger of dark tresses:
Her dawning love-look rapt Endymion blesses
With 'haviour[25] soft. Sleep yawn'd from underneath.
'Thou swan of Ganges, let us no more breathe
This murky phantasm! thou contented seem'st
Pillow'd in lovely idleness, nor dream'st
What horrors may discomfort thee and me.
Ah, shouldst thou die from my heart-treachery! –
Yet did she merely weep – her gentle soul   470
Hath no revenge in it: as it is whole
In tenderness, would I were whole in love!
Can I prize thee, fair maid, all price above,
Even when I feel as true as innocence?
I do, I do. – What is this soul then? Whence
Came it? It does not seem my own, and I
Have no self-passion or identity.
Some fearful end must be: where, where is it?
By Nemesis, I see my spirit flit
Alone about the dark – Forgive me, sweet: 480
Shall we away?' He rous'd the steeds: they beat
Their wings chivalrous into the clear air,
Leaving old Sleep within his vapoury lair.

　　The good-night blush of eve was waning slow,
And Vesper, risen star, began to throe
In the dusk heavens silverly, when they
Thus sprang direct towards the Galaxy.
Nor did speed hinder converse soft and strange –
Eternal oaths and vows they interchange,
In such wise, in such temper, so aloof   490
Up in the winds, beneath a starry roof,
So witless[26] of their doom, that verily
'Tis well nigh past man's search their hearts to see;
Whether they wept, or laugh'd, or griev'd, or toy'd –
Most like with joy gone mad, with sorrow cloy'd.

Full facing their swift flight, from ebon streak;
The moon put forth a little diamond peak,
No bigger than an unobserved star,
Or tiny point of fairy scymetar;
Bright signal that she only stoop'd to tie   500
Her silver sandals, ere deliciously
She bow'd into the heavens her timid head.
Slowly she rose, as though she would have fled,
While to his lady meek the Carian turn'd,
To mark if her dark eyes had yet discern'd
This beauty in its birth – Despair! despair!
He saw her body fading gaunt and spare
In the cold moonshine. Straight he seiz'd her wrist;
It melted from his grasp: her hand he kiss'd,
And, horror! kiss'd his own – he was alone.   510
Her steed a little higher soar'd, and then
Dropt hawkwise to the earth.

                                    There lies a den,
Beyond the seeming confines of the space
Made for the soul to wander in and trace
Its own existence, of remotest glooms.
Dark regions are around it, where the tombs
Of buried griefs the spirit sees, but scarce
One hour doth linger weeping, for the pierce
Of new-born woe it feels more inly smart:
And in these regions many a venom'd dart   520
At random flies; they are the proper home
Of every ill: the man is yet to come
Who hath not journeyed in this native hell.
But few have ever felt how calm and well
Sleep may be had in that deep den of all.
There anguish does not sting; nor pleasure pall:
Woe-hurricanes beat ever at the gate,
Yet all is still within and desolate.
Beset with plainful gusts, within ye hear
No sound so loud as when on curtain'd bier   530
The death-watch tick[27] is stifled. Enter none
Who strive therefore: on the sudden it is won.
Just when the sufferer begins to burn,

Then it is free to him; and from an urn,
Still fed by melting ice, he takes a draught –
Young Semele such richness never quaft
In her maternal longing! Happy gloom!
Dark Paradise! where pale becomes the bloom
Of health by due; where silence dreariest
Is most articulate; where hopes infest; 540
Where those eyes are the brightest far that keep
Their lids shut longest in a dreamless sleep.
O happy spirit-home! O wondrous soul!
Pregnant with such a den to save the whole
In thine own depth. Hail, gentle Carian!
For, never since thy griefs and woes began,
Hast thou felt so content: a grievous feud
Hath led thee to this Cave of Quietude.
Aye, his lull'd soul was there, although upborne
With dangerous speed: and so he did not mourn 550
Because he knew not whither he was going.
So happy was he, not the aerial blowing
Of trumpets at clear parley from the east
Could rouse from that fine relish, that high feast.
They stung the feather'd horse: with fierce alarm
He flapp'd towards the sound. Alas, no charm
Could lift Endymion's head, or he had view'd
A skyey mask,[28] a pinion'd multitude, –
And silvery was its passing: voices sweet
Warbling the while as if to lull and greet 560
The wanderer in his path. Thus warbled they,
While past the vision went in bright array.

'Who, who from Dian's feast would be away?
For all the golden bowers of the day
Are empty left? Who, who away would be
From Cynthia's wedding and festivity?
Not Hesperus: lo! upon his silver wings
He leans away for highest heaven and sings,
Snapping his lucid[29] fingers merrily! –
Ah, Zephyrus! art here, and Flora too! 570
Ye tender bibbers[30] of the rain and dew,
Young playmates of the rose and daffodil,

Be careful, ere ye enter in, to fill
          Your baskets high
With fennel green, and balm, and golden pines,
Savory, latter-mint, and columbines,
Cool parsley, basil sweet, and sunny thyme;
Yea, every flower and leaf of every clime,
All gather'd in the dewy morning: hie
          Away! fly, fly! —   580
Crystalline brother of the belt of heaven,
Aquarius! to whom king Jove has given
Two liquid pulse streams 'stead of feather'd wings,
Two fan-like fountains, — thine illuminings
          For Dian play:
Dissolve the frozen purity of air;
Let thy white shoulders silvery and bare
Show cold through watery pinions; make more bright
The Star-Queen's crescent on her marriage night:
          Haste, haste away! —   590
Castor has tamed the planet Lion, see!
And of the Bear[31] has Pollux mastery:
A third is in the race! who is the third
Speeding away swift as the eagle bird?
          The ramping Centaur!
The Lion's mane's on end: the Bear how fierce!
The Centaur's arrow ready seems to pierce
Some enemy: far forth his bow is bent
Into the blue of heaven. He'll be shent,
          Pale unrelentor,   600
When he shall hear the wedding lutes a playing. —
Andromeda! sweet woman! why delaying
So timidly among the stars: come hither!
Join this bright throng, and nimbly follow whither
          They all are going.
Danae's Son,[32] before Jove newly bow'd,
Has wept for thee, calling to Jove aloud.
Thee, gentle lady, did he disenthral:
Ye shall for ever live and love, for all
          Thy tears are flowing. —   610
By Daphne's fright, behold Apollo! — '
                              More

Endymion heard not: down his steed him bore,
Prone to the green head of a misty hill.

    His first touch of the earth went nigh to kill.
'Alas!' said he, 'were I but always borne
Through dangerous winds, had but my footsteps worn
A path in hell, for ever would I bless
Horrors which nourish an uneasiness
For my own sullen conquering: to him
Who lives beyond earth's boundary, grief is dim,   620
Sorrow is but a shadow: now I see
The grass; I feel the solid ground – Ah, me!
It is thy voice – divinest! Where? – who? who
Left thee so quiet on this bed of dew?
Behold upon this happy earth we are;
Let us aye love each other; let us fare
On forest-fruits, and never, never go
Among the abodes of mortals here below,
Or be by phantoms duped. O destiny!
Into a labyrinth now my soul would fly,   630
But with thy beauty will I deaden it.
Where didst thou melt to? By thee will I sit
For ever: let our fate stop here – a kid
I on this spot will offer: Pan will bid
Us live in peace, in love and peace among
His forest wildernesses. I have clung
To nothing, lov'd a nothing, nothing seen
Or felt but a great dream! O I have been
Presumptuous against love, against the sky,
Against all elements, against the tie   640
Of mortals each to each, against the blooms
Of flowers, rush of rivers, and the tombs
Of heroes gone! Against his proper glory
Has my own soul conspired: so my story
Will I to children utter, and repent.
There never liv'd a mortal man, who bent
His appetite beyond his natural sphere,
But starv'd and died. My sweetest Indian, here,
Here will I kneel, for thou redeemed hast
My life from too thin breathing: gone and past   650

Are cloudy phantasms. Caverns lone, farewell!
And air of visions, and the monstrous swell
Of visionary seas! No, never more
Shall airy voices cheat me to the shore
Of tangled wonder, breathless and aghast.
Adieu, my daintiest Dream! although so vast
My love is still for thee. The hour may come
When we shall meet in pure elysium.
On earth I may not love thee; and therefore
Doves will I offer up, and sweetest store   660
All through the teeming year: so thou wilt shine
On me, and on this damsel fair of mine,
And bless our silver lives.[33] My Indian bliss!
My river-lily bud! one human kiss!
One sign of real breath – one gentle squeeze,
Warm as a dove's nest among summer trees,
And warm with dew at ooze from living blood!
Whither didst melt? Ah, what of that! – all good
We'll talk about – no more of dreaming. – Now,
Where shall our dwelling be? Under the brow   670
Of some steep mossy hill, where ivy dun
Would hide us up, although spring leaves were none;
And where dark yew trees, as we rustle through,
Will drop their scarlet berry cups of dew?
O thou wouldst joy to live in such a place;
Dusk for our loves, yet light enough to grace
Those gentle limbs on mossy bed reclin'd:
For by one step the blue sky shouldst thou find,
And by another, in deep dell below,
See, through the trees, a little river go   680
All in its midday gold and glimmering.
Honey from out the gnarled hive I'll bring,
And apples, wan with sweetness, gather thee, –
Cresses that grow where no man may them see,
And sorrel untorn by the dew-claw'd[34] stag:
Pipes will I fashion of the syrinx flag,[35]
That thou mayst always know whither I roam,
When it shall please thee in our quiet home
To listen and think of love. Still let me speak;
Still let me dive into the joy I seek, –   690

For yet the past doth prison me. The rill,
Thou haply mayst delight in, will I fill
With fairy fishes from the mountain tarn,
And thou shalt feed them from the squirrel's barn.[36]
Its bottom will I strew with amber shells,
And pebbles blue from deep enchanted wells.
Its sides I'll plant with dew-sweet eglantine,
And honeysuckles full of clear bee-wine.
I will entice this crystal rill to trace
Love's silver name upon the meadow's face.   700
I'll kneel to Vesta, for a flame of fire;
And to god Phoebus, for a golden lyre;
To Empress Dian, for a hunting spear;
To Vesper, for a taper silver-clear,
That I may see thy beauty through the night;
To Flora, and a nightingale shall light[37]
Tame on thy finger; to the River-gods,
And they shall bring thee taper fishing-rods
Of gold, and lines of Naiads' long bright tress.
Heaven shield thee for thine utter loveliness!   710
Thy mossy footstool shall the altar be
Fore which I'll bend, bending, dear love, to thee:
Those lips shall be my Delphos,[38] and shall speak
Laws to my footsteps, colour to my cheek,
Trembling or steadfastness to this same voice,
And of three sweetest pleasurings the choice:
And that affectionate light, those diamond things,
Those eyes, those passions, those supreme pearl springs,
Shall be my grief, or twinkle me to pleasure.
Say, is not bliss within our perfect seizure?   720
O that I could not doubt!'

              The mountaineer
Thus strove by fancies vain and crude to clear
His briar'd path to some tranquillity.
It gave bright gladness to his lady's eye,
And yet the tears she wept were tears of sorrow;
Answering thus, just as the golden morrow
Beam'd upward from the valleys of the east:
'O that the flutter of this heart had ceas'd,

Or the sweet name of love had pass'd away.
Young feather'd tyrant![39] by a swift decay   730
Wilt thou devote this body to the earth:
And I do think that at my very birth
I lisp'd thy blooming titles inwardly;
For at the first, first dawn and thought of thee,
With uplift hands I blest the stars of heaven.
Art thou not cruel? Ever have I striven
To think thee kind, but ah, it will not do!
When yet a child, I heard that kisses drew
Favour from thee, and so I kisses gave
To the void air, bidding them find out love: 740
But when I came to feel how far above
All fancy, pride, and fickle maidenhood,
All earthly pleasure, all imagin'd good,
Was the warm tremble of a devout kiss, –
Even then, that moment, at the thought of this,
Fainting I fell into a bed of flowers,
And languish'd there three days. Ye milder powers,
Am I not cruelly wrong'd? Believe, believe
Me, dear Endymion, were I to weave
With my own fancies garlands of sweet life,   750
Thou shouldst be one of all. Ah, bitter strife!
I may not be thy love: I am forbidden –
Indeed I am – thwarted, affrighted, chidden,
By things I trembled at, and gorgon wrath.
Twice hast thou ask'd whither I went: henceforth
Ask me no more! I may not utter it,
Nor may I be thy love. We might commit
Ourselves at once to vengeance; we might die;
We might embrace and die: voluptuous thought!
Enlarge not to my hunger,[40] or I'm caught   760
In trammels of perverse deliciousness.
No, no, that shall not be: thee will I bless,
And bid a long adieu.'

The Carian

No word return'd: both lovelorn, silent, wan,
Into the vallies green together went.
Far wandering, they were perforce content

To sit beneath a fair lone beechen tree;
Nor at each other gaz'd, but heavily
Por'd on its hazel cirque of shedded leaves.

Endymion! unhappy! it nigh grieves   770
Me to behold thee thus in last extreme:
Ensky'd[41] ere this, but truly that I deem
Truth the best music in a first-born song.
Thy lute-voic'd brother[42] will I sing ere long,
And thou shalt aid – hast thou not aided me?
Yes, moonlight Emperor! felicity
Has been thy meed for many thousand years;
Yet often have I, on the brink of tears,
Mourn'd as if yet thou wert a forester; –
Forgetting the old tale.

He did not stir   780
His eyes from the dead leaves, or one small pulse
Of joy he might have felt. The spirit culls
Unfaded amaranth,[43] when wild it strays
Through the old garden-ground of boyish days.
A little onward ran the very stream
By which he took his first soft poppy dream;
And on the very bark 'gainst which he leant
A crescent he had carv'd, and round it spent
His skill in little stars. The teeming tree
Had swollen and green'd the pious charactery,   790
But not ta'en out. Why, there was not a slope
Up which he had not fear'd[44] the antelope;
And not a tree, beneath whose rooty shade
He had not with his tamed leopards play'd:
Nor could an arrow light, or javelin,
Fly in the air where his had never been –
And yet he knew it not.

O treachery!
Why does his lady smile, pleasing her eye
With all his sorrowing? He sees her not.
But who so stares on him? His sister sure!   800
Peona of the woods! – Can she endure –

Impossible – how dearly they embrace!
His lady smiles; delight is in her face;
It is no treachery.

                'Dear brother mine!
Endymion, weep not so! Why shouldst thou pine
When all great Latmos so exalt will be?
Thank the great gods, and look not bitterly;
And speak not one pale word, and sigh no more.
Sure I will not believe thou hast such store
Of grief, to last thee to my kiss again.   810
Thou surely canst not bear a mind in pain,
Come hand in hand with one so beautiful.
Be happy both of you! for I will pull
The flowers of autumn for your coronals.
Pan's holy priest for young Endymion calls;
And when he is restor'd, thou, fairest dame,
Shalt be our queen. Now, is it not a shame
To see ye thus, – not very, very sad?
Perhaps ye are too happy to be glad:
O feel as if it were a common day;   820
Free-voic'd as one who never was away.
No tongue shall ask, whence come ye? but ye shall
Be gods of your own rest imperial.
Not even I, for one whole month, will pry
Into the hours that have pass'd us by,
Since in my arbour I did sing to thee.
O Hermes! on this very night will be
A hymning up to Cynthia, queen of light;
For the soothsayers old saw yesternight
Good visions in the air, – whence will befall,   830
As say these sages, health perpetual
To shepherds and their flocks; and furthermore,
In Dian's face they read the gentle lore:
Therefore for her these vesper-carols are.
Our friends will all be there from nigh and far.
Many upon thy death have ditties[45] made;
And many, even now, their foreheads shade
With cypress, on a day of sacrifice.
New singing for our maids shalt thou devise,

And pluck the sorrow from our huntsmen's brows.   840
Tell me, my lady-queen, how to espouse
This wayward brother to his rightful joys!
His eyes are on thee bent, as thou didst poise
His fate most goddess-like. Help me, I pray,
To lure – Endymion, dear brother, say
What ails thee?' He could bear no more, and so
Bent his soul fiercely like a spiritual bow,
And twang'd it inwardly, and calmly said:
'I would have thee my only friend, sweet maid!
My only visitor! not ignorant though,   850
That those deceptions which for pleasure go
'Mong men, are pleasures real as real may be:
But there are higher ones I may not see,
If impiously an earthly realm I take.
Since I saw thee, I have been wide awake
Night after night, and day by day, until
Of the empyrean I have drunk my fill.
Let it content thee, Sister, seeing me
More happy than betides[46] mortality.
A hermit young, I'll live in mossy cave,   860
Where thou alone shalt come to me, and lave
Thy spirit in the wonders I shall tell.
Through me the shepherd realm shall prosper well;
For to thy tongue will I all health confide.
And, for my sake, let this young maid abide
With thee as a dear sister. Thou alone,
Peona, mayst return to me. I own
This may sound strangely: but when, dearest girl,
Thou seest it for my happiness, no pearl
Will trespass down those cheeks. Companion fair!   870
Wilt be content to dwell with her, to share
This sister's love with me?' Like one resign'd
And bent by circumstance, and thereby blind
In self-commitment, thus that meek unknown:
'Aye, but a buzzing by my ears has flown,
Of jubilee to Dian: – truth I heard?
Well then, I see there is no little bird,
Tender soever, but is Jove's own care.
Long have I sought for rest, and, unaware,

Behold I find it! so exalted too!   880
So after my own heart! I knew, I knew
There was a place untenanted in it:
In that same void white Chastity shall sit,
And monitor[47] me nightly to lone slumber.
With sanest lips I vow me to the number
Of Dian's sisterhood; and, kind lady,
With thy good help, this very night shall see
My future days to her fane consecrate.'

    As feels a dreamer what doth most create
His own particular fright, so these three felt: 890
Or like one who, in after ages, knelt
To Lucifer or Baal, when he'd pine
After a little sleep: or when in mine
Far under-ground, a sleeper meets his friends
Who know him not. Each diligently bends
Towards common thoughts and things for very fear;
Striving their ghastly malady to cheer,
By thinking it a thing of yes and no,[48]
That housewives talk of. But the spirit-blow
Was struck, and all were dreamers. At the last   900
Endymion said: 'Are not our fates all cast?
Why stand we here? Adieu, ye tender pair!
Adieu!' Whereat those maidens, with wild stare,
Walk'd dizzily away. Pained and hot
His eyes went after them, until they got
Near to a cypress grove, whose deadly maw
In one swift moment, would what then he saw
Engulf for ever. 'Stay!' he cried, 'ah, stay!
Turn, damsels! hist! one word I have to say.
Sweet Indian, I would see thee once again.   910
It is a thing I dote on: so I'd fain,
Peona, ye should hand in hand repair
Into those holy groves, that silent are
Behind great Dian's temple. I'll be yon,
At vesper's earliest twinkle – they are gone –
But once, once, once again – ' At this he press'd
His hands against his face, and then did rest
His head upon a mossy hillock green,

And so remain'd as he a corpse had been
All the long day; save when he scantly lifted 920
His eyes abroad, to see how shadows shifted
With the slow move of time, – sluggish and weary
Until the poplar tops, in journey dreary,
Had reach'd the river's brim. Then up he rose,
And, slowly as that very river flows,
Walk'd towards the temple grove with this lament:
'Why such a golden eve? The breeze is sent
Careful and soft, that not a leaf may fall
Before the serene father[49] of them all
Bows down his summer head below the west. 930
Now am I of breath, speech, and speed possest,
But at the setting I must bid adieu
To her for the last time. Night will strew
On the damp grass myriads of lingering leaves,
And with them shall I die; nor much it grieves
To die, when summer dies on the cold sward.
Why, I have been a butterfly, a lord
Of flowers, garlands, love-knots, silly posies,
Groves, meadows, melodies, and arbour roses;
My kingdom's at its death, and just it is 940
That I should die with it: so in all this
We miscall grief, bale, sorrow, heartbreak, woe,
What is there to plain of? By Titan's foe[50]
I am but rightly serv'd.' So saying, he
Tripp'd lightly on, in sort of deathful glee;
Laughing at the clear stream and setting sun,
As though they jests had been: nor had he done
His laugh at nature's holy countenance,
Until that grove appear'd, as if perchance,
And then his tongue with sober seemlihed[51] 950
Gave utterance as he enter'd: 'Ha!' he said,
'King of the butterflies; but by this gloom,
And by old Rhadamanthus' tongue of doom,
This dusk religion, pomp of solitude,
And the Promethean clay by thief endued,
By old Saturnus'[52] forelock, by his head
Shook with eternal palsy, I did wed
Myself to things of light from infancy;

And thus to be cast out, thus lorn[53] to die,
Is sure enough to make a mortal man   900
Grow impious.' So he inwardly began
On things for which no wording can be found;
Deeper and deeper sinking, until drown'd
Beyond the reach of music: for the choir
Of Cynthia he heard not, though rough briar
Nor muffling thicket interpos'd to dull
The vesper hymn, far swollen, soft and full,
Through the dark pillars of those sylvan aisles.
He saw not the two maidens, nor their smiles,
Wan as primroses gather'd at midnight   970
By chilly finger'd spring. Unhappy wight!
'Endymion!' said Peona, 'we are here!
What wouldst thou ere we all are laid on bier?'
Then he embrac'd her, and his lady's hand
Press'd, saying: 'Sister, I would have command,
If it were heaven's will, on our sad fate.'
At which that dark-eyed stranger stood elate
And said, in a new voice, but sweet as love,
To Endymion's amaze: 'By Cupid's dove,
And so thou shalt! and by the lily truth   980
Of my own breast thou shalt, beloved youth!'
And as she spake, into her face there came
Light, as reflected from a silver flame:
Her long black hair swell'd ampler, in display
Full golden; in her eyes a brighter day
Dawn'd blue and full of love. Aye, he beheld
Phoebe, his passion! joyous she upheld
Her lucid brow, continuing thus: 'Drear, drear
Has our delaying been; but foolish fear
Withheld me first; and then decrees of fate;   990
And then 'twas fit that from this mortal state
Thou shouldst, my love, by some unlook'd for change
Be spiritualiz'd. Peona, we shall range
These forests, and to thee they safe shall be
As was thy cradle; hither shalt thou flee
To meet us many a time.' Next Cynthia bright
Peona kiss'd, and bless'd with fair good night:
Her brother kiss'd her too, and knelt adown

Before his goddess, in a blissful swoon.
She gave her fair hands to him, and behold,   1000
Before three swiftest kisses he had told,
They vanish'd far away! – Peona went
Home through the gloomy wood in wonderment.

LAMIA, ISABELLA,
THE EVE OF ST AGNES,
and other poems
1820

Advertisement

If any apology be thought necessary for the appearance of the unfinished poem of Hyperion, the publishers beg to state that they alone are responsible, as it was printed at their particular request, and contrary to the wish of the author. The poem was intended to have been of equal length with *Endymion*, but the reception given to that work discouraged the author from proceeding.

Fleet Street, 26 June 1820

Lamia

PART I

Upon a time, before the faery broods
Drove Nymph and Satyr from the prosperous woods[1],
Before king Oberon's bright diadem,
Sceptre, and mantle, clasp'd with dewy gem,
Frighted away the Dryads and the Fauns
From rushes green, and brakes, and cowslip'd lawns,
The ever-smitten Hermes[2] empty left
His golden throne, bent warm on amorous theft:
From high Olympus had he stolen light,
On this side of Jove's clouds, to escape the sight   10
Of his great summoner, and made retreat
Into a forest on the shores of Crete.
For somewhere in that sacred island dwelt
A nymph, to whom all hoofed Satyrs knelt;
At whose white feet the languid Tritons poured
Pearls, while on land they wither'd and adored.
Fast by the springs where she to bathe was wont,
And in those meads where sometime she might haunt,
Were strewn rich gifts, unknown to any Muse,
Though Fancy's casket were unlock'd to choose.   20
Ah, what a world of love was at her feet!
So Hermes thought, and a celestial heat
Burnt from his winged heels to either ear,
That from a whiteness, as the lily clear,
Blush'd into roses 'mid his golden hair,
Fallen in jealous curls about his shoulders bare.
From vale to vale, from wood to wood, he flew,
Breathing upon the flowers his passion new,
And would with many a river to its head,
To find where this sweet nymph prepar'd her secret bed: 30
In vain; the sweet nymph might nowhere be found,
And so he rested, on the lonely ground,
Pensive, and full of painful jealousies
Of the Wood-Gods, and even the very trees.
There as he stood, he heard a mournful voice,

Such as once heard, in gentle heart, destroys
All pain but pity: thus the lone voice spake:
'When from this wreathed tomb shall I awake!
When move in a sweet body fit for life,
And love, and pleasure, and the ruddy strife   40
Of hearts and lips! Ah, miserable me!'
The God, dove-footed, glided silently
Round bush and tree, soft-brushing, in his speed,
The taller grasses and full-flowering weed,
Until he found a palpitating snake,
Bright, and cirque-couchant³ in a dusky brake.

She was a gordian⁴ shape of dazzling hue,
Vermilion-spotted, golden, green, and blue;
Striped like a zebra, freckled like a pard,
Eyed like a peacock, and all crimson barr'd;   50
And full of silver moons, that, as she breathed,
Dissolv'd, or brighter shone, or interwreathed
Their lustres with the gloomier tapestries –
So rainbow-sided, touch'd with miseries,
She seem'd, at once, some penanced lady elf,
Some demon's mistress, or the demon's self.
Upon her crest she wore a wannish fire
Sprinkled with stars, like Ariadne's tiar:⁵
Her head was serpent, but ah, bitter-sweet!
She had a woman's mouth with all its pearls complete: 60
And for her eyes: what could such eyes do there
But weep, and weep, that they were born so fair?
As Proserpine still weeps for her Sicilian air.
Her throat was serpent, but the words she spake
Came, as through bubbling honey, for Love's sake,
And thus; while Hermes on his pinions lay,
Like a stoop'd falcon ere he takes his prey.

'Fair Hermes, crown'd with feathers, fluttering light,
I had a splendid dream of thee last night:
I saw thee sitting, on a throne of gold,   70
Among the Gods, upon Olympus old,
The only sad one; for thou didst not hear
The soft, lute-finger'd Muses chanting clear.

Nor even Apollo when he sang alone,
Deaf to his throbbing throat's long, long melodious moan.
I dreamt I saw thee, robed in purple flakes,[6]
Break amorous through the clouds, as morning breaks,
And, swiftly as a bright Phoebean dart,
Strike for the Cretan isle; and here thou art!
Too gentle Hermes, hast thou found the maid?'   80
Whereat the star of Lethe[7] not delay'd
His rosy eloquence, and thus inquired:
'Thou smooth-lipp'd serpent, surely high inspired!
Thou beauteous wreath, with melancholy eyes,
Possess whatever bliss thou canst devise,
Telling me only where my nymph is fled, –
Where she doth breathe!' 'Bright planet, thou hast said,'
Return'd the snake, 'but seal with oaths, fair God!'
'I swear,' said Hermes, 'by my serpent rod,
And by thine eyes, and by thy starry crown!'   90
Light flew his earnest words, among the blossoms blown.
Then thus again the brilliance feminine:
'Too frail of heart! for this lost nymph of thine,
Free as the air, invisibly, she strays
About these thornless wilds; her pleasant days
She tastes unseen; unseen her nimble feet
Leave traces in the grass and flowers sweet;
From weary tendrils, and bow'd branches green,
She plucks the fruit unseen, she bathes unseen:
And by my power is her beauty veil'd   100
To keep it unaffronted, unassail'd
By the love-glances of unlovely eyes,
Of Satyrs, Fauns, and blear'd Silenus' sighs.
Pale grew her immortality, for woe
Of all these lovers, and she grieved so
I took compassion on her, bade her steep
Her hair in weird[8] syrops, that would keep
Her loveliness invisible, yet free
To wander as she loves, in liberty.
Thou shalt behold her, Hermes, thou alone,   110
If thou wilt, as thou swearest, grant my boon!'
Then, once again, the charmed God began
An oath, and through the serpent's ears it ran

Warm, tremulous, devout, psalterian.
Ravish'd, she lifted her Circean head,
Blush'd a live damask,[9] and swift-lisping said,
'I was a woman, let me have once more
A woman's shape, and charming as before.
I love a youth of Corinth – O the bliss!
Give me my woman's form, and place me where he is.   120
Stoop, Hermes, let me breathe upon thy brow,
And thou shalt see thy sweet nymph even now.'
The God on half-shut feathers sank serene,
She breath'd upon his eyes, and swift was seen
Of both the guarded nymph near-smiling on the green.
It was no dream; or say a dream it was,
Real are the dreams of Gods, and smoothly pass
Their pleasures in a long immortal dream.
One warm, flush'd moment, hovering, it might seem
Dash'd by the wood-nymph's beauty, so he burn'd;   130
Then, lighting on the printless verdure, turn'd
To the swoon'd serpent, and with languid arm,
Delicate, put to proof the lythe Caducean charm.[10]
So done, upon the nymph his eyes he bent
Full of adoring tears and blandishment,
And towards her stept: she, like a moon in wane,
Faded before him, cower'd, nor could restrain
Her fearful sobs, self-folding like a flower
That faints into itself at evening hour:
But the God fostering her chilled hand,   140
She felt the warmth, her eyelids open'd bland,
And, like new flowers at morning song of bees,
Bloom'd, and gave up her honey to the lees.[11]
Into the green-recessed woods they flew;
Nor grew they pale, as mortal lovers do.

   Left to herself, the serpent now began
To change; her elfin blood in madness ran,
Her mouth foam'd, and the grass, therewith besprent,[12]
Wither'd at dew so sweet and virulent;
Her eyes in torture fix'd, and anguish drear,   150
Hot, glaz'd, and wide, with lid-lashes all sear,
   Flash'd phosphor and sharp sparks, without one cooling tear.

The colours all inflam'd throughout her train,
She writh'd about, convuls'd with scarlet pain:
A deep volcanian yellow took the place
Of all her milder-mooned body's grace;
And, as the lava ravishes the mead,
Spoilt all her silver mail, and golden brede;
Made gloom of all her frecklings, streaks and bars,
Eclips'd her crescents, and lick'd up her stars: 160
So that, in moments few, she was undrest
Of all her sapphires, greens, and amethyst,
And rubious-argent:[13] of all these bereft,
Nothing but pain and ugliness were left.
Still shone her crown; that vanish'd, also she
Melted and disappear'd as suddenly;
And in the air, her new voice luting soft,
Cried, 'Lycius! gentle Lycius!' – Borne aloft
With the bright mists about the mountains hoar
These words dissolv'd: Crete's forests heard no more.   170

Whither fled Lamia, now a lady bright,
A full-born beauty new and exquisite?
She fled into that valley they pass o'er
Who go to Corinth from Cenchreas' shore;
And rested at the foot of those wild hills,
The rugged founts of the Peraean rills,
And of that other ridge whose barren back
Stretches, with all its mist and cloudy rack.
South-westward to Cleone. There she stood
About a young bird's flutter from a wood,   180
Fair, on a sloping green of mossy tread,
By a clear pool, wherein she passioned
To see herself escap'd from so sore ills,
While her robes flaunted with the daffodils.

Ah, happy Lycius! – for she was a maid
More beautiful than ever twisted braid,
Or sigh'd, or blush'd, or on spring-flowered lea
Spread a green kirtle to the minstrelsy:
A virgin purest lipp'd, yet in the lore
Of love deep learned to the red heart's core: 190

Not one hour old, yet of sciential[14] brain
To unperplex bliss from its neighbour pain;
Define their pettish limits, and estrange
Their points of contact, and swift counterchange;
Intrigue with the specious chaos, and dispart
Its most ambiguous atoms with sure art;
As though in Cupid's college she had spent
Sweet days a lovely graduate, still unshent,
And kept his rosy terms in idle languishment.

Why this fair creature chose so faerily   200
By the wayside to linger, we shall see;
But first 'tis fit to tell how she could muse
And dream, when in the serpent prison-house.
Of all she list, strange or magnificent:
How, ever, where she will'd, her spirit went;
Whether to faint Elysium, or where
Down through tress-lifting waves the Nereids fair
Wind into Thetis' bower by many a pearly stair;
Or where God Bacchus drains his cups divine,
Stretch'd out, at ease, beneath a glutinous pine;   210
Or where in Pluto's gardens palatine
Mulciber's columns gleam in far piazzian line.
And sometimes into cities she would send
Her dream, with feast and rioting to blend;
And once, while among mortals dreaming thus,
She saw the young Corinthian Lycius
Charioting foremost in the envious race.
Like a young Jove with calm uneager face,
And fell into a swooning love of him.
Now on the moth-time of that evening dim   220
He would return that way, as well she knew,
To Corinth from the shore ; for freshly blew
The eastern soft wind, and his galley now
Grated the quaystones with her brazen prow
In port Cenchreas, from Egina isle
Fresh anchor'd ; whither he had been awhile
To sacrifice to Jove, whose temple there
Waits with high marble doors for blood and incense rare.
Jove heard his vows,[15] and better'd his desire;

For by some freakful chance he made retire   230
From his companions, and set forth to walk.
Perhaps grown wearied of their Corinth talk:
Over the solitary hills he fared,
Thoughtless at first, but ere eve's star appeared
His phantasy was lost, where reason fades,
In the calm'd twilight of Platonic shades.[16]
Lamia beheld him coming, near, more near –
Close to her passing, in indifference drear,
His silent sandals swept the mossy green ;
So neighbour'd to him, and yet so unseen   240
She stood: he pass'd, shut up in mysteries,
His mind wrapp'd like his mantle, while her eyes
Follow'd his steps, and her neck regal white
Turn'd – syllabling thus, 'Ah, Lycius bright,
And will you leave me on the hills alone?
Lycius, look back! and be some pity shown.'
He did ; not with cold wonder fearingly,
But Orpheus-like at an Eurydice;
For so delicious were the words she sung,
It seem'd he had lov'd them a whole summer long: 250
And soon his eyes had drunk her beauty up,
Leaving no drop in the bewildering cup,
And still the cup was full, – while he, afraid
Lest she should vanish ere his lip had paid
Due adoration, thus began to adore;
Her soft look growing coy, she saw his chain[17] so sure:
'Leave thee alone! Look back! Ah, Goddess, see
Whether my eyes can ever turn from thee!
For pity do not this sad heart belie –
Even as thou vanishest so shall I die.   260
Stay! though a Naiad of the rivers, stay!
To thy far wishes will thy streams obey:
Stay! though the greenest woods be thy domain,
Alone they can drink up the morning rain:
Though a descended Pleiad, will not one
Of thine harmonious sisters keep in tune
Thy spheres, and as thy silver proxy shine?
So sweetly to these ravish'd ears of mine
Came thy sweet greeting, that if thou shouldst fade

Thy memory will waste me to a shade: –   270
For pity do not melt!' – 'If I should stay,'
Said Lamia, 'here, upon this floor of clay,
And pain my steps upon these flowers too rough,
What canst thou say or do of charm enough
To dull the nice remembrance of my home?
Thou canst not ask me with thee here to roam
Over these hills and vales, where no joy is, –
Empty of immortality and bliss!
Thou art a scholar, Lycius, and must know
That finer spirits cannot breathe below   280
In human climes, and live: Alas! poor youth,
What taste of purer air hast thou to soothe
My essence? What serener palaces,
Where I may all my many senses please,
And by mysterious sleights a hundred thirsts appease?
It cannot be – Adieu!' So said, she rose
Tiptoe with white arms spread. He, sick to lose
The amorous promise of her lone complain,
Swoon'd, murmuring of love, and pale with pain.
The cruel lady,[18] without any show   290
Of sorrow for her tender favourite's woe,
But rather, if her eyes could brighter be,
With brighter eyes and slow amenity,
Put her new lips to his, and gave afresh
The life she had so tangled in her mesh:
And as he from one trance was wakening
Into another, she began to sing,
Happy in beauty, life, and love, and everything,
A song of love, too sweet for earthly lyres,
While, like held breath, the stars drew in their panting fires.
And then she whisper'd in such trembling tone,   301
As those who, safe together met alone
For the first time through many anguish'd days,
Use other speech than looks; bidding him raise
His drooping head, and clear his soul of doubt,
For that she was a woman, and without
Any more subtle fluid in her veins
Than throbbing blood, and that the self-same pains
Inhabited her frail-strung heart as his.

And next she wonder'd how his eyes could miss   310
Her face so long in Corinth, where, she said,
She dwelt but half retir'd, and there had led
Days happy as the gold coin could invent
Without the aid of love; yet in content
Till she saw him, as once she pass'd him by,
Where 'gainst a column he lent thoughtfully
At Venus' temple porch, 'mid baskets heap'd
Of amorous herbs and flowers, newly reap'd
Late on that eve, as 'twas the night before
The Adonian feast; whereof she saw no more,   320
But wept alone those days, for why should she adore?
Lycius from death awoke into amaze,
To see her still, and singing so sweet lays;
Then from amaze into delight he fell
To hear her whisper woman's lore so well;
And every word she spake entic'd him on
To unperplex'd delight and pleasure known.
Let the mad poets say whate'er they please
Of the sweets of Faeries, Peris, Goddesses,
There is not such a treat among them all,   330
Haunters of cavern, lake, and waterfall,
As a real woman, lineal[19] indeed
From Pyrrha's pebbles or old Adam's seed.
Thus gentle Lamia judg'd, and judg'd aright,
That Lycius could not love in half a fright,
So threw the goddess off, and won his heart
More pleasantly by playing woman's part,
With no more awe than what her beauty gave,
That, while it smote, still guaranteed to save.
Lycius to all made eloquent reply,   340
Marrying to every word a twinborn sigh;
And last, pointing to Corinth, ask'd her sweet.
If 'twas too far that night for her soft feet.
The way was short, for Lamia's eagerness
Made, by a spell, the triple league decrease
To a few paces; not at all surmised
By blinded Lycius, so in her comprised.[20]
They pass'd the city gates, he knew not how,
So noiseless, and he never thought to know.

As men talk in a dream, so Corinth all,   350
Throughout her palaces imperial,
And all her populous streets and temples lewd,[21]
Mutter'd, like tempest in the distance brew'd,
To the wide-spreaded night above her towers.
Men, women, rich and poor, in the cool hours,
Shuffled their sandals o'er the pavement white,
Companion'd or alone; while many a light
Flared, here and there, from wealthy festivals,
And threw their moving shadows on the walls,
Or found them cluster'd in the corniced shade   360
Of some arch'd temple door, or dusky colonnade.

Muffling his face, of greeting friends in fear,
Her fingers he press'd hard, as one came near
With curl'd gray beard, sharp eyes, and smooth bald crown,
Slow-stepp'd, and robed in philosophic gown:
Lycius shrank closer, as they met and past,
Into his mantle, adding wings to haste,
While hurried Lamia trembled: 'Ah,' said he,
'Why do you shudder, love, so ruefully?
Why does your tender palm dissolve in dew?'   370
I'm wearied,' said fair Lamia: 'tell me who
Is that old man? I cannot bring to mind
His features: – Lycius! wherefore did you blind
Yourself from his quick eyes?' Lycius replied,
'Tis Apollonius sage, my trusty guide
And good instructor; but tonight he seems
The ghost of folly haunting my sweet dreams.'

While yet he spake they had arrived before
A pillar'd porch, with lofty portal door,
Where hung a silver lamp, whose phosphor glow   380
Reflected in the slabbed steps below,
Mild as a star in water; for so new,
And so unsullied was the marble's hue,
So through the crystal polish, liquid fine,
Ran the dark veins, that none but feet divine
Could e'er have touch'd there. Sounds Aeolian
Breath'd from the hinges, as the ample span

Of the wide doors disclos'd a place unknown
Some time to any, but those two alone,
And a few Persian mutes, who that same year   390
Were seen about the markets: none knew where
They could inhabit; the most curious
Were foil'd, who watch'd to trace them to their house:
And but the flitter-winged verse must tell,
For truth's sake, what woe afterwards befell,
'Twould humour many a heart to leave them thus,
Shut from the busy world of more incredulous.

Lamia – Part II

Love in a hut, with water and a crust,
Is – Love, forgive us! – cinders, ashes, dust;
Love in a palace is perhaps at last
More grievous torment than a hermit's fast: –
That is a doubtful tale from faery land,
Hard for the non-elect to understand.
Had Lycius liv'd to hand his story down,
He might have given the moral a fresh frown,
Or clench'd[1] it quite: but too short was their bliss
To breed distrust and hate, that make the soft voice hiss. 10
Beside, there, nightly, with terrific glare,
Love, jealous grown of so complete a pair,
Hover'd and buzz'd his wings, with fearful roar,
Above the lintel of their chamber door,
And down the passage cast a glow upon the floor.

    For all this came a ruin: side by side
They were enthroned, in the even tide,
Upon a couch, near to a curtaining
Whose airy texture, from a golden string,
Floated into the room, and let appear   20
Unveil'd the summer heaven, blue and clear,
Betwixt two marble shafts:[2] – there they reposed,
Where use had made it sweet, with eyelids closed,
Saving a tithe[3] which love still open kept,
That they might see each other while they almost slept;
When from the slope side of a suburb hill,
Deafening the swallow's twitter, came a thrill
Of trumpets – Lycius started – the sounds fled,
But left a thought, a buzzing in his head.
For the first time, since first he harbour'd in   30
That purple-lined palace of sweet sin,
His spirit pass'd beyond its golden bourn
Into the noisy world almost forsworn.
The lady, ever watchful, penetrant,[4]
Saw this with pain, so arguing a want
Of something more, more than her empery[5]

Of joys; and she began to moan and sigh
Because he mused beyond her, knowing well
That but a moment's thought is passion's passing bell.
'Why do you sigh, fair creature?' whisper'd he: 40
'Why do you think?' return'd she tenderly:
'You have deserted me; – where am I now?
Not in your heart while care weighs on your brow:
No, no, you have dismiss'd me; and I go
From your breast houseless: aye, it must be so.'
He answer'd, bending to her open eyes,
Where he was mirror'd small in paradise,
'My silver planet, both of eve and morn!
Why will you plead yourself so sad forlorn,
While I am striving how to fill my heart   50
With deeper crimson, and a double smart?
How to entangle, trammel up and snare
Your soul in mine, and labyrinth you there
Like the hid scent in an unbudded rose?
Aye, a sweet kiss – you see your mighty woes.
My thoughts! shall I unveil them? Listen then!
What mortal hath a prize, that other men
May be confounded and abash'd withal,
But lets it sometimes pace abroad majestical,
And triumph, as in thee I should rejoice   60
Amid the hoarse alarm of Corinth's voice.
Let my foes choke, and my friends shout afar,
While through the thronged streets your bridal car
Wheels round its dazzling spokes.' – The lady's cheek
Trembled; she nothing said, but, pale and meek,
Arose and knelt before him, wept a rain
Of sorrows at his words; at last with pain
Beseeching him, the while his hand she wrung,
To change his purpose. He thereat was stung,
Perverse, with stronger fancy to reclaim   70
Her wild and timid nature to his aim:
Besides, for all his love, in self despite,
Against his better self, he took delight
Luxurious in her sorrows, soft and new.
His passion, cruel grown, took on a hue
Fierce and sanguineous as 'twas possible

In one whose brow had no dark veins to swell.
Fine was the mitigated fury, like
Apollo's presence when in act to strike
The serpent[6] – Ha, the serpent! certes, she   80
Was none. She burnt, she lov'd the tyranny,
And, all subdued, consented to the hour
When to the bridal he should lead his paramour.
Whispering in midnight silence, said the youth,
'Sure some sweet name thou hast, though, by my truth,
I have not ask'd it, ever thinking thee
Not mortal, but of heavenly progeny,
As still I do. Hast any mortal name,
Fit appellation for this dazzling frame?
Or friends or kinsfolk on the citied earth,   90
To share our marriage feast and nuptial mirth?'
'I have no friends,' said Lamia, 'no, not one:
My presence in wide Corinth hardly known:
My parents' bones are in their dusty urns
Sepulchred, where no kindled incense burns,
Seeing all their luckless race are dead, save me,
And I neglect the holy rite for thee.
Even as you list invite your many guests;
But if, as now it seems, your vision rests
With any pleasure on me, do not bid   100
Old Apollonius – from him keep me hid.'
Lycius, perplex'd at words so blind and blank,
Made close inquiry ; from whose touch she shrank,
Feigning a sleep; and he to the dull shade
Of deep sleep in a moment was betray'd.[7]

        It was the custom then to bring away
The bride from home at blushing shut of day,
Veil'd, in a chariot, heralded along
By strewn flowers, torches, and a marriage song,
With other pageants: but this fair unknown   110
Had not a friend. So being left alone,
(Lycius was gone to summon all his kin)
And knowing surely she could never win
His foolish heart from its mad pompousness,
She set herself, high-thoughted, how to dress

The misery in fit magnificence.
She did so, but 'tis doubtful how and whence
Came, and who were her subtle[8] servitors.
About the halls, and to and from the doors,
There was a noise of wings, till in short space   120
The glowing banquet-room shone with wide-arched grace.
A haunting music, sole perhaps and lone
Supportress of the faery-roof, made moan
Throughout, as fearful the whole charm might fade.
Fresh carved cedar, mimicking a glade
Of palm and plantain, met from either side,
High in the midst, in honour of the bride:
Two palms and then two plantains, and so on,
From either side their stems branch'd one to one
All down the aisled place; and beneath all   130
There ran a stream of lamps straight on from wall to wall.
So canopied, lay an untasted feast
Teeming with odours. Lamia, regal drest,
Silently paced about, and as she went,
In pale contented sort of discontent,
Mission'd her viewless servants to enrich
The fretted[9] splendour of each nook and niche.
Between the tree-stems, marbled plain at first,
Came jasper panels; then, anon, there burst
Forth creeping imagery of slighter trees,   140
And with the larger wove in small intricacies.
Approving all, she faded at self-will,
And shut the chamber up, close, hush'd and still,
Complete and ready for the revels rude,
When dreadful guests would come to spoil her solitude.

    The day appear'd, and all the gossip rout.
O senseless Lycius! Madman! wherefore flout
The silent-blessing fate, warm cloister'd hours,
And show to common eyes these secret bowers?
The herd approach'd; each guest, with busy brain,   150
Arriving at the portal, gaz'd amain,
And enter'd marveling: for they knew the street,
Remember'd it from childhood all complete
Without a gap, yet ne'er before had seen

That royal porch, that high-built fair demesne;
So in they hurried all, maz'd, curious and keen:
Save one, who look'd thereon with eye severe,
And with calm-planted steps walk'd in austere;
'Twas Apollonius: something too he laugh'd,
As though some knotty problem, that had daft[10]   160
His patient thought, had now begun to thaw,
And solve and melt: – 'twas just as he foresaw.

    He met within the murmurous vestibule
His young disciple. ''Tis no common rule,
Lycius,' said he,'for uninvited guest
To force himself upon you, and infest
With an unbidden presence the bright throng
Of younger friends; yet must I do this wrong,
And you forgive me.' Lycius blush'd, and led
The old man through the inner doors broad-spread;   170
With reconciling words and courteous mien
Turning into sweet milk the sophist's[11] spleen.

    Of wealthy lustre was the banquet-room,
Fill'd with pervading brilliance and perfume:
Before each lucid panel fuming stood
A censer fed with myrrh and spiced wood,
Each by a sacred tripod held aloft,
Whose slender feet wide-swerv'd upon the soft
Wool-woofed carpets: fifty wreaths of smoke
From fifty censers their light voyage took   180
To the high roof, still mimick'd as they rose
Along the mirror'd walls by twin-clouds odorous.
Twelve sphered tables, by silk seats insphered,
High as the level of a man's breast rear'd
On libbard's paws, upheld the heavy gold
Of cups and goblets, and the store thrice told
Of Ceres' horn, and, in huge vessels, wine
Come from the gloomy tun with merry shine.
Thus loaded with a feast the tables stood,
Each shrining in the midst the image of a God.   190

    When in an antichamber every guest
Had felt the cold full sponge to pleasure press'd,

By minist'ring slaves, upon his hands and feet,
And fragrant oils with ceremony meet
Pour'd on his hair, they all mov'd to the feast
In white robes, and themselves in order placed
Around the silken couches, wondering
Whence all this mighty cost and blaze of wealth could spring.

    Soft went the music the soft air along,
While fluent Greek a vowel'd undersong   200
Kept up among the guests, discoursing low
At first, for scarcely was the wine at flow;
But when the happy vintage touch'd their brains,
Louder they talk, and louder come the strains
Of powerful instruments: – the gorgeous dyes,
The space, the splendour of the draperies,
The roof of awful richness, nectarous cheer,
Beautiful slaves, and Lamia's self, appear,
Now, when the wine has done its rosy deed,
And every soul from human trammels freed,   210
No more so strange; for merry wine, sweet wine,
Will make Elysian shades not too fair, too divine.
Soon was God Bacchus at meridian height;[12]
Flush'd were their cheeks, and bright eyes double bright:
Garlands of every green, and every scent
From vales deflower'd, or forest-trees branch-rent,
In baskets of bright osier'd[13] gold were brought
High as the handles heap'd, to suit the thought
Of every guest; that each, as he did please,
Might fancy-fit his brows, silk-pillow'd at his ease   220

    What wreath for Lamia? What for Lycius?
What for the sage, old Apollonius?
Upon her aching forehead be there hung
The leaves of willow and of adder's tongue;[14]
And for the youth, quick, let us strip for him
The thyrsus,[15] that his watching eyes may swim
Into forgetfulness; and, for the sage,
Let spear-grass and the spiteful thistle wage
War on his temples. Do not all charms fly
At the mere touch of cold philosophy?[16]   230
There was an awful rainbow once in heaven:

We know her woof, her texture; she is given
In the dull catalogue of common things.
Philosophy will clip an Angel's wings,
Conquer all mysteries by rule and line,
Empty the haunted air, and gnomed mine –
Unweave a rainbow, as it erewhile made
The tender-person'd Lamia melt into a shade.

By her glad Lycius sitting, in chief place,
Scarce saw in all the room another face,   240
Till, checking his love trance, a cup he took
Full brimm'd, and opposite sent forth a look
'Cross the broad table, to beseech a glance
From his old teacher's wrinkled countenance,
And pledge him. The bald-head philosopher
Had fix'd his eye, without a twinkle or stir
Full on the alarmed beauty of the bride,
Brow-beating her fair form, and troubling her sweet pride.
Lycius then press'd her hand, with devout touch,
As pale it lay upon the rosy couch: 250
'Twas icy, and the cold ran through his veins;
Then sudden it grew hot, and all the pains
Of an unnatural heat shot to his heart.
'Lamia, what means this? Wherefore dost thou start?
Know'st thou that man?' Poor Lamia answer'd not.
He gaz'd into her eyes, and not a jot
Own'd they the lovelorn piteous appeal:
More, more he gaz'd: his human senses reel:
Some hungry spell that loveliness absorbs;
'Lamia!' he cried – and no soft-toned reply.   260
The many heard, and the loud revelry
Grew hush; the stately music no more breathes;
The myrtle sicken'd in a thousand wreaths.
By faint degrees, voice, lute, and pleasure ceased;
A deadly silence step by step increased,
Until it seem'd a horrid presence there,
And not a man but felt the terror in his hair.
'Lamia!' he shriek'd; and nothing but the shriek
With its sad echo did the silence break.   270
'Begone, foul dream!' he cried, gazing again

In the bride's face, where now no azure vein
Wander'd on fair-spaced temples; no soft bloom
Misted the cheek; no passion to illume
The deep-recessed vision:[17] – all was blight;
Lamia, no longer fair, there sat a deadly white.
'Shut, shut those juggling[18] eyes, thou ruthless man!
Turn them aside, wretch! or the righteous ban
Of all the Gods, whose dreadful images
Here represent their shadowy presences,   280
May pierce them on the sudden with the thorn
Of painful blindness; leaving thee forlorn,
In trembling dotage to the feeblest fright
Of conscience, for their long offended might,
For all thine impious proud-heart sophistries,
Unlawful magic, and enticing lies.
Corinthians! look upon that grey-beard wretch!
Mark how, possess'd, his lashless eyelids stretch
Around his demon eyes! Corinthians, see!
My sweet bride withers at their potency.'   290
'Fool!' said the sophist, in an undertone
Gruff with contempt; which a death-nighing moan
From Lycius answer'd, as heart-struck and lost,
He sank supine beside the aching ghost.
'Fool! Fool!' repeated he, while his eyes still
Relented not, nor mov'd; 'from every ill
Of life have I preserv'd thee to this day,
And shall I see thee made a serpent's prey?'
Then Lamia breath'd death breath; the sophist's eye,
Like a sharp spear, went through her utterly,   300
Keen, cruel, perceant,[19] stinging: she, as well
As her weak hand could any meaning tell,
Motion'd him to be silent; vainly so,
He look'd and look'd again a level – No!
'A serpent!' echoed he; no sooner said,
Than with a frightful scream she vanished:
And Lycius' arms were empty of delight,
As were his limbs of life, from that same night.
On the high couch he lay! – his friends came round –
Supported him – no pulse, or breath they found,   310
And, in its marriage robe, the heavy body wound.

Isabella
or The Pot of Basil

A Story from Boccaccio

I.

Fair Isabel, poor simple Isabel!
   Lorenzo, a young palmer[1] in Love's eye!
They could not in the selfsame mansion dwell
   Without some stir of heart, some malady;
They could not sit at meals but feel how well
   It soothed each to be the other by;
They could not, sure, beneath the same roof sleep
But to each other dream, and nightly weep.

II

With every morn their love grew tenderer,
   With every eve deeper and tenderer still;
He might not in house, field, or garden stir.
   But her full shape would all his seeing fill;
And his continual voice was pleasanter
   To her, than noise of trees or hidden rill;
Her lute-string gave an echo of his name,
She spoilt her half-done broidery with the same.

III

He knew whose gentle hand was at the latch
   Before the door had given her to his eyes;
And from her chamber window he would catch
   Her beauty farther than the falcon spies;
And constant as her vespers would he watch,
   Because her face was turn'd to the same skies;
And with sick longing all the night outwear,
To hear her morning step upon the stair.

IV

A whole long month of May in this sad plight
    Made their cheeks paler by the break of June:
'Tomorrow will I bow to my delight,
    Tomorrow will I ask my lady's boon.' –
'O may I never see another night,
    Lorenzo, if thy lips breathe not love's tune.' –
So spake they to their pillows; but, alas,
Honeyless days and days did he let pass;

V

Until sweet Isabella's untouch'd cheek
    Fell sick within the rose's just domain,
Fell thin as a young mother's, who doth seek
    By every lull to cool her infant's pain:
'How ill she is,' said he, 'I may not speak,
    And yet I will, and tell my love all plain:
If looks speak love-laws, I will drink her tears,
And at the least 'twill startle off her cares.'

VI

So said he one fair morning, and all day
    His heart beat awfully against his side;
And to his heart he inwardly did pray
    For power to speak; but still the ruddy tide
Stifled his voice, and puls'd resolve away –
    Fever'd his high conceit of such a bride,
Yet brought him to the meekness of a child:
Alas! when passion is both meek and wild!

VII

So once more he had wak'd and anguished
    A dreary night of love and misery,
If Isabel's quick eye had not been wed
    To every symbol on his forehead high;
She saw it waxing very pale and dead,
    And straight all flush'd; so, lisped tenderly,
'Lorenzo!'– here she ceas'd her timid quest,
But in her tone and look he read the rest.

VIII

'O Isabella, I can half perceive
    That I may speak my grief into thine ear;
If thou didst ever anything believe,
    Believe how I love thee, believe how near
My soul is to its doom: I would not grieve
    Thy hand by unwelcome pressing, would not fear
Thine eyes by gazing; but I cannot live
Another night, and not my passion shrive.

IX

'Love! thou art leading me from wintry cold,
    Lady! thou leadest me to summer clime,
And I must taste the blossoms that unfold
    In its ripe warmth this gracious morning time.'
So said, his erewhile timid lips grew bold,
    And poesied with hers in dewy rhyme:
Great bliss was with them, and great happiness
Grew, like a lusty flower in June's caress.

X

Parting they seem'd to tread upon the air,
    Twin roses by the zephyr blown apart
Only to meet again more close, and share
    The inward fragrance of each other's heart.
She, to her chamber gone, a ditty fair
    Sang, of delicious love and honey'd dart;
He with light steps went up a western hill,
And bade the sun farewell, and joy'd his fill.

XI

All close they met again, before the dusk
    Had taken from the stars its pleasant veil,
All close they met, all eves, before the dusk
    Had taken from the stars its pleasant veil,
Close in a bower of hyacinth and musk,
    Unknown of any, free from whispering tale.
Ah! better had it been for ever so,
Than idle ears should pleasure in their woe.

XII

Were they unhappy then? – It cannot be –
   Too many tears for lovers have been shed,
Too many sighs give we to them in fee,
   Too much of pity after they are dead,
Too many doleful stories do we see,
   Whose matter in bright gold were best be read;
Except in such a page where Theseus' spouse[2]
Over the pathless waves towards him bows.

XIII

But, for the general award of love,
   The little sweet doth kill much bitterness;
Though Dido silent is in under-grove,
   And Isabella's was a great distress,
Though young Lorenzo in warm Indian clove
   Was not embalm'd, this truth is not the less –
Even bees, the little almsmen of spring-bowers,
Know there is richest juice in poison-flowers.

XIV

With her two brothers this fair lady dwelt,
   Enriched from ancestral merchandise,
And for them many a weary hand did swelt[3]
   In torched mines and noisy factories,
And many once proud-quiver'd loins did melt
   In blood from stinging whip; – with hollow eyes
Many all day in dazzling river stood,
To take the rich-ored driftings of the flood.

XV

For them the Ceylon[4] diver held his breath,
   And went all naked to the hungry shark;
For them his ears gush'd blood; for them in death
   The seal on the cold ice with piteous bark
Lay full of darts; for them alone did seethe
   A thousand men in troubles wide and dark:
Half-ignorant, they turn'd an easy wheel,
That set sharp racks at work, to pinch and peel.

XVI

Why were they proud? Because their marble founts
   Gush'd with more pride than do a wretch's tears? –
Why were they proud? Because fair orange-mounts
   Were of more soft ascent than lazar stairs?[5] –
Why were they proud? Because red-lin'd accounts
   Were richer than the songs of Grecian years? –
Why were they proud? again we ask aloud, .
Why in the name of Glory were they proud?

XVII

Yet were these Florentines as self-retired
   In hungry pride and gainful cowardice,
As two close Hebrews in that land inspired,[6]
   Paled in and vineyarded from beggar-spies;
The hawks of ship-mast forests – the untired
   And pannier'd mules for ducats[7] and old lies –
Quick cat's-paws on the generous stray-away, –
Great wits in Spanish, Tuscan, and Malay.

XVIII

How was it these same ledger-men could spy
   Fair Isabella in her downy nest?
How could they find out in Lorenzo's eye
   A straying from his toil? Hot Egypt's pest[8]
Into their vision covetous and sly!
   How could these moneybags see east and west? –
Yet so they did – and every dealer fair
Must see behind, as doth the hunted hare.

XIX

O eloquent and famed Boccaccio!
   Of thee we now should ask forgiving boon,
And of thy spicy myrtles as they blow,
   And of thy roses amorous of the moon,
And of thy lilies, that do paler grow
   Now they can no more hear thy ghittern's[9] tune,
For venturing syllables that ill beseem
The quiet glooms of such a piteous theme.

XX

Grant thou a pardon here, and then the tale
 Shall move on soberly, as it is meet;
There is no other crime, no mad assail
 To make old prose in modern rhyme more sweet:
But it is done – succeed the verse or fail –
 To honour thee. and thy gone spirit greet;
To stead[10] thee as a verse in English tongue,
An echo of thee in the north wind sung.

XXI

These brethren having found by many signs
 What love Lorenzo for their sister had,
And how she lov'd him too, each unconfines
 His bitter thoughts to other, well nigh mad
That he, the servant of their trade designs,
 Should in their sister's love be blithe and glad,
When 'twas their plan to coax her by degrees
To some high noble and his olive trees.

XXII

And many a jealous conference had they,
 And many times they bit their lips alone,
Before they fix'd upon a surest way
 To make the youngster for his crime atone;
And at the last, these men of cruel clay
 Cut Mercy with a sharp knife to the bone;
For they resolved in some forest dim
To kill Lorenzo, and there bury him.

XXIII

So on a pleasant morning, as he leant
 Into the sunrise, o'er the balustrade
Of the garden terrace, towards him they bent
 Their footing through the dews; and to him said,
'You seem there in the quiet of content,
 Lorenzo, and we are most loth to invade
Calm speculation; but if you are wise,
Bestride your steed while cold is in the skies.

XXIV

'Today we purpose, aye, this hour we mount
  To spur three leagues towards the Apennine;[11]
Come down, we pray thee, ere the hot sun count
  His dewy rosary on the eglantine.'
Lorenzo, courteously as he was wont,
  Bow'd a fair greeting to these serpents' whine;
And went in haste, to get in readiness,
With belt, and spur, and bracing huntsman's dress.

XXV

And as he to the courtyard pass'd along,
  Each third step did he pause, and listen'd oft
If he could hear his lady's matin-song,
  Or the light whisper of her footstep soft;
And as he thus over his passion hung,
  He heard a laugh full musical aloft;
When, looking up, he saw her features bright
Smile through an indoor lattice, all delight.

XXVI

'Love, Isabel!' said he, 'I was in pain
  Lest I should miss to bid thee a good morrow:
Ah! what if I should lose thee, when so fain
  I am to stifle all the heavy sorrow
Of a poor three hours' absence? but we'll gain
  Out of the amorous dark what day doth borrow.
Goodbye! I'll soon be back.' – 'Goodbye!' said she: –
And as he went she chanted merrily.

XXVII

So the two brothers and their murder'd man
  Rode past fair Florence, to where Arno's stream[12]
Gurgles through straiten'd banks, and the still doth fan
  Itself with dancing bulrush, and the bream
Keeps head against the freshets.[13] Sick and wan
  The brothers' faces in the ford did seem,
Lorenzo's flush with love. – They pass'd the water
Into a forest quiet for the slaughter.

XXVIII

There was Lorenzo slain and buried in,
  There in that forest did his great love cease;
Ah! when a soul doth thus its freedom win,
  It aches in loneliness – is ill at peace
As the break-covert bloodhounds of such sin:
  They dipp'd their swords in the water, and did tease
Their horses homeward, with convulsed spur,
Each richer by his being a murderer.

XXIX

They told their sister how, with sudden speed,
  Lorenzo had ta'en ship for foreign lands,
Because of some great urgency and need
  In their affairs, requiring trusty hands.
Poor Girl! put on thy stifling widow's weed,
  And 'scape at once from Hope's accursed bands;
Today thou wilt not see him, nor tomorrow,
And the next day will be a day of sorrow.

XXX

She weeps alone for pleasures not to be;
  Sorely she wept until the night came on,
And then, instead of love, O misery!
  She brooded o'er the luxury alone:
His image in the dusk she seem'd to see,
  And to the silence made a gentle moan,
Spreading her perfect arms upon the air,
And on her couch low murmuring 'Where? O where?'

XXXI

But Selfishness, Love's cousin, held not long
  Its fiery vigil in her single breast;
She fretted for the golden hour, and hung
  Upon the time with feverish unrest –
Not long – for soon into her heart a throng
  Of higher occupants, a richer zest,
Came tragic; passion not to be subdued,
And sorrow for her love in travels rude.

XXXII

In the mid days of autumn, on their eves
   The breath of Winter comes from far away,
And the sick west continually bereaves
   Of some gold tinge, and plays a roundelay
Of death among the bushes and the leaves,
   To make all bare before he dares to stray
From his north cavern. So sweet Isabel
By gradual decay from beauty fell,

XXXIII

Because Lorenzo came not. Oftentimes
   She ask'd her brothers, with an eye all pale,
Striving to be itself, what dungeon climes
   Could keep him off so long? They spake a tale
Time after time, to quiet her. Their crimes
   Came on them, like a smoke from Hinnom's vale;[14]
And every night in dreams they groan'd aloud,
To see their sister in her snowy shroud.

XXXIV

And she had died in drowsy ignorance,
   But for a thing more deadly dark than all:
It came like a fierce potion, drunk by chance,
   Which saves a sick man from the feather'd pall[15]
For some few gasping moments; like a lance,
   Waking an Indian[16] from his cloudy hall
With cruel pierce, and bringing him again
Sense of the gnawing fire at heart and brain.

XXXV

It was a vision. – In the drowsy gloom,
   The dull of midnight, at her couch's foot
Lorenzo stood, and wept: the forest tomb
   Had marr'd his glossy hair which once could shoot
Lustre into the sun, and put cold doom
   Upon his lips, and taken the soft lute
From his lorn voice, and past his loamed[17] ears
Had made a miry channel for his tears.

XXXVI

Strange sound it was, when the pale shadow spake;
  For there was striving, in its piteous tongue,
To speak as when on earth it was awake,
  And Isabella on its music hung:
Languor there was in it, and tremulous shake,
  As in a palsied Druid's harp unstrung;
And through it moan'd a ghostly under-song,
Like hoarse night gusts sepulchral briars[18] among.

XXXVII

Its eyes, though wild, were still all dewy bright
  With love, and kept all phantom fear aloof
From the poor girl by magic of their light,
  The while it did unthread the horrid woof
Of the late darken'd time, – the murderous spite
  Of pride and avarice, – the dark pine roof
In the forest, – and the sodden turfed dell,
Where, without any word, from stabs he fell.

XXXVIII

Saying moreover, 'Isabel, my sweet!
  Red whortle-berries droop above my head,
And a large flint-stone weighs upon my feet;
  Around me beeches and high chestnuts shed
Their leaves and prickly nuts; a sheep-fold bleat
  Comes from beyond the river to my bed:
Go, shed one tear upon my heather-bloom,
And it shall comfort me within the tomb.

XXXIX

'I am a shadow now, alas! alas!
  Upon the skirts of human-nature dwelling
Alone: I chant alone the holy mass,
  While little sounds of life are round me knelling,
And glossy bees at noon do fieldward pass,
  And many a chapel bell the hour is telling,
Paining me through: those sounds grow strange to me,
And thou art distant in Humanity.

XL

'I know what was, I feel full well what is,
   And I should rage, if spirits could go mad;
Though I forget the taste of earthly bliss,
   That paleness warms my grave, as though I had
A Seraph chosen from the bright abyss
   To be my spouse: thy paleness makes me glad;
Thy beauty grows upon me, and I feel
A greater love through all my essence steal.'

XLL

The Spirit mourn'd 'Adieu!' – dissolv'd and left
   The atom[19] darkness in a slow turmoil;
As when of healthful midnight sleep bereft,
   Thinking on rugged hours and fruitless toil,
We put our eyes into a pillowy cleft,
   And see the spangly gloom froth up and boil:
It made sad Isabella's eyelids ache,
And in the dawn she started up awake;

XLII

'Ha! ha!' said she, 'I knew not this hard life,
   I thought the worst was simple misery;
I thought some Fate with pleasure or with strife
   Portion'd us – happy days, or else to die;
But there is crime – a brother's bloody knife!
   Sweet Spirit, thou hast school'd my infancy:
I'll visit thee for this, and kiss thine eyes,
And greet thee morn and even in the skies.'

XLIII

When the full morning came, she had devised
   How she might secret to the forest hie;[20]
How she might find the clay, so dearly prized,
   And sing to it one latest lullaby;
How her short absence might be unsurmised,
   While she the inmost of the dream would try.
Resolv'd, she took with her an aged nurse,
And went into that dismal forest-hearse.[21]

XLIV

See, as they creep along the river side,
    How she doth whisper to that aged Dame,
And, after looking round the champaign wide,
    Shows her a knife. – 'What feverous hectic flame
'Burns in thee, child? – What good can thee betide,
    That thou should'st smile again?' – The evening came,
And they had found Lorenzo's earthy bed;
The flint was there, the berries at his head.

XLV

Who hath not loiter'd in a green churchyard,
    And let his spirit, like a demon-mole,
Work through the clayey soil and gravel hard,
    To see scull, coffin'd bones, and funeral stole;
Pitying each form that hungry Death hath marr'd,
    And filling it once more with human soul?
Ah! this is holiday to what was felt
When Isabella by Lorenzo knelt.

XLVI

She gaz'd into the fresh-thrown mould, as though
    One glance did fully all its secrets tell;
Clearly she saw, as other eyes would know
    Pale limbs at bottom of a crystal well;
Upon the murderous spot she seem'd to grow,
    Like to a native lily of the dell:
Then with her knife, all sudden, she began
To dig more fervently than misers can.

XLVII

Soon she turn'd up a soiled glove, whereon
    Her silk had play'd in purple phantasies,
She kiss'd it with a lip more chill than stone,
    And put it in her bosom, where it dries
And freezes utterly unto the bone
    Those dainties[22] made to still an infant's cries:
Then 'gan she work again; nor stay'd her care,
But to throw back at times her veiling hair.

XLVIII

That old nurse stood beside her wondering,
  Until her heart felt pity to the core
At sight of such a dismal labouring,
  And so she kneeled, with her locks all hoar,
And put her lean hands to the horrid thing:
  Three hours they labour'd at this travail sore;
At last they felt the kernel of the grave,
And Isabella did not stamp and rave.

XLIX

Ah! wherefore all this wormy circumstance?
  Why linger at the yawning tomb so long?
O for the gentleness of old Romance,
  The simple plaining of a minstrel's song!
Fair reader, at the old tale[23] take a glance,
  For here, in truth, it doth not well belong
To speak: – O turn thee to the very tale,
And taste the music of that vision pale.

L

With duller steel than the Persean sword[24]
  They cut away no formless monster's head,
But one, whose gentleness did well accord
  With death, as life. The ancient harps[25] have said,
Love never dies, but lives, immortal Lord:
  If Love impersonate was ever dead,
Pale Isabella kiss'd it, and low moan'd.
'Twas love; cold, – dead indeed, but not dethroned.

LI

In anxious secrecy they took it home,
  And then the prize was all for Isabel:
She calm'd its wild hair with a golden comb,
  And all around each eye's sepulchral cell
Pointed each fringed lash; the smeared loam
  With tears, as chilly as a dripping well,
She drench'd away: – and still she comb'd, and kept
Sighing all day – and still she kiss'd, and wept.

LII

Then in a silken scarf, – sweet with the dews
   Of precious flowers pluck'd in Araby,
And divine liquids come with odorous ooze
   Through the cold serpent-pipe refreshfully, –
She wrapp'd it up; and for its tomb did choose
   A garden-pot, wherein she laid it by,
And cover'd it with mould, and o'er it set
Sweet Basil, which her tears kept ever wet.

LIII

And she forgot the stars, the moon, and sun,
   And she forgot the blue above the trees,
And she forgot the dells where waters run,
   And she forgot the chilly autumn breeze;
She had no knowledge when the day was done,
   And the new morn she saw not: but in peace
Hung over her sweet Basil evermore,
And moisten'd it with tears unto the core.

LIV

And so she ever fed it with thin tears,
   Whence thick, and green, and beautiful it grew,
So that it smelt more balmy than its peers
   Of Basil-tufts in Florence; for it drew
Nurture besides, and life, from human fears,
   From the fast mouldering head there shut from view:
So that the jewel, safely casketed,
Came forth, and in perfumed leafits[26] spread.

LV

O Melancholy, linger here awhile!
   O Music, Music, breathe despondingly!
O Echo, Echo, from some sombre isle,
   Unknown, Lethean, sigh to us – O sigh!
Spirits in grief, lift up your heads, and smile;
   Lift up your heads, sweet Spirits, heavily,
And make a pale light in your cypress glooms,
Tinting with silver wan your marble tombs.

LVI

Moan hither, all ye syllables of woe,
    From the deep throat of sad Melpomene!
Through bronzed lyre in tragic order go,
    And touch the strings into a mystery;
Sound mournfully upon the winds and low;
    For simple Isabel is soon to be
Among the dead: She withers, like a palm
Cut by an Indian for its juicy balm.

LVII

O leave the palm to wither by itself;
    Let not quick Winter chill its dying hour! –
It may not be – those Baälites of pelf,[27]
    Her brethren, noted the continual shower
From her dead eyes; and many a curious elf,
    Among her kindred, wonder'd that such dower
Of youth and beauty should be thrown aside
By one mark'd out to be a Noble's bride.

LVIII

And, furthermore, her brethren wonder'd much
    Why she sat drooping by the Basil green,
And why it flourish'd, as by magic touch;
    Greatly they wonder'd what the thing might mean:
They could not surely give belief, that such
    A very nothing would have power to wean
Her from her own fair youth, and pleasures gay,
And even remembrance of her love's delay.

LIX

Therefore they watch'd a time when they might sift
    This hidden whim; and long they watch'd in vain;
For seldom did she go to chapel-shrift,[28]
    And seldom felt she any hunger-pain;
And when she left, she hurried back, as swift
    As bird on wing to breast its eggs again;
And, patient as a hen-bird, sat her there
Beside her Basil, weeping through her hair.

LX

Yet they contriv'd to steal the Basil-pot,
    And to examine it in secret place;
The thing was vile with green and livid spot,
    And yet they knew it was Lorenzo's face:
The guerdon of their murder they had got,
    And so left Florence in a moment's space,
Never to turn again. – Away they went,
With blood upon their heads, to banishment.

LXI

O Melancholy, turn thine eyes away!
    O Music, Music, breathe despondingly!
O Echo, Echo, on some other day,
    From isles of Lethean, sigh to us – O sigh!
Spirits of grief, sing not your 'Well-a-way!'
    For Isabel, sweet Isabel, will die;
Will die a death too lone and incomplete,
Now they have ta'en away her Basil sweet.

LXII

Piteous she look'd on dead and senseless things,
    Asking for her lost Basil amorously;
And with melodious chuckle in the strings
    Of her lorn voice, she oftentimes would cry
After the Pilgrim in his wanderings,
    To ask him where her Basil was; and why
'Twas hid from her: 'For cruel 'tis,' said she,
'To steal my Basil-pot away from me.'

LXIII

And so she pined, and so she died forlorn,
    Imploring for her Basil to the last.
No heart was there in Florence but did mourn
    In pity of her love, so overcast.
And a sad ditty of this story born
    From mouth to mouth through all the country pass'd:
Still is the burthen[29] sung – 'O cruelty,
'To steal my Basil-pot away from me!'

The Eve of St Agnes

I

St Agnes' Eve – Ah, bitter chill it was!
The owl, for all his feathers, was a-cold;
The hare limp'd trembling through the frozen grass,
And silent was the flock in woolly fold:
Numb were the Beadsman's[1] fingers, while he told
His rosary, and while his frosted breath,
Like pious incense from a censer old,
Seem'd taking flight for heaven, without a death,[2]
Past the sweet Virgin's picture, while his prayer he saith.

II

His prayer he saith, this patient, holy man;
Then takes his lamp, and riseth from his knees,
And back returneth, meagre, barefoot, wan,
Along the chapel aisle by slow degrees:
The sculptur'd dead, on each side, seem to freeze,
Emprison'd in black, purgatorial rails:
Knights, ladies, praying in dumb orat'ries,
He passeth by; and his weak spirit fails
To think how they may ache in icy hoods and mails.

III

Northward he turneth through a little door,
And scarce three steps, ere Music's golden tongue
Flatter'd to tears this aged man and poor;
But no – already had his deathbell rung:
The joys of all his life were said and sung:
His was harsh penance on St Agnes' Eve:[3]
Another way he went, and soon among
Rough ashes sat he for his soul's reprieve,
And all night kept awake, for sinners' sake to grieve.

IV

That ancient Beadsman heard the prelude soft;
And so it chanc'd, for many a door was wide,

From hurry to and fro. Soon, up aloft,
The silver, snarling trumpets 'gan to chide:
The level chambers, ready with their pride,
Were glowing to receive a thousand guests:
The carved angels, ever eager-eyed,
Star'd, where upon their heads the cornice rests,
With hair blown back, and wings put cross-wise on their breasts.

V

At length burst in the argent revelry,
With plume, tiara, and all rich array,
Numerous as shadows haunting faerily
The brain, new stuff'd, in youth, with triumphs gay
Of old romance. These let us wish away,
And turn, sole-thoughted, to one Lady there,
Whose heart had brooded, all that wintry day,
On love, and wing'd St Agnes' saintly care,
As she had heard old dames full many times declare.

VI

They told her how, upon St Agnes' Eve,
Young virgins might have visions of delight
And soft adorings from their loves receive
Upon the honey'd middle of the night,
If ceremonies due they did aright;
As, supperless to bed they must retire,
And couch supine their beauties, lily white;
Nor look behind, nor sideways, but require
Of Heaven with upward eyes for all that they desire.

VII

Full of this whim was thoughtful Madeline:
The music, yearning like a God in pain,
She scarcely heard: her maiden eyes divine,
Fix'd on the floor, saw many a sweeping train
Pass by – she heeded not at all: in vain
Came many a tiptoe, amorous cavalier,
And back retir'd; not cool'd by high disdain,
But she saw not: her heart was otherwise:
She sigh'd for Agnes' dreams, the sweetest of the year.

VIII

She danc'd along with vague, regardless eyes,
Anxious her lips, her breathing quick and short:
The hallow'd hour was near at hand: she sighs
Amid the timbrels, and the throng'd resort
Of whisperers in anger, or in sport;
'Mid looks of love, defiance, hate, and scorn,
Hoodwink'd with faery fancy; all amort.[4]
Save to St Agnes and her lambs unshorn,
And all the bliss to be before tomorrow morn.

IX

So, purposing each moment to retire,
She linger'd still. Meantime, across the moors,
Had come young Porphyro, with heart on fire
For Madeline. Beside the portal doors,
Buttress'd from moonlight, stands he, and implores
All saints to give him sight of Madeline,
But for one moment in the tedious hours,
That he might gaze and worship all unseen;
Perchance speak, kneel, touch, kiss – in sooth such
things have been.

X

He ventures in: let no buzz'd whisper tell:
All eyes be muffled, or a hundred swords
Will storm his heart, Love's fev'rous citadel:
For him, those chambers held barbarian hordes,
Hyena foemen, and hot-blooded lords,
Whose very dogs would execrations howl
Against his lineage: not one breast affords
Him any mercy, in that mansion foul,
Save one old beldame,[5] weak in body and in soul.

XI

Ah, happy chance! the aged creature came,
Shuffling along with ivory-headed wand,
To where he stood, hid from the torch's flame,
Behind a broad hall-pillar, far beyond

The sound of merriment and chorus bland:
He startled her; but soon she knew his face,
And grasp'd his fingers in her palsied hand,
Saying, 'Mercy, Porphyro! hie thee from this place:
They are all here tonight, the whole bloodthirsty race!

XII

'Get hence! get hence! there's dwarfish Hildebrand;
He had a fever late, and in the fit
He cursed thee and thine, both house and land:
Then there's that old Lord Maurice, not a whit
More tame for his gray hairs – Alas me! flit!
Flit like a ghost away.' – 'Ah, Gossip[6] dear,
We're safe enough; here in this armchair sit,
And tell me how' – 'Good Saints! not here, not here;
Follow me, child, or else these stones will be thy bier.'

XIII

He follow'd through a lowly arched way,
Brushing the cobwebs with his lofty plume,
And as she mutter'd 'Well-a – well-a-day!'
He found him in a little moonlight room,
Pale, lattic'd, chill, and silent as a tomb.
'Now tell me where is Madeline,' said he,
'O tell me, Angela, by the holy loom[7]
Which none but secret sisterhood may see,
When they St Agnes' wool are weaving piously.'

XIV

'St Agnes! Ah! it is St Agnes' Eve –
Yet men will murder upon holy days:
Thou must hold water in a witch's sieve,
And be liege lord of all the Elves and Fays,
To venture so: it fills me with amaze
To see thee, Porphyro! – St Agnes' Eve!
God's help! my lady fair the conjuror plays
This very night: good angels her deceive!
But let me laugh awhile, I've mickle time to grieve'

XV

Feebly she laugheth in the languid moon,
While Porphyro upon her face doth look,
Like puzzled urchin on an aged crone
Who keepeth clos'd a wond'rous riddle book,
As spectacled she sits in chimney nook.
But soon his eyes grew brilliant, when she told
His lady's purpose; and he scarce could brook[8]
Tears, at the thought of those enchantments cold,
And Madeline asleep in lap of legends old.

XVI

Sudden a thought came like a full-blown rose,
Flushing his brow, and in his pained heart
Made purple riot: then doth he propose
A stratagem, that makes the beldame start:
'A cruel man and impious thou art!
Sweet lady, let her pray, and sleep, and dream
Alone with her good angels, far apart
From wicked men like thee. Go, go! – I deem
Thou canst not surely be the same that thou didst seem.'

XVII

'I will not harm her, by all saints I swear,'
Quoth Porphyro: 'O may I ne'er find grace
When my weak voice shall whisper its last prayer,
If one of her soft ringlets I displace,
Or look with ruffian passion in her face:
Good Angela, believe me by these tears;
Or I will, even in a moment's space,
Awake, with horrid shout, my foemen's ears,
And beard them, though they be more fang'd than
                                        wolves and bears.'

XVIII

'Ah! why wilt thou affright a feeble soul?
A poor, weak, palsy-stricken, churchyard thing,
Whose passing-bell may ere the midnight toll;
Whose prayers for thee, each morn and evening,

Were never miss'd.' – Thus plaining, doth she bring
A gentler speech from burning Porphyro;
So woful, and of such deep sorrowing,
That Angela gives promise she will do
Whatever he shall wish, betide her weal or woe.[9]

XIX

Which was, to lead him, in close secrecy,
Even to Madeline's chamber, and there hide
Him in a closet, of such privacy
That he might see her beauty unespied,
And win perhaps that night a peerless bride,
While legion'd faeries pac'd the coverlet,
And pale enchantment held her sleepy-eyed.
Never on such a night have lovers met,
Since Merlin paid his Demon[10] all the monstrous debt.

XX

'It shall be as thou wishest,' said the Dame:
'All cates and dainties shall be stored there
Quickly on this feast-night: by the tambour frame
Her own lute thou wilt see: no time to spare,
For I am slow and feeble, and scarce dare
On such a catering trust my dizzy head.
Wait here, my child, with patience; kneel in prayer
The while: Ah! thou must needs the lady wed,
Or may I never leave my grave among the dead.'

XXI

So saying, she hobbled off with busy fear.
The lover's endless minutes slowly pass'd;
The dame return'd, and whisper'd in his ear
To follow her; with aged eyes aghast
From fright of dim[11] espial. Safe at last,
Through many a dusky gallery, they gain
The maiden's chamber, silken, hush'd, and chaste;
Where Porphyro took covert, pleas'd amain.
His poor guide hurried back with agues in her brain.

XXII

Her falt'ring hand upon the balustrade,
Old Angela was feeling for the stair,
When Madeline, St Agnes' charmed maid,
Rose, like a mission'd spirit, unaware:
With silver taper's light, and pious care,
She turn'd, and down the aged gossip led
To a safe level matting. Now prepare,
Young Porphyro, for gazing on that bed;
She comes, she comes again, like ring-dove fray'd[12] and fled.

XXIII

Out went the taper as she hurried in;
Its little smoke, in pallid moonshine, died:
She clos'd the door, she panted, all akin
To spirits of the air, and visions wide:
No uttered syllable, or, woe betide![13]
But to her heart, her heart was voluble,
Paining with eloquence her balmy side;
As though a tongueless nightingale should swell
Her throat in vain, and die, heart-stifled, in her dell.

XXIV

A casement high and triple-arch'd there was,
All garlanded with carven imag'ries
Of fruits, and flowers, and bunches of knot-grass,
And diamonded with panes of quaint device,
Innumerable of stains and splendid dyes,
As are the tiger moth's deep-damask'd wings;
And in the midst, 'mong thousand heraldries,
And twilight saints, and dim emblazonings,[14]
A shielded scutcheon blush'd with blood of queens and kings.

XXV

Full on this casement shone the wintry moon,
And threw warm gules[15] on Madeline's fair breast,
As down she knelt for heaven's grace and boon;
Rose-bloom fell on her hands, together prest,

And on her silver cross soft amethyst,
And on her hair a glory,[16] like a saint:
She seem'd a splendid angel, newly drest,
Save wings, for heaven: – Porphyro grew faint:
She knelt, so pure a thing, so free from mortal taint.

XXVI

Anon his heart revives: her vespers done,
Of all its wreathed pearls her hair she frees;
Unclasps her warmed jewels one by one;
Loosens her fragrant bodice; by degrees
Her rich attire creeps rustling to her knees:
Half-hidden, like a mermaid in seaweed,
Pensive awhile she dreams awake, and sees,
In fancy, fair St Agnes in her bed,
But dares not look behind, or all the charm is fled.

XXVII

Soon, trembling in her soft and chilly nest,
In sort of wakeful swoon, perplex'd she lay,
Until the poppied warmth of sleep oppress'd
Her soothed limbs, and soul fatigued away;
Flown, like a thought, until the morrow-day;
Blissfully haven'd both from joy and pain;
Clasp'd like a missal where swart Paynims[17] pray;
Blinded alike from sunshine and from rain,
As though a rose should shut, and be a bud again.

XXVIII

Stol'n to this paradise, and so entranced,
Porphyro gazed upon her empty dress,
And listen'd to her breathing, if it chanced
To wake into a slumberous tenderness;
Which when he heard, that minute did he bless,
And breath'd himself: then from the closet crept,
Noiseless as fear in a wide wilderness,
And over the hush'd carpet, silent, stept,
And 'tween the curtains peep'd, where, lo! – how fast she slept.

XXIX

Then by the bedside, where the faded moon
Made a dim, silver twilight, soft he set
A table, and, half anguish'd, threw thereon
A cloth of woven crimson, gold, and jet:-
O for some drowsy Morphean amulet!
The boisterous, midnight, festive clarion,
The kettledrum, and far-heard clarinet,
Affray his ears, though but in dying tone: –
The hall door shuts again, and all the noise is gone.

XXX

And still she slept an azure-lidded sleep,
In blanched linen, smooth, and lavender'd,
While he from forth the closet brought a heap
Of candied apple, quince, and plum, and gourd;
With jellies soother than the creamy curd,
And lucent syrops, tinct[18] with cinnamon;
Manna and dates, in argosy[19] transferr'd
From Fez; and spiced dainties, every one,
From silken Samarcand to cedar'd Lebanon.[20]

XXXI

These delicates he heap'd with glowing hand
On golden dishes and in baskets bright
Of wreathed silver: sumptuous they stand
In the retired quiet of the night,
Filling the chilly room with perfume light. –
'And now, my love, my seraph fair, awake!
Thou art my heaven, and I thine eremite:
Open thine eyes, for meek St Agnes' sake,
Or I shall drowse beside thee, so my soul doth ache.'

XXXII

Thus whispering, his warm, unnerved[21] arm
Sank in her pillow. Shaded was her dream
By the dusk curtains: – 'twas a midnight charm
Impossible to melt as iced stream:

The lustrous salvers in the moonlight gleam;
Broad golden fringe upon the carpet lies:
It seem'd he never, never could redeem
From such a steadfast spell his lady's eyes;
So mus'd awhile, entoil'd in woofed[22] phantasies.

XXXIII

Awakening up, he took her hollow lute, –
Tumultuous, – and, in chords that tenderest be,
He play'd an ancient ditty, long since mute,
In Provence call'd, 'La belle dame sans mercy:'[23]
Close to her ear touching the melody; –
Wherewith disturb'd, she utter'd a soft moan:
He ceased – she panted quick – and suddenly
Her blue affrayed eyes wide open shone:
Upon his knees he sank, pale as smooth-sculptured stone.

XXXIV

Her eyes were open, but she still beheld,
Now wide awake, the vision of her sleep:
There was a painful change, that nigh expell'd
The blisses of her dream so pure and deep
At which fair Madeline began to weep,
And moan forth witless words with many a sigh;
While still her gaze on Porphyro would keep;
Who knelt, with joined hands and piteous eye,
Fearing to move or speak, she look'd so dreamingly.

XXXV

'Ah, Porphyro!' said she, 'but even now
Thy voice was at sweet tremble in mine ear,
Made tuneable with every sweetest vow;
And those sad eyes were spiritual and clear:
How chang'd thou art! how pallid, chill, and drear!
Give me that voice again, my Porphyro,
Those looks immortal, those complainings dear!
Oh leave me not in this eternal woe,
For if thou diest, my Love, I know not where to go.'

XXXVI

Beyond a mortal man impassion'd far
At these voluptuous accents, he arose,
Ethereal, flush'd, and like a throbbing star
Seen mid the sapphire heaven's deep repose;
Into her dream he melted, as the rose
Blendeth its odour with the violet, –
Solution[24] sweet: meantime the frost-wind blows
Like Love's alarum pattering the sharp sleet
Against the window-panes; St Agnes' moon hath set.

XXXVII

'Tis dark: quick pattereth the flaw-blown[25] sleet:
'This is no dream, my bride, my Madeline!'
'Tis dark: the iced gusts still rave and beat:
'No dream, alas! alas! and woe is mine!
Porphyro will leave me here to fade and pine. –
 Cruel! what traitor could thee hither bring?
I curse not, for my heart is lost in thine,
Though thou forsakest a deceived thing; –
A dove forlorn and lost with sick unpruned[26] wing.'

XXXVIII

'My Madeline! sweet dreamer! lovely bride!
Say, may I be for aye thy vassal blest?
Thy beauty's shield, heart-shap'd and vermeil dyed?
Ah, silver shrine, here will I take my rest
After so many hours of toil and quest,
A famish'd pilgrim, – sav'd by miracle.
Though I have found, I will not rob thy nest
Saving of thy sweet self; if thou think'st well
To trust, fair Madeline, to no rude infidel.

XXXIX

'Hark! 'tis an elfin-storm from faery land,
Of haggard[27] seeming, but a boon indeed:
Arise – arise! the morning is at hand; –
The bloated wassailers[28] will never heed: –

Let us away, my love, with happy speed;
There are no ears to hear, or eyes to see, –
Drown'd all in Rhenish[29] and the sleepy mead:
Awake! arise! my love, and fearless be,
For o'er the southern moors I have a home for thee.'

XL

She hurried at his words, beset with fears,
For there were sleeping dragons all around,
At glaring watch, perhaps, with ready spears –
Down the wide stairs a darkling way they found. –
In all the house was heard no human sound.
A chain-droop'd lamp was flickering by each door;
The arras, rich with horseman, hawk, and hound,
Flutter'd in the besieging wind's uproar;
And the long carpets rose along the gusty floor.

XLI

They glide, like phantoms, into the wide hall;
Like phantoms, to the iron porch, they glide;
Where lay the Porter, in uneasy sprawl,
With a huge empty flagon by his side:
The wakeful bloodhound rose, and shook his hide,
But his sagacious[30] eye an inmate owns:
By one, and one, the bolts full easy slide: –
The chains lie silent on the footworn stones; –
The key turns, and the door upon its hinges groans.

XLII

And they are gone: aye, ages long ago
These lovers fled away into the storm.
That night the Baron dreamt of many a woe,
And all his warrior-guests, with shade and form
Of witch, and demon, and large coffin-worm,
Were long benightmar'd. Angela the old
Died palsy-twitch'd, with meagre face deform;
The Beadsman, after thousand aves[31] told,
For aye[32] unsought for slept among his ashes cold.

Ode to a Nightingale

I

My heart aches, and a drowsy numbness pains
  My sense, as though of hemlock I had drunk,
Or emptied some dull opiate to the drains[1]
  One minute past, and Lethe-wards had sunk:
'Tis not through envy of thy happy lot,
  But being too happy in thine happiness, –
    That thou, light-winged Dryad of the trees,
      In some melodious plot
  Of beechen green, and shadows numberless,
    Singest of summer in full-throated ease.

II

O, for a draught of vintage! that hath been
  Cool'd a long age in the deep-delved earth,
Tasting of Flora and the country green,
  Dance, and Provençal song, and sunburnt mirth!
O for a beaker full of the warm South,[2]
  Full of the true, the blushful Hippocrene,
    With beaded bubbles winking at the brim,
      And purple-stained mouth;
  That I might drink, and leave the world unseen,
    And with thee fade away into the forest dim:

III

Fade far away, dissolve, and quite forget
  What thou among the leaves hast never known,
The weariness, the fever, and the fret
  Here, where men sit and hear each other groan;
Where palsy shakes a few, sad, last gray hairs,
  Where youth grows pale, and spectre-thin, and dies;
    Where but to think is to be full of sorrow
      And leaden-eyed despairs,
  Where Beauty cannot keep her lustrous eyes,
    Or new Love pine at them beyond tomorrow.

IV

Away! away! for I will fly to thee,
  Not charioted by Bacchus and his pards,
But on the viewless[3] wings of Poesy,
  Though the dull brain perplexes and retards:
Already with thee! tender is the night,
    And haply the Queen-Moon is on her throne,
      Cluster'd around by all her starry Fays;
        But here there is no light,
    Save what from heaven is with the breezes blown
      Through verdurous glooms and winding mossy ways.

V

I cannot see what flowers are at my feet,
  Nor what soft incense hangs upon the boughs,
But, in embalmed darkness,[4] guess each sweet
  Wherewith the seasonable month endows
The grass, the thicket, and the fruit tree wild;
    White hawthorn, and the pastoral eglantine;
      Fast fading violets cover'd up in leaves;
        And mid-May's eldest child,
    The coming musk-rose, full of dewy wine,
      The murmurous haunt of flies on summer eves.

VI

Darkling I listen; and, for many a time
  I have been half in love with easeful Death,
Call'd him soft names in many a mused rhyme,
  To take into the air my quiet breath;
Now more than ever seems it rich to die,
    To cease upon the midnight with no pain,
      While thou art pouring forth thy soul abroad
        In such an ecstasy!
    Still wouldst thou sing, and I have ears in vain –
      To thy high requiem become a sod.

VII

Thou wast not born for death, immortal Bird!
  No hungry generations tread thee down;
The voice I hear this passing night was heard
  In ancient days by emperor and clown:
Perhaps the selfsame song that found a path
    Through the sad heart of Ruth,[5] when, sick for home,
      She stood in tears amid the alien corn;
        The same that oft-times hath
    Charm'd magic casements, opening on the foam
      Of perilous seas, in faery lands forlorn.

VIII

Forlorn! the very word is like a bell
  To toll me back from thee to my sole self!
Adieu! the fancy cannot cheat so well
  As she is fam'd to do, deceiving elf.
Adieu! adieu! thy plaintive anthem fades
  Past the near meadows, over the still stream,
    Up the hillside; and now 'tis buried deep
      In the next valley glades:
  Was it a vision, or a waking dream?
    Fled is that music: – Do I wake or sleep?

Ode on a Grecian Urn

I

Thou still unravish'd bride of quietness,
    Thou foster-child of silence and slow time,
Sylvan[1] historian, who canst thus express
    A flowery tale more sweetly than our rhyme:
What leaf-fring'd legend haunts about thy shape
    Of deities or mortals, or of both,
        In Tempe or the dales of Arcady?
    What men or gods are these? What maidens loth?
What mad pursuit? What struggle to escape?
        What pipes and timbrels? What wild ecstasy?

II

Heard melodies are sweet, but those unheard
    Are sweeter; therefore, ye soft pipes, play on;
Not to the sensual[2] ear, but, more endear'd,
    Pipe to the spirit ditties of no tone:
Fair youth, beneath the trees, thou canst not leave
    Thy song, nor ever can those trees be bare;
        Bold Lover, never, never canst thou kiss,
Though winning near the goal – yet, do not grieve;
    She cannot fade, though thou hast not thy bliss,
        For ever wilt thou love, and she be fair!

III

Ah, happy, happy boughs! that cannot shed
    Your leaves, nor ever bid the Spring adieu;
And, happy melodist, unwearied,
    For ever piping songs for ever new;
More happy love! more happy, happy love!
    For ever warm and still to be enjoy'd,
        For ever panting, and for ever young;
All breathing human passion for above,
    That leaves a heart high-sorrowful and cloy'd,
        A burning forehead, and a parching tongue.

IV

Who are these coming to the sacrifice?
    To what green altar, O mysterious priest,
Lead'st thou that heifer lowing at the skies,
    And all her silken flanks with garlands drest?
What little town by river or sea shore,
    Or mountain-built with peaceful citadel,
        Is emptied of this folk, this pious morn?
And, little town, thy streets for evermore
    Will silent be; and not a soul to tell
        Why thou art desolate, can e'er return.

V

O Attic shape! Fair attitude! with brede
    Of marble men and maidens overwrought,
With forest branches and the trodden weed;
    Thou, silent form, dost tease us out of thought
As doth eternity: Cold Pastoral!³
    When old age shall this generation waste,
        Thou·shalt remain, in midst of other woe
Than ours, a friend to man, to whom thou say'st,
    'Beauty is truth, truth beauty,'⁴ – that is all
        Ye know on earth, and all ye need to know.

Ode to Psyche

O Goddess! hear these tuneless numbers, wrung
   By sweet enforcement and remembrance dear,
And pardon that thy secrets should be sung
   Even into thine own soft-conched[1] ear:
Surely I dreamt today, or did I see
   The winged Psyche with awaken'd eyes?
I wander'd in a forest thoughtlessly,
   And, on the sudden, fainting with surprise,
Saw two fair creatures, couched side by side
   In deepest grass, beneath the whisp'ring roof   10
   Of leaves and trembled blossoms, where there ran
      A brooklet, scarce espied:[2]

'Mid hush'd, cool-rooted flowers, fragrant-eyed,
   Blue, silver-white, and budded Tyrian,[3]
They lay calm-breathing on the bedded grass;
   Their arms embraced, and their pinions too;
   Their lips touch'd not, but had not bade adieu,
As if disjoined by soft-handed slumber,
And ready still past kisses to outnumber
   At tender eye-dawn of aurorean love:[4]   20
      The winged boy[5] I knew;
   But who wast thou, O happy, happy dove?
      His Psyche true!

O latest born and loveliest vision far
   Of all Olympus' faded hierarchy![6]
Fairer than Phoebe's sapphire-region'd star,
   Or Vesper, amorous glow-worm of the sky;
Fairer than these, though temple thou hast none,
      Nor altar heap'd with flowers;
Nor virgin-choir to make delicious moan   30
      Upon the midnight hours;
No voice, no lute, no pipe, no incense sweet
   From chain-swung censer teeming;
No shrine, no grove, no oracle, no heat
   Of pale-mouth'd prophet dreaming.

O brightest! though too late for antique vows,
    Too, too late for the fond[7] believing lyre,
When holy were the haunted forest boughs
    Holy the air, the water, and the fire:
Yet even in these days so far retir'd   40
    From happy pieties, thy lucent[8] fans,
    Fluttering among the faint Olympians,
I see, and sing, by my own eyes inspir'd.
So let me be thy choir, and make a moan
        Upon the midnight hours;
Thy voice, thy lute, thy pipe, thy incense sweet
    From swinged censer teeming;
Thy shrine, thy grove, thy oracle, thy heat
    Of pale-mouth'd prophet dreaming.

Yes, I will be thy priest, and build a fane   50
    In some untrodden region of my mind,
Where branched thoughts, new grown with pleasant pain,
    Instead of pines shall murmur in the wind:
Far, far around shall those dark-cluster'd trees
    Fledge the wild-ridged mountains steep by steep;
And there by zephyrs, streams, and birds, and bees,
    The moss-lain Dryads shall be lull'd to sleep;
And in the midst of this wide quietness
A rosy sanctuary will I dress
With the wreath'd trellis of a working brain,   60
    With buds, and bells, and stars without a name,
With all the gardener Fancy e'er could feign,[9]
    Who breeding flowers, will never breed the same:
And there shall be for thee all soft delight
    That shadowy thought can win,
A bright torch, and a casement ope at night,
    To let the warm Love[10] in!

To Fancy

Ever let the Fancy roam,
Pleasure never is at home:
At a touch sweet Pleasure melteth,
Like to bubbles when rain pelteth;
Then let winged Fancy wander
Through the thought still spread beyond her:
Open wide the mind's cage-door,
She'll dart forth, and cloudward soar.
O sweet Fancy! let her loose;
Summer's joys are spoilt by use,   10
And the enjoying of the Spring
Fades as does its blossoming;
Autumn's red-lipp'd fruitage too,
Blushing through the mist and dew,
Cloys with tasting: What do then?
Sit thee by the ingle,[1] when
The sear faggot blazes bright,
Spirit of a winter's night;
When the soundless earth is muffled,
And the caked snow is shuffled   20
From the ploughboy's heavy shoon;[2]
When the Night doth meet the Noon
In a dark conspiracy
To banish Even from her sky.
Sit thee there, and send abroad,
With a mind self-overaw'd,
Fancy, high-commission'd: – send her!
She has vassals to attend her:
She will bring, in spite of frost,
Beauties that the earth hath lost;   30
She will bring thee, all together,
All delights of summer weather;
All the buds and bells of May,
From dewy sward or thorny spray;
All the heaped Autumn's wealth,
With a still, mysterious stealth:
She will mix these pleasures up

Like three fit wines in a cup,
And thou shalt quaff it: – thou shalt hear
Distant harvest-carols clear;   40
Rustle of the reaped corn;
Sweet birds antheming the morn:
And, in the same moment – hark!
'Tis the early April lark,
Or the rooks, with busy caw,
Foraging for sticks and straw.
Thou shalt, at one glance, behold
The daisy and the marigold;
White-plum'd lilies, and the first
Hedge-grown primrose that hath burst;   50
Shaded hyacinth, alway
Sapphire queen of the mid-May;
And every leaf, and every flower
Pearled with the selfsame shower.
Thou shalt see the field mouse peep
Meagre from its celled sleep;
And the snake all winter-thin
Cast on sunny bank its skin;
Freckled nest-eggs thou shalt see
Hatching in the hawthorn tree,   60
When the hen-bird's wing doth rest
Quiet on her mossy nest;
Then the hurry and alarm
When the beehive casts its swarm;
Acorns ripe down-pattering,
While the autumn breezes sing.

   Oh, sweet Fancy! let her loose;
Every thing is spoilt by use:
Where's the cheek that doth not fade,
Too much gaz'd at? Where's the maid   70
Whose lip mature is ever new?
Where's the eye, however blue,
Doth not weary? Where's the face
One would meet in every place?
Where's the voice, however soft,
One would hear so very oft?

At a touch sweet Pleasure melteth
Like to bubbles when rain pelteth.
Let, then, winged Fancy find
Thee a mistress to thy mind: 80
Dulcet-eyed as Ceres' daughter,[3]
Ere the God of Torment[4] taught her
How to frown and how to chide;
With a waist and with a side
White as Hebe's, when her zone
Slipt its golden clasp, and down
Fell her kirtle[5] to her feet,
While she held the goblet sweet,
And Jove grew languid. – Break the mesh
Of the Fancy's silken leash;   90
Quickly break her prison-string
And such joys as these she'll bring. –
Let the winged Fancy roam,
Pleasure never is at home.

Ode

[*Written on the blank page before Beaumont and
Fletcher's tragi-comedy 'The Fair Maid of the Inn'*]

Bards of Passion and of Mirth,
Ye have left your souls on earth!
Have ye souls in heaven too,
Double lived in regions new?
Yes, and those of heaven commune
With the spheres of sun and moon;
With the noise of fountains wond'rous,
And the parle[1] of voices thund'rous;
With the whisper of heaven's trees
And one another, in soft ease   10
Seated on Elysian lawns
Brows'd by none but Dian's fawns;
Underneath large blue bells tented,
Where the daisies are rose-scented,

And the rose herself has got
Perfume which on earth is not;
Where the nightingale doth sing
Not a senseless, tranced thing,
But divine melodious truth;
Philosophic numbers smooth;   20
Tales and golden histories
Of heaven and its mysteries.

   Thus ye live on high, and then
On the earth ye live again;
And the souls ye left behind you
Teach us, here, the way to find you,
Where your other souls are joying,
Never slumber'd, never cloying.
Here, your earth-born souls still speak
To mortals, of their little week;[2]   30
Of their sorrows and delights;
Of their passions and their spites;
Of their glory and their shame;
What doth strengthen and what maim.
Thus ye teach us, every day,
Wisdom, though fled far away.

   Bards of Passion and of Mirth,
Ye have left your souls on earth!
Ye have souls in heaven too,
Double-lived in regions new!   40

Lines on the Mermaid Tavern[1]

Souls of Poets dead and gone,
What Elysium have ye known,
Happy field or mossy cavern,
Choicer than the Mermaid Tavern?
Have ye tippled drink more fine
Than mine host's Canary wine?[2]
Or are fruits of Paradise
Sweeter than those dainty pies
Of venison? O generous food!
Drest as though bold Robin Hood   10
Would, with his maid Marian,
Sup and bowse[3] from horn and can.

I have heard that on a day
Mine host's sign-board flew away,
Nobody knew whither, till
An astrologer's old quill
To a sheepskin gave the story,
Said he saw you in your glory,
Underneath a new old sign
Sipping beverage divine,   20
And pledging with contented smack
The Mermaid in the Zodiac.[4]

Souls of Poets dead and gone,
What Elysium have ye known,
Happy field or mossy cavern,
Choicer than the Mermaid Tavern?

Robin Hood

To a friend

No! those days are gone away,
And their hours are old and gray,
And their minutes buried all
Under the downtrodden pall
Of the leaves of many years:
Many times have winter's shears,
Frozen North, and chilling Enst,
Sounded tempests to the feast
Of the forest's whispering fleeces,[1]
Since men knew nor rent nor leases   10

   No, the bugle sounds no more,
And the twanging bow no more;
Silent is the ivory[2] shrill
Past the heath and up the hill;
There is no mid-forest laugh,
Where lone Echo gives the half
To some wight, amaz'd to hear
Jesting, deep in forest drear.

   On the fairest time of June
You may go, with sun or moon,   20
Or the seven stars to light you,
Or the polar ray[3] to right you;
But you never may behold
Little John, or Robin bold;
Never one, of all the clan,
Thrumming[4] on an empty can
Some old hunting ditty, while
He doth his green way beguile[5]
To fair hostess Merriment,
Down beside the pasture Trent;[6]   30
For he left the merry tale
Messenger for spicy ale.

Gone, the merry morris din;[7]
Gone, the song of Gamelyn;[8]
Gone, the tough-belted outlaw
Idling in the 'grene shawe';[9]
All are gone away and past!
And if Robin should be cast
Sudden from his turfed grave,
And if Marian should have   40
Once again her forest days,
She would weep, and he would craze:[10]
He would swear, for all his oaks,
Fall'n beneath the dockyard strokes,
Have rotted on the briny seas;
She would weep that her wild bees
Sang not to her – strange! that honey
Can't be got without hard money!

So it is: yet let us sing,
Honour to the old bow-string!   50
Honour to the bugle-horn!
Honour to the woods unshorn!
Honour to the Lincoln green!
Honour to the archer keen!
Honour to tight[11] little John,
And the horse he rode upon!
Honour to bold Robin Hood,
Sleeping in the underwood!
Honour to maid Marian,
And to all the Sherwood-clan!   60
Though their days have hurried by
Let us two a burden try.

To Autumn

I

Season of mists and mellow fruitfulness,
   Close bosom-friend of the maturing sun;
Conspiring with him how to load and bless
   With fruit the vines that round the thatch-eves run;
To bend with apples the moss'd cottage-trees,
   And fill all fruit with ripeness to the core;
     To swell the gourd, and plump the hazel shells
   With a sweet kernel; to set budding more,
And still more, later flowers for the bees,
Until they think warm days will never cease,
     For Summer has o'er-brimm'd their clammy cells.

II

Who hath not seen thee oft amid thy store?
   Sometimes whoever seeks abroad may find
Thee sitting careless on a granary floor
   Thy hair soft-lifted by the winnowing wind;
Or on a half-reap'd furrow sound asleep,
   Drows'd with the fume of poppies, while thy hook
     Spares the next swath and all its twined flowers:
And sometimes like a gleaner thou dost keep
   Steady thy laden head across a brook;
   Or by a cider-press, with patient look,
     Thou watchest the last oozings hours by hours.

III

Where are the songs of Spring? Ay, where are they?
   Think not of them, thou hast thy music too, –
While barred clouds bloom[1] the soft-dying day,
   And touch the stubble-plains with rosy hue;
Then in a wailful choir the small gnats mourn
   Among the river sallows, borne aloft

Or sinking as the light wind lives or dies;
And full-grown lambs loud bleat from hilly bourn;[2]
  Hedge-crickets sing; and now with treble soft
  The red-breast whistles from a garden-croft;
    And gathering swallows twitter in the skies.

Ode on Melancholy

I

No, no, go not to Lethe, neither twist
  Wolf's-bane,[1] tight-rooted, for its poisonous wine;
Nor suffer thy pale forehead to be kiss'd
  By nightshade, ruby grape of Proserpine;
Make not your rosary of yew-berries,
  Nor let the beetle, nor the death-moth be
    Your mournful Psyche, nor the downy owl
A partner in your sorrow's mysteries;
  For shade to shade will come too drowsily,
    And drown the wakeful anguish of the soul.

II

But when the melancholy fit shall fall
  Sudden from heaven like a weeping cloud,
That fosters the droop-headed flowers all,
  And hides the green hill in an April shroud;
Then glut thy sorrow on a morning rose,
  Or on the rainbow of the salt sand-wave,
    Or on the wealth of globed peonies;
Or if thy mistress some rich anger shows,
  Emprison her soft hand, and let her rave,
    And feed deep, deep upon her peerless eyes.

III

She dwells with Beauty – Beauty that must die;
  And Joy, whose hand is ever at his lips
Bidding adieu; and aching Pleasure nigh,
  Turning to poison while the bee-mouth sips:

Ay, in the very temple of delight
 Veil'd Melancholy has her sovran shrine,
  Though seen of none save him whose strenuous tongue
 Can burst Joy's grape against his palate fine;
His soul shall taste the sadness of her might,
  And be among her cloudy trophies hung.

Hyperion

A Fragment

BOOK I

Deep in the shady sadness of a vale
Far sunken from the healthy breath of morn,
Far from the fiery noon, and eve's one star,
Sat grey-hair'd Saturn, quiet as a stone.
Still as the silence round about his lair;
Forest on forest hung about his head
Like cloud on cloud. No stir of air was there,
Not so much life as on a summer's day
Robs not one light seed from the feather'd grass,
But where the dead leaf fell, there did it rest.   10
A stream went voiceless by, still deadened more
By reason of his fallen divinity
Spreading a shade: the Naiad 'mid her reeds
Press'd her cold finger closer to her lips.

Along the margin-sand large footmarks went,
No further than to where his feet had stray'd,
And slept there since. Upon the sodden ground
His old right hand lay nerveless, listless, dead,
Unsceptred; and his realmless eyes were closed;
While his bow'd head seem'd list'ning to the Earth,   20
His ancient mother, for some comfort yet.

It seem'd no force could wake him from his place;
But there came one, who with a kindred hand
Touch'd his wide shoulders, after bending low
With reverence, though to one who knew it not.
She was a Goddess of the infant world;
By her in stature the tall Amazon
Had stood a pigmy's height: she would have ta'en
Achilles by the hair and bent his neck;
Or with a finger stay'd Ixion's wheel.   30
Her face was large as that of Memphian sphinx.[1]
Pedestal'd haply in a palace court,

When sages look'd to Egypt for their lore.
But oh! how unlike marble was that face:
How beautiful, if sorrow had not made
Sorrow more beautiful than Beauty's self.
There was a listening fear in her regard,
As if calamity had but begun;
As if the vanward clouds of evil days
Had spent their malice, and the sullen rear   40
Was with its stored thunder labouring up.
One hand she press'd upon that aching spot
Where beats the human heart, as if just there,
Though an immortal, she felt cruel pain:
The other upon Saturn's bended neck
She laid, and to the level of his ear
Leaning with parted lips, some words she spake
In solemn tenor and deep organ tone:
Some mourning words, which in our feeble tongue
Would come in these like accents; O how frail   50
To that large utterance of the early Gods!
'Saturn, look up! – though wherefore, poor old King?
I have no comfort for thee, no not one:
I cannot say, "O wherefore sleepest thou?"
For heaven is parted from thee, and the earth
Knows thee not, thus afflicted, for a God;
And ocean too, with all its solemn noise
Has from thy sceptre pass'd; and all the air
Is emptied of thine hoary majesty.
Thy thunder, conscious of the new command,   60
Rumbles reluctant² o'er our fallen house;
And thy sharp lightning in unpractis'd hands
Scorches and burns our once serene domain.
O aching time! O moments big as years!
All as ye pass swell out the monstrous truth,
And press it so upon our weary griefs
That unbelief has not a space to breathe.
Saturn, sleep on: – O thoughtless, why did I
Thus violate thy slumbrous solitude?
Why should I ope thy melancholy eyes?   70
Saturn, sleep on! while at thy feet I weep.'

As when, upon a tranced summer night,
Those green-rob'd senators of mighty woods,
Tall oaks, branch-charmed by the earnest stars,
Dream, and so dream all night without a stir,
Save from one gradual solitary gust
Which comes upon the silence, and dies off,
As if the ebbing air had but one wave;
So came these words and went; the while in tears
She touch'd her fair large forehead to the ground,   80
Just where her falling hair might be outspread
A soft and silken mat for Saturn's feet
One moon, with alteration slow, had shed
Her silver seasons four upon the night,
And still these two were postured motionless,
Like natural sculpture in cathedral cavern;
The frozen God still couchant[3] on the earth,
And the sad Goddess weeping at his feet:
Until at length old Saturn lifted up
His faded eyes, and saw his kingdom gone,   90
And all the gloom and sorrow of the place,
And that fair kneeling Goddess; and then spake,
As with a palsied tongue, and while his beard
Shook horrid with such aspen-malady:[4]
'O tender spouse of gold Hyperion,
Thea, I feel thee ere I see thy face;
Look up, and let me see our doom in it;
Look up, and tell me if this feeble shape
Is Saturn's; tell me, if thou hear'st the voice
Of Saturn; tell me, if this wrinkling brow,   100
Naked and bare of its great diadem,
Peers like the front of Saturn. Who had power
To make me desolate? whence came the strength?
How was it nurtur'd to such bursting forth,
While Fate seem'd strangled in my nervous[5] grasp?
But it is so; and I am smother'd up,
And buried from all godlike exercise
Of influence benign on planets pale,
Of admonitions to the winds and seas,
Of peaceful sway above man's harvesting,   110
And all those acts which Deity supreme

Doth ease its heart of love in. – I am gone
Away from my own bosom: I have left
My strong identity, my real self,
Somewhere between the throne, and where I sit
Here on this spot of earth. Search, Thea, search!
Open thine eyes eterne, and sphere them round
Upon all space: space starr'd, and lorn of[6] light;
Space region'd with life-air, and barren void;
Spaces of fire, and all the yawn of hell. –   120
Search, Thea, search! and tell me, if thou seest
A certain shape or shadow, making way
With wings or chariot fierce to repossess
A heaven he lost erewhile: it must – it must
Be of ripe progress – Saturn must be – King.
Yes, there must be a golden victory;
There must be Gods thrown down, and trumpets blown
Of triumph calm, and hymns of festival
Upon the gold clouds metropolitan,
Voices of soft proclaim, and silver stir   130
Of strings in hollow shells; and there shall be
Beautiful things made new, for the surprise
Of the sky-children;[7] I will give command:
Thea! Thea! Thea! where is Saturn?'

    This passion lifted him upon his feet,
And made his hands to struggle in the air,
His Druid locks[8] to shake and ooze with sweat,
His eyes to fever out,[9] his voice to cease.
He stood, and heard not Thea's sobbing deep;
A little time, and then again he snatch'd   140
Utterance thus. – 'But cannot I create?
 Cannot I form? Cannot I fashion forth
Another world, another universe,
To overbear and crumble this to naught?
Where is another chaos? Where?' – That word
Found way unto Olympus, and made quake
The rebel three[10] – Thea was startled up,
And in her bearing was a sort of hope,
As thus she quick-voic'd spake, yet full of awe.
'This cheers our fallen house: come to our friends,   150

O Saturn! come away, and give them heart;
I know the covert, for thence came I hither.'
Thus brief; then with beseeching eyes she went
With backward footing through the shade a space:
He follow'd, and she turn'd to lead the way
Through aged boughs, that yielded like the mist
Which eagles cleave[11] upmounting from their nest.

    Meanwhile in other realms big tears were shed,
More sorrow like to this, and such like woe,
Too huge for mortal tongue or pen of scribe: 160
The Titans fierce, self-hid, or prison-bound,
Groan'd for the old allegiance once more,
And listen'd in sharp pain for Saturn's voice.
But one of the whole mammoth brood still kept
His sov'reignty, and rule, and majesty; –
Blazing Hyperion on his orbed fire[12]
Still sat, still snuff'd[13] the incense, teeming up
From man to the sun's God; yet unsecure:
For as among us mortals omens drear
Fright and perplex, so also shuddered he –   170
Not at dog's howl, or gloom-bird's[14] hated screech,
Or the familiar visiting of one
Upon the first toll of his passing-bell,
Or prophesyings of the midnight lamp;
But horrors, portion'd[15] to a giant nerve,
Oft made Hyperion ache. His palace bright
Bastion'd with pyramids of glowing gold,
And touch'd with shade of bronzed obelisks,
Glar'd a blood-red through all its thousand courts,
Arches, and domes, and fiery galleries;   180
And all its curtains of Aurorian clouds
Flush'd angerly:[16] while sometimes eagle's wings,
Unseen before by Gods or wondering men,
Darken'd the place; and neighing steeds were heard,
Not heard before by Gods or wondering men,
Also, when he would taste the spicy wreaths
Of incense, breat'd aloft from sacred hills,
Instead of sweets, his ample palate took
Savour of poisonous brass and metal sick:

And so, when harbour'd in the sleepy west,   190
After the full completion of fair day, –
For rest divine upon exalted couch
And slumber in the arms of melody,
He pac'd away the pleasant hours of ease
With stride colossal, on from hall to hall;
While far within each aisle and deep recess,
His winged minions in close clusters stood,
Amaz'd and full of fear; like anxious men
Who on wide plains gather in panting troops,
When earthquakes jar their battlements and towers.   200
Even now, while Saturn, rous'd from icy trance,
Went step for step with Thea through the woods,
Hyperion, leaving twilight in the rear,
Came slope[17] upon the threshold of the west;
Then, as was wont, his palace door flew ope
In smoothest silence, save what solemn tubes,[18]
Blown by the serious Zephyrs, gave of sweet
And wandering sounds, slow-breathed melodies;
And like a rose in vermeil tint and shape,
In fragrance soft, and coolness to the eye,   210
That inlet to severe magnificence
Stood full blown, for the God to enter in.

He enter'd, but he enter'd full of wrath;
His flaming robes stream'd out beyond his heels,
And gave a roar, as if of earthly fire,
That scar'd away the meek ethereal Hours
And made their dove-wings tremble. On he flared,
From stately nave to nave, from vault to vault,
Through bowers of fragrant and enwreathed light,
And diamond-paved lustrous long arcades,   220
Until he reach'd the great main cupola;[19]
There standing fierce beneath, he stamped his foot,
And from the basements deep to the high towers
Jarr'd his own golden region; and before
The quavering thunder thereupon had ceas'd,
His voice leapt out, despite of godlike curb,
To this result: 'O dreams of day and night!
'O monstrous forms! O effigies of pain!

O spectres busy in a cold, cold gloom!
O lank-ear'd Phantoms of black-weeded pools!   230
Why do I know ye? why have I seen ye? why
Is my eternal essence thus distraught
To see and to behold these horrors new?
Saturn is fallen, am I too to fall?
Am I to leave this haven of my rest,
This cradle of my glory, this soft clime,
This calm luxuriance of blissful light,
These crystalline pavilions, and pure fanes,
Of all my lucent[20] empire? It is left
Deserted, void, nor any haunt of mine.   240
The blaze, the splendor, and the symmetry,
I cannot see – but darkness, death and darkness.
Even here, into my centre of repose,
The shady visions come to domineer,
Insult, and blind, and stifle up my pomp. –
Fall! – No, by Tellus and her briny robes!
Over the fiery frontier of my realms
I will advance a terrible right arm
Shall scare that infant thunderer, rebel Jove,
And bid old Saturn take his throne again.' –   250
He spake, and ceas'd, the while a heavier threat
Held struggle with his throat but came not forth;
For as in theatres of crowded men
Hubbub increases more they call out 'Hush!'
So at Hyperion's words the Phantoms pale
Bestirr'd themselves, thrice horrible and cold;
And from the mirror'd level where he stood
A mist arose, as from a scummy marsh.
At this, through all his bulk an agony
Crept gradual, from the feet unto the crown,   260
Like a lithe serpent vast and muscular
Making slow way, with head and neck convuls'd
From over-strained might. Releas'd, he fled
To the eastern gates, and full six dewy hours
Before the dawn in season due should blush,
He breath'd fierce breath against the sleepy portals,
Clear'd them of heavy vapours, burst them wide
Suddenly on the ocean's chilly streams.

The planet orb of fire, where he rode
Each day from east to west the heavens through,   270
Spun round in sable[21] curtaining of clouds;
Not therefore veiled quite, blindfold, and hid,
But ever and anon the glancing spheres,
Circles, and arcs, and broad-belting colure,[22]
Glow'd through, and wrought upon the muffling dark
Sweet-shaped lightnings from the nadir deep
Up to the zenith,[23] – hieroglyphics old
Which sages and keen-eyed astrologers
Then living on the earth, with labouring thought
Won from the gaze of many centuries: 280
Now lost, save what we find on remnants huge
Of stone, or marble swart; their import gone,
Their wisdom long since fled. – Two wings[24] this orb
Possess'd for glory, two fair argent wings,
Ever exalted at the God's approach:
And now, from forth the gloom their plumes immense
Rose, one by one, till all outspreaded were;
While still the dazzling globe maintain'd eclipse,
Awaiting for Hyperion's command.
Fain would he have commanded, fain took throne   290
And bid the day begin, if but for change.
He might not: – No, though a primeval God:[25]
The sacred seasons might not be disturb'd.
Therefore the operations of the dawn
Stay'd in their birth, even as here 'tis told.
Those silver wings expanded sisterly,
Eager to sail their orb; the porches wide
Open'd upon the dusk demesnes of night;
And the bright Titan, frenzied with new woes,
Unus'd to bend, by hard compulsion bent   300
His spirit to the sorrow of the time;
And all along a dismal rack of clouds,
Upon the boundaries of day and night,
He stretch'd himself in grief and radiance faint.
There as he lay, the Heaven with its stars
Look'd down on him with pity, and the voice
Of Coelus, from the universal space,
Thus whisper'd low and solemn in his ear.

'O brightest of my children dear, earth-born
And sky-engendered, Son of Mysteries   310
All unrevealed even to the powers
Which met at thy creating; at whose joys
And palpitations sweet, and pleasures soft,
I, Coelus, wonder, how they came and whence;
And at the fruits thereof what shapes they be,
Distinct, and visible; symbols divine,
Manifestations of that beauteous life
Diffus'd unseen throughout eternal space:
Of these new-form'd art thou, oh brightest child!
Of these, thy brethren and the Goddesses!   320
There is sad feud among ye, and rebellion
Of son against his sire. I saw him fall,
I saw my first-born[26] tumbled from his throne!
To me his arms were spread, to me his voice
Found way from forth the thunders round his head!
Pale wox I, and in vapours hid my face.
Art thou, too, near such doom? vague fear there is:
For I have seen my sons most unlike Gods.
Divine ye were created, and divine
In sad demeanour, solemn, undisturb'd,   330
Unruffled, like high Gods, ye liv'd and ruled:
Now I behold in you fear, hope, and wrath;
Actions of rage and passion; even as
I see them, on the mortal world beneath,
In men who die. – This is the grief, O Son!
Sad sign of ruin, sudden dismay, and fall!
Yet do thou strive; as thou art capable,
As thou canst move about, an evident God;
And canst oppose to each malignant hour
Ethereal presence: – I am but a voice;   340
My life is but the life of winds and tides,
No more than winds and tides can I avail: –
But thou canst. – Be thou therefore in the van
Of circumstance; yea, seize the arrow's barb
Before the tense string murmur. – To the earth!
For there thou wilt find Saturn, and his woes.
Meantime I will keep watch on thy bright sun,
And of thy seasons be a careful nurse.' –

Ere half this region-whisper[27] had come down,
Hyperion arose, and on the stars   350
Lifted his curved lids, and kept them wide
Until it ceas'd; and still he kept them wide:
And still they were the same bright, patient stars.
Then with a slow incline of his broad breast,
Like to a diver in the pearly seas,
Forward he stoop'd over the airy shore,
And plung'd all noiseless into the deep night.

Hyperion – Book II

Just at the selfsame beat of Time's wide wings
Hyperion slid into the rustled air,
And Saturn gain'd with Thea that sad place
Where Cybele and the bruised Titans mourn'd.
It was a den where no insulting light
Could glimmer on their tears; where their own groans
They felt, but heard not, for the solid roar
Of thunderous waterfalls and torrents hoarse,
Pouring a constant bulk, uncertain where.[1]
Crag jutting forth to crag, and rocks that seem'd   10
Ever as if just rising from a sleep,
Forehead to forehead held their monstrous horns;
And thus in thousand hugest phantasies
Made a fit roofing to this nest of woe.
Instead of thrones, hard flint they sat upon,
Couches of rugged stone, and slaty ridge
Stubborn'd with iron. All were not assembled:
Some chain'd in torture, and some wandering.
Coelus, and Gyges, and Briareüs,
Typhon, and Dolor, and Porphyrion,[2]   20
With many more, the brawniest in assault,
Were pent in regions of laborious breath;
Dungeon'd in opaque element,[3] to keep
Their clenched teeth still clench'd, and all their limbs
Lock'd up like veins of metal, cramp'd and screw'd;
Without a motion, save of their big hearts
Heaving in pain, and horribly convuls'd

With sanguine feverous boiling gurge of pulse.[4]
Mnemosyne was straying in the world;
Far from her moon had Phoebe wandered: 30
And many else were free to roam abroad.
But for the main, here found they covert drear.
Scarce images of life, one here, one there,
Lay vast and edgeways; like a dismal cirque
Of Druid stones, upon a forlorn moor.
When the chill rain begins at shut of eve.
In dull November, and their chancel[5] vault,
The Heaven itself, is blinded throughout night.
Each one kept shroud, nor to his neighbour gave
Or word, or look, or action of despair.   40
Creüs was one; his ponderous iron mace
Lay by him, and a shatter'd rib of rock
Told of his rage, ere he thus sank and pined.
Iäpetus another; in his grasp,
A serpent's plashy neck; its barbed tongue
Squeez'd from the gorge, and all its uncurl'd length
Dead; and because the creature could not spit
Its poison in the eyes of conquering Jove.
Next Cottus:[6] prone he lay, chin uppermost,
As though in pain; for still upon the flint   50
He ground severe his skull, with open mouth
And eyes at horrid working. Nearest him
Asia,[7] born of most enormous Caf,
Who cost her mother Tellus keener pangs,
Though feminine, than any of her sons:
More thought than woe was in her dusky face,
For she was prophesying of her glory;
And in her wide imagination stood
Palm-shaded temples, and high rival fanes,
By Oxus[8] or in Ganges' sacred isles.   60
Even as Hope upon her anchor leans,
So leant she, not so fair, upon a tusk
Shed from the broadest of her elephants.
Above her, on a crag's uneasy shelve,
Upon his elbow rais'd, all prostrate else,
Shadow'd Enceladus; once tame and mild
As grazing ox unworried in the meads;

Now tiger-passion'd, lion-thoughted, wroth,
He meditated, plotted, and even now
Was hurling mountains in that second war,   70
Not long delay'd, that scar'd the younger Gods
To hide themselves in forms of beast and bird.
Not far hence Atlas; and beside him prone
Phorcus, the sire of Gorgons. Neighbour'd close
Oceanus, and Tethys, in whose lap
Sobb'd Clymene among her tangled hair.
In midst of all lay Themis,[9] at the feet
Of Ops the queen all clouded round from sight;
No shape distinguishable, more than when
Thick night confounds the pine-tops with the clouds: 80
And many else whose names may not be told.
For when the Muse's wings are air-ward spread,
Who shall delay her flight? And she must chant
Of Saturn, and his guide, who now had climb'd
With damp and slippery footing from a depth
More horrid still. Above a sombre cliff
Their heads appear'd, and up their stature grew
Till on the level height their steps found ease:
Then Thea spread abroad her trembling arms
Upon the precincts of this nest of pain,   90
And sidelong fix'd her eye on Saturn's face:
There saw she direst strife; the supreme God
At war with all the frailty of grief,
Of rage, of fear, anxiety, revenge,
Remorse, spleen, hope, but most of all despair.
Against these plagues he strove in vain; for Fate
Had pour'd a mortal oil upon his head,
A disanointing poison: so that Thea,
Affrighted, kept her still, and let him pass
First onwards in, among the fallen tribe.   100

   As with us mortal men, the laden heart
Is persecuted more, and fever'd more,
When it is nighing to the mournful house
Where other hearts are sick of the same bruise;
So Saturn, as he walk'd into the midst,
Felt faint, and would have sunk among the rest,

But that he met Enceladus's eye,
Whose mightiness, and awe of him, at once
Came like an inspiration; and he shouted,
'Titans, behold your God!' at which some groan'd;   110
Some started on their feet; some also shouted;
Some wept, some wail'd, all bow'd with reverence;
And Ops, uplifting her black folded veil,
Show'd her pale cheeks, and all her forehead wan,
Her eyebrows thin and jet, and hollow eyes.
There is a roaring in the bleak-grown pines
When Winter lifts his voice; there is a noise
Among immortals when a God gives sign,
With hushing finger, how he means to load
His tongue with the full weight of utterless thought,   120
With thunder, and with music, and with pomp:
Such noise is like the roar of bleak-grown pines:
Which, when it ceases in this mountain'd world,
No other sound succeeds; but ceasing here,
Among these fallen, Saturn's voice therefrom
Grew up like organ, that begins anew
Its strain, when other harmonies, stopt short,
Leave the dinn'd air vibrating silverly.
Thus grew it up – 'Not in my own sad breast,
Which is its own great judge and searcher out,   130
Can I find reason why ye should be thus:
Not in the legends of the first of days,
Studied from that old spirit-leaved book[10]
Which starry Uranus with finger bright
Sav'd from the shores of darkness, when the waves
Low-ebb'd still hid it up in shallow gloom; –
And the which book ye know I ever kept
For my firm-based footstool: – Ah, infirm!
Not there, nor in sign, symbol, or portent
Of element, earth, water, air, and fire, –   140
At war, at peace, or inter-quarreling
One against one, or two, or three, or all
Each several one against the other three,
As fire with air loud warring when rain-floods
Drown both, and press them both against earth's face,
Where, finding sulphur, a quadruple wrath

Unhinges the poor world; – not in that strife,
Wherefrom I take strange lore, and read it deep,
Can I find reason why ye should be thus:
No nowhere can unriddle, though I search,   150
And pore on Nature's universal scroll
Even to swooning, why ye, Divinities,
The firstborn of all shap'd and palpable Gods.
Should cower beneath what, in comparison,
Is untremendous might. Yet ye are here,
O'erwhelm'd, and spurnd, and batter'd, ye are here!
O Titans, shall I say, "Arise!" – Ye groan:
Shall I say "Crouch!" – Ye groan. What can I then?
O Heaven wide! O unseen parent dear!
What can I? Tell me, all ye brethren Gods,   160
How we can war, how engine our great wrath![11]
O speak your counsel now, for Saturn's ear
Is all a-hunger'd. Thou, Oceanus,
Ponderest high and deep; and in thy face
I see, astonied,[12] that severe content
Which comes of thought and musing: give us help!'

   So ended Saturn; and the God of the Sea,
Sophist and sage, from no Athenian grove,
But cogitation[13] in his watery shades,
Arose, with locks not oozy, and began,   170
In mumurs, which his first-endeavouring tongue
Caught infant-like from the far-foamed sands.
'O ye, whom wrath consumes! who, passion-stung,
Writhe at defeat, and nurse your agonies!
Shut up your senses, stifle up your ears,
My voice is not a bellows unto ire.
Yet listen, ye who will, whilst I bring proof
How ye, perforce, must be content to stoop:
And in the proof much comfort will I give,
If ye will take that comfort in its truth.   180
We fall by course of Nature's law, not force
Of thunder, or of Jove. Great Saturn, thou
Hast sifted well the atom-universe;[14]
But for this reason, that thou art the King.
And only blind from sheer supremacy,

One avenue was shaded from thine eyes,
Through which I wandered to eternal truth.
And first, as thou wast not the first of powers,
So art thou not the last; it cannot be:
Thou art not the beginning nor the end. 190
From chaos and parental darkness came
Light, the first fruits of that intestine broil,[15]
That sullen ferment, which for wondrous ends
Was ripening in itself. The ripe hour came,
And with it light, and light, engendering
Upon its own producer, forthwith touch'd
The whole enormous matter into life.
Upon that very hour, our parentage,
The Heavens and the Earth, were manifest:
Then thou firstborn, and we the giant race, 200
Found ourselves ruling new and beauteous realms.
Now comes the pain of truth, to whom 'tis pain:
O folly! for to bear all naked truths,
And to envisage circumstance, all calm,
That is the top of sovereignty. Mark well!
As Heaven and Earth are fairer, fairer far
Than Chaos and blank Darkness, though once chiefs:
And as we show beyond that Heaven and Earth
In form and shape compact and beautiful,
In will, in action free, companionship, 210
And thousand other signs of purer life;
So on our heels a fresh perfection treads,
A power more strong in beauty, born of us
And fated to excel us, as we pass
In glory that old Darkness: nor are we
Thereby more conquer'd, than by us the rule
Of shapeless Chaos. Say, doth the dull soil
Quarrel with the proud forests it hath fed,
And feedeth still, more comely than itself?
Can it deny the chiefdom of green groves? 220
Or shall the tree be envious of the dove
Because it cooeth, and hath snowy wings
To wander wherewithal and find its joys?
We are such forest trees, and our fair boughs
Have bred forth, not pale solitary doves,

But eagles golden-feather'd, who do tower
Above us in their beauty, and must reign
In right thereof; for 'tis the eternal law
That first in beauty should be first in might:
Yea, by that law, another race may drive   230
Our conquerors to mourn as we do now.
Have ye beheld the young God of the Seas,[16]
My dispossessor? Have ye seen his face?
Have ye beheld his chariot, foam'd along
By noble winged creatures he hath made?
I saw him on the calmed waters scud,
With such a glow of beauty in his eyes,
That it enforc'd me to bid sad farewell
To all my empire: farewell sad I took,
And hither came, to see how dolorous fate   240
Had wrought upon ye; and how I might best
Give consolation in this woe extreme.
Receive the truth, and let it be your balm.'
Whether through pos'd[17] conviction, or disdain,
They guarded silence, when Oceanus
Left murmuring, what deepest thought can tell?
But so it was, none answer'd for a space,
Save one whom none regarded, Clymene;
And yet she answer'd not, only complain'd,
With hectic lips, and eyes up-looking mild,   250
Thus wording timidly among the fierce:
'O Father, I am here the simplest voice,
And all my knowledge is that joy is gone,
And this thing woe crept in among our hearts,
There to remain for ever, as I fear:
I would not bode of evil, if I thought
So weak a creature could turn off the help
Which by just right should come of mighty Gods;
Yet let me tell my sorrow, let me tell
Of what I heard, and how it made me weep,   260
And know that we had parted from all hope.
I stood upon a shore, a pleasant shore,
Where a sweet clime was breathed from a land
Of fragrance, quietness, and trees, and flowers.
Full of calm joy it was, as I of grief;

Too full of joy and soft delicious warmth;
So that I felt a movement in my heart
To chide, and to reproach that solitude
With songs of misery, music of our woes;
And sat me down, and took a mouthed shell[18]   270
And murmur'd into it, and made melody –
O melody no more! for while I sang,
And with poor skill let pass into the breeze
The dull shell's echo, from a bowery strand
Just opposite, an island of the sea,
There came enchantment with the shifting wind,
That did both drown and keep alive my ears.
I threw my shell away upon the sand,
And a wave fill'd it, as my sense was fill'd
With that new blissful golden melody.   280
A living death was in each gush of sounds,
Each family of rapturous hurried notes,
That fell, one after one, yet all at once,
Like pearl beads dropping sudden from their string:
And then another, then another strain,
Each like a dove leaving its olive perch,
With music wing'd instead of silent plumes,
To hover round my head, and make me sick
Of joy and grief at once. Grief overcame,
And I was stopping up my frantic ears,   290
When, past all hindrance of my trembling hands.
A voice came sweeter, sweeter than all tune,
And still it cried, "Apollo! young Apollo!
The morning-bright Apollo! young Apollo!"
I fled, it follow'd me, and cried 'Apollo!'
O Father, and O Brethren, had ye felt
Those pains of mine; O Saturn, hadst thou felt,
Ye would not call this too indulged tongue
Presumptuous, in thus venturing to be heard.'

       So far her voice flow'd on, like timorous brook   300
That, lingering along a pebbled coast,
Doth fear to meet the sea: but sea it met,
And shudder'd; for the overwhelming voice
Of huge Enceladus swallow'd it in wrath:

The ponderous syllables, like sullen waves
In the half-glutted hollows of reef-rocks,
Came booming thus, while still upon his arm
He lean'd; not rising, from supreme contempt.
'Or shall we listen to the over-wise,
Or to the over-foolish, Giant-Gods?   310
Not thunderbolt on thunderbolt, till all
That rebel Jove's whole armoury were spent,
Not world on world upon these shoulders piled,
Could agonise me more than baby words
In midst of this dethronement horrible.
Speak! roar! shout! yell! ye sleepy Titans all
Do ye forget the blows, the buffets vile?
Are ye not smitten by a youngling arm?
Dost thou forget, sham Monarch of the Waves,
Thy scalding in the seas? What, have I rous'd   320
Your spleens with so few simple words as these?
O joy! for now I see ye are not lost:
O joy! for now I see a thousand eyes
Wide-glaring for revenge!' – As this he said,
He lifted up his stature vast, and stood,
Still without intermission speaking thus:
'Now ye are flames, I'll tell you how to burn,
And purge the ether of our enemies;
How to feed fierce the crooked stings of fire,
And singe away the swollen clouds of Jove,   330
Stifling that puny essence in its tent.
O let him feel the evil he hath done;
For though I scorn Oceanus's lore,
Much pain have I for more than loss of realms:
The days of peace and slumberous calm are fled;
Those days, all innocent of scathing war,
When all the fair Existences of heaven
Came open-eyed to guess what we would speak: –
That was before our brows were taught to frown,
Before our lips knew else but solemn sounds;   340
That was before we knew the winged thing,
Victory,[19] might be lost, or might be won.
And be ye mindful that Hyperion,
Our brightest brother, still is undisgraced –

Hyperion, lo! his radiance is here!'

    All eyes were on Enceladus's face,
And they beheld, while still Hyperion's name
Flew from his lips up to the vaulted rocks,
A pallid gleam across his features stern:
Not savage, for he saw full many a God   350
Wroth as himself. He look'd upon them all,
And in each face he saw a gleam of light,
But splendider in Saturn's, whose hoar locks
Shone like the bubbling foam about a keel
When the prow sweeps into a midnight cove.
In pale and silver silence they remain'd,
Till suddenly a splendour, like the morn,
Pervaded all the beetling gloomy steeps,
All the sad spaces of oblivion,
And every gulf, and every chasm old,   360
And every height, and every sullen depth,
Voiceless, or hoarse with loud tormented streams:
And all the everlasting cataracts,
And all the headlong torrents far and near,
Mantled[20] before in darkness and huge shade,
Now saw the light and made it terrible.
It was Hyperion: – a granite peak
His bright feet touch'd, and there he stay'd to view
The misery his brilliance had betray'd
To the most hateful seeing of itself.   370
Golden his hair of short Numidian curl,[21]
Regal his shape majestic, a vast shade
In midst of his own brightness, like the bulk
Of Memnon's image at the set of sun
To one who travels from the dusking East:
Sighs, too, as mournful as that Memnon's harp[22]
He utter'd, while his hands contemplative
He press'd together, and in silence stood.
Despondence seiz'd again the fallen Gods
At sight of the dejected King of Day,   380
And many hid their faces from the light:
But fierce Enceladus sent forth his eyes
Among the brotherhood; and, at their glare,

Uprose Iäpetus, and Creüs too,
And Phorcus, sea-born, and together strode
To where he towered on his eminence.
There those four shouted forth old Saturn's name;
Hyperion from the peak loud answered, 'Saturn!'
Saturn sat near the Mother of the Gods,
In whose face was no joy, though all the Gods   390
Gave from their hollow throats the name of 'Saturn!'

Hyperion – Book III

Thus in alternate uproar and sad peace,
Amazed were those Titans utterly.
O leave them, Muse! O leave them to their woes;
For thou art weak to sing such tumults dire:
A solitary sorrow best befits
Thy lips, and antheming a lonely grief.
Leave them, O Muse! for thou anon wilt find
Many a fallen old Divinity
Wandering in vain about bewildered shores.
Meantime touch piously the Delphic harp,   10
And not a wind of heaven but will breathe
In aid soft warble from the Dorian flute;[1]
For lo! 'tis for the Father of all verse.
Flush every thing that hath a vermeil hue,
Let the rose glow intense and warm the air,
And let the clouds of even and of morn
Float in voluptuous fleeces o'er the hills;
Let the red wine within the goblet boil,
Cold as a bubbling well; let faint-lipp'd shells,
On sands, or in great deeps, vermilion turn   20
Through all their labyrinths; and let the maid
Blush keenly, as with some warm kiss surpris'd.
Chief isle of the embowered Cyclades,
Rejoice, O Delos, with thine olives green,
And poplars, and lawn-shading palms, and beech,
In which the Zephyr breathes the loudest song,
And hazels thick, dark-stemm'd beneath the shade:
Apollo is once more the golden theme!

Where was he, when the Giant of the Sun[2]
Stood bright, amid the sorrow of his peers?   30
Together had he left his mother fair
And his twin-sister sleeping in their bower,
And in the morning twilight wandered forth
Beside the osiers of a rivulet,[3]
Full ankle-deep in lilies of the vale.
The nightingale had ceas'd, and a few stars
Were lingering in the heavens, while the thrush
Began calm-throated. Throughout all the isle
There was no covert, no retired cave
Unhaunted by the murmurous noise of waves,   40
Though scarcely heard in many a green recess.
He listen'd, and he wept, and his bright tears
Went trickling down the golden bow he held.
Thus with half-shut suffused eyes he stood,
While from beneath some cumbrous boughs hard by
With solemn step an awful Goddess came,
And there was purport in her looks for him
Which he with eager guess began to read
Perplex'd, the while melodiously he said:
'How cam'st thou over the unfooted[4] sea?   50
Or hath that antique mien[5] and robed form
Mov'd in these vales invisible till now?
Sure I have heard those vestments sweeping o'er
The fallen leaves, when I have sat alone
In cool mid-forest. Surely I have traced
The rustle of those ample skirts about
These grassy solitudes, and seen the flowers
Lift up their heads, as still the whisper pass'd.
Goddess! I have beheld those eyes before,
And their eternal calm, and all that face,   60
Or I have dream'd.' – 'Yes,' said the supreme shape,
'Thou hast dream'd of me; and awaking up
Didst find a lyre all golden by thy side,
Whose strings touch'd by thy fingers, all the vast
Unwearied ear of the whole universe
Listen'd in pain and pleasure at the birth
Of such new tuneful wonder. Is't not strange
That thou shouldst weep, so gifted? Tell me, youth,

What sorrow thou canst feel; for I am sad
When thou dost shed a tear: explain thy griefs   70
To one who in this lonely isle hath been
The watcher of thy sleep and hours of life,
From the young day when first thy infant hand
Pluck'd witless the weak flowers, till thine arm
Could bend that bow heroic to all times.
Show thy heart's secret to an ancient Power
Who hath forsaken old and sacred thrones
For prophecies of thee, and for the sake
Of loveliness new born.' – Apollo then,
With sudden scrutiny and gloomless eyes,   80
Thus answer'd, while his white melodious throat
Throbb'd with the syllables. – 'Mnemosyne!
Thy name is on my tongue, I know not how;
Why should I tell thee what thou so well seest?
Why should I strive to show what from thy lips
Would come no mystery? For me, dark, dark,
And painful vile oblivion seals my eyes:
I strive to search wherefore I am so sad,
Until a melancholy numbs my limbs;
And then upon the grass I sit, and moan,   90
Like one who once had wings. – O why should I
Feel curs'd and thwarted, when the liegeless[6] air
Yields to my step aspirant?[7] why should I
Spurn the green turf as hateful to my feet?
Goddess benign, point forth some unknown thing:
Are there not other regions than this isle?
What are the stars? There is the sun, the sun!
And the most patient brilliance of the moon!
And stars by thousands! Point me out the way
To any one particular beauteous star,   100
And I will flit into it with my lyre,
And make its silvery splendour pant with bliss.
I have heard the cloudy thunder: Where is power?
Whose hand, whose essence, what divinity
Makes this alarum in the elements,
While I here idle listen on the shores
In fearless yet in aching ignorance?
O tell me, lonely Goddess, by thy harp,

That waileth every morn and eventide,
Tell me why thus I rave, about these groves!   110
Mute thou remainest – mute! yet I can read
A wondrous lesson in thy silent face:
Knowledge enormous makes a God of me.
Names, deeds, grey legends, dire events, rebellions,
Majesties, sovran voices, agonies,
Creations and destroyings, all at once
Pour into the wide hollows of my brain,
And deify me, as if some blithe wine
Or bright elixir peerless[8] I had drunk,
And so become immortal.' – Thus the God,   120
While his enkindled[9] eyes, with level glance
Beneath his white soft temples, steadfast kept
Trembling with light upon Mnemosyne.
Soon wild commotions shook him, and made flush
All the immortal fairness of his limbs;
Most like the struggle at the gate of death;
Or liker still to one who should take leave
Of pale immortal death, and with a pang
As hot as death's is chill, with fierce convulse[10]
Die into life: so young Apollo anguish'd: 130
His very hair, his golden tresses famed
Kept undulation round his eager neck.
During the pain Mnemosyne upheld
Her arms as one who prophesied. – At length
Apollo shriek'd; – and lo! from all his limbs
Celestial . . .

POSTHUMOUS AND
FUGITIVE POEMS

On Death

I

Can death be sleep, when life is but a dream,
And scenes of bliss pass as a phantom by?
The transient pleasures as a vision seem,
And yet we think the greatest pain's to die.

II

How strange it is that man on earth should roam,
And lead a life of woe, but not forsake
His rugged path; nor dare he view alone
His future doom which is but to awake.

Women, Wine, and Snuff

Give me women, wine and snuff
Until I cry out 'hold, enough!'
You may do so sans objection
Till the day of resurrection;
For bless my beard they aye shall be
My beloved Trinity.

Fill for me a brimming bowl

Fill for me a brimming bowl
And let me in it drown my soul:
But put therein some drug, designed
To banish women from my mind:
For I want not the stream inspiring
That fills the mind with – fond desiring,
But I want as deep a draught
As e'er from Lethe's wave was quaff'd;
From my despairing heart to charm
The image of the fairest form
That e'er my reveling eyes beheld,

10

That e'er my wandering fancy spell'd.
In vain! away I cannot chase
The melting softness of that face,
The beaminess of those bright eyes,
That breast-earth's only Paradise.
My sight will never more be blest;
For all I see has lost its zest:
Nor with delight can I explore
The Classic page, or Muse's lore.   20
Had she but known how beat my heart,
And with one smile reliev'd its smart
I should have felt sweet relief,
I should have felt 'the joy of grief.'¹
Yet as the Tuscan mid the snow
Of Lapland thinks on sweet Arno,
Even so for ever shall she be
The Halo of my Memory.

August 1814

Sonnet on Peace

O Peace!¹ and dost thou with thy presence bless
    The dwellings of this war-surrounded Isle;
Soothing with placid brow our late distress,
    Making the triple kingdom brightly smile?
Joyful I hail thy presence; and I hail
    The sweet companions that await on thee;
Complete my joy – let not my first wish fail,
    Let the sweet mountain nymph thy favourite be,
With England's happiness proclaim Europa's Liberty.
O Europe! let not sceptred tyrants see   10
    That thou must shelter in thy former state;
Keep thy chains burst, and boldly say thou art free;
    Give thy kings law – leave not uncurbed the great;
    So with the horrors past thou'lt win thy happier fate!

Sonnet to Byron

Byron! how sweetly sad thy melody!
   Attuning still the soul to tenderness,
   As if soft Pity, with unusual stress,
Had touch'd her plaintive lute, and thou, being by,
Hadst caught the tones, nor suffer'd them to die.
   O'ershadowing sorrow doth not make thee less
   Delightful: thou thy griefs dost dress
With a bright halo, shining beamily,
As when a cloud the golden moon doth veil,
   Its sides are ting'd with a resplendent glow,   10
Through the dark robe oft amber rays prevail,
   And like fair veins in sable marble flow;
Still warble, dying swan! still tell the tale,
   The enchanting tale, the tale of pleasing woe.

Sonnet to Chatterton

O Chatterton! how very sad thy fate!
   Dear child of sorrow – son of misery!
   How soon the film of death obscur'd that eye,
Whence Genius mildly flash'd, and high debate.
How soon that voice, majestic and elate,
   Melted in dying numbers! Oh! how nigh
   Was night to thy fair morning. Thou didst die
A half-blown flow'ret which cold blasts amate.[1]
But this is past: thou art among the stars
   Of highest Heaven: to the rolling spheres   10
Thou sweetly singest: naught thy hymning mars,
   Above the ingrate[2] world and human fears.
On earth the good man base detraction bars
   From thy fair name, and waters it with tears.

Sonnet to Spenser

Spenser! a jealous honourer[1] of thine,
　　A forester deep in thy midmost trees,
Did last eve ask my promise to refine
　　Some English that might strive thine ear to please.
But Elfin Poet[2] 'tis impossible
　　For an inhabitant of wintry earth
To rise like Phoebus with a golden quell[3]
　　Fire-wing'd and make a morning in his mirth.
It is impossible to escape from toil
　　O' the sudden and receive thy spiriting:　　　　　　10
The flower must drink the nature of the soil
　　Before it can put forth its blossoming:
Be with me in the summer days and I
Will for thine honour and his pleasure try.

Ode to Apollo

In thy western halls of gold[1]
　　When thou sittest in thy state,
Bards, that erst[2] sublimely told
　　Heroic deeds, and sang of fate,
With fervour seize their adamantine[3] lyres,
Whose chords are solid rays, and twinkle radiant fires.

Here Homer with his nervous arms
　　Strikes the twanging harp of war,
And even the western splendour warms,
　　While the trumpets sound afar:　　　　　　10
But, what creates the most intense surprise,
His soul looks out through renovated eyes.

Then, through thy Temple wide, melodious swells
　　The sweet majestic tone of Maro's[4] lyre:
The soul delighted on each accent dwells, –
　　Enraptur'd dwells, – not daring to respire,
The while he tells of grief around a funeral pyre.

'Tis awful silence then again;
   Expectant stand the spheres;
   Breathless the laurell'd peers,   20
 Nor move, till ends the lofty strain,
 Nor move till Milton's tuneful thunders cease,
And leave once more the ravish'd heavens in peace.

 Thou biddest Shakespeare wave his hand,
   And quickly forward spring
The Passions – a terrific[5] band –
   And each vibrates the string
 That with its tyrant temper best accords,
While from their Master's lips pour forth the inspiring words.

 A silver trumpet Spenser blows,   30
   And, as its martial notes to silence flee,
 From a virgin chorus flows
   A hymn in praise of spotless Chastity.[6]
 'Tis still! Wild warblings from the Aeolian lyre
Enchantment softly breathe, and tremblingly expire.

 Next thy Tasso's ardent numbers
   Float along the pleased air,
 Calling youth from idle slumbers,
   Rousing them from Pleasure's lair: –
 Then o'er the strings his fingers gently move,   40
 And melt the soul to pity and to love.

 But when *Thou* joinest with the Nine,[7]
 And all the powers of song combine,
   We listen here on earth:
 The dying tones that fill the air,
 And charm the ear of evening fair,
From thee, great God of Bards, receive their heavenly birth.

To a Young Lady who Sent Me a Laurel Crown

Fresh morning gusts have blown away all fear
  From my glad bosom, – now from gloominess
  I mount for ever – not an atom less
Than the proud laurel shall content my bier.
No! by the eternal stars! or why sit here
  In the Sun's eye, and 'gainst my temples press
  Apollo's very leaves, woven to bless
By thy white fingers and thy spirit clear.
Lo! who dares say, 'Do this'? Who dares call down
  My will from its high purpose? Who say, 'Stand,'   10
Or 'Go'? This mighty moment I would frown
  On abject Caesars – not the stoutest band
Of mailed heroes should tear off my crown:
  Yet would I kneel and kiss thy gentle hand!

On Receiving a Laurel Crown from Leigh Hunt

Minutes are flying[1] swiftly, and as yet
  Nothing unearthly has enticed my brain
  Into a delphic labyrinth – I would fain
Catch an unmortal thought to pay the debt
I owe to the kind Poet who has set
  Upon my ambitious head a glorious gain.[2]
  Two bending laurel sprigs – 'tis nearly pain
To be conscious of such a Coronet.
Still time is fleeting, and no dream arises
  Gorgeous as I would have it – only I see   10
A trampling down of what the world most prizes
  Turbans and Crowns, and blank regality;
And then I run into most wild surmises
  Of all the many glories that may be.

To the Ladies who Saw Me Crown'd

What is there in the universal Earth
   More lovely than a Wreath from the bay tree?
   Haply a Halo round the Moon – a glee
Circling from three sweet pair of lips in mirth;
And haply you will say the dewy birth
   Of morning roses – riplings tenderly
   Spread by the Halcyon's breast upon the sea –
But these comparisons are nothing worth –
Then is there nothing in the world so fair?
   The silvery tears of April? – Youth of May?   10
Or June that breaths out life for butterflies?
   No – none of these can from my favourite bear
Away the Palm – yet shall it ever pay
   Due reverence to your most sovereign eyes.

Hymn to Apollo

   God of the golden bow,
      And of the golden lyre,
   And of the golden hair,
      And of the golden fire,
         Charioteer
         Of the patient year,
     Where – where slept thine ire,
When like a blank idiot I put on thy wreath,
      Thy laurel, thy glory,
      The light of thy story,   10
Or was I a worm – too low crawling, for death?
     O Delphic Apollo!

   The Thunderer[1] grasp'd and grasp'd,
      The Thunderer frown'd and frown'd;
   The eagle's feathery mane
      For wrath became stiffen'd – the sound
         Of breeding thunder
         Went drowsily under,

Muttering to be unbound.
O why didst thou pity, and for a worm   20
Why touch thy soft lute
Till the thunder was mute,
Why was not I crush'd – such a pitiful germ?
O Delphic Apollo!

The Pleiades were up,
Watching the silent air;
The seeds and roots in the Earth
Were swelling for summer fare;
The Ocean, its neighbour,
Was at its old labour,   30
When, who – who did dare
To tie, like a madman, thy plant round his brow.
And grin and look proudly,
And blaspheme so loudly,
And live for that honour, to stoop to thee now?
O Delphic Apollo!

Sonnet

As from the darkening gloom a silver dove
Upsoars, and darts into the eastern light,
On pinions that naught moves but pure delight,
So fled thy soul[1] into the realms above,
Regions of peace and everlasting love;
Where happy spirits, crown'd with circlets bright
Of starry beam, and gloriously bedight,[2]
Taste the high joy none but the blest can prove.
There thou or joinest the immortal quire
In melodies that even heaven fair   10
Fill with superior bliss, or, at desire
Of the omnipotent Father, cleavest the air
On holy message sent – What pleasures higher?
Wherefore does any grief our joy impair?

Stanzas to Miss Wylie

O come Georgiana![1] the rose is full blown,
The riches of Flora are lavishly strown,
The air is all softness, and crystal the streams,
The West is resplendently clothed in beams.
O come! let us haste to the freshening shades,
The quaintly carv'd seats, and the opening glades;
Where the faeries are chanting their evening hymns,
And in the last sunbeam the sylph lightly swims.
And when thou art weary I'll find thee a bed,
Of mosses and flowers to pillow thy head: 10
And there Georgiana I'll sit at thy feet,
While my story of love I enraptur'd repeat.
So fondly I'll breathe, and so softly I'll sigh,
Thou wilt think that some amorous Zephyr is nigh:
Yet no – as I breathe I will press thy fair knee,
And then thou wilt know that the sigh comes from me.
Ah! why dearest girl should we lose all these blisses?
That mortal's a fool who such happiness misses:
So smile acquiescence, and give me thy hand,
With love looking eyes, and with voice sweetly bland.   20

Sonnet

Oh! how I love, on a fair summer's eve,
    When streams of light pour down the golden west,
    And on the balmy zephyrs tranquil rest
The silver clouds, far – far away to leave
All meaner thoughts, and take a sweet reprieve
    From little cares; to find, with easy quest,
    A fragrant wild,[1] with Nature's beauty drest,
And there into delight my soul deceive.
There warm my breast with patriotic lore,
    Musing on Milton's fate – on Sydney's bier –   10
        Till their stern forms before my mind arise:
Perhaps on wing of Poesy upsoar,
    Full often dropping a delicious tear,
        When some melodious sorrow spells mine eyes.

Sonnet

Before he went to feed with owls and bats
    Nebuchadnezzar[1] had an ugly dream,
    Worse than an hus'if's[2] when she thinks her cream
Made a naumachia[3] for mice and rats.
So scared, he sent for that 'Good King of Cats'
    Young Daniel, who soon did pluck away the beam
    From out his eye, and said he did not deem
The sceptre worth a straw – his cushions old door-mats.
A horrid nightmare similar somewhat
    Of late has haunted a most motley crew,   1●
        Most loggerheads and chapmen[4] – we are told
That any Daniel tho' he be a sot
    Can make the lying lips turn pale of hue
        By belching out 'ye are that head of gold.'[5]

Sonnet Written in Disgust of Vulgar Superstition

The church bells toll a melancholy round,
    Calling the people to some other prayers,
    Some other gloominess, more dreadful cares,
More hearkening to the sermon's horrid sound.
Surely the mind of man is closely bound
    In some black spell; seeing that each one tears
    Himself from fireside joys, and Lydian airs,
And converse high of those with glory crown'd.
Still, still they toll, and I should feel a damp, –
    A chill as from a tomb, did I not know   1●
That they are dying like an outburnt lamp;
    That 'tis their sighing, wailing ere they go
    Into oblivion; – that fresh flowers will grow,
And many glories of immortal stamp.

Sonnet

After dark vapours have oppress'd our plains
   For a long dreary season, comes a day
   Born of the gentle South, and clears away
From the sick heavens all unseemly stains.
The anxious month, relieved of its pains,
   Takes as a long-lost right the feel of May;
   The eyelids with the passing coolness play
Like rose leaves with the drip of summer rains.
The calmest thoughts come round us; as of leaves
   Budding – fruit ripening in stillness – autumn suns   10
Smiling at eve upon the quiet sheaves –
Sweet Sappho's cheek – a smiling infant's breath –
   The gradual sand that through an hourglass runs –
A woodland rivulet – a Poet's death.

Sonnet

[*Written at the end of 'The Floure and the Lefe'*][1]

This pleasant tale is like a little copse:
   The honied lines do freshly interlace
   To keep the reader in so sweet a place,
So that he here and there full-hearted stops;
And oftentimes he feels the dewy drops
   Come cool and suddenly against his face,
   And by the wandering melody may trace
Which way the tender-legged linnet hops.
Oh! what a power hath white simplicity!
   What mighty power has this gentle story!   10
   I that for ever feel athirst for glory
Could at this moment be content to lie
   Meekly upon the grass, as those whose sobbings[2]
   Were heard of none beside the mournful robins.

Two Sonnets

I

To Haydon, with a Sonnet Written on Seeing
the Elgin Marbles

Haydon! forgive me that I cannot speak
   Definitively on these mighty things;
   Forgive me that I have not Eagle's wings –
That what I want I know not where to seek:
And think that I would not be over meek
   In rolling out upfollow'd thunderings,[1]
   Even to the steep of Heliconian springs,
Were I of ample strength for such a freak[2] –
Think too, that all those numbers should be thine;
   Whose else? In this who touch thy vesture's hem?   10
For when men star'd at what was most divine
   With browless idiotism – o'erwise phlegm –
Thou hadst beheld the Hesperean shine
   Of their star in the east,[3] and gone to worship them.

II

On Seeing the Elgin Marbles[4]

My spirit is too weak – mortality
   Weighs heavily on me like unwilling sleep.
   And each imagin'd pinnacle and steep
Of godlike hardship, tells me I must die
Like a sick Eagle looking at the sky.
   Yet 'tis a gentle luxury to weep
   That I have not the cloudy winds to keep,
Fresh for the opening of the morning's eye.
Such dim-conceived glories of the brain
   Bring round the heart an undescribable feud: 10
So do these wonders a most dizzy pain,
   That mingles Grecian grandeur with the rude
Wasting of old Time – with a billowy main –
   A sun – a shadow of a magnitude.[5]

Sonnet on a Picture of Leander

Come hither all sweet maidens soberly,
   Down-looking aye, and with a chasten'd light,
   Hid in the fringes of your eyelids white,
And meekly let your fair hands joined be,
As if so gentle that ye could not see,
   Untouch'd, a victim of your beauty bright,
   Sinking away to his young spirit's night, –
Sinking bewilder'd 'mid the dreary sea:
'Tis young Leander toiling to his death;
   Nigh swooning, he doth purse his weary lips   10
      For Hero's cheek, and smiles against[1] her smile.
   O horrid dream! see how his body dips
      Dead-heavy; arms and shoulders gleam awhile:
He's gone: up bubbles all his amorous breath!

To —

Think not of it, sweet one, so; –
   Give it not a tear;
Sigh thou mayst, and bid it go
   Any – anywhere.

Do not look so sad, sweet one, –
   Sad and fadingly;
Shed one drop, then it is gone,
   O 'twas born to die.

Still so pale? then dearest weep;
   Weep, I'll count the tears,   10
And each one shall be a bliss
   For thee in after years.

Brighter has it left thine eyes
   Than a sunny rill;
And thy whispering melodies
   Are tenderer still.

Yet – as all things mourn awhile
    At fleeting blisses,
Let us too! but be our dirge
    A dirge of kisses.   20

Lines

I

Unfelt, unheard, unseen,
I've left my little queen,
Her languid arms in silver slumber lying:
    Ah! through their nestling touch,
    Who – who could tell how much
There is for madness – cruel, or complying?

II

Those faery lids how sleek!
Those lips how moist! – they speak,
In ripest quiet, shadows of sweet sounds:
    Into my fancy's ear
    Melting a burden dear,
How 'Love doth know no fullness nor no bounds.'

III

True! – tender monitors!
I bend unto your laws:
This sweetest day for dalliance was born!
    So, without more ado,
    I'll feel my heaven anew,
For all the blushing of the hasty morn.

Sonnet on the Sea

It keeps eternal whisperings around
    Desolate shores, and with its mighty swell
    Gluts twice ten thousand Caverns, till the spell
Of Hecate[1] leaves them their old shadowy sound.
Often 'tis in such gentle temper found,
    That scarcely will the very smallest shell
    Be mov'd for days from where it sometime fell,
When last the winds of Heaven were unbound.
Oh ye! who have your eyeballs vex'd and tir'd,
    Feast them upon the wideness of the Sea;   10
      Oh ye! whose ears are dinn'd with uproar rude,
    Or fed too much with cloying melody –
      Sit ye near some old cavern's mouth, and brood
Until ye start, as if the sea-nymphs quir'd![2]

Sonnet on Leigh Hunt's Poem 'The Story of Rimini'

Who loves to peer up at the morning sun,
    With half-shut eyes and comfortable cheek.
    Let him, with this sweet tale, full often seek
For meadows where the little rivers run;
Who loves to linger with that brightest one
    Of Heaven – Hesperus – let him lowly speak
    These numbers to the night, and starlight meek.
Or moon, if that her hunting be begun.
He who knows these delights, and too is prone
    To moralise upon a smile or tear,   10
Will find at once a region of his own,
    A bower for his spirit, and will steer
To alleys where the fir tree drops its cone,
    Where robins hop, and fallen leaves are sear.

On Oxford – A Parody

I

The Gothic looks solemn,
　　The plain Doric column
Supports an old Bishop and Crosier;
　　The mouldering arch,
　　Shaded o'er by a larch
Stands next door to Wilson the Hosier.

II

　　Vicè – that is, by turns, –
　　O'er pale faces mourns
The black tassell'd trencher[1] and common hat;
　　The Chantry[2] boy sings,
　　The Steeple-bell rings,
And as for the Chancellor – *dominat*.[3]

III

　　There are plenty of trees,
　　And plenty of ease,
And plenty of fat deer for parsons:
　　And when it is venison,
　　Short is the benison, –
Then each on a leg or thigh fastens.

The Poet – A Fragment

Where's the Poet? show him! show him,
Muses nine! that I may know him!
'Tis the man who with a man
 Is an equal, be he King,
Or poorest of the beggar-clan,
 Or any other wondrous thing
A man may be 'twixt ape and Plato;
 'Tis the man who with a bird,
Wren or Eagle, finds his way to
 All its instincts; he hath heard   10
The Lion's roaring, and can tell
 What his horny throat expresseth,
And to him the Tiger's yell
 Comes articulate and presseth
On his ear like mother tongue.

Modern Love

And what is love? It is a doll dress'd up
For idleness to cosset, nurse, and dandle;
A thing of soft misnomers, so divine
That silly youth doth think to make itself
Divine by loving, and so goes on
Yawning and doting a whole summer long,
Till Miss's comb is made a pearl tiara,
And common Wellingtons turn Romeo boots;
Then Cleopatra lives at number seven,
And Antony resides in Brunswick Square.   10
Fools! if some passions high have warm'd the world,
If Queens and Soldiers have play'd deep for hearts,
It is no reason why such agonies
Should be more common than the growth of weeds.
Fools! make me whole again that weighty pearl
The Queen of Egypt melted,[1] and I'll say
That ye may love in spite of beaver hats.

The Castle Builder – Fragments of a Dialogue

CASTLE BUILDER   In short, convince you that however wise
You may have grown from convent libraries,
I have, by many yards at least, been carding
A longer skein of wit in convent garden.

BERNADINE   A very Eden that same place must be!
Pray what demesne? Whose Lordship's legacy?
What, have you convents in that Gothic Isle?
Pray pardon me, I cannot help but smile.

CASTLE BUILDER   Sir, Convent Garden[1] is a monstrous beast
From morning, four o'clock, to twelve at noon,   10
It swallows cabbages without a spoon,
And then, from twelve till two, this Eden made is
A promenade for cooks and ancient ladies;
And then for supper, 'stead of soup and poaches,
It swallows chairmen, damns, and Hackney coaches.[2]
In short, Sir, 'tis a very place for monks,
For it containeth twenty thousand punks,
Which any man may number for his sport,
By following fat elbows up a court.
In such like nonsense would I pass an hour   20
With random Friar, or Rake upon his tour,
Or one of few of that imperial host[3]
Who came unmaimed from the Russian frost./
Tonight I'll have my friar – let me think
About my room, – I'll have it in the pink;[4]
It should be rich and sombre, and the moon,
Just in its mid-life in the midst of June,
Should look thro' four large windows and display
Clear, but for gold-fish vases in the way,
Their glassy diamonding on Turkish floor;[5]   30
The tapers keep aside, an hour and more,
To see what else the moon alone can show;
While the night-breeze doth softly let us know
My terrace is well bower'd with oranges.
Upon the floor the dullest spirit sees
A guitar-ribband and a lady's glove

Beside a crumple-leaved tale of love;
A tambour-frame, with Venus sleeping there,
All finish'd but some ringlets of her hair;
A viol, bow-strings torn, crosswise upon   40
A glorious folio of Anacreon;
A skull upon a mat of roses lying,
Ink'd purple with a song concerning dying;
An hourglass on the turn, amid the trails
Of passion-flower; – just in time there sails
A cloud across the moon, – the lights bring in!
And see what more my phantasy can win.
It is a gorgeous room, but somewhat sad;
The draperies are so, as tho' they had
Been made for Cleopatra's winding-sheet;[6]   50
And opposite the steadfast eye doth meet
A spacious looking-glass, upon whose face,
In letters raven-sombre, you may trace
Old 'Mene, Mene, Tekel, Upharsin.'[7]
Greek busts and statuary have ever been
Held, by the finest spirits, fitter far
Than vase grotesque and Siamesian[8] jar;
Therefore 'tis sure a want of Attic taste
That I should rather love a Gothic waste
Of eyesight on cinque-coloured[9] potter's clay,   60
Than on the marble fairness of old Greece.
My table-coverlets of Jason's fleece[10]
And black Numidian[11] sheep-wool should be wrought,
Gold, black, and heavy, from the Lama brought.
My ebon sofas should delicious be
With down from Leda's cygnet progeny.
My pictures all Salvator's, save a few
Of Titian's portraiture, and one, though new,
Of Haydon's in its fresh magnificence.
My wine – O good! 'tis here at my desire,   70
And I must sit to supper with my friar.

A Song of Opposites

> Under the flag
> Of each his faction, they to battle bring
> Their embryon atoms.[1]
>
> *Milton*

Welcome joy, and welcome sorrow,
   Lethe's weed and Hermes' feather;
Come today, and come tomorrow,
    I do love you both together!
    I love to mark sad faces in fair weather;
And hear a merry laugh amid the thunder;
    Fair and foul I love together.
Meadows sweet where flames are under,
And a giggle at a wonder;
Visage sage at pantomime;   10
Funeral, and steeple-chime;
Infant playing with a skull;
Morning fair, and shipwreck'd hull;
Nightshade with the woodbine kissing;
Serpents in red roses hissing;
Cleopatra regal-dress'd
With the aspic at her breast;
Dancing music, music sad,
Both together, sane and mad;
Muses bright and muses pale;   20
Sombre Saturn, Momus hale; –
Laugh and sigh, and laugh again;
Oh the sweetness of the pain!
Muses bright, and muses pale,
Bare your faces of the veil;
Let me see; and let me write
Of the day, and of the night –
Both together: – let me slake
All my thirst for sweet hearache!
Let my bower be of yew,   30
Interwreath'd with myrtles new;
Pines and lime-trees full in bloom,
And my couch a low grass-tomb.

Sonnet to a Cat

Cat! who hast pass'd thy grand climacteric,[1]
  How many mice and rats hast in thy days
  Destroy'd? – How many tit bits stolen? Gaze
With those bright languid segments green, and prick
Those velvet ears – but pr'ythee do not stick
  Thy latent talons in me – and upraise
  Thy gentle mew – and tell me all thy frays
Of fish and mice, and rats and tender chick.
Nay, look not down, nor lick thy dainty wrists –
  For all the wheezy asthma, – and for all   10
Thy tail's tip is nick'd off – and though the fists
  Of many a maid have given thee many a maul,
Still is that fur as soft as when the lists[2]
  In youth thou enter'dst on glass bottled wall.

Lines On Seeing a Lock of Milton's Hair

Chief of organic[1] numbers!
  Old Scholar of the Spheres!
Thy spirit never slumbers,
  But rolls about our ears,
For ever, and for ever!
O what a mad endeavour
  Worketh he,
Who to thy sacred and ennobled hearse
Would offer a burnt sacrifice of verse
  And melody.   10

How heavenward thou soundest,
  Live Temple of sweet noise,
And Discord unconfoundest,
  Giving Delight new joys,
And Pleasure nobler pinions!
O, where are thy dominions?
  Lend thine ear

To a young Delian[2] oath, – aye, by thy soul,
By all that from thy mortal lips did roll,
And by the kernel of thine earthly love,   20
Beauty, in things on earth, and things above
        I swear!

  When every childish fashion
    Has vanish'd from my rhyme,
  Will I, grey-gone in passion,
    Leave to an after-time,
       Hymning and harmony
Of thee, and of thy works, and of thy life;
But vain is now the burning and the strife,
Pangs are in vain, until I grow high-rife   30
      With old Philosophy,
And mad with glimpses of futurity!

For many years my offering must be hush'd;
  When I do speak, I'll think upon this hour,
Because I feel my forehead hot and flush'd,
  Even at the simplest vassal of thy power, –
    A lock of thy bright hair, –
    Sudden it came,
And I was startled, when I caught thy name
    Coupled so unaware;   40
Yet, at the moment, temperate was my blood.
I thought I had beheld it from the flood.

Sonnet on Sitting Down to Read King Lear Once Again

O golden tongued Romance, with serene lute!
    Fair plumed Syren, Queen of far-away!
    Leave melodising on this wintry day,
Shut up thine olden pages, and be mute:
Adieu! for, once again, the fierce dispute
    Betwixt damnation and impassion'd clay[1]
    Must I burn through; once more humbly assay[2]
The bitter-sweet of this Shakespearian fruit:
Chief Poet! and ye clouds of Albion,
    Begetters of our deep eternal theme!   10
When through the old oak forest I am gone,
    Let me not wander in a barren dream,
But, when I am consumed in the fire,
Give me new Phoenix wings[3] to fly at my desire.

Sonnet

When I have fears that I may cease to be
    Before my pen has glean'd my teeming brain,
Before high-piled books, in charactery,[1]
    Hold like rich garners[2] the full ripen'd grain;
When I behold, upon the night's starr'd face,
    Huge cloudy symbols of a high romance,
And think that I may never live to trace
    Their shadows, with the magic hand of chance;
And when I feel, fair creature of an hour,
    That I shall never look upon thee more,   10
Never have relish in the faery power
    Of unreflecting love; – then on the shore
Of the wide world I stand alone, and think
Till love and fame to nothingness do sink.

Sharing Eve's Apple

I

O blush not so! O blush not so!
  Or I shall think you knowing;
And if you smile the blushing while,
  Then maidenheads are going.

II

There's a blush for won't, and a blush for shan't,
  And a blush for having done it:
There's a blush for thought and a blush for naught,
  And a blush for just begun it.

III

O sigh not so! O sigh not so!
  For it sounds of Eve's sweet pippin;
By these loosen'd lips you have tasted the pips
  And fought in an amorous nipping.

IV

Will you play once more at nice-cut-core,
  For it only will last our youth out,
And we have the prime of the kissing time,
  We have not one sweet tooth out.

V

There's a sigh for yes, and a sigh for no,
  And a sigh for I can't bear it!
O what can be done, shall we stay or run?
  O cut the sweet apple and share it!

A Draught of Sunshine

Hence Burgundy, Claret, and Port,
   Away with old Hock and Madeira,
Too earthly ye are for my sport;
   There's a beverage brighter and clearer.
Instead of a pitiful rummer,[1]
My wine overbrims a whole summer;
   My bowl is the sky,
   And I drink at my eye,
   Till I feel in the brain
   A Delphian pain –   10
Then follow, my Caius![2] then follow:
   On the green of the hill
   We will drink our fill
   Of golden sunshine,
   Till our brains intertwine
With the glory and grace of Apollo!
   God of the meridian,
     And of the east and west,
To thee my soul is flown,
     And my body is earthward press'd. –   20
   It is an awful mission,
   A terrible division;
   And leaves a gulf austere
   To be fill'd with worldly fear.
   Aye, when the soul is fled
   To high above our head,
   Affrighted do we gaze
   After its airy maze,
   As doth a mother wild,
   When her young infant child   30
   Is in an eagle's claws –
   And is not this the cause
   Of madness? – God of Song,
   Thou bearest me along
   Through sights I scarce can bear:
   O let me, let me share
   With the hot lyre and thee.

The staid Philosophy.
Temper my lonely hours,
And let me see thy bowers   40
More unalarm'd!

Sonnet to the Nile

Son of the old moon-mountains[1] African!
  Chief of the Pyramid and Crocodile!
  We call thee fruitful, and, that very while,
A desert fills our seeing's inward span;
Nurse of swart nations since the world began,
  Art thou so fruitful? or dost thou beguile
  Such men to honour thee, who, worn with toil,
Rest for a space 'twixt Cairo and Decan?[2]
O may dark fancies err! they surely do;
  'Tis ignorance that makes a barren waste   10
Of all beyond itself, thou dost bedew
  Green rushes like our rivers, and dost taste
The pleasant sunrise, green isles hast thou too,
  And to the sea as happily dost haste.

Sonnet to a Lady Seen for a Few Moments at Vauxhall

Time's sea hath been five years at its slow ebb,
  Long hours have to and fro let creep the sand,
Since I was tangled in thy beauty's web,
  And snared by the ungloving of thine hand.
And yet I never look on midnight sky,
  But I behold thine eyes' well memory'd light;
I cannot look upon the rose's dye,
  But to thy cheek my soul doth take its flight.
I cannot look on any building flower,
  But my fond ear, in fancy at thy lips   10
And hearkening for a love-sound, doth devour
  Its sweets in the wrong sense: – Thou dost eclipse
Every delight with sweet remembering,
And grief unto my darling joys dost bring.

Sonnet Written in Answer to a Sonnet Ending thus:

Dark eyes are dearer far
Than those that mock the hyacinthine bell!
J. H. Reynolds

Blue! 'Tis the life of heaven, – the domain
   Of Cynthia, – the wide palace of the sun, –
The tent of Hesperus, and all his train, –
   The bosomer of clouds, gold, grey and dun.
Blue! 'Tis the life of waters: – Ocean
   And all its vassal streams, pools numberless,
May rage, and foam, and fret, but never can
   Subside, if not to dark blue nativeness.
Blue! Gentle cousin of the forest-green,
   Married to green in all the sweetest flowers, –   10
Forget-me-not, – the bluebell, – and, that queen
   Of secrecy, the violet: what strange powers
Hast thou, as a mere shadow! But how great,
When in an Eye thou art, alive with fate!

Sonnet to John Hamilton Reynolds[1x]

O that a week could be an age, and we
   Felt parting and warm meeting every week,
Then one poor year a thousand years would be,
   The flush of welcome ever on the cheek:
So could we live long life in little space,
   So time itself would be annihilate,
So a day's journey in oblivious haze
   To serve our joys would lengthen and dilate.
O to arrive each Monday morn from Ind!
   To land each Tuesday from the rich Levant![2]   10
In little time a host of joys to bind,
   And keep our souls in one eternal pant!
This morn, my friend, and yester-evening taught
Me how to harbour such a happy thought.

What the Thrush Said

Lines From a Letter to John Hamilton Reynolds

O Thou whose face hath felt the Winter's wind,
   Whose eye has seen the snow-clouds hung in mist,
   And the black elm tops 'mong the freezing stars,
   To thee the spring will be a harvest-time.
O thou, whose only book has been the light
   Of supreme darkness which thou feddest on
   Night after night when Phoebus was away,
   To thee the Spring shall be a triple morn.
O fret not after knowledge – I have none,
   And yet my song comes native with the warmth.   10
O fret not after knowledge – I have none,
   And yet the Evening listens. He who saddens
At thought of idleness cannot be idle,
And he's awake who thinks himself asleep.

Sonnet – The Human Seasons

Four seasons fill the measure of the year;
   There are four seasons in the mind of man:
He has his lusty Spring, when fancy clear
   Takes in all beauty with an easy span:
He has his Summer, when luxuriously
   Spring's honied cud of youthful thought he loves
To ruminate, and by such dreaming nigh
   His nearest unto heaven: quiet coves
His soul has in its Autumn, when his wings
   He furleth close; contented so to look   10
On mists in idleness – to let fair things
   Pass by unheeded as a threshold brook.[1]
He has his Winter too of pale misfeature,[2]
Or else he would forego his mortal nature.

Extracts from an Opera

O! Were I one of the Olympian twelve,
Their godships should pass this into a law, –
That when a man doth set himself in toil
After some beauty veiled far away,
Each step he took should make his lady's hand
More soft, more white, and her fair cheek more fair;
And for each briar-berry he might eat,
A kiss should bud upon the tree of love,
And pulp and ripen richer every hour,
To melt away upon the traveller's lips.   10
. . .

Daisy's Song

I

The sun, with his great eye,
Sees not so much as I;
And the moon, all silver-proud,
Might as well be in a cloud.

II

And O the spring – the spring!
I lead the life of a king!
Couch'd in the teeming grass,
I spy each pretty lass.

III

I look where no one dares,
And I stare where no one stares,
And when the night is nigh,
Lambs bleat my lullaby.
. . .

Folly's Song

When wedding fiddles are a-playing,
                Huzza for folly O!

And when maidens go a-maying,
      Huzza for folly O!
When a milk-pail is upset,
      Huzza for folly O!
And the clothes left in the wet,
      Huzza for folly O!
When the barrel's set abroach,[1]
      Huzza for folly O!
When Kate Eyebrow keeps a coach,
      Huzza for folly O!
When the pig is over-roasted,
      Huzza for folly O!
And the cheese is over-toasted,
      Huzza for folly O!
When Sir Snap is with his lawyer,
      Huzza for folly O!
And Miss Chip has kiss'd the sawyer,
      Huzza for folly O!

. . .

Oh, I am frighten'd with most hateful thoughts!
Perhaps her voice is not a nightingale's,
Perhaps her teeth are not the fairest pearl;
Her eye-lashes may be, for aught I know,
Not longer than the mayfly's small fan-horns;
There may not be one dimple on her hand;
And freckles many; ah! a careless nurse,
In haste to teach the little thing to walk,
May have crumpt[2] up a pair of Dian's legs,
And warpt the ivory of a Juno's neck.

. . .

Song

I

The stranger lighted from his steed,
And ere he spake a word,
He seiz'd my lady's lily hand,
And kiss'd it all unheard.

II

The stranger walk'd into the hall,
And ere he spake a word,
He kiss'd my lady's cherry lips,
And kiss'd 'em all unheard.

III

The stranger walk'd into the bower, –
But my lady first did go, –
Aye hand in hand into the bower,
Where my lord's roses blow.

IV

My lady's maid had a silken scarf,
And a golden ring had she,
And a kiss from the stranger, as off he went
Again on his fair palfrey.
. . .
Asleep! O sleep a little while, white pearl!
And let me kneel, and let me pray to thee,
And let me call Heaven's blessing on thine eyes,
And let me breathe into the happy air,
That doth enfold and touch thee all about,
Vows of my slavery, my giving up,
My sudden adoration, my great love!

Faery Songs

I

Shed no tear – O shed no tear!
The flower will bloom another year.
Weep no more – O weep no more!
Young buds sleep in the root's white core.
Dry your eyes – O dry your eyes,
For I was taught in Paradise
To ease my breast of melodies –
            Shed no tear.

Overhead – look overhead
'Mong the blossoms white and red –   10
Look up, look up – I flutter now
On this flush pomegranate bough –
See me – 'tis this silvery bill
Ever cures the good man's ill –
Shed no tear – O shed no tear!
The flower will bloom another year,
Adieu – Adieu – I fly, adieu,
I vanish in the heaven's blue –
          Adieu, Adieu!

II

Ah! woe is me! poor silver-wing!
    That I must chant thy lady's dirge,
And death to this fair haunt of spring,
    Of melody, and streams of flowery verge, –
Poor silver-wing! ah! woe is me!
          That I must see
These blossoms snow upon thy lady's pall!
    Go, pretty page! and in her ear
    Whisper that the hour is near!
    Softly tell her not to fear   10
Such calm favonian[1] burial!
    Go, pretty page! and soothly tell, –
    The blossoms hang by a melting spell,
And fall they must, ere a star wink thrice
          Upon her closed eyes,
That now in vain are weeping their last tears,
    At sweet life leaving, and these arbours green, –
Rich dowry from the Spirit of the Spheres, –
    Alas! poor Queen!

Sonnet to Homer

Standing aloof in giant ignorance,
   Of thee I hear and of the Cyclades,
As one who sits ashore and longs perchance
   To visit dolphin-coral in deep seas.
So thou wast blind; – but then the veil was rent,
   For Jove uncurtain'd Heaven to let thee live,
And Neptune made for thee a spumy tent,
   And Pan made sing for thee his forest-hive;
Aye on the shores of darkness there is light,
   And precipices show untrodden green,   10
There is a budding morrow in midnight,
   There is a triple sight in blindness keen;
Such seeing hadst thou, as it once befell
To Dian, Queen of Earth, and Heaven, and Hell.

Song

*[Written on a blank page in
Beaumont and Fletcher's Works, between
'Cupid's Revenge' and 'The Two Noble Kinsmen']*

I

Spirit here that reignest!
Spirit here that painest!
Spirit here that burnest!
Spirit here that mournest!
   Spirit, I bow
   My forehead low,
Enshaded with thy pinions.
   Spirit, I look
   All passion-struck
Into thy pale dominions.

II

Spirit here that laughest!
Spirit here that quaffest!
Spirit here that dancest!
Noble soul that prancest!
  Spirit, with thee
  I join in the glee
A-nudging the elbow of Momus.
  Spirit, I flush
  With a Bacchanal blush
Just fresh from the Banquet of Comus.[1]

Teignmouth

'Some doggerel' sent in a letter to B. R. Haydon

I

Here all the summer could I stay.
  For there's Bishop's teign
  And King's teign
And Coomb[1] at the clear teign head –
  Where close by the stream
  You may have your cream
All spread upon barley bread.

II

  There's Arch Brook
  And there's Larch Brook
Both turning many a mill;
  And cooling the drouth
  Of the salmon's mouth,
And fattening his silver gill.

III

  There is Wild wood,
  A mild hood
To the sheep on the lea o' the down,
  Where the golden furze,

With its green, thin spurs,
Doth catch at the maiden's gown.

IV

There is Newton marsh
    With its spear grass harsh –
A pleasant summer level
    Where the maidens sweet
    Of the Market Street,
Do meet in the dusk to revel.

V

There's the Barton rich
    With dyke and ditch
And hedge for the thrush to live in
    And the hollow tree
    For the buzzing bee
And a bank for the wasp to hive in.

VI

And O, and O
    The daisies blow
And the primroses are waken'd,
    And violets white
    Sit in silver plight,[2]
And the green bud's as long as the spike[3] end.

VII

Then who would go
    Into dark Soho,
And chatter with dack'd[4] hair'd critics,
    When he can stay
    For the new-mown hay,
And startle the dappled Prickets?[5]

The Devon Maid

Stanzas sent in a letter to B. R. Haydon

I

Where be ye going, you Devon maid?
    And what have ye there in the basket?
Ye tight little fairy just fresh from the dairy,
    Will ye give me some cream if I ask it?

II

I love your meads, and I love your flowers,
    And I love your junkets[1] mainly,
But 'hind the door I love kissing more,
    O look not so disdainly.

III

I love your hills, and I love your dales,
    And I love your flocks a-bleating –
But O, on the heather to lie together,
    With both our hearts a-beating!

IV

I'll put your basket all safe in a nook,
    Your shawl I hang up on the willow,
And we will sigh in the daisy's eye
    And kiss on a grass green pillow.

Epistle to John Hamilton Reynolds

Dear Reynolds! as last night I lay in bed,
There came before my eyes that wonted thread
Of shapes, and shadows, and remembrances,
That every other minute vex and please:
Things all disjointed come from north and south, –
Two Witch's eyes above a Cherub's mouth,
Voltaire[1] with casque[2] and shield and habergeon,
And Alexander with his nightcap on;
Old Socrates a-tying his cravat,
And Hazlitt playing with Miss Edgeworth's[3] cat;   10
And Junius Brutus, pretty well so so,[4]
Making the best of's way towards Soho.

   Few are there who escape these visitings, –
Perhaps one or two whose lives have patent wings,
And thro' whose curtains peeps no hellish nose,
No wild-boar tushes,[5] and no mermaid's toes;
But flowers bursting out with lusty pride,
And young Aeolian harps personified;
Some Titian colours touch'd into real life, –
The sacrifice goes on; the pontiff knife   20
Gleams in the sun, the milk-white heifer lows,
The pipes go shrilly, the libation flows:
A white sail shows above the green-head cliff,
Moves round the point, and throws her anchor stiff;
The mariners join hymn with those on land.

   You know the Enchanted Castle, – it doth stand
Upon a rock, on the border of a lake,
Nested in trees, which all do seem to shake
From some old magic-like Urganda's Sword.[6]
O Phoebus! that I had thy sacred word   30
To show this castle, in fair dreaming wise,
Unto my friend, while sick and ill he lies!

   You know it well enough, where it doth seem
A mossy place, a Merlin's Hall, a dream;

You know the clear lake, and the little isles,
The mountains blue, and cold near neighbour rills.
All which elsewhere are but half animate;
There do they look alive to love and hate,
To smiles and frowns; they seem a lifted mound
Above some giant, pulsing underground.   40

    Part of the Building was a chosen See,
Built by a banish'd Santon of Chaldee;[7]
The other part, two thousand years from him.
Was built by Cuthbert de Saint Aldebrim;[8]
Then there's a little wing, far from the sun,
Built by a Lapland witch[9] turn'd maudlin nun:
And many other juts of aged stone
Founded with many a mason-devil's groan.

    The doors all look as if they op'd themselves,
The windows as if latch'd by fays and elves,   50
And from them comes a silver flash of light,
As from the westward of a summer's night;
Or like a beauteous woman's large blue eyes
Gone mad thro' olden songs and poesies.

    See! what is coming from the distance dim!
A golden galley all in silken trim!
Three rows of oars are lightening, moment whiles,[10]
Into the verd'rous bosoms of those isles;
Towards the shade, under the castle wall.
It comes in silence, – now 'tis hidden all.   60
The clarion sounds, and from a postern-gate
An echo of sweet music doth create
A fear in the poor herdsman, who doth bring
His beast to trouble the enchanted spring. –
He tells of the sweet music, and the spot,
To all his friends, and they believe him not.

    O that our dreamings all, of sleep or wake,
Would all their colours from the sunset take:
From something of material sublime,
Rather than shadow our own soul's daytime   70

In the dark void of night. For in the world
We jostle, – but my flag is not unfurl'd[11]
On the Admiral-staff, – and so philosophise
I dare not yet! Oh, never will the prize,
High reason, and the love of good and ill,
Be my award! Things cannot to the will
Be settled, but they tease us out of thought;
Or is it that imagination brought
Beyond its proper bound, yet still confin'd,
Lost in a sort of purgatory blind,   80
Cannot refer to any standard law
Of either earth or heaven? It is a flaw
In happiness, to see beyond our bourn, –
It forces us in summer skies to mourn,
It spoils the singing of the nightingale.

   Dear Reynolds! I have a mysterious tale,
And cannot speak it: the first page I read
Upon a lampit[12] rock of green seaweed
Among the breakers; 'twas a quiet eve,
The rocks were silent, the wide sea did weave   90
An untumultuous fringe of silver foam
Along the flat brown sand; I was at home
And should have been most happy, – but I saw
Too far into the sea, where every maw
The greater on the less feeds evermore. –
But I saw too distinct into the core
Of an eternal fierce destruction,
And so from happiness I far was gone.
Still am I sick of it, and tho', today,
I've gather'd young spring-leaves, and flowers gay   100
Of periwinkle and wild strawberry,
Still do I that most fierce destruction see, –
The shark at savage prey, – the hawk at pounce, –
The gentle robin, like a pard or ounce,[13]
Ravening a worm, – Away, ye horrid moods!
Moods of one's mind! You know I hate them well.
You know I'd sooner be a clapping bell
To some Kamtschatcan[14] missionary church,
Than with these horrid moods be left i' the lurch.

Dawlish Fair

Over the hill and over the dale,
    And over the bourne to Dawlish,
Where ginger-bread wives have a scanty sale,
    And gingerbread nuts are smallish.

Fragment of an Ode to Maia,
Written on May Day, 1818

Mother of Hermes! and still youthful Maia!
        May I sing to thee
As thou wast hymned on the shores of Baiae?
        Or may I woo thee
In earlier Sicilian? or thy smiles
Seek as they once were sought, in Grecian isles,
By bards who died content on pleasant sward,
    Leaving great verse unto a little clan?
O, give me their old vigour, and unheard
    Save of the quiet primrose, and the span   10
        Of heaven and few ears,
Rounded by thee, my song should die away
        Content as theirs,
Rich in the simple worship of a day.

Acrostic

Georgiana Augusta Keats

Give me your patience Sister while I frame
Exact in capitals your golden name
Or sue the fair Apollo and he will
Rouse from his heavy slumber and instil
Great love in me for thee and Poesy.
Imagine not that greatest mastery
And kingdom over all the realms of verse
Nears more to heaven in aught than when we nurse
And surety give to love and brotherhood.

Anthropophagi[1] in Othello's mood;   10
Ulysses stormed, and his enchanted belt[2]
Glow with the Muse, but they are never felt
Unbosom'd so[3] and so eternal made,
Such tender incense in their laurel shade,
To all the regent sisters of the Nine
As this poor offering to you, sister mine.

Kind sister! aye, this third name says you are;
Enchanted has it been the Lord knows where.
And may it taste to you like good old wine,
Take you to real happiness and give   20
Sons, daughters and a home like honied hive.

Sonnet on Visiting the Tomb of Burns

The town, the churchyard, and the setting sun,
   The clouds, the trees, the rounded hills all seem,
   Though beautiful, cold – strange – as in a dream,
I dreamed long ago, now new begun.
The short-liv'd, paly summer is but won
   From winter's ague, for one hour's gleam;
   Though sapphire-warm, their stars do never beam:
All is cold beauty; pain is never done:
For who has mind to relish, Minos-wise,
   The real of beauty, free from that dead hue   10
     Sickly imagination and sick pride
   Cast wan upon it! Burns! with honour due
     I oft have honour'd thee. Great shadow, hide
Thy face; I sin against thy native skies.

Meg[1] Merrilies

I

Old Meg[1] she was a gipsy,
   And liv'd upon the moors:
Her bed it was the brown heath turf,
   And her house was out of doors.

II

Her apples were swart blackberries,
   Her currants pods o' broom;
Her wine was dew of the wild white rose,
   Her book a churchyard tomb.

III

Her brothers were the craggy hills,
   Her sisters larchen trees –
Alone with her great family
   She liv'd as she did please.

IV

No breakfast had she many a morn,
    No dinner many a noon,
And 'stead of supper she would stare
    Full hard against the moon.

V

But every morn of woodbine fresh
    She made her garlanding,
And every night the dark glen yew
    She wove, and she would sing.

VI

And with her fingers old and brown
    She plaited mats o'rushes,
And gave them to the cottagers
    She met among the bushes.

VII

Old Meg was brave as Margaret Queen[2]
    And tall as Amazon:
An old red blanket cloak she wore;
    A chip hat[3] had she on.
God rest her aged bones somewhere –
    She died full long agone!

A Song About Myself

From a Letter to Fanny Keats

I

There was a naughty boy,
    A naughty boy was he,
He would not stop at home,
    He could not quiet be –
        He took
        In his knapsack
        A book
        Full of vowels
        And a shirt
        With some towels –   10
        A slight cap
        For night cap –
        A hair brush,
        Comb ditto,
        New stockings
        For old ones
        Would split O!
        This knapsack
        Tight at's back
        He rivetted close   20
And followed his nose
        To the north,
        To the north,
And follow'd his nose
        To the north.

II

There was a naughty boy
    And a naughty boy was he,
For nothing would he do
    But scribble poetry –
        He took
        An ink stand
        In his hand

And a pen
Big as ten
In the other,   10
And away
In a pother
He ran
To the mountains
And fountains
And ghostes
And postes[1]
And witches
And ditches
And wrote   20
In his coat
When the weather
Was cool,
Fear of gout,
And without
When the weather
Was warm –
Och the charm
When we choose
To follow one's nose   30
   To the north,
   To the north,
To follow one's nose
   To the north!

III

There was a naughty boy
  And a naughty boy was he,
He kept little fishes
  In washing tubs three
    In spite
    Of the might
    Of the maid
    Nor afraid
    Of his Granny-good
    He often would   10

Hurly burly
Get up early
And go
By hook or crook
To the brook
And bring home
Miller's thumb,[2]
Tittlebat
Not over fat,
Minnows small   20
As the stall
Of a glove,
Not above
The size
Of a nice
Little baby's
Little fingers –
O he made
'Twas his trade
Of fish a pretty kettle   30
A kettle –
A kettle
Of fish a pretty kettle
A kettle!

IV

There was a naughty boy,
And a naughty boy was he,
He ran away to Scotland
The people for to see –
Then he found
That the ground
Was as hard,
That a yard
Was as long,
That a song   10
Was as merry,
That a cherry
Was as red –

That lead
Was as weighty,
That fourscore
Was as eighty,
That a door
Was as wooden
As in England –   20
So he stood in his shoes
And he wonder'd,
He wonder'd,
He stood in his shoes
And he wonder'd.

A Galloway Song

From a Letter to Tom Keats

Ah! ken ye what I met the day
    Out oure[1] the mountains
A coming down by craggies grey
    An mossie fountains –
Ah goud hair'd Marie yeve[2] I pray
    Ane[3] minute's guessing –
For that I met upon the way
    Is past expressing.
As I stood where a rocky brig
    A torrent crosses   10
I spied upon a misty rig
    A troup o' horses –
And as they trotted down the glen
    I sped to meet them
To see if I might know the men
    To stop and greet them.
First Willie on his sleek mare came
    At canting gallop
His long hair rustled like a flame
    On board a shallop.   20
Then came his brother Rab and then
    Young Peggy's mither

And Peggy too – adown the glen
   They went together –
I saw her wrappit in her hood
   Fra wind and raining –
Her cheek was flush wi' timid blood
   Twixt growth and waning –
She turn'd her dazed head full oft
   For there her brithers   30
Came riding with her bridegroom soft
   And mony ithers.
Young Tam came up an' eyed me quick
   With reddened cheek –
Braw[4] Tam was daffed[5] like a chick –
   He coud na speak –
Ah Marie they are all gane hame
   Through blustering weather
An' every heart is full on flame
   A' light as feather.   40
Ah! Marie they are all gone hame
   Fra happy wedding,
Whilst I – Ah is it not a shame?
   Sad tears am shedding.

Sonnet to Ailsa Rock[1]

Hearken, thou craggy ocean pyramid!
   Give answer from thy voice, the sea-fowls' screams!
   When were thy shoulders mantled in huge streams?
When, from the sun, was thy broad forehead hid?
How long is't since the mighty power bid
   Thee heave to airy sleep from fathom dreams?
   Sleep in the lap of thunder or sunbeams,
Or when grey clouds are thy cold coverlid.
Thou answer'st not; for thou art dead asleep;
   Thy life is but two dead eternities –   10
The last in air, the former in the deep;
   First with the whales, last with the eagle-skies –
Drown'd wast thou till an earthquake made thee steep,
   Another cannot wake thy giant size.

Sonnet Written in the Cottage where Burns was Born

This mortal body of a thousand days
    Now fills, O Burns, a space in thine own room,
Where thou didst dream alone on budded bays,[1]
    Happy and thoughtless of thy day of doom!
My pulse is warm with thine own barley-bree,[2]
    My head is light with pledging a great soul,
My eyes are wandering, and I cannot see,
    Fancy is dead and drunken at its goal;
Yet can I stamp my foot upon thy floor,
    Yet can I ope thy window-sash to find   10
The meadow thou hast tramped o'er and o'er, –
    Yet can I think of thee till thought is blind, –
Yet can I gulp a bumper to thy name, –
O smile among the shades, for this is fame!

Lines Written in the Highlands after a
Visit to Burns's Country

There is a charm in footing slow across a silent plain,
Where patriot battle has been fought, where glory had the gain;
There is a pleasure on the heath where druids old have been,
Where mantles grey have rustled by and swept the nettles green;
There is a joy in every spot made known by times of old,
New to the feet, although each tale a hundred times be told;
There is a deeper joy than all, more solemn in the heart,
More parching to the tongue than all, of more divine a smart,
When weary steps forget themselves upon a pleasant turf,
Upon hot sand, or flinty road, or seashore iron scurf,   10
Toward the castle or the cot, where long ago was born
One who was great through mortal days, and died of fame unshorn,
Light heather-bells may tremble then, but they are far away;
Wood-lark may sing from sandy fern, – the sun may hear his lay;
Runnels may kiss the grass on shelves and shallows clear,
But their low voices are not heard, though come on travels drear;
Blood-red the sun may set behind black mountain peaks;

Blue tides may sluice and drench their time in caves and
                                         weedy creeks;
Eagles may seem to sleep wing-wide upon the air;
Ring-doves may flyconvuls'd across to some high-cedar'd lair;   20
But the forgotten eye is still fast lidded to the ground,
As Palmer's, that with weariness, mid-desert shrine hath found.
At such a time the soul's a child, in childhood is the brain;
Forgotten is the worldly heart – alone, it beats in vain. –
Aye, if a madman could have leave to pass a healthful day
To tell his forehead's swoon and faint when first began decay,
He might make tremble many a one whose spirit had gone forth
To find a Bard's low cradle-place about the silent North!
Scanty the hour and few the steps beyond the bourn of care,
Beyond the sweet and bitter world, – beyond it unaware!   30
Scanty the hour and few the steps, because a longer stay
Would bar return, and make a man forget his mortal way:
O horrible! to lose the sight of well remember'd face,
Of Brother's eyes, of Sister's brow – constant to every place;
Filling the air, as on we move, with portraiture intense;
More warm than those heroic tints that pain a painter's sense,
When shapes of old come striding by, and visages of old,
Locks shining black, hair scanty grey, and passions manifold.
No, no, that horror cannot be, for at the cable's length
Man feels the gentle anchor pull and gladdens in its strength: –   40
One hour, half-idiot, he stands by mossy waterfall,
But in the very next he reads his soul's memorial: –
He reads it on the mountain's height, where chance he
                                        may sit down
Upon rough marble diadem – that hill's eternal crown.
Yet be his anchor e'er so fast, room is there for a prayer
That man may never lose his mind on mountains black and bare;
That he may stray league after league some great birth place to find
And keep his vision clear from speck, his inward sight unblind.

The Gadfly

From a Letter to Tom Keats

I

All gentle folks who owe a grudge
   To any living thing
Open your ears and stay your trudge
   Whilst I in dudgeon sing.

II

The Gadfly he hath stung me sore –
   O may he ne'er sting you!
But we have many a horrid bore
   He may sting black and blue.

III

Has any here an old grey Mare
   With three legs all her store,
O put it to her Buttocks bare
   And straight she'll run on four.

IV

Has any here a Lawyer suit
   Of Seventeen-Forty-Three,[1]
Take Lawyer's nose and put it to 't
   And you the end will see.

V

Is there a Man in Parliament
   Dum[b-]founder'd in his speech,
O let his neighbour make a rent
   And put one in his breech.

VI

O Lowther[2] how much better thou
   Hadst figur'd t'other day
When to the folks thou mad'st a bow
   And hadst no more to say

VII

If lucky Gadfly had but ta'en
  His seat . . .[3]
And put thee to a little pain
  To save thee from a worse.

VIII

Better than Southey it had been,
  Better than Mr D—,
Better than Wordsworth too, I ween,
  Better than Mr V—.[4]

IX

Forgive me pray good people all
  For deviating so –
In spirit sure I had a call –
  And now I on will go.

X

Has any here a daughter fair
  Too fond of reading novels,
Too apt to fall in love with care
  And charming Mister Lovels,[5]

XI

O put a Gadfly to that thing
  She keeps so white and pert –
I mean the finger for the ring,
  And it will breed a wort.

XII

Has any here a pious spouse
  Who seven times a day
Scolds as King David pray'd,[6] to chouse
  And have her holy way –

XIII

O let a Gadfly's little sting
   Persuade her sacred tongue
That noises are a common thing.
   But that her bell has rung.

XIV

And as this is the summmum bo-
   num[7] of all conquering,
I leave 'withouten wordes mo'[8]
   The Gadfly's little sting.

Sonnet on Hearing the Bagpipe and Seeing 'The Stranger' Played at Inverary

Of late two dainties were before me plac'd
   Sweet, holy, pure, sacred and innocent,
   From the ninth sphere[1] to me benignly sent
That Gods might know my own particular taste:
First the soft Bagpipe mourn'd with zealous haste,
   The Stranger[2] next with head on bosom bent
   Sigh'd; rueful again the piteous Bagpipe went,
Again the Stranger sighings fresh did waste.
O Bagpipe thou didst steal my heart away –
   O Stranger thou my nerves from Pipe didst charm –   10
O Bagpipe thou didst reassert thy sway –
   Again thou Stranger gav'st me fresh alarm –
Alas! I could not choose. Ah! my poor heart.
Mum chance[3] art thou with both oblig'd to part.

Staffa[1]

Not Aladdin magian
Ever such a work began;
Not the wizard of the Dee[2]
Ever such a dream could see;
Not St John,[3] in Patmos' Isle,
In the passion of his toil,
When he saw the churches seven,
Golden aisl'd, built up in heaven,
Gaz'd at such a rugged wonder.
As I stood its roofing under,   10
Lo! I saw one sleeping there,
On the marble cold and bare.
While the surges wash'd his feet.
And his garments white did beat
Drench'd about the sombre rocks,
On his neck his well-grown locks,
Lifted dry above the main,
Were upon the curl again.
'What is this? and what art thou?'
Whisper'd I, and touch'd his brow;   20
'What art thou? and what is this?'
Whisper'd I, and strove to kiss
The spirit's hand, to wake his eyes;
Up he started in a trice:
'I am Lycidas,' said he,
'Fam'd in funeral minstrelsy!
This was architectur'd thus
By the great Oceanus! –
Here his mighty waters play
Hollow organs all the day;   30
Here by turns his dolphins all,
Finny palmers great and small,
Come to pay devotion due –
Each a mouth of pearls must strew.
Many a mortal of these days,
Dares to pass our sacred ways,
Dares to touch audaciously

This Cathedral of the Sea!
I have been the pontiff-priest
Where the waters never rest, 40
Where a fledgy sea-bird choir
Soars for ever; holy fire
I have hid from mortal man;
Proteus is my Sacristan.[4]
But the dulled eye of mortal
Hath pass'd beyond the rocky portal;
So for ever will I leave
Such a taint, and soon unweave
All the magic of the place.'
. . .
So saying, with a Spirit's glance 50
He dived!

Sonnet Written upon the Top of Ben Nevis

Read me a lesson, Muse, and speak it loud
   Upon the top of Nevis, blind in mist!
I look into the chasms, and a shroud
   Vapourous doth hide them, – just so much I wist
Mankind do know of hell; I look o'erhead,
   And there is sullen mist, – even so much
Mankind can tell of heaven; mist is spread
   Before the earth, beneath me, – even such,
Even so vague is man's sight of himself!
   Here are the craggy stones beneath my feet, – 10
Thus much I know that, a poor witless elf,
   I tread on them, – that all my eye doth meet
Is mist and crag, not only on this height,
But in the world of thought and mental might!

Ben Nevis – a Dialogue

[Persons: MRS CAMERON[1] and BEN NEVIS]

MRS CAMERON   Upon my life Sir Nevis I am pique'd
That I have so far panted tugg'd and reek'd
To do an hono[u]r to your old bald pate
And now am sitting on you just to bate,[2]
Without your paying me one compliment.
Alas 'tis so with all, when our intent
Is plain, and in the eye of all Mankind
We fair ones show a preference, too blind!
You gentle man immediately turn tail –
O let me then my hapless fate bewail!   10
Ungrateful baldpate, have I not disdain'd
The pleasant valleys – have I not, madbrain'd,
Deserted all my pickles and preserves,
My china closet too – with wretched nerves
To boot – say, wretched ingrate, have I not
Le[f]t my soft cushion chair and caudle[3] pot?
'Tis true I had no corns – no! thank the fates,
My shoemaker was always Mr Bates.
And if not Mr Bates why I'm not old!
Still dumb, ungrateful Nevis – still so cold!   20

*Here the Lady took some more w[h]iskey and was putting even more to
her lips when she dashed [it] to the ground for the mountain began to
grumble – which continued for a few minutes before he thus began,*

BEN NEVIS   What whining bit of tongue and mouth thus dares
Disturb my slumber of a thousand years?
Even so long my sleep has been secure –
And to be so awaked I'll not endure.
Oh pain – for since the eagle's earliest scream
I've had a dam[n]'d confounded ugly dream,
A nightmare sure. What, Madam, was it you?
It cannot be! My old eyes are not true!
Red-Crag,[4] my spectacles! Now let me see!
Good Heavens, Lady, how the gemini   30
Did you get here? O I shall split my sides!

I shall earthquake –

MRS CAMERON Sweet Nevis, do not quake, for though I love
You[r] honest countenance all things above,
Truly I should not like to be convey'd
So far into your bosom-gentle maid
Loves not too rough a treatment, gentle Sir –
Pray thee be calm and do not quake nor stir,
No not a stone, or I shall go in fits –

BEN NEVIS I must – I shall – I meet not such titbits –   40
I meet not such sweet creatures every day –
By my old nightcap, nightcap night and day,
I must have one sweet buss – I must and shall!
Red-Crag! – What, Madam, can you then repent
Of all the toil and vigour you have spent
To see Ben Nevis and to touch his nose?
Red-Crag, I say! O I must have them close!
Red-Crag, there lies beneath my farthest toe
A vein of sulphur – go dear Red-Crag, go –
And rub your flinty back against it – budge!   50
Dear Madam, I must kiss you, faith I must!
I must embrace you with my dearest gust![5]
Block-head, d'ye hear – Block-head,[6] I'll make her feel –
There lies beneath my east leg's northern heel
A cave of young earth dragons – well, my boy,
Go thither quick and so complete my joy;
Take you a bundle of the largest pines
And when the sun on fiercest phosphor shines
Fire them and ram them in the dragon's nest,
Then will the dragons fry and fizz their best   60
Until ten thousand now no bigger than
Poor alligators – poor things of one span –
Will each one swell to twice ten times the size
Of northern whale – then for the tender prize –
The moment then – for then will Red-Crag rub
His flinty back – and I shall kiss and snub
And press my dainty morsel to my breast.
Block-head, make haste!
                              O Muses weep the rest –
The lady fainted and he thought her dead
So pulled the clouds again about his head   70

And went to sleep again – soon she was rous'd
By her affrighted servants – next day hous'd
Safe on the lowly ground she bless'd her fate
That fainting fit was not delayed too late.

Translation from a Sonnet of Ronsard[1]

Nature withheld Cassandra in the skies,
    For more adornment, a full thousand years;
She took their cream of beauty's fairest dyes,
    And shap'd and tinted her above all Peers'
Meanwhile Love kept her dearly with his wings,
    And underneath their shadow fill'd her eyes
With such a richness that the cloudy Kings
    Of high Olympus utter'd slavish sighs.
When from the heavens I saw her first descend,
    My heart took fire, and only burning pains,   10
They were my pleasures – they my life's sad end;
    Love pour'd her beauty into my warm veins . . .

A Prophecy: to George Keats in America

'Tis the witching hour[1] of night,
Orbed is the moon and bright,
And the stars they glisten, glisten,
Seeming with bright eyes to listen –
        For what listen they?
For a song and for a charm,
See they glisten in alarm,
And the moon is waxing warm
        To hear what I shall say.
Moon! keep wide thy golden ears –   10
Hearken, stars! and hearken, spheres! –
Hearken, thou eternal sky!
I sing an infant's lullaby,
        A pretty lullaby.
Listen, listen, listen, listen,
Glisten, glisten, glisten, glisten,

And hear my lullaby!
Though the rushes that will make
Its cradle still are in the lake –
Though the linen that will be   20
Its swathe, is on the cotton tree –
Though the woollen that will keep
It warm, is on the silly[2] sheep –
Listen, starlight, listen, listen,
Glisten, glisten, glisten, glisten,
    And hear my lullaby!
Child, I see thee! Child, I've found thee
Midst of the quiet all around thee!
Child, I see thee! Child, I spy thee!
And thy mother sweet is nigh thee!   30
Child, I know thee! Child no more,
But a Poet evermore!
See, see, the lyre, the lyre,
In a flame of fire,
Upon the little cradle's top
Flaring, flaring, flaring,
Past the eyesight's bearing.
Awake it from its sleep,
And see if it can keep
Its eyes upon the blaze –   40
    Amaze, amaze!
It stares, it stares, it stares,
It dares what no one dares!
It lifts its little hand into the flame
Unharm'd, and on the strings
Paddles a little tune, and sings,
With dumb endeavour sweetly –
Bard art thou completely!
    Little child
    O'th' western wild,   50
Bard art thou completely!
Sweetly with dumb endeavour,
A Poet now or never,
    Little child
    O' th' western wild,
A Poet now or never!

Stanzas

I

In a drear-nighted December,
    Too happy, happy tree,
Thy branches ne'er remember
    Their green felicity:
  The north cannot undo them,
  With a sleety whistle through them;
  Nor frozen thawings[1] glue them
      From budding at the prime.

II

In a drear-nighted December,
    Too happy, happy brook,
Thy bubblings ne'er remember
    Apollo's summer look;
  But with a sweet forgetting,
  They stay their crystal fretting,
  Never, never petting[2]
      About the frozen time.

III

Ah! would 'twere so with many
    A gentle girl and boy!
But were there ever any
    Writh'd not at passed joy?
  To know the change and feel it,
  When there is none to heal it,
  Nor numbed sense to steel it,
      Was never said in rhyme.

Spenserian Stanza

[*Written at the close of Canto II, Book V, of 'The Faerie Queene'.*]

In after-time, a sage of mickle lore
Yclep'd[1] Typographus,[2] the Giant[3] took,
And did refit his limbs as heretofore,
And made him read in many a learned book,
And into many a lively legend look;
Thereby in goodly themes so training him,
That all his brutishness he quite forsook,
When, meeting Artegall and Talus grim,
The one he struck stone-blind, the other's eyes wox dim.

The Eve of Saint Mark[1]

Upon a Sabbath-day it fell;
Twice holy was the Sabbath-bell,
That call'd the folk to evening prayer;
The city streets were clean and fair
From wholesome drench of April rains;
And, on the western window panes,
The chilly sunset faintly told
Of unmatur'd green valleys cold,
Of the green thorny bloomless hedge,
Of rivers new with spring-tide sedge,   10
Of primroses by shelter'd rills,
And daisies on the aguish hills.
Twice holy was the Sabbath-bell:
The silent streets were crowded well
With staid and pious companies,
Warm from their fireside orat'ries;
And moving, with demurest air,
To evensong, and vesper prayer.
Each arched porch, and entry low,
Was fill'd with patient folk and slow,   20
With whispers hush, and shuffling feet,
While play'd the organ loud and sweet.

The bells had ceas'd, the prayers begun,
And Bertha had not yet half done
A curious volume, patch'd and torn,
That all day long, from earliest morn,
Had taken captive her two eyes,
Among its golden broideries;[2]
Perplex'd her with a thousand things, –
The stars of Heaven, and angels' wings.   30
Martyrs in a fiery blaze,
Azure saints in silver rays,
Moses' breastplate,[3] and the seven
Candlesticks[4] John saw in Heaven.
The winged Lion[5] of Saint Mark,
And the Covenantal Ark,
With its many mysteries,
Cherubim and golden mice.[6]

Bertha was a maiden fair,
Dwelling in the old Minster Square;   40
From her fireside she could see,
Sidelong, its rich antiquity,
Far as the Bishop's garden wall;
Where sycamores and elm-trees tall,
Full-leav'd, the forest had outstript,
By no sharp north- wind ever nipt,
So shelter'd by the mighty pile.
Bertha arose, and read awhile,
With forehead 'gainst the window-pane.
Again she try'd, and then again,   50
Until the dusk eve left her dark
Upon the legend of St Mark.
From plaited lawn-frill, fine and thin,
She lifted up her soft warm chin,
With aching neck and swimming eyes,
And daz'd with saintly imageries.

All was gloom, and silent all,
And now and then the still footfall
Of one returning homewards late,
Past the echoing minstergate.   60

The clamorous daws,[7] that all the day
Above tree-tops and towers play,
Pair by pair had gone to rest,
Each in its ancient belfry nest,
Where asleep they fall betimes,
To music of the drowsy chimes.

All was silent, all was gloom,
Abroad and in the homely room:
Down she sat, poor cheated soul!
And struck a lamp from the dismal coal;   70
Lean'd forward, with bright drooping hair
And slant book, full against the glare.
Her shadow, in uneasy guise,
Hover'd about, a giant size,
On ceiling-beam and old oak chair,
The parrot's cage, and panel square;
And the warm angled winter screen,
On which were many monsters seen,
Call'd doves of Siam, Lima mice,
And legless birds of Paradise,   80
Macaw, and tender Avadavat,[8]
And silken-furr'd Angora cat.
Untir'd she read, her shadow still
Glower'd about, as it would fill
The room with wildest forms and shades,
As though some ghostly queen of spades[9]
Had come to mock behind her back,
And dance, and ruffle her garments black.
Untir'd she read the legend page,
Of holy Mark, from youth to age,   90
On land, on sea, in pagan chains,
Rejoicing for his many pains.
Sometimes the learned eremite,
With golden star, or dagger bright,[10]
Referr'd to pious poesies
Written in smallest crow-quill[11] size
Beneath the text; and thus the rhyme
Was parcell'd out from time to time:
 – 'Als writith he of swevenis,[12]

Men han beforne they wake in bliss,   100
Whanne that hir friendes thinke hem bound
In crimped shroude farre under grounde;
And how a litling child mote be
A saint er its nativitie,
Gif that the modre (God her blesse!)
Kepen in solitarinesse,
And kissen devoute the holy croce.
Of Goddes love, and Sathan's force, –
He writith; and thinges many mo:
Of swiche thinges I may not show.   110
Bot I must tellen verilie
Somdel[13] of Sainte Cicilie,[14]
And chieflie what he auctorethe[15]
Of Sainte Markis life and dethe:'

    At length her constant eyelids come
Upon the fervent martyrdom;
Then lastly to his holy shrine,[16]
Exalt amid the tapers' shine
At Venice, –

Ode to Fanny

I

Physician Nature! let my spirit blood![1]
  O ease my heart of verse and let me rest;
Throw me upon thy Tripod,[2] till the flood
  Of stifling numbers ebbs from my full breast.
A theme! a theme! great nature! give a theme;
      Let me begin my dream.
I come – I see thee, as thou standest there,
Beckon me out[3] into the wintry air.

II

Ah! dearest love, sweet home of all my fears,
  And hopes, and joys, and panting miseries. –
Tonight, if I may guess, thy beauty wears
      A smile of such delight,
      As brilliant and as bright.
  As when with ravished, aching, vassal eyes,
      Lost in soft amaze,
      I gaze, I gaze!

III

Who now, with greedy looks, eats up my feast?
  What stare outfaces now my silver moon!
Ah! keep that hand unravished at the least;
      Let, let, the amorous burn –
      But, pr'ythee, do not turn
  The current of your heart from me so soon
      O! save, in charity,
      The quickest pulse for me.

IV

Save it for me, sweet love! though music breathe
  Voluptuous visions into the warm air;
Though swimming through the dance's dangerous
                                        wreath,
      Be like an April day,

> Smiling and cold and gay,
> A temperate lily, temperate as fair;
>   Then, Heaven! there will be
>   A warmer June for me.

V

> Why, this – you'll say, my Fanny! is not true
>   Put your soft hand upon your snowy side,
> Where the heart beats: confess – 'tis nothing new –
>   Must not a woman be
>   A feather on the sea,
>   Sway'd to and fro by every wind and tide?
>   Of as uncertain speed
>   As blow-ball[4] from the mead?

VI

> I know it – and to know it is despair
>   To one who loves you as I love, sweet Fanny!
> Whose heart goes fluttering for you everywhere,
>   Nor, when away you roam,
>   Dare keep its wretched home,
>   Love, love alone, his pains severe and many:
>   Then, loveliest! keep me free,
>   From torturing jealousy.

VII

> Ah! if you prize my subdued soul above
>   The poor, the fading, brief, pride of an hour;
> Let none profane my Holy See of love,
>   Or with a rude hand break
>   The sacramental cake:
>   Let none else touch the just new-budded flower;
>   If not – may my eyes close,
>   Love! on their lost repose.

Sonnet to Sleep

O soft embalmer of the still midnight,
  Shutting, with careful fingers and benign,
Our gloom – pleas'd eyes, embower'd from the light,
  Enshaded in forgetfulness divine:
O soothest Sleep! if so it please thee, close
  In midst of this thine hymn my willing eyes,
Or wait the 'Amen,' ere thy poppy throws
  Around my bed its lulling charities.
Then save me, or the passed day will shine
Upon my pillow, breeding many woes, –   10
  Save me from curious conscience, that still lords
Its strength for darkness, burrowing like a mole;
  Turn the key deftly in the oiled wards,
And seal the hushed casket of my Soul.

Song

I

Hush, hush! tread softly! hush, hush my dear!
  All the house is asleep, but we know very well
That the jealous, the jealous old bald-pate may hear,
  Tho' you've padded his nightcap – O sweet Isabel!
    Tho' your feet are more light than a Fairy's feet,
    Who dances on bubbles where brooklets meet. –
Hush, hush! soft tiptoe! hush, hush my dear!
For less than a nothing the jealous can hear.

II

No leaf doth tremble, no ripple is there
  On the river, – all's still, and the night's sleepy eye
Closes up, and forgets all its Lethean care,
  Charm'd to death by the drone of the humming Mayfly;
    And the moon, whether prudish or complaisant,
    Has fled to her bower, well knowing I want
No light in the dusk, no torch in the gloom,
But my Isabel's eyes, and her lips pulp'd with bloom.

III

Lift the latch! ah gently! ah tenderly – sweet!
　We are dead if that latchet gives one little clink!
Well done – now those lips, and a flowery seat –
　The old man may sleep, and the planets may wink;
　　The shut rose shall dream of our loves, and awake
　　Full blown, and such warmth for the morning's take
The stock-dove shall hatch her soft brace and shall coo,
While I kiss to the melody, aching all through!

Song

I had a dove and the sweet dove died;
　And I have thought it died of grieving:
O, what could it grieve for? Its feet were tied,
　With a silken thread of my own hand's weaving;
Sweet little red feet! why should you die –
Why should you leave me, sweet bird! why?
You liv'd alone in the forest-tree,
Why, pretty thing! would you not live with me?
I kiss'd you oft and gave you white peas;
Why not live sweetly, as in the green trees?   10

Ode on Indolence

They toil not, neither do they spin.[1]

I

One morn before me were three figures seen,
　With bowed necks, and joined hands, side-faced;
And one behind the other stepp'd serene,
　In placid sandals, and in white robes graced;
They pass'd, like figures on a marble urn,
　When shifted round to see the other side;
　　They came again; as when the urn once more
Is shifted round, the first seen shades return;
　And they were strange to me, as may betide
　　With vases, to one deep in Phidian lore.[2]

II

How is it, Shadows! that I knew ye not?
  How came ye muffled in so hush a mask?
Was it a silent deep-disguised plot
  To steal away, and leave without a task
My idle days? Ripe was the drowsy hour;
  The blissful cloud of summer-indolence
    Benumb'd my eyes; my pulse grew less and less;
Pain had no sting, and pleasure's wreath no flower:
  O, why did ye not melt, and leave my sense
    Unhaunted quite of all but – nothingness?

III

A third time pass'd they by, and, passing, turn'd
  Each one the face a moment whiles to me;
Then faded, and to follow them I burn'd
  And ach'd for wings because I knew the three;
The first was a fair Maid, and Love her name;
  The second was Ambition, pale of cheek,
    And ever watchful with fatigued eye;
The last, whom I love more, the more of blame
  Is heap'd upon her, maiden most unmeek, –
    I knew to be my demon[3] Poesy.

IV

They faded, and, forsooth! I wanted wings:
  O folly! What is love! and where is it?
And for that poor Ambition! it springs
  From a man's little heart's short fever-fit;
For Poesy! – no, – she has not a joy, –
  At least for me, – so sweet as drowsy noons,
    And evenings steep'd in honied indolence;
O, for an age so shelter'd from annoy,
  That I may never know how change the moons,
    Or hear the voice of busy commonsense!

V

And once more came they by; – alas! wherefore?
  My sleep had been embroider'd with dim dreams;

My soul had been a lawn besprinkled o'er
   With flowers, and stirring shades, and baffled beams:
The morn was clouded, but no shower fell,
    Tho' in her lids hung the sweet tears of May;
      The open casement press'd a new-leav'd vine,
    Let in the budding warmth and throstle's lay;[4]
O Shadows! 'twas a time to bid farewell!
    Upon your skirts had fallen no tears of mine.

VI

So, ye three Ghosts, adieu! Ye cannot raise
   My head cool-bedded in the flowery grass;
For I would not be dieted with praise,
   A pet-lamb in a sentimental farce!
Fade softly from my eyes, and be once more
   In masque-like figures on the dreamy urn;
    Farewell! I yet have visions for the night,
And for the day faint visions there is store;
    Vanish, ye Phantoms! from my idle spright,
   Into the clouds, and never more return!

Sonnet

Why did I laugh tonight? No voice will tell:
   No God, no Demon of severe response,
Deigns to reply from heaven or from hell.
   Then to my human heart I turn at once.
Heart! Thou and I are here sad and alone;
   I say, why did I laugh! O mortal pain!
O Darkness! Darkness! ever must I moan,
   To question Heaven and Hell and Heart in vain.
Why did I laugh? I know this Being's lease,
   My fancy to its utmost blisses spreads;   10
Yet would I on this very midnight cease,
   And the world's gaudy ensigns[1] see in shreds;
Verse, Fame, and Beauty are intense indeed,
But Death intenser – Death is Life's high meed.

Sonnet

A Dream, after Reading Dante's Episode of Paulo and Francesca[1]

As Hermes once took to his feathers light,
· When lulled Argus, baffled, swoon'd and slept,
So on a Delphic reed, my idle spright
    So play'd, so charm'd, so conquer'd, so bereft
The dragon-world[2] of all its hundred eyes;
    And, seeing it asleep, so fled away –
Not to pure Ida[3] with its snow-cold skies,
    Nor unto Tempe where Jove griev'd[4] a day;
But to that second circle[5] of sad hell,
    Where 'mid the gust, the whirlwind, and the flaw   10
Of rain and hailstones, lovers need not tell
    Their sorrows. Pale were the sweet lips I saw,
Pale were the lips I kiss'd, and fair the form
I floated with, about that melancholy storm.

An Extempore

From a Letter to George Keats and His Wife

When they were come into the Faery's Court
They rang – no one at home – all gone to sport
And dance and kiss and love as faeries do
For Fa[e]ries be as humans, lovers true –
Amid the woods they were, so lone and wild,
Where even the Robin feels himself exil'd
And where the very brooks as if afraid
Hurry along to some less magic shade.
'No one at home!' the fretful princess cried
'And all for nothing such a dre[a]ry ride,   10
And all for nothing my new diamond cross,
No one to see my Persian feathers[1] toss,
No one to see my Ape, my Dwarf, my Fool,[2]
Or how I pace my Otaheitan[3] mule.
Ape, Dwarf and Fool, why stand you gaping there?

Burst the door open, quick – or I declare
I'll switch you soundly and in pieces tear.'
The dwarf began to tremble and the ape
Star'd at the fool, the fool was all agape,
The Princess grasp'd her switch, but just in time   20
The dwarf with piteous face began to rhyme.
'O mighty Princess did you ne'er hear tell
What your poor servants know but too too well?
Know you the three great crimes in faery land?
The first, alas! poor Dwarf, I understand –
I made a whipstock of a faery's wand –
The next is snoring in their company –
The next, the last, the direst of the three
Is making free when they are not at home.
I was a Prince – a baby prince – my doom   30
You see, I made a whipstock of a wand –
My top has henceforth slept in faery land.
He was a Prince, the Fool, a grown up Prince,
But he has never been a King's son since
He fell a-snoring at a faery Ball –
Your poor Ape was a prince and he, poor thing,
Picklock'd a faery's boudour – now no king,
But ape – so pray your highness stay awhile;
'Tis sooth indeed, we know it to our sorrow –
Persist and *you* may be an ape tomorrow' –   40
While the Dwarf spake the Princess all for spite
Peal'd [*sic*] the brown hazel twig to lily white,
Clench'd her small teeth, and held her lips apart,
Try'd to look unconcern'd with beating heart.
They saw her highness had made up her mind
And quaver'd[4] like the reeds before the wind,
And they had had it, but, O happy chance!
The Ape for very fear began to dance
And grin'd as all his ugliness did ache –
She staid her vixen fingers for his sake,   50
He was so very ugly: then she took
Her pocket glass mirror and began to look
First at herself and [then] at him and then
She smil'd at her own beauteous face again.
Yet for all this – for all her pretty face

She took it in her head to see the place.
Women gain little from experience
Either in Lovers, husbands or expense.
The more the beauty, the more fortune too,
Beauty before the wide world never knew.
So each fair reasons – tho' it oft miscarries.   60
She thought *her* pretty face would please the fa[e]ries.
'My darling Ape I won't whip you today –
Give me the Picklock, sirrah, and go play.'
They all three wept – but counsel was as vain
As crying cup biddy⁵ to drops of rain.
Yet lingeringly did the sad Ape forth draw
The Picklock from the Pocket in his Jaw.
The Princess took it and dismounting straight
Trip'd in blue silver'd slippers to the gate   70
And touch'd the wards, the door full cou[r]teou[s]ly
Opened – she enter'd with her servants three.
Again it clos'd and there was nothing seen
But the Mule grazing on the herbage green.

End of Canto xii

CANTO THE XIII

The Mule no sooner saw himself alone
Than he prick'd up his ears – and said 'well done!
At least, unhappy Prince, I may be free –
No more a Princess shall side-saddle me.
O King of Othaietè – tho' a Mule
"Aye every inch a King" – tho' "Fortune's fool"⁶ –   80
Well done – for by what Mr Dwarfy said
I would not give a sixpence for her head.'
Even as he spake he trotted in high glee
To the knotty side of an old pollard tree
And rub['d] his sides against the mossed bark
Till his girths burst and left him naked stark
Except his bridle – how get rid of that,
Buckled and tied with many a twist and plait?
At last it struck him to pretend to sleep
And then the thievish monkeys down would creep   90

And filch[7] the unpleasant trammels[8] quite away.
No sooner thought of than adown he lay,
Sham'd a good snore – the monkey-men descended
And whom they thought to injure they befriended.
They hung his bridle on a topmost bough
And of[f] he went, run, trot, or anyhow –
    Brown is gone to bed – and I am tired of rhyming
. . .

Spenserian Stanzas on Charles Armitage Brown[1]

I

He is to weet[2] a melancholy carle:[3]
Thin in the waist, with bushy head of hair,
As hath the seeded thistle when in parle
It holds the Zephyr, ere it sendeth fair
Its light balloons into the summer air;
Therto his beard had not begun to bloom,
No brush had touch'd his chin or razor sheer;
No care had touch'd his cheek with mortal doom,
But new he was and bright as scarf from Persian loom.

II

Ne cared he for wine, or half-and-half[4]
Ne cared he for fish or flesh or fowl,
And sauces held he worthless as the chaff;
He 'sdeigned[5] the swine-head at the wassail-bowl;[6]
Ne with lewd ribbalds sat he cheek by jowl;
Ne with sly Lemans[7] in the scorner's chair;
But after water-brooks this Pilgrim's soul
Panted, and all his food was woodland air
Though he would oft-times feast on gilliflowers rare.

III

The slang of cities in no wise he knew,
Tipping the wink to him was heathen Greek;
He sipp'd no olden Tom or ruin blue,[8]
Or nantz or cherry-brandy drank full meek

By many a damsel hoarse and rouge of cheek;
Nor did he know each aged watchman's beat,
Nor in obscured purlieus would he seek
For curled Jewesses, with ankles neat,
Who as they walk abroad make tinkling with their feet.

Two or Three

From a Letter to His Sister

Two or three posies
With two or three simples[1] –
Two or three noses
With two or three pimples –
Two or three wise men
And two or three ninny's –
Two or three purses
And two or three guineas –
Two or three raps
At two or three doors –   10
Two or three naps
Of two or three hours –
Two or three cats
And two or three mice
Two or three sprats
At a very great price –
Two or three sandies
And two or three tabbies –
Two or three dandies
And two Mrs —[2] mum!   20
Two or three smiles
And two or three frowns –
Two or three miles
To two or three towns –
Two or three pegs
For two or three bonnets –
Two or three dove eggs
To hatch into sonnets.

La Belle Dame Sans Merci[1]

I

Ah, what can ail thee, wretched wight,
    Alone and palely loitering;
The sedge is wither'd from the lake,
    And no birds sing.

II

Ah, what can ail thee, wretched wight,
    So haggard and so woebegone?
The squirrel's granary is full,
    And the harvest's done.

III

I see a lily on thy brow,
    With anguish moist and fever dew;
And on thy cheek a fading rose
    Fast withereth too.

IV

I met a lady in the meads
    Full beautiful, a faery's child;
Her hair was long, her foot was light,
    And her eyes were wild.

V

I set her on my pacing steed,
    And nothing else saw all day long;
For sideways would she lean, and sing
    A feary's song.

VI

I made a garland for her head,
    And bracelets too, and fragrant zone;
She look'd at me as she did love,
    And made sweet moan.

VII

She found me roots of relish sweet,
   And honey wild, and manna dew;
And sure in language strange she said,
   I love thee true.

VIII

She took me to her elfin grot,
   And there she gaz'd and sighed deep,
And there I shut her wild sad eyes –
   So kiss'd to sleep.

IX

And there we slumber'd on the moss,
   And there I dream'd, ah woe betide,
The latest dream I ever dream'd
   On the cold hillside.

X

I saw pale kings, and princes too,
   Pale warriors, death-pale were they all;
Who cry'd – 'La belle Dame sans merci
   Hath thee in thrall!'[2]

XI

I saw their starv'd lips in the gloam[3]
   With horrid warning gaped wide,
And I awoke, and found me here
   On the cold hillside.

XII

And this is why I sojourn here
   Alone and palely loitering,
Though the sedge is wither'd from the lake,
   And no birds sing.

Song of Four Faeries – Fire, Air, Earth, and Water –
Salamander, Zephyr, Dusketha and Breama[1]

SALAMANDER	Happy, happy glowing fire!
ZEPHYR	Fragrant air! delicious light!
DUSKETHA	Let me to my glooms retire!
BREAMA	I to green-weed rivers bright!

SALAMANDER   Happy, happy glowing fire!
Dazzling bowers of soft retire,
Ever let my nourish'd wing,
Like a bat's, still wandering.
Faintless fan your fiery spaces,
Spirit sole in deadly places.   10
In unhaunted roar and blaze,
Open eyes that never daze,
Let me see the myriad shapes
Of men, and beasts, and fish, and apes,
Portray'd in many a fiery den,
And wrought by spumy bitumen.
On the deep intenser roof,
Arched every way aloof,
Let me breathe upon their skies,
And anger their live tapestries;[2]   20
Free from cold, and every care,
Of chilly rain, and shivering air.

ZEPHYR   Spirit of Fire – away! away!
Or your very roundelay
Will sear my plumage newly budded
From its quilled sheath, all studded
With the selfsame dews that fell
On the May-grown Asphodel.
Spirit of Fire – away! away!

BREAMA   Spirit of Fire – away! away!   30
Zephyr, blue-eyed Faery, turn,
And see my cool sedge-bury'd urn,

Where it rests its mossy brim
'Mid water-mint and cresses dim;
And the flowers, in sweet troubles,
Lift their eyes above the bubbles,
Like our Queen,[3] when she would please
To sleep, and Oberon *will* tease.
Love me, blue-eyed Faery, true!
Soothly I am sick for you.   40

ZEPHYR   Gentle Breama! by the first
Violet young nature nurst,
I will bathe myself with thee,
So you sometimes follow me
To my home, far, far, in west,
Beyond the nimble-wheeled quest
Of the golden-browed sun:
Come with me, o'er tops of trees.
To my fragrant palaces,
Where they ever floating are   50
Beneath the cherish of a star
Call'd Vesper, who with silver veil
Ever hides his brilliance pale,
Ever gently-drows'd doth keep
Twilight for the Fayes to sleep.
Fear not that your watery hair
Will thirst in drouthy ringlets there;
Clouds of stored summer rains
Thou shalt taste, before the stains
Of the mountain soil they take,   60
And too unlucent[4] for thee make.
I love thee, crystal Faery, true!
Sooth I am as sick for you!

SALAMANDER   Out, ye aguish[5] Faeries, out!
Chilly lovers, what a rout
Keep ye with your frozen breath.
Colder than the mortal death.
Adder-eyed[6] Dusketha, speak,
Shall we leave these, and go seek
In the earth's wide entrails old   70
Couches warm as their's are cold?

O for a fiery gloom and thee,
Dusketha, so enchantingly
Freckle-wing'd and lizard-sided!

DUSKETHA   By thee, Sprite, will I be guided!
I care not for cold or heat;
Frost and flame, or sparks, or sleet,
To my essence are the same; –
But I honour more the flame.
Sprite of Fire, I follow thee   80
Wheresoever it may be,
To the torrid spouts and fountains,
Underneath earth-quaked mountains;
Or, at thy supreme desire,
Touch the very pulse of fire
With my bare unlidded eyes.

SALAMANDER   Sweet Dusketha! paradise!
Off, ye icy Spirits, fly!
Frosty creatures of the sky!

DUSKETHA   Breathe upon them, fiery sprite!   90

ZEPHYR AND DUSKETHA   Away! away to our delight!

SALAMANDER   Go, feed on icicles, while we
Bedded in tongue-flames will be.

DUSKETHA   Lead me to those feverous glooms,
Sprite of Fire!

BREAMA   Me to the blooms,
Blue-eyed Zephyr, of those flowers
Far in the west where the May-cloud lowers:
And the beams of still Vesper, when winds are all wist,[7]
Are shed thro' the rain and the milder mist,
And twilight your floating bowers.   100

Two Sonnets on Fame

I

Fame, like a wayward Giri, will still be coy
　　To those who woo her with too slavish knees,
But makes surrender to some thoughtless boy,
　　And dotes the more upon a heart at ease;
She is a Gipsey, will not speak to those
　　Who have not learnt to be content without her;
A Jilt, whose ear was never whisper'd close,
　　Who thinks they scandal her who talk about her;
A very Gipsey is she, Nilus-born,[1]
　　Sister-in-law to jealous Potiphar;[2]   10
Ye lovesick Bards, repay her scorn for scorn,
　　Ye Artists lovelorn, madmen that ye are!
Make your best bow to her and bid adieu,
Then, if she likes it, she will follow you.

II

You cannot eat your cake and have it too. – *Proverb*

How fever'd is the man, who cannot look
　　Upon his mortal days with temperate blood,
Who vexes all the leaves of his life's book,
　　And robs his fair name of its maidenhood;
It is as if the rose should pluck herself,
　　Or the ripe plum finger its misty bloom,
As if a Naiad, like a meddling elf,
　　Should darken her pure grot with muddy gloom,
But the rose leaves herself upon the briar,
　　For winds to kiss and grateful bees to feed,   10
And the ripe plum still wears its dim attire
　　The undisturbed lake has crystal space,
　　Why then should man, teasing the world for grace,
Spoil his salvation for a fierce miscreed?[3]

Sonnet on the Sonnet

If by dull rhymes our English must be chain'd,
And, like Andromeda, the Sonnet sweet
Fetter'd, in spite of pained loveliness,
Let us find out, if we must be constrain'd,
Sandals more interwoven and complete
To fit the naked foot of Poesy:
Let us inspect the Lyre, and weigh the stress
Of every chord, and see what may be gain'd
By ear industrious, and attention meet;
Misers of sound and syllable, no less   10
Than Midas of his coinage, let us be
Jealous of dead leaves in the bay wreath crown;[1]
So, if we may not let the Muse be free,
She will be bound with garlands of her own.

Apollo and the Graces

Written to the Tune of the Air in 'Don Giovanni'[1]

APOLLO   Which of the fairest three
                 Today will ride with me?
My steeds are all pawing at the threshold of the morn:
                 Which of the fairest three
                 Today will ride with me
Across the gold Autumn's whole Kingdom of corn?

THE GRACES *all answer*   I will, I – I – I –
                 O young Apollo let me fly
                   Along with thee,
                 I will – I, I, I,
                   The many wonders see
                 I – I – I – I –   10
And thy lyre shall never have a slackened string
                   I, I, I, I,
Thro the golden day will sing.

You Say You Love

I

You say you love; but with a voice
   Chaster than a nun's, who singeth
The soft vespers to herself
   While the chime-bell ringeth –
     O love me truly!

II

You say you love; but with a smile
   Cold as sunrise in September,
As you were Saint Cupid's nun,
   And kept his weeks of Ember.[1]
     O love me truly!

III

You say you love – but then your lips
   Coral tinted teach no blisses.
More than coral in the sea –
   They never pout for kisses –
     O love me truly!

IV

You say you love; but then your hand
   No soft squeeze for squeeze returneth,
It is like a statue's dead –
   While mine to passion burneth –
     O love me truly!

V

O breathe a word or two of fire!
   Smile, as if those words should burn me,
Squeeze as lovers should – O kiss
   And in thy heart inurn me!
     O love me truly!

Otho the Great[1]
A Tragedy in Fve Acts

Dramatis Personae

OTHO THE GREAT, *Emperor of Germany*

LUDOLPH, *his son*

CONRAD, *Duke of Franconia*

ALBERT, *a knight, favoured by Otho*

SIGIFRED, *an officer, friend of Ludolph*

THEODORE ⎱
GONFRED ⎰ *officers*

ETHELBERT, *an abbot*

GERSA, *Prince of Hungary*

An Hungarian Captain

Physician

Page

Nobles, Knights, Attendants, and Soldiers

ERMINIA, *niece of Otho*

AURANTHE, *Conrad's sister*

Ladies and Attendants

SCENE. *The Castle of Friedburg, its vicinity,
and the Hungarian Camp*

TIME. *One Day*

ACT 1   SCENE 1

An apartment in the castle. Enter CONRAD

CONRAD   So, I am safe emerged from these broils!
           Amid the wreck of thousands I am whole;
           For every crime I have a laurel-wreath,
           For every lie a lordship. Nor yet has
           My ship of fortune furl'd her silken sails, –
           Let her glide on! This danger'd neck is saved,
           By dexterous policy, from the rebel's axe;
           And of my ducal palace not one stone
           Is bruised by the Hungarian petards.[2]
           Toil hard, ye slaves, and from the miser-earth   10
           Bring forth once more my bullion, treasured deep,
           With all my jewell'd salvers, silver and gold,
           And precious goblets that make rich the wine.
           But why do I stand babbling to myself?
           Where is Auranthe? I have news for her
           Shall –

Enter AURANTHE

AURANTHE   Conrad! what tidings? Good, if I may guess
           From your alert eyes and high-lifted brows.
           What tidings of the battle? Albert? Ludolph? Otho?
CONRAD   You guess aright. And, sister, slurring o'er
           Our bygone quarrels, I confess my heart   20
           Is beating with a child's anxiety,
           To make our golden fortune known to you.
AURANTHE   So serious?
CONRAD   Yes, so serious, that before
           I utter even the shadow of a hint
           Concerning what will make that sin-worn cheek
           Blush joyous blood through every lineament,
           You must make here a solemn vow to me.
AURANTHE   I prythee, Conrad, do not overact
           The hypocrite – what vow would you impose?

CONRAD	Trust me for once, – that you may be assur'd	30

CONRAD
Trust me for once, – that you may be assur'd   30
'Tis not confiding to a broken reed,
A poor court-bankrupt, outwitted and lost,
Revolve these facts in your acutest mood,
In such a mood as now you listen to me: –
A few days since, I was an open rebel
Against the Emperor, had suborn'd his son,
Drawn off his nobles to revolt, and shown
Contented fools causes for discontent
Fresh hatch'd in my ambition's eagle nest –
So thriv'd I as a rebel, and behold   40
Now I am Otho's favourite, his dear friend,
His right hand, his brave Conrad.

AURANTHE   I confess
You have intrigued with these unsteady times
To admiration;[3] but to be a favourite –

CONRAD
I saw my moment. The Hungarians,
Collected silently in holes and corners,
Appear'd, a sudden host, in the open day.
I should have perish'd in our empire's wreck,
But, calling interest loyalty, swore faith
To most believing Otho; and so help'd   50
His bloodstain'd ensigns to the victory
In yesterday's hard fight, that it has turn'd
The edge of his sharp wrath to eager kindness.

AURANTHE
So far yourself. But what is this to me
More than that I am glad? I gratulate you.

CONRAD
Yes, sister, but it does regard you greatly,
Nearly, momentously, – aye, painfully!
Make me this vow –

AURANTHE   Concerning whom or what?

CONRAD   Albert!

AURANTHE   I would inquire somewhat of him:
You had a letter from me touching him?   60
No treason 'gainst his head in deed or word!
Surely you spar'd him at my earnest prayer?
Give me the letter – it should not exist!

CONRAD
At one pernicious charge of the enemy,
I, for a moment – whiles, was prisoner ta'en
And rifled,[4] – stuff! the horses' hoofs have minc'd it!

AURANTHE He is alive?
CONRAD He is! but here make oath
To alienate him from your scheming brain,
Divorce him from your solitary thoughts,
And cloud him in such utter banishment,
That when his person meets again your eye,
Your vision shall quite lose its memory,
And wander past him as through vacancy.
AURANTHE I'll not be perjured.
CONRAD No, nor great, nor mighty;
You would not wear a crown, or rule a kingdom.
To you it is indifferent.
AURANTHE What means this?
CONRAD You'll not be perjured! Go to Albert then.
That camp-mushroom – dishonour of our house.
Go, page his dusty heels upon a march,
Furbish his jingling baldric[5] while he sleeps,
And share his mouldy ration in a siege.
Yet stay, – perhaps a charm may call you back,
And make the widening circlets of your eyes
Sparkle with healthy fevers. – The Emperor
Hath given consent that you should marry Ludolph!
AURANTHE Can it be, brother? For a golden crown
With a queen's awful lips I doubly thank you!
This is to wake in Paradise! Farewell
Thou clod of yesterday – 'twas not myself!
Not till this moment did I ever feel
My spirit's faculties! I'll flatter you
For this, and be you ever proud of it;
Thou, Jove-like, struck'dst thy forehead,
And from the teeming marrow of thy brain
I spring complete Minerva! But the prince –
His highness Ludolph – where is he?
CONRAD I know not:
When, lackeying my counsel at a beck,[6]
The rebel lords, on bended knees, received
The Emperor's pardon, Ludolph kept aloof.
Sole, in a stiff, foolhardy, sulky pride;
Yet, for all this, I never saw a father
In such a sickly longing for his son.

We shall soon see him, for the Emperor
He will be here this morning.

AURANTHE   That I heard
Among the midnight rumours from the camp.

CONRAD   You give up Albert to me?

AURANTHE   Harm him not!
E'en for his highness Ludolph's sceptry hand,
I would not Albert suffer any wrong.

CONRAD   Have I not laboured, plotted –?

AURANTHE   See you spare him:
Nor be pathetic, my kind benefactor,   110
On all the many bounties of your hand, –
'Twas for yourself you laboured – not for me!
Do you not count, when I am queen, to take
Advantage of your chance discoveries
Of my poor secrets, and so hold a rod
Over my life?

CONRAD   Let not this slave – this villain –
Be cause of feud between us. See! he comes!
Look, woman, look, your Albert is quite safe!
In haste it seems. Now shall I be in the way,
And wish'd with silent curses in my grave,   120
Or side by side with 'whelmed' mariners.

Enter ALBERT

ALBERT   Fair on your graces fall this early morrow!
So it is like to do, without my prayers,
For your right noble names, like favourite tunes,
Have fall'n full frequent from our Emperor's lips,
High commented with smiles.

AURANTHE   Noble Albert!

CONRAD   [*aside*]   Noble!

AURANTHE   Such salutation argues a glad heart
In our prosperity. We thank you, sir.

ALBERT   Lady! O, would to Heaven your poor servant
Could do you better service than mere words!   130
But I have other greeting than mine own,
From no less man than Otho, who has sent
This ring as pledge of dearest amity;[7]
'Tis chosen I hear from Hymen's jewel'ry,

	And you will prize it, lady, I doubt not,
	Beyond all pleasures past, and all to come.
	To you great duke –
CONRAD	To me! What of me, ha?
ALBERT	What pleas'd your grace to say?
CONRAD	Your message, sir!
ALBERT	You mean not this to me?
CONRAD	Sister, this way;

For there shall be no 'gentle Alberts' now,   [*aside*
No 'sweet Auranthes!'   141

[*exeunt* CONRAD *and* AURANTHE

ALBERT   [*solus*][8] The duke is out of temper; if he knows
More than a brother of a sister ought,
I should not quarrel with his peevishness.
Auranthe – Heaven preserve her always fair! –
Is in the heady, proud, ambitious vein;
I bicker not with her, – bid her farewell!
She has taken flight from me, then let her soar, –
He is a fool who stands at pining gaze!
But for poor Ludolph, he is food for sorrow: 150
No levelling bluster of my licens'd thoughts,
No military swagger of my mind,
Can smother from myself the wrong I've done him, –
Without design, indeed, – yet it is so, –
And opiate for the conscience have I none!

[*exit*

SCENE 2

The courtyard of the castle

Martial music. Enter, from the outer gate, OTHO, *nobles, knights, and attendants. The soldiers halt at the gate, with banners in sight.*

OTHO   Where is my noble herald?

Enter CONRAD, *from the castle, attended by two knights and servants.* ALBERT *following*

                           Well, hast told
Auranthe our intent imperial?
Lest our rent banners, too o' the sudden shown,
Should fright her silken casements, and dismay
Her household to our lack of entertainment.
A victory!

CONRAD   God save illustrious Otho!

OTHO   Aye, Conrad, it will pluck out all grey hairs;
It is the best physician for the spleen;
The courtliest inviter to a feast;
The subtlest excuser of small faults;   10
And a nice judge in the age and smack of wine.

Enter, from the castle, AURANTHE, *followed by pages holding up her robes, and a train of women. She kneels*

Hail my sweet hostess! I do thank the stars,
Or my good soldiers, or their ladies' eyes,
That, after such a merry battle fought,
I can, all safe in body and in soul,
Kiss your fair hand and lady fortune's too.
My ring! now, on my life, it doth rejoice
These lips to feel't on this soft ivory!
Keep it, my brightest daughter; it may prove
The little prologue to a line of kings.   20
I strove against thee and my hot-blood son,
Dull blockhead that I was to be so blind,
But now my sight is clear; forgive me, lady.

AURANTHE   My lord, I was a vassal to your frown,

And now your favour makes me but more humble;
In wintry winds the simple snow is safe,
But fadeth at the greeting of the sun:
Unto thine anger I might well have spoken,
Taking on me a woman's privilege,
But this so sudden kindness makes me dumb.   30

OTHO   What need of this? Enough, if you will be
A potent tutoress to my wayward boy,
And teach him, what it seems his nurse could not,
To say, for once, I thank you. Sigifred!

ALBERT   He has not yet return'd, my gracious liege.

OTHO   What then! No tidings of my friendly Arab?[9]

CONRAD   None, mighty Otho.   [to one of his knights, who goes out
                    Send forth instantly
An hundred horsemen from my honoured gates,
To scour the plains and search the cottages.
Cry a reward, to him who shall first bring   40
News of that vanished Arabian,
A full-heap'd helmet of the purest gold.

OTHO   More thanks, good Conrad; for, except my son's,
There is no face I rather would behold
Than that same quick-eyed pagan's. By the saints,
This coming night of banquets must not light
Her dazzling torches; nor the music breathe
Smooth, without clashing cymbal, tones of peace
And indoor melodies; nor the ruddy wine
Ebb spouting to the lees;[10] if I pledge not,   50
In my first cup, that Arab!

ALBERT   Mighty Monarch,
I wonder not this stranger's victor-deeds
So hang upon your spirit. Twice in the fight
It was my chance to meet his olive brow,
Triumphant in the enemy's shatter'd rhomb;[11]
And, to say truth, in any Christian arm
I never saw such prowess.

OTHO   Did you ever?
O, 'tis a noble boy! – tut! – what do I say?
I mean a triple Saladin,[12] whose eyes,
When in the glorious scuffle they met mine,   60
Seem'd to say – 'Sleep, old man, in safety sleep;

	I am the victory!'
CONRAD	Pity he's not here.
OTHO	And my son too, pity he is not here.
	Lady Auranthe, I would not make you blush,
	But can you give a guess where Ludolph is?
	Know you not of him?
AURANTHE	Indeed, my liege, no secret –
OTHO	Nay, nay, without more words, dost know of him?
AURANTHE	I would I were so over-fortunate,
	Both for his sake and mine, and to make glad
	A father's ears with tidings of his son.

OTHO   I see 'tis like to be a tedious day.
          Were Theodore and Gonfred and the rest
          Sent forth with my commands?
ALBERT   Aye, my lord.
OTHO   And no news! No news! 'Faith! 'tis very strange
          He thus avoids us. Lady, is't not strange?
          Will he be truant to you too? It is a shame.
CONRAD   Will't please your highness enter, and accept
          The unworthy welcome of your servant's house?
          Leaving your cares to one whose diligence
          May in few hours make pleasures of them all.
OTHO   Not so tedious, Conrad. No, no, no, –
          I must see Ludolph or the – What's that shout!
VOICES WITHOUT   Huzza! huzza! Long live the Emperor!
OTHER VOICES   Fall back! Away there!
OTHO   Say, what noise is that?
          [ALBERT *advancing from the back of the stage,*
                   whither he had hastened on hearing
                         the cheers of the soldiery

ALBERT   It is young Gersa, the Hungarian prince,
          Pick'd like a red stag from the fallow herd
          Of prisoners. Poor prince, forlorn he steps,
          Slow, and demure, and proud in his despair.
          If I may judge by his so tragic bearing,
          His eye not downcast, and his folded arm,
          He doth this moment wish himself asleep
          Among his fallen captains on yon plains.

70

80

90

Enter GERSA, *in chains and guarded*

OTHO   Well said, Sir Albert.

GERSA   Not a word of greeting,
No welcome to a princely visitor,
Most mighty Otho? Will not my great host
Vouchsafe a syllable, before he bids
His gentlemen conduct me with all care
To some securest lodging? – cold perhaps!

OTHO   What mood is this? Hath fortune touch'd thy brain?

GERSA   O kings and princes of this fev'rous world,
What abject things, what mockeries must ye be,   101
What nerveless minions of safe palaces!
When here, a monarch, whose proud foot is used
To fallen princes' necks, as to his stirrup,
Must needs exclaim that I am mad forsooth,
Because I cannot flatter with bent knees
My conqueror!

OTHO   Gersa, I think you wrong me:
I think I have a better fame abroad.

GERSA   I prythee mock me not with gentle speech,
But, as a favour, bid me from thy presence;   110
Let me no longer be the wondering food
Of all these eyes; prythee command me hence!

OTHO   Do not mistake me, Gersa. That you may not,
Come, fair Auranthe, try if your soft hands
Can manage those hard rivets to set free
So brave a prince and soldier.

AURANTHE   [*sets him free*]   Welcome task!

GERSA   I am wound up in deep astonishment!
Thank you, fair lady. Otho! emperor!
You rob me of myself; my dignity
Is now your infant; I am a weak child.   120

OTHO   Give me your hand, and let this kindly grasp
Live in our memories.

GERSA   In mine it will.
I blush to think of my unchasten'd tongue;
But I was haunted by the monstrous ghost
Of all our slain battalions. Sire, reflect,
And pardon you will grant, that, at this hour,

The bruised remnants of our stricken camp
Are huddling undistinguish'd my dear friends,
With common thousands, into shallow graves.

OTHO   Enough, most noble Gersa. You are free   130
To cheer the brave remainder of your host
By your own healing presence, and that too,
Not as their leader merely, but their king;
For, as I hear, the wily enemy,
Who eas'd the crownet from your infant brows,
Bloody Taraxa, is among the dead.

GERSA   Then I retire, so generous Otho please,
Bearing with me a weight of benefits
Too heavy to be borne.

OTHO   It is not so;
Still understand me, King of Hungary,   140
Nor judge my open purposes awry.
Though I did hold you high in my esteem
For your self's sake, I do not personate
The stage-play emperor to entrap applause,
To set the silly sort o' the world agape,
And make the politic smile; no, I have heard
How in the Council you condemn'd this war,
Urging the perfidy of broken faith, –
For that I am your friend.

GERSA   If ever, sire,
You are mine enemy, I dare here swear   150
'Twill not be Gersa's fault. Otho, farewell!

OTHO   Will you return, Prince, to our banqueting?

GERSA   As to my father's board[13] I will return.

OTHO   Conrad, with all due ceremony, give
The prince a regal escort to his camp;
Albert, go thou and bear him company.
Gersa; farewell!

GERSA   All happiness attend you!

OTHO   Return with what good speed you may; for soon
We must consult upon our terms of peace.
                    [exeunt GERSA *and* ALBERT *with others*
And thus a marble column do I build   160
To prop my empire's dome. Conrad, in thee
I have another steadfast one, to uphold

The portals of my state; and, for my own
Pre-eminence and safety, I will strive
To keep thy strength upon its pedestal.
For, without thee, this day I might have been
A show-monster about the streets of Prague,
In chains, as just now stood that noble prince:
And then to me no mercy had been shown,
For when the conquer'd lion is once dungeon'd,   170
Who lets him forth again? or dares to give
An old lion sugar-cates of mild reprieve?
Not to thine ear alone I make confession,
But to all here, as, by experience,
I know how the great basement[14] of all power
Is frankness, and a true tongue to the world;
And how intriguing secrecy is proof
Of fear and weakness, and a hollow state.
Conrad, I owe thee much.

CONRAD   To kiss that hand,
My emperor, is ample recompense,   180
For a mere act of duty.

OTHO   Thou art wrong;
For what can any man on earth do more?
We will make trial of your house's welcome,
My bright Auranthe!

CONRAD   How is Friedburg honoured!

Enter ETHELBERT *and six monks*

ETHELBERT   The benison of heaven on your head,
Imperial Otho!

OTHO   Who stays me? Speak! Quick!

ETHELBERT   Pause but one moment, mighty conqueror
Upon the threshold of this house of joy.

OTHO   Pray, do not prose, good Ethelbert, but speak
What is your purpose.   190

ETHELBERT   The restoration of some captive maids,
Devoted to Heaven's pious ministries,
Who, being driven from their religious cells,
And kept in thraldom by our enemy,
When late this province was a lawless spoil,
Still weep amid the wild Hungarian camp,

	Though hemm'd around by thy victorious arms.	
OTHO	Demand the holy sisterhood in our name	
	From Gersa's tents. Farewell, old Ethelbert.	
ETHELBERT	The saints will bless you for this pious care.	200
OTHO	Daughter, your hand; Ludolph's would fit it best.	
CONRAD	Ho! let the music sound!	

> [*Music.* ETHELBERT *raises his raises his*
> *hands, as in benediction of* OTHO.
> *Exeunt severally. The scene closes on them*

SCENE 3

The country, with the castle in the distance

Enter LUDOLPH *and* SIGIFRED

LUDOLPH	You have my secret; let it not be breath'd.	
SIGIFRED	Still give me leave to wonder that the Prince	
	Ludolph and the swift Arab are the same;	
	Still to rejoice that 'twas a German arm	
	Death doing in a turban'd masquerade.	
LUDOLPH	The Emperor must not know it, Sigifred.	
SIGIFRED	I prythee, why? What happier hour of time	
	Could thy pleas'd star point down upon from heaven	
	With silver index, bidding thee make peace?	
LUDOLPH	Still it must not be known, good Sigifred;	10
	The star may point oblique.	
SIGIFRED	If Otho knew	
	His son to be that unknown Mussulman[15]	
	After whose spurring heels he sent me forth,	
	With one of his well-pleas'd Olympian oaths,	
	The charters of man's greatness, at this hour	
	He would be watching round the castle walls,	
	And, like an anxious warder,[16] strain his sight	
	For the first glimpse of such a son return'd –	
	Ludolph that blast of the Hungarians,	
	That Saracenic[17] meteor of the fight,	20
	That silent fury, whose fell scymitar[18]	
	Kept danger all aloof from Otho's head,	
	And left him space for wonder.	

LUDOLPH   Say no more.
        Not as a swordsman would I pardon claim,
        But as a son. The bronz'd centurion,
        Long toil'd in foreign wars, and whose high deeds
        Are shaded in a forest of tall spears,
        Known only to his troop, hath greater plea
        Of favour with my sire than I can have.

SIGIFRED   My lord, forgive me that I cannot see   30
        How this proud temper with clear reason squares.
        What made you then, with such an anxious love,
        Hover around that life, whose bitter days
        You vext with bad revolt? Was't opium,
        Or the mad-fumed wine? Nay, do not frown,
        I rather would grieve with you than upbraid.

LUDOLPH   I do believe you. No, 'twas not to make
        A father his son's debtor, or to heal
        His deep heart-sickness for a rebel child.
        'Twas done in memory of my boyish days,   40
        Poor cancel[19] for his kindness to my youth,
        For all his calming of my childish griefs,
        And all his smiles upon my merriment.
        No, not a thousand foughten fields could sponge
        Those days paternal from my memory,
        Though now upon my head he heaps disgrace.

SIGIFRED   My Prince, you think too harshly –
LUDOLPH   Can I so?
        Hath he not gall'd my spirit to the quick?
        And with a sullen rigour obstinate
        Pour'd out a phial of wrath upon my faults?   50
        Hunted me as the Tartar[20] does the boar,
        Driven me to the very edge o' the world,
        And almost put a price upon my head?

SIGIFRED   Remember how he spar'd the rebel lords.
LUDOLPH   Yes, yes, I know he hath a noble nature
        That cannot trample on the fallen. But his
        Is not the only proud heart in his realm.
        He hath wrong'd me, and I have done him wrong;
        He hath lov'd me, and I have shown him kindness;
        We should be almost equal.

SIGIFRED   Yet, for all this,   60

I would you had appear'd among those lords,
And ta'en his favour.

LUDOLPH   Ha! till now I thought
My friend had held poor Ludolph's honour dear.
What! would you have me sue before his throne
And kiss the courtier's missal, its silk steps?
Or hug the golden housings[21] of his steed,
Amid a camp, whose steeled swarms I dar'd
But yesterday? And, at the trumpet sound,
Bow like some unknown mercenary's flag,
And lick the soiled grass? No, no, my friend,   70
I would not, I, be pardon'd in the heap,
And bless indemnity with all that scum, –
Those men I mean, who on my shoulders propp'd
Their weak rebellion, winning me with lies,
And pitying forsooth my many wrongs;
Poor self-deceived wretches, who must think
Each one himself a king in embryo,
Because some dozen vassals cry'd – my lord!
Cowards, who never knew their little hearts,
Till flurried danger held the mirror up,   80
And then they own'd themselves without a blush,
Curling, like spaniels, round my father's feet.
Such things deserted me and are forgiven,
While I, least guilty, am an outcast still,
And will be, for I love such fair disgrace.

SIGIFRED   I know the clear truth; so would Otho see,
For he is just and noble. Fain would I
Be pleader for you –

LUDOLPH   He'll hear none of it;
You know his temper, hot, proud, obstinate;
Endanger not yourself so uselessly.   90
I will encounter his thwart spleen[22] myself,
Today, at the Duke Conrad's, where he keeps
His crowded state after the victory.
There will I be, a most unwelcome guest,
And parley with him, as a son should do,
Who doubly loathes a father's tyranny;
Tell him how feeble is that tyranny;
How the relationship of father and son

	Is no more valid than a silken leash	
	Where lions tug adverse, if love grow not	100
	From interchanged love through many years.	
	Aye, and those turreted Franconian walls,	
	Like to a jealous casket, hold my pearl –	
	My fair Auranthe! Yes, I will be there.	

SIGIFRED   Be not so rash; wait till his wrath shall pass,
Until his royal spirit softly ebbs
Self-influenced; then, in his morning dreams
He will forgive thee, and awake in grief
To have not thy good morrow.

LUDOLPH   Yes, today
I must be there, while her young pulses beat   110
Among the new-plum'd minions of the war.
Have you seen her of late? No? Auranthe,
Franconia's fair sister, 'tis I mean.
She should be paler for my troublous[23] days –
And there it is – my father's iron lips
Have sworn divorcement 'twixt me and my right.

SIGIFRED   [*aside*] Auranthe! I had hop'd this whim had pass'd.

LUDOLPH   And, Sigifred, with all his love of justice,
When will he take that grandchild in his arms,
That, by my love I swear, shall soon be his?   120
This reconcilement is impossible.
For see – but who are these?

SIGIFRED   They are messengers
From our great emperor; to you, I doubt not,
For couriers are abroad to seek you out.

Enter THEODORE *and* GONFRED

THEODORE   Seeing so many vigilant eyes explore
The province to invite your highness back
To your high dignities, we are too happy.

GONFRED   We have no eloquence to colour justly
The emperor's anxious wishes.

LUDOLPH   Go. I follow you.
[*exeunt* THEODORE *and* GONFRED
I play the prude: it is but venturing –   130
Why should he be so earnest? Come, my friend,
Let us to Friedburg castle.

ACT 2   SCENE 1

An ante-hamber in the castle

Enter LUDOLPH *and* SIGIFRED

LUDOLPH   No more advices, no more cautioning:
             I leave it all to fate – to anything!
             I cannot square my conduct to time, place,
             Or circumstance; to me 'tis all a mist!

SIGIFRED   I say no more.

LUDOLPH   It seems I am to wait
             Here in the ante-room; – that may be a trifle.
             You see now how I dance attendance here,
             Without that tyrant temper, you so blame,
             Snapping the rein. You have medicin'd me
             With good advices; and I here remain,   10
             In this most honourable ante-room,
             Your patient scholar.

SIGIFRED   Do not wrong me, Prince.
             By Heavens, I'd rather kiss Duke Conrad's slipper,
             When in the morning he doth yawn with pride,
             Than see you humbled but a half-degree!
             Truth is, the Emperor would fain dismiss
             The nobles ere he sees you.

Enter GONFRED *from the council-room*

LUDOLPH   Well, sir! what?

GONFRED   Great honour to the Prince! The Emperor,
             Hearing that his brave son had reappeared,
             Instant dismiss'd the Council from his sight,   20
             As Jove fans off the clouds. Even now they pass.

                                                          [*exit*

Enter the Nobles from the council-room. They cross the stage,
bowing with respect to LUDOLPH, *he frowing on them.*
                CONRAD follows. Exeunt Nobles

LUDOLPH   Not the discoloured poisons of a fen,
             Which he who breathes feels warning of his death,

Could taste so nauseous to the bodily sense,
As these prodigious sycophants disgust
The soul's fine palate.

CONRAD   Princely Ludolph, hail!
Welcome, thou younger sceptre to the realm!
Strength to thy virgin crownet's golden buds,
That they, against the winter of thy sire,
May burst, and swell, and flourish round thy brows,   30
Maturing to a weighty diadem!
Yet be that hour far off; and may he live,
Who waits for thee, as the chapp'd earth for rain.
Set my life's star! I have lived long enough,
Since under my glad roof, propitiously,
Father and son each other repossess.

LUDOLPH Fine wording, Duke! but words could never yet
Forestall the fates; have you not learnt that yet?
Let me look well: your features are the same;
Your gait the same; your hair of the same shade;   40
As one I knew some passed weeks ago,
Who sung far different notes into mine ears.
I have mine own particular comments on 't;
You have your own, perhaps.

CONRAD   My gracious Prince,
All men may err. In truth I was deceived
In your great father's nature, as you were.
Had I known that of him I have since known.
And what you soon will learn, I would have turn'd
My sword to my own throat, rather than held
Its threatening edge against a good King's quiet: 50
Or with one word fever'd[24] you, gentle Prince,
Who seem'd to me, as rugged times then went,
Indeed too much oppress'd. May I be bold
To tell the Emperor you will haste to him?

LUDOLPH Your Dukedom's privilege will grant so much.

                           [*exit* CONRAD

He's very close to Otho, a tight leech!
Your hand – I go. Ha! here the thunder comes
Sullen against the wind! If in two angry brows
My safety lies, then Sigifred, I'm safe.

Enter OTHO *and* CONRAD

OTHO	Will you make Titan play the lackey-page	60
	To chattering pigmies? I would have you know	
	That such neglect of our high Majesty	
	Annuls all feel of kindred. What is son, –	
	Or friend, – or brother, – or all ties of blood, –	
	When the whole kingdom, centred in ourself,	
	Is rudely slighted? Who am I to wait?	
	By Peter's chair![25] I have upon my tongue	
	A word to fright the proudest spirit here! –	
	Death! – and slow tortures to the hardy fool,	
	Who dares take such large charter from our smiles!	70
	Conrad, we would be private. Sigifred!	
	Off! And none pass this way on pain of death!	

[*exeunt* CONRAD *and* SIGIFRED

LUDOLPH	This was but half expected, my good sire.
	Yet I am griev'd at it, to the full height,
	As though my hopes of favour had been whole.
OTHO	How you indulge yourself! What can you hope for?
LUDOLPH	Nothing, my liege; I have to hope for nothing.
	I come to greet you as a loving son,
	And then depart, if I may be so free,
	Seeing that blood of yours in my warm veins
	Has not yet mitigated into milk.[26]
OTHO	What would you, sir?
LUDOLPH	A lenient banishment;
	So please you let me unmolested pass
	This Conrad's gates, to the wide air again.
	I want no more. A rebel wants no more.
OTHO	And shall I let a rebel loose again
	To muster kites and eagles 'gainst my head?
	No, obstinate boy, you shall be kept cag'd up,
	Serv'd with harsh food, with scum for Sunday-drink.
LUDOLPH	Indeed!
OTHO	And chains too heavy for your life:
	I'll choose a gaoler, whose swart monstrous face
	Shall be a hell to look upon, and she –
LUDOLPH	Ha!
OTHO	Shall be your fair Auranthe.
LUDOLPH	Amaze! Amaze!

The line numbers 80 and 90 appear at the right margin aligned with "Seeing that blood of yours in my warm veins" (80) and "And chains too heavy for your life:" (90).

OTHO	Today you marry her.
LUDOLPH	This is a sharp jest!
OTHO	No. None at all. When have I said a lie?
LUDOLPH	If I sleep not, I am a waking wretch.
OTHO	Not a word more. Let me embrace my child.
LUDOLPH	I dare not. 'Twould pollute so good a father!

O heavy crime! that your son's blinded eyes
Could not see all his parent's love aright,   100
As now I see it. Be not kind to me –
Punish me not with favour.

OTHO	Are you sure,

Ludolph, you have no saving plea in store?

LUDOLPH	My father, none!
OTHO	Then you astonish me.
LUDOLPH	No, I have no plea. Disobedience,

Rebellion, obstinacy, blasphemy,
Are all my counsellors. If they can make
My crooked deeds show good and plausible,
Then grant me loving pardon, but not else,
Good Gods! not else, in any way, my liege!   110

OTHO	You are a most perplexing, noble boy.
LUDOLPH	You not less a perplexing noble father.
OTHO	Well, you shall have free passport through the gates.

Farewell!

LUDOLPH	Farewell! and by these tears believe,

And still remember, I repent in pain
All my misdeeds!

OTHO	Ludolph, I will! I will!

But, Ludolph, ere you go, I would enquire
If you, in all your wandering, ever met
A certain Arab haunting in these parts.

LUDOLPH	No, my good lord, I cannot say I did. 120
OTHO	Make not your father blind before his time;

Nor let these arms paternal hunger more
For an embrace, to dull the appetite
Of my great love for thee, my supreme child!
Come close, and let me breathe into thine ear.
I knew you through disguise. You are the Arab!
You can't deny it.   [*embracing him*

LUDOLPH	Happiest of days!

OTHO	We'll make it so.
LUDOLPH	'Stead of one fatted calf

LUDOLPH   'Stead of one fatted calf
Ten hecatombs shall bellow out their last,
Smote 'wixt the horns by the death-stunning mace   130
Of Mars, and all the soldiery shall feast
Nobly as Nimrod's masons, when the towers
Of Nineveh new kiss'd the parted clouds![27]

OTHO Large as a God speak out, where all is thine.

LUDOLPH Aye, father, but the fire in my sad breast
Is quench'd with inward tears! I must rejoice
For you, whose wings so shadow over me
In tender victory, but for myself
I still must mourn. The fair Auranthe mine!
Too great a boon! I prythee let me ask   140
What more than I know of could so have changed
Your purpose touching her?

OTHO   At a word, this:
In no deed did you give me more offence
Than your rejection of Erminia.
To my appalling, I saw too good proof
Of your keen-eyed suspicion, – she is naught!

LUDOLPH You are convinc'd?

OTHO   Aye, spite of her sweet looks.
O, that my brother's daughter should so fall!
Her fame has pass'd into the grosser lips
Of soldiers in their cups.[28]

LUDOLPH   'Tis' very sad.   150

OTHO No more of her. Auranthe – Ludolph, come!
This marriage be the bond of endless peace!

                                       [exeunt

SCENE 2

The entrance of Gersa's tent in the Hungarian camp

Enter ERMINIA

ERMINIA   Where! where! where shall I find a messenger?
A trusty soul? A good man in the camp?
Shall I go myself? Monstrous wickedness!
O cursed Conrad! devilish Auranthe!
Here is proof palpable as the bright sun!
O for a voice to reach the Emperor's ears!

                           [*shouts in the camp*

Enter a Hungarian Captain

CAPTAIN   Fair prisoner, hear you those joyous shouts?
The king – aye, now our king, – but still your slave,
Young Gersa, from a short captivity
Has just return'd. He bids me say, bright Dame,   10
That even the homage of his ranged chiefs
Cures not his keen impatience to behold
Such beauty once again. What ails you, lady?

ERMINIA   Say, is not that a German, yonder? There!

CAPTAIN   Methinks by his stout bearing he should be –
Yes – 'tis one Albert; a brave German knight,
And much in the emperor's favour.

ERMINIA   I would fain
Enquire of friends and kinsfolk; how they fared
In these rough times. Brave soldier, as you pass
To royal Gersa with my humble thanks,   20
Will you send yonder knight to me?

CAPTAIN   I will.   [*exit*

ERMINIA   Yes, he was ever known to be a man
Frank, open, generous; Albert I may trust.
O proof! proof! proof! Albert's an honest man;
Not Ethelbert the monk, if he were here,
Would I hold more trustworthy. Now!

Enter ALBERT

ALBERT   Good Gods!

Lady Erminia! are you prisoner
In this beleaguer'd camp? Or are you here
Of your own will? You pleas'd to send for me.
By Venus, 'tis' a pity I knew not   30
Your plight before, and, by her son,[29] I swear
To do you every service you can ask.
What would the fairest –?

ERMINIA   Albert, will you swear?

ALBERT   I have. Well?

ERMINIA   Albert, you have fame to lose.
If men, in court and camp, lie not outright,
You should be, from a thousand, chosen forth
To do an honest deed. Shall I confide –?

ALBERT   Aye, anything to me, fair creature. Do;
Dictate my task. Sweet woman, –

ERMINIA   Truce with that.
You understand me not; and, in your speech,   40
I see how far the slander is abroad.
Without proof could you think me innocent?

ALBERT   Lady, I should rejoice to know you so.

ERMINIA   If you have any pity for a maid,
Suffering a daily death from evil tongues;
Any compassion for that Emperor's niece,
Who, for your bright sword and clear honesty,
Lifted you from the crowd of common men
Into the lap of honour; – save me, knight!

ALBERT   How? Make it clear; if it be possible,   50
I, by the banner of Saint Maurice,[30] swear
To right you.

ERMINIA   Possible! – Easy. O my heart!
This letter's not so soil'd but you may read it: –
Possible! There – that letter! Read – read it.
                                [gives him a letter

ALBERT   [reading] 'To the Duke Conrad. – Forget the threat you
made at parting, and I will forget to send the Emperor
letters and papers of yours I have become possessed of.
His life is no trifle to me; his death you shall find none
to yourself.' [speaks to himself] 'Tis me – my life that's
pleaded for! [reads] 'He, for his own sake, will be dumb

as the grave. Erminia has my shame fix'd upon her, sure
as a wen.[31] We are safe.

	AURANTHE'

A she-devil! A dragon! I her imp!
Fire of Hell! Auranthe – lewd demon!
Where got you this? Where? When?

| ERMINIA | I found it in the tent, among some spoils |

Which, being noble, fell to Gersa's lot.
Come in, and see.   [they go in and return

| ALBERT | Villainy! Villainy! |

Conrad's sword, his corslet,[32] and his helm,   70
And his letter. Caitiff, he shall feel –

ERMINIA	I see you are thunderstruck. Haste, haste away!
ALBERT	O I am tortured by this villainy.
ERMINIA	You needs must be. Carry it swift to Otho;

Tell him, moreover, I am prisoner
Here in this camp, where all the sisterhood,
Forc'd from their quiet cells, are parcell'd out
For slaves among these Huns. Away! Away!

| ALBERT | I am gone. |
| ERMINIA | Swift be your steed! Within this hour |

The Emperor will see it.

| ALBERT | Ere I sleep: 80 |

That I can swear.   [hurries out

| GERSA | [without]   Brave captains! thanks. Enough |

Of loyal homage now!

Enter GERSA

| ERMINIA | Hail, royal Hun! |
| GERSA | What means this, fair one? Why in such alarm? |

Who was it hurried by me so distract?
It seem'd you were in deep discourse together;
Your doctrine has not been so harsh to him
As to my poor deserts. Come, come, be plain.
I am no jealous fool to kill you both,
Or, for such trifles, rob the adorned world
Of such a beauteous vestal.[33]

| ERMINIA | I grieve, my Lord,   90 |

To hear you condescend to ribald phrase.

| GERSA | This is too much! Hearken, my lady pure! |

ERMINIA   Silence! and hear the magic of a name –
Erminia! I am she, – the Emperor's niece!
Prais'd be the Heavens, I now dare own myself!

GERSA   Erminia! Indeed! I've heard of her.
Prythee, fair lady, what chance brought you here?

ERMINIA   Ask your own soldiers.

GERSA   And you dare own your name.
For loveliness you may – and for the rest
My vein is not censorious.

ERMINIA   Alas! poor me!   100
'Tis false indeed.

GERSA   Indeed you are too fair:
The swan, soft leaning on her fledgy[34] breast,
When to the stream she launches, looks not back
With such a tender grace; nor are her wings
So white as your soul is, if that but be
Twin-picture to your face. Erminia!
Today, for the first day, I am a king,
Yet would I give my unworn crown away
To know you spotless.

ERMINIA   Trust me one day more,
Generously, without more certain guarantee,   110
Than this poor face you deign to praise so much;
After that, say and do whate'er you please.
If I have any knowledge of you, sir,
I think, nay I am sure, you will grieve much
To hear my story. O be gentle to me,
For I am sick and faint with many wrongs,
Tir'd out, and weary-worn with contumelies.[35]

GERSA   Poor lady!

Enter ETHELBERT

ERMINIA   Gentle Prince, 'tis false indeed.
Good morrow, holy father! I have had
Your prayers, though I look'd for you in vain.   120

ETHELBERT   Blessings upon you, daughter! Sure you look
Too cheerful for these foul pernicious days.
Young man, you heard this virgin say 'twas false,
'Tis false, I say. What! can you not employ
Your temper elsewhere, 'mong these burly tents.

But you must taunt this dove, for she hath lost
The Eagle Otho to beat off assault?
Fie! fie! But I will be her guard myself;
In the Emperor's name. I here demand of you
Herself, and all her sisterhood. She false!   130

GERSA   Peace! peace, old man! I cannot think she is.

ETHELBERT Whom I have known from her first infancy,
Baptis'd her in the bosom of the Church,
Watch'd her, as anxious husbandmen[36] the grain,
From the first shoot till the unripe mid-May,
Then to the tender ear of her June days,
Which, lifting sweet abroad its timid green.
Is blighted by the touch of calumny;
You cannot credit such a monstrous tale.

GERSA   I cannot. Take her. Fair Erminia,   140
I follow you to Friedburg, – is't not so?

ERMINIA   Aye, so we purpose.

ETHELBERT   Daughter, do you so?
How's this? I marvel! Yet you look not mad.

ERMINIA   I have good news to tell you, Ethelbert.

GERSA   Ho! ho, there! Guards!
Your blessing, father! Sweet Erminia,
Believe me, I am well nigh sure –

ERMINIA   Farewell!
Short time will show.

Enter Chiefs

                      Yes, father Ethelbert,
I have news precious as we pass along.

ETHELBERT Dear daughter, you shall guide me.

ERMINIA   To no ill.   150

GERSA   Command an escort to the Friedburg lines.

[exeunt Chiefs

Pray let me lead. Fair lady, forget not
Gersa, how he believ'd you innocent.
I follow you to Friedburg with all speed.

[exeunt

ACT 3   SCENE 1

The country

Enter ALBERT

ALBERT   O that the earth were empty, as when Cain[37]
                Had no perplexity to hide his head!
                Or that the sword of some brave enemy
                Had put a sudden stop to my hot breath,
                And hurl'd me down the illimitable gulf
                Of times past, unremember'd! Better so
                Than thus fast-limed in a cursed snare,[38]
                The white limbs of a wanton.[39] This the end
                Of an aspiring life! My boyhood past
                In feud with wolves and bears, when no eye saw   10
                The solitary warfare, fought for love
                Of honour 'mid the growling wilderness.
                My sturdier youth, maturing to the sword,
                Won by the syren-trumpets, and the ring
                Of shields upon the pavement, when bright-mail'd
                Henry the Fowler[40] pass'd the streets of Prague.
                Was't to this end I louted and became
                The menial of Mars,[41] and held a spear
                Sway'd by command, as corn is by the wind?
                Is it for this, I now am lifted up   20
                By Europe's throned Emperor, to see
                My honour be my executioner, –
                My love of fame, my prided honesty
                Put to the torture for confessional?
                Then the damn'd crime of blurting to the world
                A woman's secret! – Though a fiend she be,
                Too tender of my ignominious life;
                But then to wrong the generous Emperor
                In such a searching point, were to give up
                My soul for football at Hell's holiday!   30
                I must confess, – and cut my throat, – today?
                Tomorrow? Ho! some wine!

Enter SIGIFRED

SIGIFRED   A fine humour –

ALBERT   Who goes there? Count Sigifred? Ha! Ha!

SIGIFRED   What, man, do you mistake the hollow sky
For a throng'd tavern, – and these stubbed trees
For old serge[42] hangings, – me, your humble friend,
For a poor waiter? Why, man, how you stare!
What gipsies have you been carousing with?
No, no more wine; methinks you've had enough.

ALBERT   You well may laugh and banter. What a fool   40
An injury may make of a staid man!
You shall know all anon.

SIGIFRED   Some tavern brawl?

ALBERT   'Twas with some people out of common reach;
Revenge is difficult.

SIGIFRED   I am your friend;
We meet again today, and can confer
Upon it. For the present I'm in haste.

ALBERT   Whither?

SIGIFRED   To fetch King Gersa to the feast.
The Emperor on this marriage is so hot,
Pray Heaven it end not in apoplexy!
The very porters, as I pass'd the doors,   50
Heard his loud laugh, and answer'd in full choir.
I marvel, Albert, you delay so long
From those bright revelries; go, show yourself,
You may be made a duke.

ALBERT   Aye, very like:
Pray, what day has his Highness fix'd upon?

SIGIFRED   For what?

ALBERT   The marriage. What else can I mean?

SIGIFRED   Today! O, I forgot, you could not know;
The news is scarce a minute old with me.

ALBERT   Married today! Today! You did not say so?

SIGIFRED   Now, while I speak to you, their comely heads   60
Are bow'd before the mitre.[43]

ALBERT   O! monstrous!

SIGIFRED   What is this?

ALBERT   Nothing, Sigifred. Farewell!
We'll meet upon our subject. Farewell, count!

                                          [*exit*

SIGIFRED   Is this clear-headed Albert? He brain-turn'd!
        'Tis as portentous as a meteor.

                                                [exit

SCENE 2

An apartment in the castle

Enter, as from the marriage, OTHO, LUDOLPH, AURANTHE,
    CONRAD, *nobles, knights, ladies, etc. music*

OTHO   Now, Ludolph! Now, Auranthe! Daughter fair!
        What can I find to grace your nuptial day
        More than my love, and these wide realms in fee?[44]
LUDOLPH   I have too much.
AURANTHE   And I, my liege, by far.
LUDOLPH   Auranthe! I have! O, my bride, my love!
        Not all the gaze upon us can restrain
        My eyes, too long poor exiles from thy face,
        From adoration, and my foolish tongue
        From uttering soft responses to the love
        I see in thy mute beauty beaming forth!   10
        Fair creature, bless me with a single word!
        All mine!
AURANTHE   Spare, spare me, my Lord; I swoon else.
LUDOLPH   Soft beauty! by tomorrow I should die,
        Wert thou not mine.   *[they talk apart*
FIRST LADY   How deep she has bewitch'd him!
FIRST KNIGHT Ask you for her recipe for love philtres.[45]
SECOND LADY They hold the Emperor in admiration.
OTHO   If ever king was happy, that am I!
        What are the cities 'yond the Alps to me,
        The provinces about the Danube's mouth,
        The promise of fair soil beyond the Rhone;   20
        Or routing out of Hyperborean[46] hordes.
        To these fair children, stars of a new age?
        Unless perchance I might rejoice to win
        This little ball of earth, and chuck it them

	To play with!	
AURANTHE	Nay, my Lord, I do not know.	
LUDOLPH	Let me not famish.	
OTHO	(*to Conrad*) Good Franconia,	

You heard what oath I sware,[47] as the sun rose,
That unless Heaven would send me back my son,
My Arab, – no soft music should enrich
The cool wine, kiss'd off with a soldier's smack;   30
Now all my empire, baster'd for one feast,
Seems poverty.

CONRAD   Upon the neighbour-plain
The heralds have prepar'd a royal lists;[48]
Your knights, found war-proof in the bloody field,
Speed to the game.

OTHO   Well, Ludolph, what say you?

LUDOLPH My lord!

OTHO   A tourney?[49]

CONRAD   Or, if 't please you best –

LUDOLPH I want no more!

FIRST LADY   He soars!

SECOND LADY   Past all reason.

LUDOLPH Though heaven's choir
Should in a vast circumference descend
And sing for my delight, I'd stop my ears!   40
Though bright Apollo's car stood burning here,
And he put out an arm to bid me mount,
His touch an immortality, not I!
This earth, this palace, this room, Auranthe!

OTHO This is a little painful; just too much.
Conrad, if he flames longer in this wise,
I shall believe in wizard-woven loves
And old romances; but I'll break the spell.
Ludolph!

CONRAD   He will be calm, anon.

LUDOLPH   You call'd?
Yes, yes, yes, I offend. You must forgive me;   50
Not being quite recover'd from the stun
Of your large bounties. A tourney, is it not?

                   [*a senet*[50] *heard faintly*

CONRAD	The trumpets reach us.
ETHELBERT	[*without*] On your peril, sirs,
	Detain us!
FIRST VOICE	[*without*] Let not the abbot pass.
SECOND VOICE	[*without*] No,
	On your lives!
FIRST VOICE	[*without*] Holy father, you must not.
ETHELBERT	[*without*] Otho!
OTHO	Who calls on Otho?
ETHELBERT	[*without*] Ethelbert!
OTHO	Let him come in.

Enter ETHELBERT *leading in* ERMINIA

	Thou cursed abbot, why
	Hast brought pollution to our holy rites?
	Hast thou no fear of hangman, or the faggot?[51]
LUDOLPH	What portent – what strange prodigy is this? 60
CONRAD	Away!
ETHELBERT	You, Duke?
ERMINIA	Albert has surely fail'd me!
	Look at the Emperor's brow upon me bent!
ETHELBERT	A sad delay!
CONRAD	Away, thou guilty thing!
ETHELBERT	You again, Duke? Justice, most mighty Otho!
	You – go to your sister there and plot again,
	A quick plot, swift as thought to save your heads;
	For lo! the toils are spread around your den.
	The world is all agape to see dragg'd forth
	Two ugly monsters.
LUDOLPH	What means he, my lord?
CONRAD	I cannot guess.
ETHELBERT	Best ask your lady sister, 70
	Whether the riddle puzzles her beyond
	The power of utterance.
CONRAD	Foul barbarian, cease:
	The Princess faints!
LUDOLPH	Stab him! O, sweetest wife!
	[*attendants bear off* AURANTHE
ERMINIA	Alas!
ETHELBERT	Your wife?

LUDOLPH	Aye, Satan! does that yerk[32] ye?
ETHELBERT	Wife! so soon!
LUDOLPH	Aye, wife! Oh, impudence!

Thou bitter mischief! Venomous mad priest!
How dar'st thou lift those beetle brows at me?
Me – the prince Ludolph, in this presence here,
Upon my marriage-day, and scandalise
My joys with such opprobrious surprise?   80
Wife! Why dost linger on that syllable,
As if it were some demon's name pronounc'd
To summon harmful lightning, and make roar
The sleepy thunder? Hast no sense of fear?
No ounce of man in thy mortality?
Tremble! for, at my nod, the sharpen'd axe
Will make thy bold tongue quiver to the roots,
Those grey lids wink, and thou not know it more!

ETHELBERT O, poor deceived Prince! I pity thee!
Great Otho! I claim justice –

LUDOLPH   Thou shalt have't!   90
Thine arms from forth a pulpit of hot fire
Shall sprawl distracted! O that that dull cowl
Were some most sensitive portion of thy life,
That I might give it to my hounds to tear!
Thy girdle some fine zealous-pained[53] nerve
To girth my saddle! And those devil's beads[54]
Each one a life, that I might, every day,
Crush one with Vulcan's hammer!

OTHO   Peace, my son;
You far outstrip my spleen in this affair.
Let us be calm, and hear the abbot's plea   100
For this intrusion.

LUDOLPH   I am silent, sire.

OTHO Conrad, see all depart not wanted here.
                    [exeunt knights, ladies, etc.
Ludolph, be calm. Ethelbert, peace awhile.
This mystery demands an audience
Of a just judge, and that will Otho be.

LUDOLPH Why has he time to breathe another word?

OTHO Ludolph, old Ethelbert, be sure, comes not
To beard us for no cause; he's not the man

To cry himself up an ambassador
Without credentials.

LUDOLPH   I'll chain up myself.[55]   110

OTHO   Old Abbot, stand here forth. Lady Erminia,
Sit. And now, Abbot! what have you to say?
Our ear is open. First we here denounce
Hard penalties against thee, if't be found
The cause for which you have disturb'd us here,
Making our bright hours muddy, be a thing
Of little moment.

ETHELBERT   See this innocent!
Otho! thou father of the people call'd,
Is her life nothing? Her fair honour nothing?
Her tears from matins[56] until evensong   120
Nothing? Her burst heart nothing? Emperor!
Is this your gentle niece – the simplest flower
Of the world's herbal – this fair lily blanch'd
Still with the dews of piety, this meek lady
Here sitting like an angel newly-shent,
Who veils its snowy wings and grows all pale, –
Is she nothing?

OTHO   What more to the purpose, abbot?

LUDOLPH   Whither is he winding?

CONRAD   No clue yet!

ETHELBERT   You have heard, my Liege, and so, no doubt, all here,
Foul, poisonous, malignant whisperings;   130
Nay open speech, rude mockery grown common,
Against the spotless nature and clear fame
Of the princess Erminia, your niece.
I have intruded here thus suddenly,
Because I hold those base weeds, with tight hand,
Which now disfigure her fair growing stem,
Waiting but for your sign to pull them up
By the dark roots, and leave her palpable,
To all men's sight, a Lady, innocent.
The ignominy of that whisper'd tale   140
About a midnight gallant, seen to climb
A window to her chamber neighbour'd near,
I will from her turn off, and put the load
On the right shoulders; on that wretch's head,

	Who, by close stratagems, did save herself,
	Chiefly by shifting to this lady's room
	A rope-ladder for false witness.
LUDOLPH	Most atrocious!
OTHO	Ethelbert, proceed.
ETHELBERT	With sad lips I shall:

For, in the healing of one wound, I fear
To make a greater. His young highness here   150
Today was married.

| LUDOLPH | Good. |
| ETHELBERT | Would it were good! |

Yet why do I delay to spread abroad
The names of those two vipers, from whose jaws
A deadly breath went forth to taint and blast
This guileless lady?

| OTHO | Abbot, speak their names. |
| ETHELBERT | A minute first. It cannot be – but may |

I ask, great judge, if you today have put
A letter by unread?

OTHO	Doesn't end in this?
CONRAD	Out with their names!
ETHELBERT	Bold sinner, say you so?
LUDOLPH	Out, tedious monk!
OTHO	Confess, or by the wheel – 160
ETHELBERT	My evidence cannot be far away

And, though it never come, be on my head
The crime of passing an attaint[57] upon
The slanderers of this virgin.

LUDOLPH	Speak aloud!
ETHELBERT	Auranthe, and her brother there.
CONRAD	Amaze!
LUDOLPH	Throw them from the windows!
OTHO	Do what you will!
LUDOLPH	What shall I do with them?

Something of quick dispatch, for should she hear.
My soft Auranthe, her sweet mercy would
Prevail against my fury. Damned priest!   170
What swift death wilt thou die? As to the lady
I touch her not.

| ETHELBERT | Illustrious Otho, stay! |

An ample store of misery thou hast,
Choke not the granary of thy noble mind
With more bad bitter grain, too difficult
A cud for the repentance of a man
Grey-growing. To thee only I appeal,
Not to thy noble son, whose yeasting youth
Will clear itself, and crystal turn again.[58]
A young man's heart, by Heaven's blessing, is   180
A wide world, where a thousand new-born hopes
Empurple fresh the melancholy blood:
But an old man's is narrow, tenantless
Of hopes, and stuff'd with many memories,
Which, being pleasant, ease the heavy pulse –
Painful, clog up and stagnate. Weigh this matter
Even as a miser balances his coin;
And, in the name of mercy, give command
That your knight Albert be brought here before you.
He will expound this riddle; he will show   190
A noon-day proof[59] of bad Auranthe's guilt.

OTHO   Let Albert straight be summon'd.

                                        [exit one of the nobles

LUDOLPH   Impossible!
I cannot doubt – I will not – no – to doubt
Is to be ashes! – wither'd up to death!

OTHO   My gentle Ludolph, harbour not a fear;
You do yourself much wrong.

LUDOLPH   O, wretched dolt![60]
Now, when my foot is almost on thy neck,
Wilt thou infuriate me? Proof! Thou fool!
Why wilt thou tease impossibility
With such a thick-skull'd persevering suit?   200
Fanatic obstinacy! Prodigy!
Monster of folly! Ghost of a turn'd brain!
You puzzle me, – you haunt me, – when I dream
Of you my brain will split! Bald sorcerer!
Juggler! May I come near you? On my soul
I know not whether to pity, curse, or laugh.

                    Enter ALBERT, *and the nobleman*

Here, Albert, this old phantom wants a proof!

	Give him his proof! A camel's load of proofs!	
OTHO	Albert, I speak to you as to a man	
	Whose words once utter'd pass like current gold;	210

And therefore fit to calmly put a close
To this brief tempest. Do you stand possess'd
Of any proof against the honourableness
Of Lady Auranthe, our new-spoused daughter?

ALBERT   You chill me with astonishment. How's this?
My Liege, what proof should I have 'gainst a fame
Impossible of slur?   [OTHO *rises*

ERMINIA   O wickedness!

ETHELBERT   Deluded monarch, 'tis a cruel lie.

OTHO   Peace, rebel-priest!

CONRAD   Insult beyond credence!

ERMINIA   Almost a dream!

LUDOLPH   We have awaken'd from   220
A foolish dream that from my brow hath wrung
A wrathful dew. O folly! why did I
So act the lion with this silly gnat?
Let them depart. Lady Erminia!
I ever griev'd for you, as who did not?
But now you have, with such a brazen front,
So most maliciously, so madly striven
To dazzle the soft moon, when tenderest clouds
Should be unloop'd around to curtain her;
I leave you to the desert of the world   230
Almost with pleasure. Let them be set free
For me! I take no personal revenge
More than against a nightmare, which a man
Forgets in the new dawn.   [*exit* LUDOLPH

OTHO   Still in extremes! No, they must not be loose.

ETHELBERT   Albert, I must suspect thee of a crime
So fiendish –

OTHO   Fear'st thou not my fury, monk?
Conrad, be they in your sure custody
Till we determine some fit punishment.
It is so mad a deed, I must reflect   240
And question them in private; for perhaps,
By patient scrutiny, we may discover

Whether they merit death, or should be placed
In care of the physicians.

         [exeunt OTHO *and nobles,* ALBERT *following*

CONRAD   My guards, ho!

ERMINIA   Albert, wilt thou follow there?
Wilt thou creep dastardly behind his back,
And slink away from a weak woman's eye?
Turn, thou court-Janus![61] thou forget'st thyself;
Here is the Duke, waiting with open arms,

             Enter guards

To thank thee; here congratulate each other;   250
Wring hands; embrace; and swear how lucky 'twas
That I, by happy chance, hit the right man
Of all the world to trust in.

ALBERT   Trust! to me!

CONRAD   *[aside]* He is the sole one in this mystery.

ERMINIA   Well, I give up, and save my prayers for Heaven!
You, who could do this deed, would ne'er relent,
Though, at my words, the hollow prison-vaults
Would groan for pity.

CONRAD   Manacle them both!

ETHELBERT   I know it – it must be – I see it all!
Albert, thou art the minion![62]

ERMINIA   Ah! too plain –   260

CONRAD   Silence! Gag up their mouths! I cannot bear
More of this brawling. That the Emperor
Had plac'd you in some other custody!
Bring them away.   *[exeunt all but* ALBERT

ALBERT   Though my name perish from the book of honour,
Almost before the recent ink is dry,
And be no more remember'd after death,
Than any drummer's in the muster-roll;
Yet shall I season high my sudden fall
With triumph o'er that evil-witted duke!   270
He shall feel what it is to have the hand
Of a man drowning, on his hateful throat.

            Enter GERSA *and* SIGIFRED

GERSA   What discord is at ferment in this house?

SIGIFRED	We are without conjecture; not a soul
	We met could answer any certainty.
GERSA	Young Ludolph, like a fiery arrow, shot
	By us.
SIGIFRED	The Emperor, with cross'd arms, in thought.
GERSA	In one room music, in another sadness,
	Perplexity every where!
ALBERT	A trifle more!
	Follow; your presences will much avail
	To tune our jarred spirits. I'll explain.

280

[exeunt

ACT 4   SCENE 1

Auranthe's apartment

AURANTHE *and* CONRAD *discovered*

CONRAD   Well, well, I know what ugly jeopardy
            We are cag'd in; you need not pester that
            Into my ears. Prythee, let me be spared
            A foolish tongue, that I may bethink me
            Of remedies with some deliberation.
            You cannot doubt but 'tis in Albert's power
            To crush or save us?

AURANTHE   No, I cannot doubt.
            He has, assure yourself, by some strange means,
            My secret; which I ever hid from him,
            Knowing his mawkish honesty.

CONRAD   Curs'd slave!   10

AURANTHE   Ay, I could almost curse him now myself.
            Wretched impediment! Evil genius!
            A glue upon my wings, that cannot spread,
            When they should span the provinces! A snake,
            A scorpion, sprawling on the first gold step,
            Conducting to the throne, high canopied.

CONRAD   You would not hear my council, when his life
            Might have been trodden out, all sure and hush'd;
            Now the dull animal forsooth must be
            Entreated, managed! When can you contrive   20
            The interview he demands?

AURANTHE   As speedily
            It must be done as my brib'd woman can
            Unseen conduct him to me; but I fear
            'Twill be impossible, while the broad day
            Comes through the panes with persecuting glare.
            Methinks, if 't now were night I could intrigue
            With darkness, bring the stars to second me,
            And settle all this trouble.

CONRAD   Nonsense! Child!
            See him immediately; why not now?

AURANTHE   Do you forget that even the senseless doorposts   30
Are on the watch and gape through all the house?
How many whisperers there are about,
Hungry for evidence to ruin me;
Men I have spurn'd, and women I have taunted?
Besides, the foolish prince sends, minute whiles,[63]
His pages – so they tell me – to enquire
After my health, entreating, if I please,
To see me.

CONRAD   Well, suppose this Albert here;
What is your power with him?

AURANTHE   He should be
My echo, my taught parrot! but I fear   40
He will be cur[64] enough to bark at me;
Have his own say, read me some silly creed
'Bout shame and pity.

CONRAD   What will you do then?

AURANTHE   What I shall do, I know not: what I would
Cannot be done; for see, this chamber-floor
Will not yield to the pick-axe and the spade, –
Here is no quiet depth of hollow ground.

CONRAD   Sister, you have grown sensible and wise,
Seconding, ere I speak it, what is now,
I hope, resolv'd between us.

AURANTHE   Say, what is 't?   50

CONRAD   You need not be his sexton[65] too: a man
May carry that with him shall make him die
Elsewhere, – give that to him; pretend the while
You will tomorrow succumb to his wishes,
Be what they may, and send him from the Castle
On some fool's errand; let his latest groan
Frighten the wolves!

AURANTHE   Alas! he must not die!

CONRAD   Would you were both hears'd up in stifling lead!
Detested –

AURANTHE   Conrad, hold! I would not bear
The little thunder of your fretful tongue,   60
Tho' I alone were taken in these toils.
And you could free me; but remember, Sir,
You live alone in my security:

	So keep your wits at work, for your own sake,
	Not mine, and be more mannerly.
CONRAD	Thou wasp!
	If my domains were emptied of these folk,
	And I had thee to starve –
AURANTHE	O, marvellous!

But Conrad, now be gone; the Host is look'd for;
Cringe to the Emperor, entertain the Lords,
And, do ye mind, above all things, proclaim   70
My sickness, with a brother's sadden'd eye,
Condoling with Prince Ludolph. In fit time
Return to me.

CONRAD   I leave you to your thoughts.   [exit

AURANTHE   [sola][66] Down, down, proud temper! down,
                              Auranthe's pride!
Why do I anger him when I should kneel?
Conrad! Albert! help! help! What can I do?
O wretched woman! lost, wreck'd, swallow'd up,
Accursed, blasted! O, thou golden Crown,
Orbing along the serene firmament
Of a wide empire, like a glowing moon;   80
And thou, bright sceptre! lustrous in my eyes, –
There – as the fabled fair Hesperian tree,[67]
Bearing a fruit more precious! graceful thing,
Delicate, godlike, magic! must I leave
Thee to melt in the visionary air,
Ere, by one grasp, this common hand is made
Imperial? I do not know the time
When I have wept for sorrow; but methinks
I could now sit upon the ground, and shed
Tears, tears of misery. O, the heavy day!   90
How shall I bear my life till Albert comes?
Ludolph! Erminia! Proofs! O heavy day!
Bring me some mourning weeds,[68] that I may 'tire
Myself, as fits one wailing her own death:
Cut off these curls, and brand this lily hand,
And throw these jewels from my loathing sight, –
Fetch me a missal, and a string of beads, –
A cup of bitter'd water, and a crust, –
I will confess, O holy Abbot! – How!

What is this? Auranthe! thou fool, dolt,　　　　　　100
Whimpering idiot! up! up! act and quell!
I am safe! Coward! why am I in fear?
Albert! he cannot stickle,[69] chew the cud
In such a fine extreme, – impossible!
Who knocks?　　　　*[goes to the door, listens, and opens it*

Enter ALBERT

Albert, I have been waiting for you here
With such an aching heart, such swooning throbs
On my poor brain, such cruel – cruel sorrow,
That I should claim your pity! Art not well?

ALBERT　　Yes, lady, well.

AURANTHE　　　　　　　You look not so, alas!　　　　110
But pale, as if you brought some heavy news.

ALBERT　　You know full well what makes me look so pale.

AURANTHE　　No! Do I? Surely I am still to learn
Some horror; all I know, this present, is
I am near hustled to a dangerous gulf,
Which you can save me from, – and therefore safe,
So trusting in thy love; that should not make
Thee pale, my Albert.

ALBERT　　　　　　　It doth make me freeze.

AURANTHE　　Why should it, love?

ALBERT　　　　　　　You should not ask me that,
But make your own heart monitor, and save　　　　120
Me the great pain of telling. You must know.

AURANTHE　　Something has vext you, Albert. There are times
When simplest things put on a sombre cast;
A melancholy mood will haunt a man,
Until most easy matters take the shape
Of unachievable tasks; small rivulets
Then seem impassable.

ALBERT　　　　　　　Do not cheat yourself
With hope that gloss of words, or suppliant action,
Or tears, or ravings, or self-threaten'd death,
Can alter my resolve.

AURANTHE　　　　　　　You make me tremble;　　　　130
Not so much at your threats, as at your voice,
Untun'd, and harsh, and barren of all love.

ALBERT You suffocate me! Stop this devil's parley,
And listen to me; know me once for all.
AURANTHE I thought I did. Alas! I am deceiv'd.
ALBERT No, you are not deceiv'd. You took me for
A man detesting all inhuman crime;
And therefore kept from me your demon's plot
Against Erminia. Silent? Be so still;
For ever! Speak no more; but hear my words,
Thy fate. Your safety I have bought today
By blazoning[70] a lie, which in the dawn
I'll expiate with truth.
AURANTHE O cruel traitor!
ALBERT For I would not set eyes upon thy shame;
I would not see thee dragg'd to death by the hair;
Penanc'd, and taunted on a scaffolding!
Tonight, upon the skirts of the blind wood
That blackens northward of these horrid towers,
I wait for you with horses. Choose your fate.
Farewell.
AURANTHE Albert, you jest; I'm sure you must.
You, an ambitious Soldier! I, a Queen,
One who could say, – Here, rule these Provinces!
Take tribute from those cities for thyself!
Empty these armouries, these treasuries,
Muster thy warlike thousands at a nod!
Go! conquer Italy!
ALBERT Auranthe, you have made
The whole world chaff to me. Your doom is fix'd.
AURANTHE Out, villain! dastard!
ALBERT Look there to the door!
Who is it?
AURANTHE Conrad, traitor!
ALBERT Let him in.

Enter CONRAD

Do not affect amazement, hypocrite,
At seeing me in this chamber.
CONRAD Auranthe?
ALBERT Talk not with eyes, but speak your curses out
Against me, who would sooner crush and grind

A brace of toads, than league with them to oppress
An innocent lady, gull an Emperor
More generous to me than autumn's sun
To ripening harvests.

AURANTHE   No more insult, sir!

ALBERT   Aye, clutch your scabbard; but, for prudence sake,
Draw not the sword; 'twould make an uproar, Duke,
You would not hear the end of. At nightfall   170
Your lady sister, if I guess aright,
Will leave this busy castle. You had best
Take farewell too of worldly vanities.

CONRAD   Vassal!

ALBERT   Tomorrow, when the Emperor sends
For loving Conrad, see you fawn on him.
Good even![71]

AURANTHE   You'll be seen!

ALBERT   See the coast clear then.

AURANTHE   [as he goes] Remorseless Albert! Cruel, cruel wretch!
                                                        [she lets him out

CONRAD   So, we must lick the dust?

AURANTHE   I follow him.

CONRAD   How? Where? The plan of your escape?

AURANTHE   He waits
For me with horses by the forest-side,   180
Northward.

CONRAD   Good, good! he dies. You go, say you?

AURANTHE   Perforce.[72]

CONRAD   Be speedy, darkness! Till that comes,
Fiends keep you company!   [exit

AURANTHE   And you! And you!
And all men! Vanish!

                                        [retires to an inner apartment

SCENE 2

An apartment in the castle

Enter LUDOLPH *and* Page

PAGE　　　　　Still very sick, my Lord; but now I went
　　　　　　Knowing my duty to so good a Prince;
　　　　　　And there her women in a mournful throng
　　　　　　Stood in the passage whispering: if any
　　　　　　Mov'd 'twas with careful steps and hush'd as death;
　　　　　　They bid me stop.

LUDOLPH　　　　　　　　　Good fellow, once again
　　　　　　Make some enquiry; prythee be not stay'd
　　　　　　By any hindrance, but with gentlest force
　　　　　　Break through her weeping servants, till thou com'st
　　　　　　E'en to her chamber door, and there, fair boy,　　　　10
　　　　　　If with thy mother's milk thou hast suck'd in
　　　　　　Any diviner eloquence; woo her ears
　　　　　　With plaints[73] for me more tender than the voice
　　　　　　Of dying Echo, echoed.

PAGE　　　　　　　　　　Kindest master!
　　　　　　To know thee sad thus, will unloose my tongue
　　　　　　In mournful syllables. Let but my words reach
　　　　　　Her ears and she shall take them coupled with
　　　　　　Moans from my heart and sighs not counterfeit.
　　　　　　May I speed better!　　　　　　　　*[exit Page*

LUDOLPH　　　　　　　　Auranthe! My Life!
　　　　　　Long have I lov'd thee, yet till now not lov'd:　　　　20
　　　　　　Remembering, as I do, hard-hearted times
　　　　　　When I had heard even of thy death perhaps,
　　　　　　And thoughtless, suffered to pass alone
　　　　　　Into Elysium! now I follow thee
　　　　　　A substance or a shadow, wheresoe'er
　　　　　　Thou leadest me, – whether thy white feet press,
　　　　　　With pleasant weight, the amorous-aching earth,
　　　　　　Or thro' the air thou pioneerest me,
　　　　　　A shade! Yet sadly I predestinate!
　　　　　　O unbenignest Love, why will thou let　　　　　　30

Darkness steal out upon the sleepy world
So wearily; as if night's chariot wheels
Were clog'd in some thick cloud. O, changeful Love,
Let not her steeds with drowsy-footed pace
Pass the high stars, before sweet embassage[74]
Comes from the pillow'd beauty of that fair
Completion of all delicate nature's wit.
Pout her faint lips anew with rubious[75] health
And with thine infant fingers lift the fringe
Of her sick eyelids; that those eyes may glow   40
With wooing light upon me, ere the Morn
Peers with disrelish, grey, barren, and cold.

Enter GERSA *and courtiers*

Otho calls me his Lion – should I blush
To be so tam'd, so –

GERSA   Do me the courtesy
Gentlemen to pass on.

COURTIER   We are your servants.
                              [*exeunt courtiers*

LUDOLPH   It seems then, Sir, you have found out the man
You would confer with; me?

GERSA   If I break not
Too much upon your thoughtful mood, I will
Claim a brief while your patience.

LUDOLPH   For what cause
Soe'er I shall be honour'd

GERSA   I not less.   50

LUDOLPH   What may it be? No trifle can take place
Of such deliberate prologue, serious 'haviour.
But be it what it may I cannot fail
To listen with no common interest –
For though so new your presence is to me,
I have a soldier's friendship for your fame –
Please you explain.

GERSA   As thus – for, pardon me,
I cannot in plain terms grossly assault
A noble nature; and would faintly sketch
What your quick apprehension will fill up   60

	So finely I esteem you.	
LUDOLPH	I attend –	
GERSA	Your generous Father, most illustrious Otho,	

              Sits in the Banquet room among his chiefs –
              His wine is bitter, for you are not there –
              His eyes are fix'd still on the open doors,
              And every passer in he frowns upon
              Seeing no Ludolph comes.

LUDOLPH   I do neglect –

GERSA   And for your absence, may I guess the cause?

LUDOLPH   Stay there! no – guess? more princely you must be –
              Than to make guesses at me. 'Tis enough,   70
              I'm sorry I can hear no more.

GERSA   And I
              As griev'd to force it on you so abrupt;
              Yet one day you must know a grief whose sting
              Will sharpen more the longer 'tis conceal'd.

LUDOLPH   Say it at once, sir, dead, dead, is she dead?

GERSA   Mine is a cruel task: she is not dead –
              And would for your sake she were innocent –

LUDOLPH   Thou liest! thou amazest me beyond
              All scope of thought; convulsest my heart's blood
              To deadly churning – Gersa you are young   80
              As I am; let me observe you face to face;
              Not grey-brow'd like the poisonous Ethelbert,
              No rheumed[76] eyes, no furrowing of age,
              No wrinkles where all vices nestle in
              Like crannied vermin – no, but fresh and young
              And hopeful featur'd. Ha! by heaven you weep
              Tears, human tears – Do you repent you then
              Of a curs'd torturer's office! Why shouldst join –
              Tell me, the league of Devils? Confess – confess
              The Lie. –

GERSA   Lie! – but begone all ceremonious point   90
              Of honour battailous.[77] I could not turn
              My wrath against thee for the orbed world.

LUDOLPH   Your wrath, weak boy? Tremble at mine unless
              Retraction follow close upon the heels
              Of that late astounding insult: why has my sword

Not done already a sheer judgment on thee?
Despair, or eat thy words. Why, thou wast nigh
Whimpering away my reason: hark ye, Sir,
It is no secret; – that Erminia,
Erminia, Sir, was hidden in your tent;   100
O bless'd asylum! comfortable home!
Begone, I pity thee, thou art a Gull –
Erminia's last new puppet –

GERSA   Furious fire!
Thou mak'st me boil as hot as thou canst flame!
And in thy teeth I give thee back the lie!
Thou liest! Thou, Auranthe's fool, a wittol[78] –

LUDOLPH   Look! look at this bright sword;
There is no part of it to the very hilt
But shall indulge itself about thine heart –
Draw – but remember thou must cower thy plumes,   110
As yesterday the Arab made thee stoop –

GERSA   Patience! not here, I would not spill thy blood
Here underneath this roof where Otho breathes,
Thy father – almost mine –

LUDOLPH   O faltering coward –

               Re-enter Page

Stay, stay, here is one I have half a word with –
Well – What ails thee child?

PAGE   My lord,

LUDOLPH   Good fellow!

PAGE   They are fled!

LUDOLPH   They – who?

PAGE   When anxiously
I hasten'd back, your grieving messenger,
I found the stairs all dark, the lamps extinct,
And not a foot or whisper to be heard.   120
I thought her dead, and on the lowest step
Sat listening; when presently came by
Two muffled up, – one sighing heavily,
The other cursing low, whose voice I knew
For the Duke Conrad's. Close I follow'd them
Thro' the dark ways they chose to the open air;
And, as I follow'd, heard my lady speak.

LUDOLPH	Thy life answers the truth!
PAGE	The chamber's empty!
LUDOLPH	As I will be of mercy! So, at last,
	This nail is in my temples!
GERSA	Be calm in this.

130

LUDOLPH	I am.
GERSA	And Albert too has disappear'd;
	Ere I met you, I sought him everywhere;
	You would not hearken.
LUDOLPH	Which way went they, boy?
GERSA	I'll hunt with you.
LUDOLPH	No, no, no. My senses are
	Still whole. I have surviv'd. My arm is strong –
	My appetite sharp – for revenge! I'll no sharer
	In my feast; my injury is all my own,
	And so is my revenge, my lawful chattels!
	Terrier, ferret them out! Burn – burn the witch!
	Trace me their footsteps! Away!

140

[exeunt

ACT 5   SCENE 1

A part of the forest

Enter CONRAD *and* AURANTHE

AURANTHE   Go no further; not a step more; thou art
            A master-plague in the midst of miseries.
            Go – I fear thee. I tremble every limb,
            Who never shook before. There's moody death
            In thy resolved looks – Yes, I could kneel
            To pray thee far away. Conrad, go, go –
            There! yonder underneath the boughs I see
            Our horses!

CONRAD   Aye, and the man.

AURANTHE   Yes, he is there.
            Go, go, – no blood, no blood; go, gentle Conrad!

CONRAD   Farewell!

AURANTHE   Farewell, for this Heaven pardon you.   10

                                                [exit AURANTHE

CONRAD   If he survive one hour, then may I die
            In unimagined tortures – or breathe through
            A long life in the foulest sink of the world!
            He dies – 'tis well she do not advertise
            The caitiff of the cold steel at his back.

                                                [exit CONRAD

Enter LUDOLPH *and Page*

LUDOLPH   Miss'd the way, boy, say not that on your peril!

PAGE   Indeed, indeed I cannot trace them further.

LUDOLPH   Must I stop here? Here solitary die?
            Stifled beneath the thick oppressive shade
            Of these dull boughs, – this oven of dark thickets, –   20
            Silent, – without revenge? – pshaw! – bitter end, –
            A bitter death, – a suffocating death, –
            A gnawing – silent – deadly, quiet death!
            Escap'd? – fled? – vanish'd? melted into air?
            She's gone! I cannot clutch her! no revenge!
            A muffled death, ensnar'd in horrid silence!

Suck'd to my grave amid a dreamy calm!
O, where is that illustrious noise of war,
To smother up this sound of labouring breath,
This rustle of the trees!

                 [AURANTHE *shrieks at a distance*

PAGE   My Lord, a noise!
This way – hark!

LUDOLPH   Yes, yes! A hope! A music!
A glorious clamour! How I live again!

                         [*exeunt*

SCENE 2

Another part of the forest

Enter ALBERT (*wounded*)

ALBERT   O for enough life to support me on
To Otho's feet –

Enter LUDOLPH

LUDOLPH   Thrice villainous, stay there!
Tell me where that detested woman is
Or this is through thee!

ALBERT   My good Prince, with me
The sword has done its worst; not without worst
Done to another – Conrad has it home –
I see you know it all –

LUDOLPH   Where is his sister?

AURANTHE *rushes in*

AURANTHE   Albert!

LUDOLPH   Ha! There! there! – He is the paramour![79] –
There – hug him – dying! O, thou innocence,
Shrine him and comfort him at his last gasp,   10
Kiss down his eyelids! Was he not thy love?
Wilt thou forsake him at his latest hour?
Keep fearful and aloof from his last gaze,
His most uneasy moments, when cold death

Stands with the door ajar to let him in?

ALBERT   O that that door with hollow slam would close
Upon me sudden, for I cannot meet,
In all the unknown chambers of the dead,
Such horrors –

LUDOLPH   Auranthe! what can he mean?
What horrors? Is it not a joyous time?   20
Am I not married to a paragon
'Of personal beauty and untainted soul?'
A blushing fair-eyed Purity! A Sylph,
Whose snowy timid hand has never sin'd
Beyond a flower pluck'd, white as itself?
Albert, you do insult my Bride – your Mistress –
To talk of horrors on our wedding night.

ALBERT   Alas! poor Prince, I would you knew my heart.
'Tis not so guilty –

LUDOLPH   Hear you he pleads not guilty –
You are not? or if so what matters it?   30
You have escap'd me, – free as the dusk air –
Hid in the forest – safe from my revenge;
I cannot catch you – You should laugh at me,
Poor cheated Ludolph, – make the forest hiss
With jeers at me – You tremble; faint at once,
You will come to again. O Cockatrice,[80]
I have you. Whither wander those fair eyes
To entice the Devil to your help, that he
May change you to a Spider, so to crawl
Into some cranny to escape my wrath?   40

ALBERT   Sometimes the counsel of a dying man
Doth operate quietly when his breath is gone –
Disjoin those hands – part – part, do not destroy
Each other – forget her – our miseries
Are equal shar'd, and mercy is –

LUDOLPH   A boon
When one can compass it. Auranthe, try
Your oratory – your breath is not so hitch'd –
Aye, stare for help –   [ALBERT *groans and dies*
            There goes a spotted soul
Howling in vain along the hollow night –

	Hear him – he calls you – Sweet Auranthe, come!	50
AURANTHE	Kill me.
LUDOLPH	No! What? upon our marriage-night!

The earth would shudder at so foul a deed –
A fair Bride, a sweet Bride, an innocent Bride!
No, we must revel it, as 'tis in use
In times of delicate brilliant ceremony:
Come, let me lead you to our halls again –
Nay, linger not – make no resistance sweet –
Will you – Ah wretch, thou canst not, for I have
The strength of twenty lions 'gainst a lamb –
Now one adieu for Albert – come away. –   60

[exeunt

SCENE 3

An inner court of the castle

Enter SIGIFRED, GONFRED, *and* THEODORE *meeting*

| THEODORE | Was ever such a night? |
| SIGIFRED | What horrors more? |

Things unbeliev'd one hour, so strange they are,
The next hour stamps with credit.

| THEODORE | Your last news? |
| GONFRED | After the Page's story of the death |

Of Albert and Duke Conrad?

| SIGIFRED | And the return |

Of Ludolph with the Princess.

| GONFRED | No more save |

Prince Gersa's freeing Abbot Ethelbert,
And the sweet lady, fair Erminia,
From prison.

| THEODORE | Where are they now? hast yet heard? |
| GONFRED | With the sad Emperor they are closeted;   10 |

I saw the three pass slowly up the stairs,
The lady weeping, the old Abbot cowl'd.

SIGIFRED	What next?
THEODORE	I ache to think on 't.
GONFRED	'Tis with fate.
THEODORE	One while these proud towers are hush'd as death.
GONFRED	The next our poor Prince fills the arched rooms
	With ghastly ravings.
SIGIFRED	I do fear his brain.
GONFRED	I will see more. Bear you so stout a heart?

[*exeunt into the castle*

SCENE 4

A cabinet, opening towards a terrace

OTHO, ERMINIA, ETHELBERT, *and a Physician, discovered*

OTHO	O, my poor boy! my Son! my Son! my Ludolph!	
	Have ye no comfort for me, ye Physicians	
	Of the weak body and soul?	
ETHELBERT	'Tis not the medicine	
	Either of heaven or earth can cure unless	
	Fit time be chosen to administer –	
OTHO	A kind forbearance, holy Abbot – come	
	Erminia, here sit by me, gentle girl;	
	Give me thy hand – hast thou forgiven me?	
ERMINIA	Would I were with the saints to pray for you!	
OTHO	Why will ye keep me from my darling child?	10
PHYSICIAN	Forgive me, but he must not see thy face –	
OTHO	Is then a father's countenance a Gorgon?	
	Hath it not comfort in it? Would it not	
	Console my poor boy, cheer him, heal his spirits?	
	Let me embrace him, let me speak to him –	
	I will – who hinders me? Who's Emperor?	
PHYSICIAN	You may not, Sire – 'twould overwhelm him quite,	
	He is so full of grief and passionate wrath,	
	Too heavy a sigh would kill him – or do worse.	
	He must be sav'd by fine contrivances –	20
	And most especially we must keep clear	
	Out of his sight a Father whom he loves –	

	His heart is full, it can contain no more,	
	And do its ruddy office.	
ETHELBERT	Sage advice;	
	We must endeavour how to ease and slacken	
	The tight wound energies of his despair,	
	Not make them tenser –	
OTHO	Enough! I hear, I hear.	
	Yet you were about to advise more – I listen.	
ETHELBERT	This learned doctor will agree with me,	
	That not in the smallest point should he be thwarted	30
	Or gainsaid[81] by one word – his very motions,	
	Nods, becks and hints, should be obey'd with care,	
	Even on the moment: so his troubled mind	
	May cure itself –	
PHYSICIAN	There is no other means.	
OTHO	Open the door: let's hear if all is quiet –	
PHYSICIAN	Beseech you, Sire, forbear.	
ERMINIA	Do, do.	
OTHO	I command!	
	Open it straight – hush! – quiet – my lost boy!	
	My miserable child!	
LUDOLPH	(indistinctly without) Fill, fill my goblet, –	
	Here's a health!	
ERMINIA	O, close the door!	
OTHO	Let, let me hear his voice; this cannot last –	40
	And fain would I catch up his dying words	
	Though my own knell[82] they be – this cannot last –	
	O let me catch his voice – for lo! I hear	
	This silence whisper me that he is dead!	
	It is so. Gersa?	

Enter GERSA

PHYSICIAN	Say, how fares the prince?	
GERSA	More calm – his features are less wild and flush'd –	
	Once he complain'd of weariness –	
PHYSICIAN	Indeed!	
	'Tis good – 'tis good – let him but fall asleep,	
	That saves him.	
OTHO	Gersa, watch him like a child –	
	Ward him from harm – and bring me better news –	50

PHYSICIAN	Humour him to the height. I fear to go;
	For should he catch a glimpse of my dull garb,
	It might affright him – fill him with suspicion
	That we believe him sick, which must not be –
GERSA	I will invent what soothing means I can.

[*exit* GERSA

PHYSICIAN	This should cheer up your Highness – weariness
	Is a good symptom, and most favourable –
	It gives me pleasant hopes. Please you walk forth
	Onto the Terrace; the refreshing air
	Will blow one half of your sad doubts away. 60

[*Exeunt*

SCENE 5

*A banquetting hall, brilliantly illuminated, and set forth with
all costly magnificence, with supper tables, laden with
services of gold and silver. A door in the back scene, guarded
by two soldiers. Lords, ladies, knights, gentlemen, etc.,
whispering sadly, and ranging themselves; part
entering and part discovered.*

FIRST KNIGHT	Grievously are we tantalis'd, one and all –
	Sway'd here and there, commanded to and fro
	As though we were the shadows of a dream
	And link'd to a sleeping fancy. What do we here?
GONFRED	I am no Seer – you know we must obey
	The prince from A to Z – though it should be
	To set the place in flames. I pray hast heard
	Where the most wicked Princess is?
FIRST KNIGHT	There, Sir,
	In the next room – have you remark'd those two
	Stout soldiers posted at the door?
GONFRED	For what? 10

[*they whisper*

FIRST LADY	How ghast[83] a train!
SECOND LADY	Sure this should be some splendid burial.
FIRST LADY	What fearful whispering! See, see, – Gersa there!

Enter GERSA

GERSA   Put on your brightest looks; smile if you can;
     Behave as all were happy; keep your eyes
     From the least watch upon him; if he speaks
     To any one, answer collectedly,
     Without surprise, his questions, howe'er strange.
     Do this to the utmost, – though, alas! with me[84]
     The remedy grows hopeless! Here he comes, –   20
     Observe what I have said, – show no surprise.

Enter LUDOLPH, *followed by* SIGIFRED *and Page*

LUDOLPH   A splendid company! rare beauties here!
     I should have Orphean lips, and Plato's fancy,
     Amphion's utterance, toned with his lyre,
     Or the deep key of Jove's sonorous mouth,
     To give fit salutation. Methought I heard,
     As I came in, some whispers, – what of that?
     'Tis natural men should whisper; at the kiss
     Of Psyche given by Love, there was a buzz
     Among the gods! – and silence is as natural.   30
     These draperies are fine, and, being a mortal,
     I should desire no better; yet, in truth,
     There must be some superior costliness,
     Some wider-domed high magnificence!
     I would have, as a mortal I may not,
     Hanging of heaven's clouds, purple and gold,
     Slung from the spheres; gauzes of silver mist,
     Loop'd up with cords of twisted wreathed light,
     And tassell'd round with weeping meteors!
     These pendent lamps and chandeliers are bright   40
     As earthly fires from dull dross can be cleansed;
     Yet could my eyes drink up intenser beams
     Undazzled, – this is darkness, – when I close
     These lids, I see far fiercer brilliances, –
     Skies full of splendid moons, and shooting stars,
     And spouting exhalations, diamond fires,
     And panting fountains quivering with deep glows!
     Yes – this is dark – is it not dark?

SIGIFRED   My Lord,

          'Tis late; the lights of festival are ever
          Quench'd in the morn.

LUDOLPH   'Tis not tomorrow then?   50

SIGIFRED   'Tis early dawn.

GERSA   ·   Indeed full time we slept;
          Say you so, Prince?

LUDOLPH   I say I quarrell'd with you;
          We did not tilt[85] each other, – that's a blessing, –
          Good gods! no innocent blood upon my head!

SIGIFRED   Retire, Gersa!

LUDOLPH   There should be three more here:
          For two of them, they stay away perhaps,
          Being gloomy-minded, haters of fair revels, –
          They know their own thoughts best.

                           As for the third,
          Deep blue eyes – semi-shaded in white lids,
          Finish'd with lashes fine for more soft shade,   60
          Completed by her twin-arch'd ebon brows –
          White temples of exactest elegance,
          Of even mould felicitous and smooth –
          Cheeks fashion'd tenderly on either side,
          So perfect, so divine that our poor eyes
          Are dazzled with the sweet proportioning,
          And wonder that 'tis so, – the magic chance!
          Her nostrils, small, fragrant, faery-delicate;
          Her lips – I swear no human bones e'er wore
          So taking a disguise – you shall behold her!   70
          We'll have her presently; aye, you shall see her,
          And wonder at her, friends, she is so fair –
          She is the world's chief Jewel, and by heaven
          She's mine by right of marriage – she is mine!
          Patience, good people, in fit time I send
          A summoner – she will obey my call,
          Being a wife most mild and dutiful.
          First I would hear what music is prepared
          To herald and receive her – let me hear!

SIGIFRED   Bid the musicians soothe him tenderly.   80
                         [*a soft strain of music*

LUDOLPH   Ye have none better – no – I am content;
          'Tis a rich sobbing melody, with reliefs

Full and majestic; it is well enough,
And will be sweeter, when ye see her pace
Sweeping into this presence, glisten'd o'er
With emptied caskets, and her train upheld
By ladies, habited in robes of lawn,
Sprinkled with golden crescents; (others bright
In silks, with spangles shower'd,) and bow'd to
By Duchesses and pearled Margravines[86] –   90
Sad, that the fairest creature of the earth –
I pray you mind me not – 'tis sad, I say,
That the extremest beauty of the world
Should so entrench herself away from me,
Behind a barrier of engender'd guilt!

SECOND LADY   Ah! what a moan!

FIRST KNIGHT   Most piteous indeed!

LUDOLPH   She shall be brought before this company,
And then – then –

FIRST LADY   He muses.

GERSA   O, Fortune, where will this end?

SIGIFRED   I guess this purpose! Indeed he must not have
That pestilence brought in, – that cannot be,   100
There we must stop him.

GERSA   I am lost! Hush, hush!
He is about to rave again.

LUDOLPH   A barrier of guilt! I was the fool,
She was the cheater! Who's the cheater now,
And who the fool? The entrapp'd, the caged fool,
The bird-lim'd[87] raven? She shall croak to death
Secure! Methinks I have her in my fist,
To crush her with my heel! Wait, wait! I marvel
My father keeps away: good friend, ah! Sigifred!
Do bring him to me – and Erminia   110
I fain would see before I sleep – and Ethelbert,
That he may bless me, as I know he will
Though I have curs'd him.

SIGIFRED   Rather suffer me
To lead you to them –

LUDOLPH   No, excuse me, no –
The day is not quite done – go bring them hither.

                                        [*exit* SIGIFRED

	Certes, a father's smile should, like sunlight,	
	Slant on my sheafed harvest of ripe bliss –	
	Besides, I thirst to pledge my lovely Bride	
	In a deep goblet: let me see – what wine?	
	The strong Iberian juice,[88] or mellow Greek?	120
	Or pale Calabrian?[89] Or the Tuscan grape?	
	Or of old Aetna's[90] pulpy wine presses	
	Black stain'd with the fat vintage, as it were	
	The purple slaughter-house, where Bacchus' self	
	Prick'd his own swollen veins? Where is my Page?	
PAGE	Here, here!	
LUDOLPH	Be ready to obey me; anon thou shalt	
	Bear a soft message for me – for the hour	
	Draws near when I must make a winding up	
	Of bridal Mysteries – a fine-spun vengeance!	
	Carve it on my tomb, that when I rest beneath	130
	Men shall confess – This Prince was gull'd and cheated,	
	But from the ashes of disgrace he rose	
	More than a fiery Phoenix – and did burn	
	His ignominy up in purging fires –	
	Did I not send, Sir, but a moment past.	
	For my Father?	
GERSA	You did.	
LUDOLPH	Perhaps 'twould be	
	Much better he came not.	
GERSA	He enters now!	

Enter OTHO, ERMINIA, ETHELBERT, SIGIFRED, *and Physician*

LUDOLPH	O thou good Man, against whose sacred head	
	I was a mad conspirator, chiefly too	
	For the sake of my fair newly wedded wife,	140
	Now to be punish'd, do not look so sad!	
	Those charitable eyes will thaw my heart,	
	Those tears will wash away a just resolve,	
	A verdict, ten times sworn! Awake – awake –	
	Put on a judge's brow, and use a tongue	
	Made iron-stern by habit! Thou shalt see	
	A deed to be applauded, 'scribed in gold!	
	Join a loud voice to mine, and so denounce	

What I alone will execute!

OTHO   Dear son,
What is it? By your father's love, I sue   150
That it be nothing merciless!

LUDOLPH   To that demon?
Not so! No! She is in temple-stall
Being garnish'd for the sacrifice, and I,
The Priest of Justice, will immolate[91] her
Upon the altar of wrath! She stings me through! –
Even as the worm doth feed upon the nut,
So she, a scorpion, preys upon my brain!
I feel her gnawing here! Let her but vanish,
Then, father, I will lead your legions forth,
Compact in steeled squares, and speared files,[92]   160
And bid our trumpets speak a fell rebuke
To nations drows'd in peace!

OTHO   Tomorrow, Son,
Be your word law – forget today –

LUDOLPH   I will
When I have finish'd it – now! now! I'm pight,
Tight-footed for the deed!

ERMINIA   Alas! Alas!

LUDOLPH What angel's voice is that? Erminia!
Ah! gentlest creature, whose sweet innocence
Was almost murder'd; I am penitent,
Wilt thou forgive me? And thou, holy man,
Good Ethelbert, shall I die in peace with you?   170

ERMINIA Die, my lord!

LUDOLPH   I feel it possible.

OTHO   Physician?

PHYSICIAN I fear me he is past my skill.

OTHO   Not so!

LUDOLPH I see it, I see it – I have been wandering –
Half-mad – not right here – I forget my purpose.
Bestir, bestir, Auranthe! ha! ha! ha!
Youngster! Page! go bid them drag her to me!
Obey! This shall finish it!   [*Draws a dagger*

OTHO   O my Son! my Son!

SIGIFRED This must not be – stop there!

LUDOLPH   Am I obey'd?

A little talk with her – no harm – haste! haste!

                              [*exit Page*

Set her before me – never fear I can strike.   180

SEVERAL VOICES My Lord! My Lord!

GERSA   Good Prince!

LUDOLPH Why do ye trouble me? out – out – out away!
There she is! take that! and that! no, no –
That's not well done – Where is she?

      The doors open. Enter Page. Several women
  are seen grouped about AURANTHE *in the inner room*

PAGE Alas! My Lord, my Lord! they cannot move her!
Her arms are stiff, – her fingers clench'd and cold –

LUDOLPH She's dead!

                [*staggers and falls into their arms*

ETHELBERT   Take away the dagger.

GERSA   Softly; so!

OTHO Thank God for that!

SIGIFRED   I fear it could not harm him.

GERSA No! – brief be his anguish!

LUDOLPH She's gone – I am content – Nobles, good night!   190
We are all weary – faint – set ope the doors –
I will to bed! – Tomorrow –

                         [*dies*

        The Curtain Falls

King Stephen[1]

A fragment of a tragedy written in November 1819

ACT 1   SCENE 1

Field of battle

Alarum. Enter KING STEPHEN, *knights, and soldiers*

STEPHEN If shame can on a soldier's vein-swoll'n front
Spread deeper crimson than the battle's toil,
Blush in your casing helmets! for see, see!
Yonder my chivalry, my pride of war,
Wrench'd with an iron hand from firm array,
Are routed loose about the plashy meads,[2]
Of honour forfeit. O that my known voice
Could reach your dastard ears, and fright you more!
Fly, cowards, fly! 'Glocester[3] is at your backs!
Throw your slack bridles o'er the flurried manes,   10
Ply well the rowel[4] with faint trembling heels,
Scampering to death at last!

KNIGHT 1   The enemy
Bears his flaunt[5] standard close upon their rear.

KNIGHT 2 Sure of a bloody prey, seeing the fens
Will swamp them girth-deep.

STEPHEN   Over head and ears,
No matter! 'Tis a gallant enemy;
How like a comet he goes streaming on.
But we must plague him in the flank, – hey, friends?
We are well breathed, – follow!

Enter EARL BALDWIN *and soldiers, as defeated*

STEPHEN   De Redvers![6]
What is the monstrous bugbear that can fright Baldwin?   20

BALDWIN No scarecrow, but the fortunate star
Of boisterous Chester,[7] whose fell truncheon now
Points level to the goal of victory.
This way he comes, and if you would maintain
Your person unaffronted by vile odds,

Take horse, my Lord.

STEPHEN   And which way spur for life?
Now I thank heaven I am in the toils,
That soldiers may bear witness how my arm
Can burst the meshes. Not the eagle more
Loves to beat up against a tyrannous blast,   30
Than I to meet the torrent of my foes.
This is a brag, – be't so, – but if I fall,
Carve it upon my 'scutcheon'd sepulchre.
On, fellow soldiers! Earl of Redvers, back!
Not twenty Earls of Chester shall browbeat
The diadem.

                              [*exeunt. alarum*

SCENE 2

Another part of the field

Trumpets sounding a victory. Enter GLOCESTER, *knights, and forces*

GLOCESTER   Now may we lift our bruised vizors up,
And take the flattering freshness of the air.
While the wide din of battle dies away
Into times past, yet to be echoed sure
In the silent pages of our chroniclers.

KNIGHT 1   Will Stephen's death be mark'd there, my good Lord,
Or that we gave him lodging in yon towers?

GLOCESTER   Fain would I know the great usurper's fate.

Enter two Captains severally

CAPTAIN 1   My Lord!

CAPTAIN 2   Most noble Earl!

CAPTAIN 1   The King –

CAPTAIN 2   The Empress[8] greets –

GLOCESTER   What of the King?

CAPTAIN 1   He sole and lone maintains   10
A hopeless bustle mid our swarming arms,
And with a nimble savageness attacks,
Escapes, makes fiercer onset, then anew

Eludes death, giving death to most that dare
Trespass within the circuit of his sword!
He must by this have fallen. Baldwin is taken:
And for the Duke of Bretagnes,[9] like a stag
He flies, for the Welsh beagles[10] to hunt down.
God save the Empress!

GLOCESTER   Now our dreaded Queen:
What message from her Highness?

CAPTAIN 2   Royal Maud   20
From the throng'd towers of Lincoln hath look'd down,
Like Pallas from the walls of Ilion,[11]
And seen her enemies havock'd at her feet.
She greets most noble Glocester from her heart,
Entreating him, his captains, and brave knights,
To grace a banquet. The high city gates
Are envious which shall see your triumph pass;
The streets are full of music.

                        Enter Second Knight

GLOCESTER   Whence come you?
KNIGHT 2   From Stephen, my good Prince, – Stephen! Stephen!
GLOCESTER   Why do you make such echoing of his name?   30
KNIGHT 2   Because I think, my lord, he is no man,
              But a fierce demon, 'nointed safe from wounds,
              And misbaptised with a Christian name.
GLOCESTER   A mighty soldier! – Does he still hold out?
KNIGHT 2   He shames our victory. His valour still
              Keeps elbow-room amid our eager swords.
              And holds our bladed falchions[12] all aloof –
              His gleaming battle-axe being slaughter-sick,
              Smote on the morion[13] of a Flemish knight.
              Broke short in his hand; upon the which he flung   40
              The heft away with such a vengeful force,
              It paunch'd the Earl of Chester's horse, who then
              Spleen-hearted came in full career at him.
GLOCESTER   Did no one take him at a vantage then?
KNIGHT 2   Three then with tiger leap upon him flew,
              Whom, with his sword swift-drawn and nimbly held,
              He stung away again, and stood to breathe,
              Smiling. Anon upon him rush'd once more

A throng of foes, and in this renew'd strife,
My sword met his and snapp'd off at the hilts.   50

GLOCESTER   Come, lead me to this Mars – and let us move
In silence, not insulting his sad doom
With clamourous trumpets. To the Empress bear
My salutations as befits the time.

[*exceunt* GLOCESTER *and forces*

SCENE 3

The field of battle

Enter STEPHEN *unarmed*

STEPHEN   Another sword! And what if I could seize
One from Bellona's gleaming armoury,
Or choose the fairest of her sheaved spears!
Where are my enemies? Here, close at hand,
Here come the testy brood. O for a sword!
I'm faint – a biting sword! A noble sword!
A hedge-stake – or a ponderous stone to hurl
With brawny vengeance, like the labourer Cain.[14]
Come on! Farewell my kingdom, and all hail
Thou superb, plum'd, and helmeted renown,   10
All hail – I would not truck[15] this brilliant day
To rule in Pylos with a Nestor's beard [16]–
Come on!

Enter DE KAIMS *and knights, etc.*

DE KAIMS   Is't madness, or a hunger after death,
That makes thee thus unarm'd throw taunts at us?
Yield, Stephen, or my sword's point dip in
The gloomy current of a traitor's heart.

STEPHEN   Do it, De Kaims,[17] I will not budge an inch.

DE KAIMS   Yes, of thy madness thou shalt take the meed.

STEPHEN   Darest thou?

DE KAIMS   How dare, against a man disarm'd?

STEPHEN   What weapons has the lion but himself?   20
Come not near me, De Kaims, for by the price

Of all the glory I have won this day,
Being a king, I will not yield alive
To any but the second man of the realm,
Robert of Glocester.

DE KAIMS   Thou shalt vail to me.

STEPHEN   Shall I, when I have sworn against it, sir?
Thou think'st it brave to take a breathing king,
That, on a court-day bow'd to haughty Maud,
The awed presence-chamber[18] may be bold
To whisper, there's the man who took alive   30
Stephen – me – prisoner. Certes, De Kaims,
The ambition is a noble one.

DE KAIMS   'Tis true,
And, Stephen, I must compass[19] it.

STEPHEN   No, no,
Do not tempt me to throttle you on the gorge,
Or with my gauntlet crush your hollow breast,
Just when your knighthood is grown ripe and full
For lordship.

A SOLDIER   Is an honest yeoman's spear
Of no use at a need? Take that.

STEPHEN   Ah, dastard!

DE KAIMS   What, you are vulnerable! my prisoner!

STEPHEN   No, not yet. I disclaim it, and demand   40
Death as a sovereign right unto a king
Who 'sdains to yield to any but his peer,
If not in title, yet in noble deeds,
The Earl of Glocester. Stab to the hilts, De Kaims,
For I will never by mean hands be led
From this so famous field. Do ye hear! Be quick!

        [*Trumpets. Enter the* EARL OF CHESTER *and Knights*

SCENE 4

A presence chamber

QUEEN MAUD *in a chair of state, the Earls of*
GLOCESTER *and* CHESTER, *lords, attendants*

MAUD   Glocester, no more: I will behold that Boulogne:[20]
              Set him before me. Not for the poor sake
              Of regal pomp and a vain-glorious hour,
              As thou with wary speech, yet near enough,
              Hast hinted.

GLOCESTER   Faithful counsel have I given ;
              If wary, for your Highness' benefit.

MAUD   The heavens forbid that I should not think so,
              For by thy valour have I won this realm,
              Which by thy wisdom I will ever keep.
              To sage advisers let me ever bend   10
              A meek attentive ear, so that they treat
              Of the wide kingdom's rule and government,
              Not trenching[21] on our actions personal.
              Advis'd, not school'd, I would be; and henceforth
              Spoken to in clear, plain, and open terms,
              Not sideways sermon'd at.

GLOCESTER   Then, in plain terms,
              Once more for the fallen king –

MAUD   Your pardon, Brother,
              I would no more of that; for, as I said
              'Tis not for worldly pomp I wish to see
              The rebel, but as dooming judge to give   20
              A sentence something worthy of his guilt.

GLOCESTER   If't must be so, I'll bring him to yourpresence.
                                              [*exit* GLOCESTER

MAUD   A meaner summoner might do as well –
              My Lord of Chester, is't true what I hear
              Of Stephen of Boulogne, our prisoner,
              That he, as a fit penance for his crimes,
              Eats wholesome, sweet, and palatable food
              Off Glocester's golden dishes – drinks pure wine,

	Lodges soft?	
CHESTER	More than that, my gracious Queen,	
	Has anger'd me. The noble Earl, methinks,	30
	Full soldier as he is, and without peer	
	In counsel, dreams too much among his books.	
	It may read well, but sure 'tis out of date	
	To play the Alexander with Darius.[22]	
MAUD	Truth! I think so. By heavens it shall not last!	
CHESTER	It would amaze your Highness now to mark	
	How Glocester overstrains his courtesy	
	To that crime-loving rebel, that Boulogne –	
MAUD	That ingrate!	
CHESTER	For whose vast ingratitude	
	To our late sovereign lord, your noble sire,[23]	40
	The generous Earl condoles in his mishaps,	
	And with a sort of lackeying friendliness,	
	Talks off the mighty frowning from his brow,	
	Woos him to hold a duet in a smile,	
	Or, if it please him, play an hour at chess –	
MAUD	A perjured slave!	
CHESTER	And for his perjury,	
	Glocester has fit rewards – nay, I believe,	
	He sets his bustling household's wits at work	
	For flatteries to ease this Stephen's hours,	
	And make a heaven of his purgatory ;	50
	Adorning bondage with the pleasant gloss	
	Of feasts and music, and all idle shows	
	Of indoor pageantry ; while syren whispers,	
	Predestin'd for his ear, 'scape as half-check'd	
	From lips the courtliest and rubiest	
	Of all the realm, admiring of his deeds.	
MAUD	A frost upon his summer!	
CHESTER	A queen's nod	
	Can make his June December. Here he comes.	

POEMS
written late in 1819

A Party of Lovers

'A few Nonsense Verses' sent in a Letter to George Keats

Pensive they sit, and roll their languid eyes,
Nibble their toast and cool their tea with sighs ;
Or else forget the purpose of the night,
Forget their tea, forget their appetite.
See, with cross'd arms they sit – Ah! happy crew,
The fire is going out and no one rings
For coals, and therefore no coals Betty brings.
A fly is in the milk-pot. Must he die
Circled by a humane society?[1]
No, no; there, Mr Werter[2] takes his spoon,   10
Inserts it, dips the handle, and lo! soon
The little straggler, sav'd from perils dark,
Across the teaboard draws a long wet mark.

    Romeo! Arise, take snuffers by the handle,
There is a large cauliflower[3] in each candle.
A winding sheet[4] – ah, me! I must away
To No. 7, just beyond the circus gay.[5]
Alas, my friend, your coat sits very well ;
Where may your tailor live? I may not tell.
O pardon me. I'm absent now and then.   20
Where might my tailor live? I say again
I cannot tell, let me no more be teased ;
He lives in Wapping,[6] might live where he pleased.

Sonnet

The day is gone, and all its sweets are gone!
  Sweet voice, sweet lips, soft hand, and softer breast,
Warm breath, light whisper, tender semi-tone,
  Bright eyes, accomplish'd shape, and lang'rous waist!
Faded the flower and all its budded charms,
  Faded the sight of beauty from my eyes,
Faded the shape of beauty from my arms,
  Faded the voice, warmth, whiteness, paradise –
Vanish'd unseasonably at shut of eve,
  When the dusk holiday – or holinight   10
Of fragrant-curtain'd love begins to weave
  The woof[1] of darkness thick, for hid delight ;
But, as I've read love's missal through today,
He'll let me sleep, seeing I fast and pray.

Lines to Fanny

What can I do to drive away
Remembrance from my eyes? for they have seen,
Aye, an hour ago, my brilliant Queen!
Touch has a memory. O say, love, say,
What can I do to kill it and be free
In my old liberty?
When every fair one that I saw was fair,
Enough to catch me in but half a snare,
Not keep me there:
When, howe'er poor or particolour'd[1] things,   10
My muse had wings,
And ever ready was to take her course
Whither I bent her force,
Unintellectual, yet divine to me; –
Divine, I say! – What sea-bird o'er the sea
Is a philosopher the while he goes
Winging along where the great water throes?[2]

How shall I do
   To get anew
Those moulted feathers, and so mount once more   20
   Above, above
   The reach of fluttering Love,
And make him cower lowly while I soar?
Shall I gulp wine? No, that is vulgarism,
A heresy and schism,
   Foisted into the canon law[3] of love; –
No, – wine is only sweet to happy men:
   More dismal cares
   Seize on me unawares, –
Where shall I learn to get my peace again?   30
To banish thoughts of that most hateful land,[4]
Dungeoner of my friends, that wicked strand
Where they were wreck'd and live a wrecked life;
That monstrous region, whose dull rivers pour,
Ever from their sordid urns unto the shore,
Unown'd of any weedy-haired gods;
Whose winds, all zephyrless, hold scourging rods,
Iced in the great lakes, to afflict mankind;
Whose rank-grown forests, frosted, black, and blind,
Would fright a Dryad; whose harsh herbag'd meads   40
Make lean and lank the starv'd ox while he feeds;
There bad flowers have no scent, birds no sweet song,
And great unerring Nature once seems wrong.

O, for some sunny spell
To dissipate the shadows of this hell!
Say they are gone, – with the new dawning light
Steps forth my lady bright!
O, let me once more rest
My soul upon that dazzling breast!
Let once again these aching arms be plac'd,   50
The tender gaolers of thy waist!
And let me feel that warm breath here and there
To spread a rapture in my very hair, –
O, the sweetness of the pain!
Give me those lips again!
Enough! Enough! it is enough for me
To dream of thee!

Sonnet to Fanny

I cry your mercy – pity – love! – aye, love!
   Merciful love that tantalises not,
One-thoughted, never-wandering, guileless love,
   Unmask'd, and being seen – without a blot!
O! let me have thee whole, – all – all – be mine!
   That shape, that fairness, that sweet minor zest
Of love, your kiss, – those hands, those eyes divine,
   That warm, white, lucent, million-pleasured breast, –
Yourself – your soul – in pity give me all,
   Withhold no atom's atom or I die,   10
Or living on perhaps, your wretched thrall,
   Forget, in the mist of idle misery,
Life's purposes, – the palate of my mind
Losing its gust, and my ambition blind!

The Fall of Hyperion

A Dream

CANTO I

Fanatics have their dreams, wherewith they weave
A paradise for a sect; the savage too
From forth the loftiest fashion of his sleep
Guesses at Heaven; pity these have not
Trac'd upon vellum or wild Indian leaf
The shadows of melodious utterance.
But bare of laurel they live, dream, and die;
For Poesy alone can tell her dreams,
With the fine spell of words alone can save
Imagination from the sable chain   10
And dumb enchantment. Who alive can say,
'Thou art no Poet – may'st not tell thy dreams?'
Since every man whose soul is not a clod
Hath visions, and would speak, if he had loved,
And been well nurtured in his mother tongue.
Whether the dream now purpos'd to rehearse
Be poet's or fanatic's will be known
When this warm scribe my hand is in the grave.

Methought I stood where trees of every clime,
Palm, myrtle, oak, and sycamore, and beech,   20
With plantain, and spice-blossoms, made a screen;
In neighbourhood of fountains (by the noise
Soft-showering in my ears), and, (by the touch
Of scent,) not far from roses. Turning round
I saw an arbour with a drooping roof
Of trellis vines, and bells, and larger blooms,
Like floral censers, swinging light in air;
Before its wreathed doorway, on a mound
Of moss, was spread a feast of summer fruits,
Which, nearer seen, seem'd refuse of a meal   30
By angel tasted or our Mother Eve;[1]
For empty shells were scattered on the grass,
And grape-stalks but half bare, and remnants more,

Sweet-smelling, whose pure kinds I could not know.
Still was more plenty than the fabled horn[2]
Thrice emptied could pour forth, at banqueting
For Proserpine return'd to her own fields,
Where the white heifers low. And appetite
More yearning than on Earth I ever felt
Growing within, I ate deliciously;   40
And, after not long, thirsted, for thereby
Stood a cool vessel of transparent juice
Sipp'd by the wander'd bee, the which I took,
And, pledging all the mortals of the world,
And all the dead whose names are in our lips,
Drank. That full draught is parent of my theme.
No Asian poppy nor elixir fine
Of the soon-fading jealous Caliphat;[3]
No poison gender'd in close monkish cell,
To thin the scarlet conclave[4] of old men,   50
Could so have rapt unwilling life away.
Among the fragrant husks and berries crush'd,
Upon the grass I struggled hard against
The domineering potion; but in vain:
The cloudy swoon came on, and down I sank,
Like a Silenus on an antique vase.
How long I slumber'd 'tis a chance to guess.
When sense of life return'd, I started up
As if with wings; but the fair trees were gone,
The mossy mound and arbour were no more: 60
I look'd around upon the carved sides
Of an old sanctuary with roof august,
Builded so high, it seem'd that filmed clouds
Might spread beneath, as o'er the stars of heaven:
So old the place was, I remember'd none
The like upon the Earth: what I had seen
Of grey cathedrals, buttress'd walls, rent towers,
The superannuations[5] of sunk realms,
Or Nature's rocks toil'd hard in waves and winds,
Seem'd but the faulture[6] of decrepit things   70
To that eternal domed Monument. –
Upon the marble at my feet there lay
Store of strange vessels and large draperies,

Which needs had been of dyed asbestos[7] wove,
Or in that place the moth could not corrupt,
So white the linen, so, in some, distinct
Ran imageries from a sombre loom.
All in a mingled heap confus'd there lay
Robes, golden tongs, censer and chafing-dish,[8]
Girdles, and chains, and holy jewelries.   80

Turning from these with awe, once more I rais'd
My eyes to fathom the space every way;
The embossed roof, the silent massy range
Of columns north and south, ending in mist
Of nothing, then to eastward, where black gates
Were shut against the sunrise evermore. –
Then to the west I look'd, and saw far off
An image, huge of feature as a cloud,
At level of whose feet an altar slept,
To be approach'd on either side by steps,   90
And marble balustrade, and patient travail
To count with toil the innumerable degrees.
Towards the altar sober-paced I went,
Repressing haste, as too unholy there;
And, coming nearer, saw beside the shrine
One minist'ring; and there arose a flame. –
When in mid-way the sickening East wind
Shifts sudden to the south, the small warm rain
Melts out the frozen incense from all flowers,
And fills the air with so much pleasant health   100
That even the dying man forgets his shroud; –
Even so that lofty sacrificial fire,
Sending forth Maian incense,[9] spread around
Forgetfulness of everything but bliss,
And clouded all the altar with soft smoke;
From whose white fragrant curtains thus I heard
Language pronounc'd: 'If thou canst not ascend
These steps, die on that marble where thou art.
Thy flesh, near cousin to the common dust,
Will parch for lack of nutriment – thy bones   110
Will wither in few years, and vanish so
That not the quickest eye could find a grain

Of what thou now art on that pavement cold.
The sands of thy short life are spent this hour,
And no hand in the universe can turn
Thy hourglass, if these gummed leaves[10] be burnt
Ere thou canst mount up these immortal steps.'
I heard, I look'd: two senses both at once,
So fine, so subtle, felt the tyranny
Of that fierce threat and the hard task proposed.   120
Prodigious seem'd the toil; the leaves were yet
Burning – when suddenly a palsied chill
Struck from the paved level up my limbs,
And was ascending quick to put cold grasp
Upon those streams that pulse beside the throat:[11]
I shriek'd, and the sharp anguish of my shriek
Stung my own ears – I strove hard to escape
The numbness; strove to gain the lowest step.
Slow, heavy, deadly was my pace: the cold
Grew stifling, suffocating, at the heart;   130
And when I clasp'd my hands I felt them not.
One minute before death, my iced foot touch'd
The lowest stair; and as it touch'd, life seem'd
To pour in at the toes: I mounted up,
As once fair angels on a ladder flew[12]
From the green turf to Heaven – 'Holy Power,'
Cried I, approaching near the horned shrine,
'What am I that should so be saved from death?
What am I that another death come not
To choke my utterance sacrilegious, here?'   140
Then said the veiled shadow – 'Thou hast felt
What 'tis to die and live again before
Thy fated hour, that thou hadst power to do so
Is thy own safety; thou hast dated on[13]
Thy doom.' – 'High Prophetess,' said I, 'purge off,
Benign, if so it please thee, my mind's film.' –
'None can usurp this height,' return'd that shade.
'But those to whom the miseries of the world
Are misery, and will not let them rest.
All else who find a haven in the world,   150
Where they may thoughtless sleep away their days.
If by a chance into this fane they come,

Rot on the pavement where thou rottedst half.' –
'Are there not thousands in the world,' said I,
Encourag'd by the sooth voice of the shade,
'Who love their fellows even to the death,
Who feel the giant agony of the world,
And more, like slaves to poor humanity,
Labour for mortal good? I sure should see
Other men here; but I am here alone.'   160
'Those whom thou spak'st of are no vision'ries,'
Rejoin'd that voice – 'They are no dreamers weak,
They seek no wonder but the human face;
No music but a happy-noted voice –
They come not here, they have no thought to come –
And thou art here, for thou art less than they –
What benefit canst thou, or all thy tribe,
To the great world? Thou art a dreaming thing,
A fever of thyself – think of the Earth;
What bliss even in hope is there for thee?   170
What haven? every creature hath its home;
Every sole man hath days of joy and pain,
Whether his labours be sublime or low –
The pain alone; the joy alone; distinct:
Only the dreamer venoms all his days,
Bearing more woe than all his sins deserve.
Therefore, that happiness be somewhat shar'd,
Such things as thou art are admitted oft
Into like gardens thou didst pass erewhile,
And suffer'd in[14] these temples: for that cause   180
Thou standest safe beneath this statue's knees.'
'That I am favour'd for unworthiness,
By such propitious parley medicin'd
In sickness not ignoble, I rejoice,
Aye, and could weep for love of such award.'
So answer'd I, continuing, 'If it please,
Majestic shadow, tell me: sure not all
Those melodies sung into the World's ear
Are useless: sure a poet is a sage;
A humanist,[15] physician to all men.   190
That I am none I feel, as vultures feel
They are no birds when eagles are abroad.

What am I then: Thou spakest of my tribe:
What tribe?' The tall shade veil'd in drooping white
Then spake, so much more earnest, that the breath
Moved the thin linen folds that drooping hung
About a golden censer from the hand
Pendent – 'Art thou not of the dreamer tribe?
The poet and the dreamer are distinct,
Diverse, sheer opposite, antipodes.[16]   200
The one pours out a balm upon the World,
The other vexes it.' Then shouted I
Spite of myself, and with a Pythia's spleen[17]
'Apollo! faded! O far flown Apollo!
Where is thy misty pestilence[18] to creep
Into the dwellings, through the door crannies
Of all mock lyrists, large self worshippers
And careless hectorers in proud bad verse.
Though I breathe death with them it will be life
To see them sprawl before me into graves.   210
Majestic shadow, tell me where I am,
Whose altar this; for whom this incense curls;
What image this whose face I cannot see,
For the broad marble knees; and who thou art,
Of accent feminine so courteous?'
Then the tall shade, in drooping linens veil'd,
Spoke out, so much more earnest, that her breath
Stirr'd the thin folds of gauze that drooping hung
About a golden censer from her hand
Pendent; and by her voice I knew she shed   220
Long-treasured tears. 'This temple, sad and lone,
Is all spar'd from the thunder of a war[19]
Foughten long since by giant hierarchy
Against rebellion: this old image here,
Whose carved features wrinkled as he fell.
Is Saturn's; I Moneta, left supreme
Sole Priestess of this desolation.' –
I had no words to answer, for my tongue,
Useless, could find about its roofed home
No syllable of a fit majesty   230
To make rejoinder to Moneta's mourn.
There was a silence, while the altar's blaze

Was fainting for sweet food: I look'd thereon,
And on the paved floor, where nigh were piled
Faggots of cinnamon, and many heaps
Of other crisped spice-wood – then again
I look'd upon the altar, and its horns
Whiten'd with ashes, and its lang'rous flame,
And then upon the offerings again;
And so by turns – till sad Moneta cried,   240
'The sacrifice is done, but not the less
Will I be kind to thee for thy good will.
My power, which to me is still a curse,
Shall be to thee a wonder; for the scenes
Still swooning vivid through my globed brain,
With an electral[20] changing misery,
Thou shalt with these dull mortal eyes behold,
Free from all pain, if wonder pain thee not.'
As near as an immortal's sphered words
Could to a mother's soften, were these last: 250
And yet I had a terror of her robes,
And chiefly of the veils, that from her brow
Hung pale, and curtain'd her in mysteries,
That made my heart too small to hold its blood.
This saw that Goddess, and with sacred hand
Parted the veils. Then saw I a wan face,
Not pin'd by human sorrows, but bright-blanch'd
By an immortal sickness which kills not;
It works a constant change, which happy death
Can put no end to; deathwards progressing   260
To no death was that visage; it had past
The lily and the snow; and beyond these
I must not think now, though I saw that face –
But for her eyes I should have fled away.
They held me back, with a benignant light,
Soft mitigated by divinest lids
Half-closed, and visionless entire they seem'd
Of all external things; – they saw me not,
But in blank splendour, beam'd like the mild moon,
Who comforts those she sees not, who knows not   270
What eyes are upward cast. As I had found
A grain of gold upon a mountain's side,

And twing'd with avarice strain'd out my eyes
To search its sullen[21] entrails rich with ore,
So at the view of sad Moneta's brow,
I ask'd to see what things the hollow brain
Behind environed:[22] what high tragedy
In the dark secret chambers of her skull
Was acting, that could give so dread a stress
To her cold lips, and fill with such a light   280
Her planetary eyes; and touch her voice
With such a sorrow – 'Shade of Memory!' –
Cried I, with act adorant at her feet,
'By all the gloom hung round thy fallen house,
By this last temple, by the golden age,[23]
By great Apollo, thy dear Foster Child,
And by thyself, forlorn divinity,
The pale Omega[24] of a withered race,
Let me behold, according as thou saidst,
What in thy brain so ferments to and fro!'   290
No sooner had this conjuration pass'd
My devout lips, than side by side we stood
(Like a stunt bramble by a solemn pine)
Deep[25] in the shady sadness of a vale,
Far sunken from the healthy breath of morn,
Far from the fiery noon and eve's one star.
Onward I look'd beneath the gloomy boughs.
And saw, what first I thought an image huge,
Like to the image pedestal'd so high
In Saturn's temple. Then Moneta's voice   300
Came brief upon mine ear – 'So Saturn sat
When he had lost his Realms – 'whereon there grew
A power within me of enormous ken[26]
To see as a god sees, and take the depth
Of things as nimbly as the outward eye
Can size and shape pervade.[27] The lofty theme
At those few words hung vast before my mind,
With half-unravel'd web. I set myself
Upon an eagle's watch, that I might see,
And seeing ne'er forget. No stir of life   310
Was in this shrouded vale, not so much air
As in the zoning[28] of a summer's day

Robs not one light seed from the feather'd grass,
But where the dead leaf fell there did it rest:
A stream went voiceless by, still deaden'd more
By reason of the fallen divinity
Spreading more shade; the Naiad 'mid her reeds
Prest her cold finger closer to her lips.

    Along the margin-sand large footmarks went
No farther than to where old Saturn's feet   320
Had rested, and there slept, how long a sleep!
Degraded, cold, upon the sodden ground
His old right hand lay nerveless, listless, dead,
Unsceptred; and his realmless eyes were clos'd,
While his bow'd head seem'd listening to the Earth,
His ancient mother, for some comfort yet.

    It seem'd no force could wake him from his place;
But there came one who, with a kindred hand
Touch'd his wide shoulders after bending low
With reverence, though to one who knew it not.   330
Then came the griev'd voice of Mnemosyne,
And griev'd I hearken'd. 'That divinity
Whom thou saw'st step from yon forlornest wood,
And with slow pace approach our fallen King,
Is Thea, softest-natur'd of our Brood.'
I mark'd the Goddess in fair statuary[29]
Surpassing wan Moneta by the head,
And in her sorrow nearer woman's tears.
There was a listening fear in her regard,
As if calamity had but begun;   340
As if the vanward clouds of evil days
Had spent their malice, and the sullen rear
Was with its stored thunder labouring up.
One hand she press'd upon that aching spot
Where beats the human heart, as if just there,
Though an immortal, she felt cruel pain;
The other upon Saturn's bended neck
She laid, and to the level of his hollow ear
Leaning with parted lips, some words she spake
In solemn tenor and deep organ tune;   350
Some mourning words, which in our feeble tongue

Would come in this-like accenting; how frail
To that large utterance of the early Gods!

'Saturn! look up – and for what, poor lost King?
I have no comfort for thee; no not one;
I cannot say, wherefore thus sleepest thou?
For Heaven is parted from thee, and the Earth
Knows thee not, so afflicted, for a God;
And Ocean too, with all its solemn noise,
Has from thy sceptre pass'd, and all the air   360
Is emptied of thine hoary majesty:
Thy thunder, captious[30] at the new command,
Rumbles reluctant[31] o'er our fallen house;
And thy sharp lightning, in unpracticed hands,
Scorches and burns our once serene domain.
With such remorseless speed still come new woes,
That unbelief has not a space to breathe.
Saturn! sleep on: – Me thoughtless, why should I
Thus violate thy slumbrous solitude?
Why should I ope thy melancholy eyes?   370
Saturn, sleep on, while at thy feet I weep.'
As when upon a tranced summer-night
Forests, branch-charmed by the earnest stars,
Dream, and so dream all night without a noise,
Save from one gradual solitary gust,
Swelling upon the silence; dying off;
As if the ebbing air had but one wave;
So came these words, and went; the while in tears
She prest her fair large forehead to the earth,
Just where her fallen hair might spread in curls,   380
A soft and silken mat for Saturn's feet.
Long, long these two were postured motionless,
Like sculpture builded-up upon the grave
Of their own power. A long awful time
I look'd upon them: still they were the same;
The frozen God still bending to the earth,
And the sad Goddess weeping at his feet,
Moneta silent. Without stay or prop,[32]
But my own weak mortality, I bore
The load of this eternal quietude,   390

The unchanging gloom, and the three fixed shapes
Ponderous upon my senses, a whole moon.
For by my burning brain I measured sure
Her silver seasons shedded on the night,
And every day by day methought I grew
More gaunt and ghostly. – Oftentimes I pray'd
Intense, that Death would take me from the Vale
And all its burthens – gasping with despair
Of change, hour after hour I curs'd myself;
Until old Saturn rais'd his faded eyes,   400
And look'd around and saw his kingdom gone,
And all the gloom and sorrow of the place,
And that fair kneeling Goddess at his feet.
As the moist scent of flowers, and grass, and leaves,
Fills forest dells with a pervading air,
Known to the woodland nostril, so the words
Of Saturn fill'd the mossy glooms around,
Even to the hollows of time-eaten oaks,
And to the windings of the foxes' hole,
With sad low tones, while thus he spake, and sent   410
Strange musings to the solitary Pan.
'Moan, brethren, moan; for we are swallow'd up
And buried from all Godlike exercise
Of influence benign on planets pale,
And peaceful sway above man's harvesting,
And all those acts which Deity supreme
Doth ease its heart of love in. Moan and wail,
Moan, brethren, moan; for lo, the rebel spheres
Spin round, the stars their ancient courses keep,
Clouds still with shadowy moisture haunt the earth,   420
Still suck their fill of light from sun and moon;
Still buds the tree, and still the sea-shores murmur;
There is no death in all the Universe,
No smell of death – there shall be death – Moan, moan,
Moan, Cybele, moan; for thy pernicious Babes[33]
Have changed a god into an aching Palsy.
Moan, brethren, moan, for I have no strength left.
Weak as the reed – weak – feeble as my voice –
O, O, the pain, the pain of feebleness.
Moan, moan, for still I thaw – or give me help;   430

Throw down those imps,[34] and give me victory.
Let me hear other groans, and trumpets blown
Of triumph calm, and hymns of festival,
From the gold peaks of Heaven's high-piled clouds;
Voices of soft proclaim, and silver stir
Of strings in hollow shells; and there shall be
Beautiful things made new for the surprise
Of the sky-children.' So he feebly ceas'd,
With such a poor and sickly sounding pause,
Methought I heard some old man of the earth   440
Bewailing earthly loss; nor could my eyes
And ears act with that pleasant unison of sense
Which marries sweet sound with the grace of form.
And dolorous accent from a tragic harp
With large-limb'd visions. – More I scrutinised:
Still fix'd he sat beneath the sable trees,
Whose arms spread straggling in wild serpent forms,
With leaves all hush'd; his awful presence there
(Now all was silent) gave a deadly lie
To what I erewhile[35] heard – only his lips   450
Trembled amid the white curls of his beard.
They told the truth, though, round, the snowy locks
Hung nobly, as upon the face of heaven
A mid-day fleece of clouds. Thea arose.
And stretched her white arm through the hollow dark.
Pointing some whither: whereat he too rose
Like a vast giant, seen by men at sea
To grow pale from the waves[36] at dull midnight.
They melted from my sight into the woods;
Ere I could turn, Moneta cried, 'These twain   460
Are speeding to the families of grief,
Where roof'd in by black rocks they waste, in pain
And darkness, for no hope.' – And she spake on,
As ye may read who can unwearied pass
Onward from th' Antichamber of this dream.
Where even at the open doors awhile
I must delay, and glean my memory
Of her high phrase: – perhaps no further dare.

End of Canto I

Canto II

'Mortal, that thou may'st understand aright,
I humanise my sayings to thine ear,
Making comparisons of earthly things;
Or thou might'st better listen to the wind,
Whose language is to thee a barren noise,
Though it blows legend-laden thro' the trees. –
In melancholy realms big tears are shed,
More sorrow like to this, and such like woe,
Too huge for mortal tongue, or pen of scribe.
The Titans fierce, self hid or prison bound,   10
Groan for the old allegiance once more,
Listening in their doom for Saturn's voice.
But one of our whole eagle-brood still keeps
His sov'reignty, and rule, and majesty;
Blazing Hyperion on his orbed fire
Still sits, still snuffs the incense teeming up
From Man to the Sun's God: yet unsecure.
For as upon the earth dire prodigies
Fright and perplex, so also shudders he:
Nor at dog's howl or gloom-bird's[1] Even screech,   20
Or the familiar visitings of one
Upon the first toll of his passing bell:
But horrors, portioned[2] to a giant nerve,
Make great Hyperion ache. His palace bright,
Bastion'd with pyramids of glowing gold,
And touch'd with shade of bronzed obelisks,
Glares a blood-red thro' all the thousand courts,
Arches, and domes, and fiery galleries:
And all its curtains of Aurorian clouds
Flush angerly; when he would taste the wreaths   30
Of incense breathed aloft from sacred hills,
Instead of sweets, his ample palate takes
Savour of poisonous brass and metals sick.
Wherefore when harbour'd in the sleepy West,
After the full completion of fair day,
For rest divine upon exalted couch
And slumber in the arms of melody,

He paces through the pleasant hours of ease
With strides colossal, on from hall to hall;
While far within each aisle and deep recess   40
His winged minions in close clusters stand
Amaz'd, and full of fear; like anxious men,
Who on a wide plain gather in sad troops,
When earthquakes jar their battlements and towers.
Even now, while Saturn, roused from icy trance,
Goes, step for step, with Thea from yon woods,
Hyperion, leaving twilight in the rear,
Is sloping to the threshold of the West. –
Thither we tend.' – Now in clear light I stood,
Reliev'd from the dusk vale. Mnemosyne   50
Was sitting on a square-edg'd polish'd stone,
That in its lucid depth reflected pure
Her priestess-garments. – My quick eyes ran on
From stately nave to nave, from vault to vault,
Through bow'rs of fragrant and enwreathed light
And diamond-paved lustrous long arcades.
Anon rush'd by the bright Hyperion;
His flaming robes stream'd out beyond his heels,
And gave a roar, as if of earthly fire,
That scared away the meek ethereal hours,   60
And made their dove-wings tremble. On he flared.

The Cap and Bells
or the Jealousies

A Faery Tale – Unfinished

I

In midmost Ind, beside Hydaspes[1] cool,
There stood, or hover'd, tremulous in the air,
A faery city, 'neath the potent rule
Of Emperor Elfinan;[2] fam'd ev'rywhere
For love of mortal women, maidens fair,
Whose lips were solid, whose soft hands were made
Of a fit mould and beauty, ripe and rare,
To pamper his slight wooing, warm yet staid:
He lov'd girls smooth as shades, but hated a mere shade.

II

This was a crime forbidden by the law;
And all the priesthood of his city wept,
For ruin and dismay they well foresaw,
If impious prince no bound or limit kept,
And faery Zendervester[3] overstept;
They wept, he sin'd, and still he would sin on,
They dreamt of sin, and he sin'd while they slept;
In vain the pulpit thunder'd at the throne,
Caricature was vain, and vain the tart[4] lampoon.

III

Which seeing, his high court of parliament
Laid a remonstrance at his Highness' feet,
Praying his royal senses to content
Themselves with what in faery land was sweet,
Befitting best that shade with shade should meet
Whereat, to calm their fears, he promis'd soon
From mortal tempters all to make retreat, –
Aye, even on the first of the new moon,
An immaterial wife to espouse[5] as heaven's boon.

IV

Meantime he sent a fluttering embassy
To Pigmio, of Imaus[6] sovereign,
To half beg, and half demand, respectfully,
The hand of his fair daughter Bellanaine;[7]
An audience had, and speeching done, they gain
Their point, and bring the weeping bride away;
Whom, with but one attendant, safely lain
Upon their wings, they bore in bright array,
While little harps were touch'd by many a lyric fay.

V

As in old pictures tender cherubim
A child's soul thro' the sapphir'd[8] canvas bear,
So, thro' a real heaven, on they swim
With the sweet princess on her plumag'd lair,
Speed giving to the winds her lustrous hair;
And so she journey'd, sleeping or awake,
Save when, for healthful exercise and air,
She chose to *promener à l'aile*,[9] or take
A pigeon's somerset,[10] for sport or change's sake.

VI

'Dear Princess, do not whisper me so loud,'
Quoth Corallina,[11] nurse and confidant,
'Do not you see there, lurking in a cloud,
Close at your back, that sly old Crafticant?[12]
He hears a whisper plainer than a rant:
Dry up your tears, and do not look so blue;
He's Elfinan's great state-spy militant,
His running, lying, flying footman too –
Dear mistress, let him have no handle against you!

VII

'Show him a mouse's tail, and he will guess,
With metaphysic swiftness, at the mouse;
Show him a garden, and with speed no less,
He'll surmise sagely of a dwelling house,

And plot, in the same minute, how to chouse
    The owner out of it; show him a' – 'Peace!
    Peace! nor contrive thy mistress' ire to rouse!'
      Return'd the Princess, 'my tongue shall not cease
Till from this hated match I get a free release.

VIII

'Ah, beauteous mortal!'[13] 'Hush!' quoth Coralline,
    'Really you must not talk of him, indeed.'
    'You hush!' replied the mistress, with a shine
      Of anger in her eyes, enough to breed
      In stouter hearts than nurse's fear and dread:
    'Twas not the glance itself made nursey flinch,
      But of its threat she took the utmost heed;
    Not liking in her heart an hour-long pinch,
Or a sharp needle run into her back an inch.

IX

So she was silenc'd, and fair Bellanaine,
    Writhing her little body with ennui,
    Continued to lament and to complain,
      That Fate, cross-purposing, should let her be
      Ravish'd away far from her dear countree;
    That all her feelings should be set at naught,
      In trumping up this match so hastily,
    With lowland blood;[14] and lowland blood she thought
Poison, as every staunch true-born Imaian ought.

X

Sorely she griev'd, and wetted three or four
    White Provence rose-leaves with her faery tears,
    But not for this cause; – alas! she had more
      Bad reasons for her sorrow, as appears
      In the fam'd memoirs of a thousand years,
    Written by Crafticant, and published
      By Parpaglion and Co., (those sly compeers
    Who rak'd up ev'ry fact against the dead,)
In Scarab Street, Panthea, at the Jubal's Head.[15]

XI

Where, after a long hypercritic howl
Against the vicious manners of the age
He goes on to expose, with heart and soul,
What vice in this or that year was the rage,
Backbiting all the world in every page;
With special strictures on the horrid crime,
(Section'd and subsection'd with learning sage,)
Of faeries stooping on their wings sublime
To kiss a mortal's lips, when such were in their prime.

XII

Turn to the copious index, you will find
Somewhere in the column, headed letter B,
The name of Bellanaine, if you're not blind;
Then pray refer to the text, and you will see
An article made up of calumny
Against this highland princess, rating her
For giving way, so over fashionably,
To this new-fangled vice, which seems a burr
Stuck in his moral throat, no coughing e'er could stir.

XIII

There he says plainly that she lov'd a man!
That she around him flutter'd, flirted, toy'd,
Before her marriage with great Elfinan;
That after marriage too, she never joy'd
In husband's company, but still employ'd
Her wits to 'scape away to Angle-land;
Where liv'd the youth, who worried and annoy'd
Her tender heart, and its warm ardours fann'd
To such a dreadful blaze, her side would scorch her hand.

XIV

But let us leave this idle tittle-tattle[16]
To waiting-maids, and bedroom coteries,
Nor till fit time against her fame wage battle.
Poor Elfinan is very ill at ease,

Let us resume his subject if you please:
For it may comfort and console him much
To rhyme and syllable his miseries;
Poor Elfinan! whose cruel fate was such,
He sat and curs'd a bride he knew he could not touch.

XV

Soon as (according to his promises)
The bridal embassy had taken wing,
And vanish'd, bird-like, o'er the suburb trees,
The Emperor, empierc'd with the sharp sting
Of love, retired, vex'd and murmuring
Like any drone shut from the fair bee-queen,
Into his cabinet, and there did fling
His limbs upon a sofa, full of spleen,
And damn'd his House of Commons,[17] in complete chagrin.

XVI

'I'll trounce some of the members,' cried the Prince,
'I'll put a mark against some rebel names,
I'll make the Opposition benches wince,
I'll show them very soon, to all their shames,
What 'tis to smother up a Prince's flames;
That ministers should join in it, I own,
Surprises me! – they too at these high games!
Am I an Emperor? Do I wear a crown?
Imperial Elfinan, go hang thyself or drown!

XVII

'I'll trounce 'em! – there's the square-cut chancellor,[18]
His son shall never touch that bishopric;
And for the nephew of old Palfior,
I'll show him that his speech has made me sick,
And give the colonelcy to Phalaric;[19]
The tiptoe marquis, moral and gallant,
Shall lodge in shabby taverns upon tick;[20]
And for the Speaker's second cousin's aunt,
She sha'n't be maid of honour, – by heaven that she sha'n't!

XVIII

'I'll shirk the Duke of A.; I'll cut his brother;
I'll give no garter[21] to his eldest son;
I won't speak to his sister or his mother!
The Viscount B. shall live at cut-and-run;
But how in the world can I contrive to stun
That fellow's voice, which plagues me worse than any,
That stubborn fool, that impudent state-dun,
Who sets down ev'ry sovereign as a zany,[22] –
That vulgar commoner, Esquire Biancopany?[23]

XIX

'Monstrous affair! Pshaw! pah! what ugly minx
Will they fetch from Imaus for my bride?
Alas! my wearied heart within me sinks,
To think that I must be so near allied
To a cold dullard fay, – ah, woe betide!
Ah, fairest of all human loveliness!
Sweet Bertha! what crime can it be to glide
About the fragrant pleatings of thy dress,
Or kiss thine eyes, or count thy locks, tress after tress?'

XX

So said, one minute's while his eyes remain'd
Half lidded, piteous, languid, innocent;
But, in a wink, their splendour they regain'd,
Sparkling revenge with amorous fury blent.
Love thwarted in bad temper oft has vent:
He rose, he stampt his foot, he rang the bell,
And order'd some death-warrants to be sent
For signature: – somewhere the tempest fell,
As many a poor felon does not live to tell.

XXI

'At the same time Eban,'[24] – (this was his page,
A fay of colour, slave from top to toe,
Sent as a present, while yet under age,
From the Viceroy of Zanguebar, – wise, slow,

His speech, his only words were 'yes' and 'no,'
But swift of look, and foot, and wing was he, –)
'At the same time, Eban, this instant go
To Hum the soothsayer,[25] whose name I see
Among the fresh arrivals in our empery.

XXII

'Bring Hum to me! But stay – here, take my ring,
The pledge of favour, that he not suspect
Any foul play, or awkward murdering,
Tho' I have bowstrung[26] many of his sect;
Throw in a hint, that if he should neglect
One hour, the next shall see him in my grasp,
And the next after that shall see him neck'd,[27]
Or swallow'd by my hunger-starved asp, –
And mention ('tis as well) the torture of the wasp.'

XXIII

These orders given, the Prince, in half a pet,
Let o'er the silk his propping elbow slide,
Caught up his little legs, and, in a fret,
Fell on the sofa on his royal side.
The slave retreated backwards, humble-eyed,
And with a slave-like silence clos'd the door,
And to old Hum thro' street and alley hied;
He 'knew the city,' as we say, of yore,
And for short cuts and turns, was nobody knew more.

XXIV

It was the time when wholesale houses close
Their shutters with a moody sense of wealth,
But retail dealers, diligent, let loose
The gas[28] (objected to on score of health),
Convey'd in little solder'd pipes by stealth,
And make it flare in many a brilliant form,
That all the powers of darkness it repell'th,
Which to the oil-trade doth great scaith and harm,
And supersedeth quite the use of the glow-worm.

XXV

Eban, untempted by the pastry-cooks,
(Of pastry he got store within the palace,)
With hasty steps, wrapp'd cloak, and solemn looks,
Incognito upon his errand sallies,
His smelling-bottle[29] ready for the allies;
He pass'd the hurdy-gurdies[30] with disdain,
Vowing he'd have them sent aboard the gallies;[31]
Just as he made his vow, it 'gan to rain,
Therefore he call'd a coach, and bade it drive amain.

XXVI

'I'll pull the string,'[32] said he, and further said,
'Polluted Jarvey! [33]Ah, thou filthy hack!
Whose springs of life are all dried up and dead,
Whose linsey-woolsey[34] lining hangs all slack,
Whose rug is straw, whose wholeness is a crack;
And evermore thy steps go clatter-clitter;
Whose glass once up can never be got back,
Who prov'st, with jolting arguments and bitter,
That 'tis of modern use to travel in a litter.[35]

XXVII

'Thou inconvenience! thou hungry crop
For all corn![36] thou snail-creeper to and fro,
Who while thou goest ever seem'st to stop,
And fiddle-faddle[37] standest while you go;
I' the morning, freighted with a weight of woe,
Unto some lazar-house[38] thou journeyest,
And in the evening tak'st a double row
Of dowdies,[39] for some dance or party drest,
Besides the goods meanwhile thou movest east and west.

XXVIII

'By thy ungallant bearing and sad mien,
An inch appears the utmost thou couldst budge;
Yet at the slightest nod, or hint, or sign,
Round to the curb-stone patient dost thou trudge,

School'd in a beckon, learned in a nudge,
A dull-eyed Argus watching for a fare;
Quiet and plodding, thou dost bear no grudge
To whisking Tilburies, or Phaetons rare,
Curricles,[40] or Mail-coaches, swift beyond compare.'

XXIX

Philosophizing thus, he pull'd the check,
And bade the coachman wheel to such a street,
Who, turning much his body, more his neck,
Louted full low, and hoarsely did him greet:
'Certes, Monsieur were best take to his feet,
Seeing his servant can no further drive
For press of coaches, that tonight here meet
Many as bees about a straw-capp'd hive,
When first for April honey into faint flowers they dive.'

XXX

Eban then paid his fare, and tiptoe went
To Hum's hotel; and, as he on did pass
With head inclin'd, each dusky lineament
Show'd in the pearl-pav'd street, as in a glass;
His purple vest, that ever peeping was
Rich from the fluttering crimson of his cloak,
His silvery trousers, and his silken sash
Tied in a burnish'd knot, their semblance took
Upon the mirror'd walls, wherever he might look.

XXXI

He smil'd at self, and, smiling, show'd his teeth,
And seeing his white teeth, he smil'd the more:
Lifted his eyebrows, spurn'd the path beneath,
Show'd teeth again, and smil'd as heretofore,
Until he knock'd at the magician's door;
Where, till the porter answer'd, might be seen,
In the clear panel more he could adore, –
His turban wreath'd of gold, and white, and green.
Mustachios, earring, nosering, and his sabre keen.

XXXII

'Does not your master give a rout[41] tonight?'
Quoth the dark page. 'Oh, no!' return'd the Swiss,
'Next door but one to us, upon the right,
The *Magazin des Modes* now open is
Against the Emperor's wedding; – and, sir, this
My master finds a monstrous horrid bore;
As he retir'd, an hour ago I wis,[42]
With his best beard and brimstone, to explore
And cast a quiet figure[43] in his second floor.

XXXIII

'Gad! he's oblig'd to stick to business!
For chalk, I hear, stands at a pretty price;
And as for aqua vitae[44] – there's a mess!
The *dentes sapientiae*[45] of mice,
Our barber[46] tells me too, are on the rise, –
Tinder's a lighter article, – nitre[47] pure
Goes off like lightning, – grains of Paradise[48]
At an enormous figure! – stars not sure! –
Zodiac will not move without a sly douceur![49]

XXXIV

'Venus won't stir a peg[50] without a fee,
And master is too partial, *entre nous*,
To' – 'Hush – hush!' cried Eban, 'sure that is he
Coming down stairs, – by St Bartholomew!
As backwards as he can, – is't something new?
Or is't his custom, in the name of fun?'
'He always comes down backward, with one shoe' –
Return'd the porter – 'off, and one shoe on,
Like, saving shoe for sock or stocking, my man John!'[51]

XXXV

It was indeed the great Magician,
Feeling, with careful toe, for every stair,
And retrograding careful as he can,
Backwards and downwards from his own two pair:

'Salpietro!'[52] exclaim'd Hum, 'is the dog there?
He's always in my way upon the mat!'
'He's in the kitchen, or the Lord knows where,' –
Replied the Swiss, – 'the nasty, yelping brat!'
'Don't beat him!' return'd Hum, and on the floor came pat.

XXXVI

Then facing right about, he saw the Page,
And said: 'Don't tell me what you want, Eban;
The Emperor is now in a huge rage, –
'Tis nine to one he'll give you the rattan![53]
Let us away!' Away together ran
The plain-dress'd sage and spangled blackamoor,
Nor rested till they stood to cool, and fan,
And breathe themselves at the Emperor's chamber door
When Eban thought he heard a soft imperial snore.

XXXVII

'I thought you guess'd, foretold, or prophesied,
That's Majesty was in a raving fit?'
'He dreams,' said Hum, 'or I have ever lied,
That he is tearing you, sir, bit by bit.'
'He's not asleep, and you have little wit,'
Replied the page: 'that little buzzing noise,
Whate'er your palmistry may make of it,
Comes from a plaything of the Emperor's choice,
From a Man-Tiger-Organ,[54] prettiest of his toys.'

XXXVIII

Eban then usher'd in the learned Seer:
Elfinan's back was turn'd, but, ne'ertheless,
Both, prostrate on the carpet, ear by ear,
Crept silently, and waited in distress,
Knowing the Emperor's moody bitterness;
Eban especially, who on the floor 'gan
Tremble and quake to death, – he feared less
A dose of senna-tea or nightmare Gorgon
Than the Emperor when he play'd on his Man-Tiger-Organ.

XXXIX

They kiss'd nine times the carpet's velvet face
Of glossy silk, soft, smooth, and meadow-green,
Where the close eye in deep rich fur might trace
A silver tissue, scantly to be seen,
As daisies lurk'd in June-grass, buds in treen;[55]
Sudden the music ceased, sudden the hand
Of majesty, by dint of passion keen,
Doubled into a common fist, went grand,
And knock'd down three cut glasses, and his best inkstand.

XL

Then turning round, he saw those trembling two:
'Eban,' said he, 'as slaves should taste the fruits
Of diligence, I shall remember you
Tomorrow, or the next day, as time suits,
In a finger conversation with my mutes, –
Begone! – for you, Chaldean! here remain!
Fear not, quake not, and as good wine recruits
A conjurer's spirits, what cup will you drain?
Sherry in silver, hock in gold, or glass'd champagne?'

XLI

'Commander of the Faithful!' answer'd Hum,
'In preference to these, I'll merely taste
A thimbleful of old Jamaica rum.'
'A simple boon!' said Elfinan; 'thou may'st
Have Nantz, with which my morning coffee's lac'd.'
'I'll have a glass of Nantz, then,' – said the Seer, –
'Made racy – (sure my boldness is misplac'd!) –
With the third part – (yet that is drinking dear!) –
Of the least drop of crème de citron, crystal clear.'

XLII

'I pledge you, Hum! and pledge my dearest love,
My Bertha! ' 'Bertha! Bertha!' cried the sage,
'I know a many Berthas!' 'Mine's above
All Berthas!' sighed the Emperor. 'I engage,'

Said Hum, 'in duty, and in vassalage,
To mention all the Berthas in the Earth; –
There's Bertha Watson, – and Miss Bertha Page, –
This fam'd for languid eyes, and that for mirth, –
There's Bertha Blount of York, – and Bertha Knox of Perth.'

XLIII

'You seem to know' – 'I do know,' answer'd Hum,
'Your Majesty's in love with some fine girl
Named Bertha; but her surname will not come,
Without a little conjuring.' ''Tis Pearl,
'Tis Bertha Pearl that makes my brains so whirl;
And she is softer, fairer than her name!'
'Where does she live?' ask'd Hum. 'Her fair locks curl
So brightly, they put all our fays to shame! –
Live? – O! at Canterbury, with her old grand-dame.'

XLIV

'Good! good!' cried Hum, 'I've known her from a child!
She is a changeling[56] of my management;
She was born at midnight in an Indian wild;
Her mother's screams with the striped tiger's blent,
While the torch-bearing slaves a halloo sent
Into the jungles; and her palanquin,[57]
Rested amid the desert's dreariment,
Shook with her agony, till fair were seen
The little Bertha's eyes oped on the stars serene.'

XLV

'I can't say,' said the monarch; 'that may be
Just as it happen'd, true or else a bam![58]
Drink up your brandy, and sit down by me,
Feel, feel my pulse, how much in love I am;
And if your science is not all a sham,
Tell me some means to get the lady here.'
'Upon my honour!' said the son of Cham,[59]
'She is my dainty changeling, near and dear,
Although her story sounds at first a little queer.'

XLVI

'Convey her to me, Hum, or by my crown,
My sceptre, and my cross-surmounted globe,
I'll knock you' – 'Does your majesty mean – down?
No, no, you never could my feelings probe
To such a depth!' The Emperor took his robe,
And wept upon its purple palatine,
While Hum continued, shamming half a sob, –
'In Canterbury doth your lady shine?
But let me cool your brandy with a little wine.'

XLVII

Whereat a narrow Flemish glass he took,
That once belong'd to Admiral de Witt,[60]
Admir'd it with a connoisseuring look,
And with the ripest claret crowned it,
And, ere one lively bead could burst and flit,
He turn'd it quickly, nimbly upside down,
His mouth being held conveniently fit
To catch the treasure: 'Best in all the town!'
He said, smack'd his moist lips, and gave a pleasant frown.

XLVIII

'Ah! good my Prince, weep not!' And then again
He fill'd a bumper. 'Great Sire, do not weep!
Your pulse is shocking, but I'll ease your pain.'
'Fetch me that Ottoman,[61] and prithee keep
Your voice low,' said the Emperor; 'and steep
Some lady's-fingers[62] nice in Candy wine;[63]
And prithee, Hum, behind the screen do peep
For the rose-water vase, magician mine!
And sponge my forehead, – so my love doth make me pine.

XLIX

'Ah, cursed Bellanaine!' 'Don't think of her,'
Rejoin'd the Mago, 'but on Bertha muse;
For, by my choicest best barometer,
You shall not throttled be in marriage noose;

I've said it, Sire; you only have to choose
Bertha or Bellanaine.' So saying, he drew
From the left pocket of his threadbare hose,
A sampler[64] hoarded slyly, good as new,
Holding it by his thumb and finger full in view.

L

'Sire, this is Bertha Pearl's neat handiwork,
Her name, see here, Midsummer, ninety-one.'
Elfinan snatch'd it with a sudden jerk,
And wept as if he never would have done,
Honouring with royal tears the poor homespun;
Whereon were broider'd tigers with black eyes,
And long-tail'd pheasants, and a rising sun,
Plenty of posies, great stags, butterflies
Bigger than stags, – a moon, – with other mysteries.

LI

The monarch handled o'er and o'er again
These day-school hieroglyphics with a sigh;
Somewhat in sadness, but pleas'd in the main.
Till this oracular couplet met his eye
Astounded – *Cupid I, do thee defy!*
It was too much. He shrunk back in his chair,
Grew pale as death, and fainted – very nigh!
'Pho! nonsense!' exclaim'd Hum, 'now don't despair;
She does not mean it really. Cheer up hearty there!

LII

'And listen to my words. You say you won't,
On any terms, marry Miss Bellanaine;
It goes against your conscience – good! Well, don't.
You say you love a mortal. I would fain
Persuade your honour's highness to refrain
From peccadilloes. But, Sire, as I say,
What good would that do? And, to be more plain,
You would do me a mischief some odd day,
Cut off my ears and hands, or head too, by my fay![65]

LIII

'Besides, manners forbid that I should pass any
Vile strictures on the conduct of a prince
Who should indulge his genius, if he has any,
Not, like a subject, foolish matters mince.[66]
Now I think on't, perhaps I could convince
Your Majesty there is no crime at all
In loving pretty little Bertha, since
She's very delicate, – not over tall, –
A fairy's hand, and in the waist, why – very small.'

LIV

'Ring the repeater,[67] gentle Hum!' ''Tis five,'
Said gentle Hum; 'the nights draw in space;
The little birds I hear are all alive;
I see the dawning touch'd upon your face;
Shall I put out the candles, please your Grace?'
'Do put them out, and, without more ado,
Tell me how I may that sweet girl embrace, –
How you can bring her to me.' 'That's for you,
Great Emperor! to adventure, like a lover true.'

LV

'I fetch her!' – 'Yes, an't like your Majesty;
And as she would be frighten'd wide awake
To travel such a distance through the sky,
Use of some soft manoeuvre you must make,
For your convenience, and her dear nerves' sake;
Nice way would be to bring her in a swoon,
Anon, I'll tell what course were best to take;
You must away this morning.' 'Hum! so soon?'
'Sire, you must be in Kent by twelve o'clock at noon.'

LVI

At this great Caesar started on his feet,
Lifted his wings, and stood attentive-wise.
'Those wings to Canterbury you must beat,
If you hold Bertha as a worthy prize.
Look in the Almanack – *Moore*[68] never lies –

April the twenty-fourth, – this coming day,
  Now breathing its new bloom upon the skies,
  Will end in St Mark's Eve;[69] – you must away,
For on that eve alone can you the maid convey.'

LVII

Then the magician solemnly 'gan frown,
  So that his frost-white eyebrows, beetling low,
  Shaded his deep-green eyes, and wrinkles brown
Plaited upon his furnace-scorched brow :
  Forth from the hood that hung his neck below,
  He lifted a bright casket of pure gold,
  Touch'd a spring-lock, and there in wool, or snow
  Charm'd into ever-freezing, lay an old
And legend-leaved book, mysterious to behold.

LVIII

'Take this same book, – it will not bite you, Sire ;
  There, put it underneath your royal arm ;
  Though it's a pretty weight it will not tire,
But rather on your journey keep you warm :
  This is the magic, this the potent charm,
  That shall drive Bertha to a fainting fit!
  When the time comes, don't feel the least alarm,
  Uplift her from the ground, and swiftly flit
Back to your palace, where I wait for guerdon fit.'

LIX

'What shall I do with this same book?' 'Why merely
  Lay it on Bertha's table, close beside
  Her workbox, and 'twill help your purpose dearly;
I say no more.' 'Or good or ill betide,
  Through the wide air to Kent this morn I glide!'
  Exclaim'd the Emperor. 'When I return,
  Ask what you will, – I'll give you my new bride!
  And take some more wine, Hum; – O Heavens! I burn
To be upon the wing! Now, now, that minx I spurn!'

LX

'Leave her to me,' rejoin'd the magian:
'But how shall I account, illustrious fay!
For thine imperial absence? Pho! I can
Say you are very sick, and bar the way
To your so loving courtiers for one day ;
If either of their two archbishops' graces
Should talk of extreme unction,[70] I shall say
You do not like cold pig[71] with Latin phrases,
Which never should be used but in alarming cases.'

LXI

'Open the window, Hum ; I'm ready now!'
'Zooks!'[72] exclaim'd Hum, as up the sash he drew,
'Behold, your Majesty, upon the brow
Of yonder hill, what crowds of people!' 'Whew!
The monster's[73] always after something new,'
Return'd his Highness, 'they are piping hot
To see my pigsny[74] Bellanaine. Hum! do
Tighten my belt a little, – so, so, – not
Too tight, – the book! – my wand! – so, nothing is forgot.'

LXII

'Wounds! how they shout!' said Hum, 'and there, –
see, see!
The Ambassadors return'd from Pigmio!
The morning's very fine, – uncommonly!
See, past the skirts of yon white cloud they go,
Tinging it with soft crimsons! Now below
The sable-pointed heads of firs and pines
They dip, move on, and with them moves a glow
Along the forest side! Now amber lines
Reach the hill top, and now throughout the valley shines.'

LXIII

'Why, Hum, you're getting quite poetical!
Those *nows* you managed in a special style.'
'If ever you have leisure, Sire, you shall
See scraps of mine will make it worth your while,

Titbits for Phoebus! – yes, you well may smile.
Hark! Hah! the bells!' 'A little further yet,
Good Hum, and let me view this mighty coil.'
Then the great Emperor full graceful set
His elbow for a prop, and snuff'd his mignonnette.[75]

LXIV

The morn is full of holiday; loud bells
With rival clamours ring from every spire;
Cunningly-station'd music dies and swells
In echoing places; when the winds respire,
Light flags stream out like gauzy tongues of fire;
A metropolitan murmur, lifeful, warm,
Comes from the northern suburbs; rich attire;
Freckles with red and gold the moving swarm;
While here and there clear trumpets blow a keen alarm.

LXV

And now the fairy escort was seen clear,
Like the old pageant of Aurora's train,
Above a pearl-built minster, hovering near;
First wily Crafticant, the chamberlain,
Balanc'd upon his grey-grown pinions twain,
His slender wand officially reveal'd;
Then black gnomes scattering sixpences like rain;
Then pages three and three; and next, slave-held,
The Imaian 'scutcheon[76] bright, – one mouse in argent field.

LXVI

Gentlemen pensioners[77] next; and after them,
A troop of winged Janizaries[78] flew;
Then slaves, as presents bearing many a gem;
Then twelve physicians fluttering two and two;
And next a chaplain in a cassock new;
Then lords in waiting; then (what head not reels
For pleasure?) – the fair Princess in full view,
Borne upon wings, – and very pleas'd she feels
To have such splendour dance attendance at her heels.

LXVII

For there was more magnificence behind:
She wav'd her handkerchief. 'Ah, very grand!'
Cried Elfinan, and clos'd the window-blind;
'And, Hum, we must not shilly-shally stand. –
Adieu! adieu! I'm off for Angle-land![79]
I say, old Hocus,[80] have you such a thing
About you, – feel your pockets, I command, –
I want, this instant, an invisible ring,[81] –
Thank you, old mummy! – now securely I take wing.'

LXVIII

Then Elfinan swift vaulted from the floor,
And lighted graceful on the window-sill;
Under one arm the magic book he bore,
The other he could wave about at will;
Pale was his face, he still look'd very ill:
He bow'd at Bellanaine, and said – 'Poor Bell!
Farewell! farewell! and if for ever! still
For ever fare thee well!'[82] – and then he fell
A laughing! – snapp'd his fingers! – shame it is to tell!

LXIX

'By'r Lady! he is gone!' cries Hum, 'and I –
(I own it) – have made too free with his wine;
Old Crafticant will smoke me.[83] By the bye –
This room is full of jewels as a mine, –
Dear valuable creatures, how ye shine!
Sometime today I must contrive a minute,
If Mercury propitiously incline,
To examine his scrutoire,[84] and see what's in it,
For of superfluous diamonds I as well may thin it.

LXX

'The Emperor's horrid bad; yes, that's my cue!'
Some histories say that this was Hum's last speech;
That, being fuddled, he went reeling through
The corridor, and scarce upright could reach

The stair-head; that being glutted as a leech,[85]
And us'd, as we ourselves have just now said,
To manage stairs reversely, like a peach
Too ripe, he fell, being puzzled in his head
With liquor and the staircase: verdict – *found stone dead*.

LXXI

This as a falsehood Crafticanto treats;
And as his style is of strange elegance,
Gentle and tender, full of soft conceits,
(Much like our Boswell's,)[86] we will take a glance
At his sweet prose, and, if we can, make dance
His woven periods into careless rhyme;
O, little faery Pegasus! rear – prance –
Trot round the quarto – ordinary time!
March, little Pegasus, with pawing hoof sublime!

LXXII

Well, let us see, – *tenth book and chapter nine*, –
Thus Crafticant pursues his diary: –
''Twas twelve o'clock at night, the weather fine,
Latitude thirty-six; our scouts descry
A flight of starlings making rapidly
Towards Thibet. Mem.: – birds fly in the night;
From twelve to half-past – wings not fit to fly
For a thick fog – the Princess sulky quite
Call'd for an extra shawl, and gave her nurse a bite.

LXXIII

'Five minutes before one – brought down a moth
With my new double-barrel – stew'd the thighs
And made a very tolerable broth –
Princess turn'd dainty; – to our great surprise,
Alter'd her mind, and thought it very nice:
Seeing her pleasant, tried her with a pun,
She frown'd; a monstrous owl across us flies
About this time, – a sad old figure of fun;
Bad omen – this new match can't be a happy one.

LXXIV

'From two till half-past, dusky way we made,
Above the plains of Gobi,[87] – desert, bleak;
Beheld afar off, in the hooded shade
Of darkness, a great mountain (strange to speak),
Spitting, from forth its sulphur-baken peak,
A fan-shap'd burst of blood-red, arrowy fire,
Turban'd with smoke, which still away did reek,
Solid and black from that eternal pyre,
Upon the laden wind that scantly could respire.

LXXV

'Just upon three o'clock a falling star
Created an alarm among our troop,
Kill'd a man-cook, a page, and broke a jar,
A tureen, and three dishes, at one swoop,
Then passing by the Princess, singed her hoop:[88]
Could not conceive what Coralline was at,
She clapp'd her hands three times and cried out 'Whoop!'
Some strange Imaian custom. A large bat
Came sudden 'fore my face, and brush'd against my hat.

LXXVI

'Five minutes thirteen seconds after three,
Far in the west a mighty fire broke out,
Conjectur'd, on the instant, it might be
The city of Balk[89] – 'twas Balk beyond all doubt:
A Griffin,[90] wheeling here and there about,
Kept reconnoitring us – doubled our guard –
Lighted our torches, and kept up a shout,
Till he sheer'd off – the Princess very scar'd –
And many on their marrow-bones[91] for death prepar'd.

LXXVII

'At half-past three arose the cheerful moon –
Bivouack'd for four minutes on a cloud –
Where from the earth we heard a lively tune
Of tambourines and pipes, serene and loud,

While on a flowery lawn a brilliant crowd
Cinque-parted[92] danc'd, some half asleep reposed
Beneath the green-fan'd cedars, some did shroud
In silken tents, and 'mid light fragrance dozed,
Or on the open turf their soothed eyelids closed.

LXXVIII

'Dropp'd my gold watch, and kill'd a kettledrum[93] –
It went for apoplexy – foolish folks! –
Left it to pay the piper – a good sum –
(I've got a conscience, maugre[94] people's jokes;)
To scrape a little favour 'gan to coax
Her Highness' pugdog – got a sharp rebuff –
She wish'd a game at whist – made three revokes –
Turn'd from myself, her partner, in a huff;
His majesty will know her temper time enough.

LXXIX

'She cried for chess – I play'd a game with her –
Castled her king with such a vixen look,
It bodes ill to his Majesty – (refer
To the second chapter of my fortieth book,
And see what hoity-toity airs she took).
At half-past four the morn essay'd to beam –
Saluted, as we pass'd, an early rook –
The Princess fell asleep, and, in her dream,
Talk'd of one Master Hubert, deep in her esteem.

LXXX

'About this time, – making delightful way, –
Shed a quill-feather from my larboard wing –
Wish'd, trusted, hop'd 'twas no sign of decay –
Thank heaven, I'm hearty yet! – 'twas no such thing; –
At five the golden light began to spring,
With fiery shudder through the bloomed east;
At six we heard Panthea's churches ring –
The city all her unhiv'd swarms had cast,
To watch our grand approach, and hail us as we pass'd.

LXXXI

'As flowers turn their faces to the sun,
  So on our flight with hungry eyes they gaze,
And, as we shap'd our course, this, that way run,
  With madcap pleasure, or hand-clasp'd amaze;
Sweet in the air a mild-ton'd music plays,
  And progresses through its own labyrinth;
Buds gather'd from the green spring's middle-days,
  They scatter'd, – daisy, primrose, hyacinth, –
Or round white columns wreath'd from capital to plinth.

LXXXII

'Onward we floated o'er the panting streets,
  That seem'd throughout with upheld faces paved;
Look where we will, our bird's-eye vision meets
  Legions of holiday; bright standards waved,
And fluttering ensigns emulously[95] craved
  Our minute's glance; a busy thunderous roar,
From square to square, among the buildings raved,
  As when the sea, at flow, gluts up once more
The craggy hollowness of a wild reefed shore.

LXXXIII

'And "Bellanaine for ever!" shouted they,
  While that fair Princess, from her winged chair,
Bow'd low with high demeanour, and, to pay
  Their new-blown loyalty with guerdon fair,
Still emptied, at meet distance, here and there,
  A plenty horn[96] of jewels. And here I
(Who wish to give the devil her due) declare
  Against that ugly piece of calumny,
Which calls them Highland pebble-stones not worth a fly.

LXXXIV

'Still "Bellanaine!" they shouted, while we glide
  'Slant to a light Ionic[97] portico,
The city's delicacy, and the pride
  Of our Imperial Basilic;[98] a row
Of lords and ladies, on each hand, make show

Submissive of knee-bent obeisance,
All down the steps; and, as we enter'd, lo!
The strangest sight – the most unlook'd-for chance –
All things turn'd topsy-turvy in a devil's dance.

LXXXV

' 'Stead of his anxious Majesty and court
At the open doors, with wide saluting eyes,
Congées and scape-graces[99] of every sort,
And all the smooth routine of gallantries,
Was seen, to our immoderate surprise,
A motley crowd thick gather'd in the hall,
Lords, scullions,[100] deputy-scullions, with wild cries
Stunning the vestibule from wall to wall,
Where the Chief Justice on his knees and hands doth crawl.

LXXXVI

'Counts of the palace, and the state purveyor
Of moth's-down, to make soft the royal beds,
The Common Council and my fool Lord Mayor
Marching a-row, each other slipshod treads;
Powder'd bag-wigs and ruffy-tuffy heads[101]
Of cinder wenches meet and soil each other;
Toe crush'd with heel ill-natur'd fighting breeds,
Frill-rumpling elbows brew up many a bother,
And fists in the short ribs keep up the yell and pother.

LXXXVII

'A Poet, mounted on the Court-Clown's back,
Rode to the Princess swift with spurring heels,
And close into her face, with rhyming clack,
Began a Prothalamion;[102] – she reels,
She falls, she faints! while laughter peals
Over her woman's weakness. "Where!" cried I,
"Where is his Majesty?" No person feels
Inclind'd to answer; wherefore instantly
I plung'd into the crowd to find him or to die.

LXXXVIII

'Jostling my way I gain'd the stairs, and ran
To the first landing, where, incredible!
I met, far gone in liquor, that old man,
That vile impostor Hum, – '
So far so well, –
For we have prov'd the Mago never fell
Down stairs on Crafticanto's evidence;
And therefore duly shall proceed to tell,
Plain in our own original mood and tense,
The sequel of this day, though labour 'tis immense!

. . .

Lines Supposed to Have Been Addressed to Fanny Brawne

This living hand, now warm and capable
Of earnest grasping, would, if it were cold
And in the icy silence of the tomb,
So haunt thy days and chill thy dreaming nights
That thou would[st] wish thine own heart dry of blood
So in my veins red life might stream again,
And thou be conscience-calm'd – see here it is –
I hold it towards you.

Sonnet

*Written on a Blank Page in Shakespeare's Poems,
facing 'A Lover's Complaint'*

Bright star, would I were steadfast as thou art –
　Not in lone splendour hung aloft the night
And watching, with eternal lids apart,
　Like nature's patient, sleepless Eremite,
The moving waters at their priestlike task
　Of pure ablution[1] round earth's human shores,
Or gazing on the new soft-fallen mask
　Of snow upon the mountains and the moors –
No – yet still steadfast, still unchangeable,
　Pillow'd upon my fair love's ripening breast,　　　　10
To feel for ever its soft fall and swell,
　Awake for ever in a sweet unrest,
Still, still to hear her tender-taken breath,
And so live ever – or else swoon to death.

Glossary

Achilles the hero of the *Iliad*, dipped in the river Styx by his mother and thus granted invulnerability, except in the heel where she held him; subsequently injured in this one vulnerable spot, he died

Adonis a youth loved by Venus who was killed by a boar, but was revived for at least part of the year; his story represents seasonal cycles; he is also associated with a beautiful garden

Aeolus god of the winds. In the eighteenth century Aoelian harps or lyres, instruments played by the wind, became popular. For the Romantics they suggested the highest form of natural inspiration.

Aethon one of Apollo's horses

Albion England

Alexander Alexander the Great (356–323 BC); King of Macedon and military leader, conqueror of Greece, Persia and Egypt; founder of Alexandria

Alfred Alfred the Great (849–99), scholar and lawmaker who repelled the Danes and helped to unify England

Alpheus a river god of Arcadia who loved Arethusa

amain greatly, with full force or intensity

Amalthea a Cretan princess and Jupiter's nurse

Amazons a mythical race of warrior women renowned for their strength and courage

ambrosia the food of the gods

Amphion the mythical inventor of music, whose music could move objects

Amphitrite Neptune's wife, and Triton's mother

Anacreon sixth-century-BC Greek lyric poet

Andromeda a princess punished by the gods for claiming to be more beautiful than them; rescued by the hero Perseus; also a constellation

Apollo the god of poetry, medicine and, as Phoebus-Apollo, the sun

Apollonius a first-century philosopher and magician, who upheld strict moral and religious codes

Aquarius the constellation of the water carrier

Araby Arabia

Arcadia or **Arcady** a region in southern Greece; the ideal pastoral world

Archimago the wizard in Spenser's *The Faerie Queene*

Arethusa a nymph, attendant to Diana, loved by Alpheus and changed into a fountain

argent silver

Argonauts the crew of the Argo which sailed under Jason in search of the Golden Fleece

Argus the hundred-eyed guardian of the nymph Io, lulled to sleep by Hermes

Ariadne the daughter of King Minos of Crete, who helped Theseus defeat the Minotaur but was abandoned by him on the island of Naxos, where she was comforted by Bacchus

Arion a poet from Lesbos who was saved from drowning by singing to dolphins

asphodel an immortal flower grown in the Elysian fields

Atlas the mythical figure who held up the world

Attic Grecian

Aurora goddess of the dawn
aurorian rose-coloured like the dawn

Baal a fertility god of Asia Minor

Bacchus the Roman god of wine

Baiae's shore the Bay of Naples

beard to defy

Beaumont and Fletcher Francis Beaumont (1584–1616) and John Fletcher (1579–1625), playwriting partnership

Bellona the Roman goddess of war

benison blessing

bland gentle, mild

blent blended

Boccaccio Giovanni Boccaccio (1313–75), Italian writer whose most famous work is *The Decameron* (1351–3), a series of a hundred tales set against the backdrop of the Black Death

Boileau Nicolas Boileau (1636–1711), French poet and critic, prime supporter of Neo-classical principles

boon favour or request

Boreas the north wind

bourn boundary

Brahma the supreme god in Hindu mythology

brede a poeticism for anything woven or plaited

Britomartis the warrior heroine in Spenser's *The Faerie Queene*

bumper a glass

burden song

Burns Robert Burns (1759–96), Romantic poet from humble Scottish background with whom Keats identified

caitiff a despicable coward

Calidore hero of Spenser's *The Faerie Queene*

calumny false accusation

Cassandra prophetess who, amongst other things, foretold the fall of Troy

cassia honeysuckle

Castor and Pollux twins sons of Jupiter and Leda; transformed into the constellation Gemini

cates and dainties Elizabethan terms for edible delicacies

censers vessels in which incense is burned

centaur a mythical creature, half-man half-horse

Ceres mother of Proserpine, goddess of harvest

certes certainly

Chaldean a Babylonian, or an astrologer

champaign countryside

Chapman George Chapman (1559–1634), poet and dramatist whose translation of Homer (1614) was read by Keats

Charon the ferryman of the dead who was paid an obol by each soul for his services

Chatterton Thomas Chatterton (1752–70), poet who committed suicide, becoming something of a Romantic symbol for youthful neglected genius

charter privilege

Chaucer Geoffrey Chaucer (*c.*1340–1400), regarded as the greatest English medieval poet; writer of *The Canterbury Tales* (1387–1400)

chouse cheat

Circe daughter of the sun who lived on an island, sometimes Aeaea, and bewitched passing sailors, turning them into beasts

cirque circle

Clio the muse of history

Clymene one of the Nereids, often associated with the **Titans**

Coelus the father of the **Titans**

covert hiding place

Cressid or **Cressida** a Trojan women, who first returns the love of Troilus and then forsakes him; the subject of literary works by Chaucer, Shakespeare and others

cuirass a breastplate

Cupid the winged god of love

Cybele the wife of Chronos, or Saturn, and mother of the gods

Cyclades an island group, part of Greece

Cyclops a one-eyed giant tricked and blinded by Odysseus or Ulysses

Cynthia the moon goddess, linked to poetic inspiration

Cytheria another name for Venus

Daphne a nymph turned into a laurel tree to protect her from Apollo's amorous advances

darkling dark, in the dark

dastard coward(ly)

Deaucalion He and his wife were the only humans spared by Zeus from a great flood and went on to found a new race of humans.

Delos the island birthplace of Apollo, in the Cyclades

demesne dominion

descry to discover by looking

diadem jewelled crown

Diana goddess of hunting, and in some accounts Apollo's sister

Dido the queen of Carthage

Dis god of the underworld, identified with Pluto

Doris the daughter of Oceanus

drouth drought

Dryad female Nature spirit

Dryope a hamadryad, mother of Pan

ebon black

Echo a nymph whose unrequited love for Narcissus caused her to pine away until she became only an echoing voice

eglantine sweetbriar

eld old age

elf person

Elysium the resting place of virtuous souls after death

empyrean heaven or heavenly

Enceladus the most belligerent of the **Titans**

Endymion a shepherd king who fell in love with, or in some versions was seduced by, the moon goddess Cynthia

Erebus son of Chaos, whose name came to stand for Hell itself

eremite hermit

Eros see **Cupid**

eterne eternal

ethereal transcending the earthly

Eurydice the wife of Orpheus

Fancy common eighteenth-century term for imagination

fane a temple

Fanny Fanny Brawne (1800–65), engaged to Keats; the subject of some late poems

Fate(s) the mythical force(s) which control(s) human lives

Faun male Nature spirit

Flora the goddess of flowers and everything that blooms

front brow or forehead

Furies infernal spirits of vengeance

Ganymede a beautiful youth who became cupbearer to the gods

Georgiana Georgiana Keats, née Wylie (1798–1879), married Keats's brother George in May 1818.

Golden Age a mythic period of peace and prosperity

Gorgons three women monsters whose stare turned people to stone
gorgon monstrous

Glaucus a shepherd transformed into a sea deity who unsuccessfully pursued Scylla; in some versions the son of Neptune

glut to fill, to enjoy to the full

Graces three mythical figures who represented the refinements of life

guerdon reward, result

halcyon the kingfisher; halcyon days, a time of peace

hamadryad a tree-dwelling nymph

haply perhaps

Haydon Benjamin Robert Haydon (1786–1846), a painter of historical scenes, and a friend of Keats, who campaigned for the purchase of the Elgin Marbles

Hazlitt William Hazlitt (1778–1830), painter, philosopher, and most importantly literary critic; part of the Leigh Hunt circle

Hebe goddess of youth, cupbearer to the gods

Hecate goddess of the night and witchcraft, associated with the moon

hecatomb a vast amount

hectic feverish, exhibiting the symptoms of consumption or tuberculosis

Helicon a spring sacred to the Muses

Hellebore the Christmas rose

Hercules mythical warrior famed for his strength

Hermes see **Mercury**

Hesperides the daughters of Hesperus, who traditionally guarded Atlas's tree which bore golden apples

Hesperus the evening star

Hippocrene a spring on Mount Helicon, sacred to the Muses

Homer (c.850 BC) thought to be the greatest of classical Greek poets; traditionally thought to have been blind; the *Iliad* and the *Odyssey* are attributed to him

Hours nymphs attendant on the sun

Hunt James Henry Leigh Hunt (1784–1859), liberal literary figure, publisher of *The Examiner* in which Keats's first published poem appeared; criticised as founder of 'Cockney School' of poetry

Hyacinthus a Spartan loved by Apollo whose quoit, blown by Zephyr, killed him; in grief Apollo turned him into a flower

Hybla a Sicilian mountain famous for its bees and honey

Hymen the Greek god of marriage

Hyperion the Titan god of the sun; married his sister Thea

Imageries embroidered designs

Ind, Inde India

Iris the goddess of the rainbow, and also a sea nymph

Ixion a king punished by Zeus for ingratitude by being bound to a wheel to suffer eternal torment

Juno the wife of Jupiter and the queen of heaven

Jupiter or **Jove** Roman king of the gods, often depicted astride an eagle carrying a thunderbolt

Kosciusko Tadeusz Kosciusko (1746–1817), Polish leader who led an uprising against Russia (1791–4)

Lamia a monstrous snake-woman

Latmos a mountain in Asia Minor traditionally associated with Endymion; its inhabitants are Latmians

Latona the mother of Apollo and Cynthia

Leander swam the Hellespont to be with Hero

Leda daughter of the king of Aetolia whom Zeus, in the form of a swan, seduced or raped

Lethe the river of forgetfulness in Hades, or Hell; or Hell itself

Libertas Leigh Hunt

louted bowed

Lucifer the morning star

Lycean a mountain in Arcadia sacred to Pan

Lycidas or **Lycid** Milton's friend Edward King who drowned, and for whom he wrote an elegiac poem of that name (1637)

Lydian airs sensuous songs – see Milton's *L'Allegro*, ll. 135–6

magian magical

Maia daughter of Atlas, mother of Mercury or Hermes, identified with May and with spring in general

Manna miraculous food supplied to the Israelites in the wilderness – see Exodus 17:21; used by Keats in the sense of any exotic food

Mars the Roman god of war

maw mouth, opening

Meander a river in Asia Minor, famous for its winding course

meed reward

Melpomene the muse of tragedy

Mercury the winged messenger of the gods

mickle much

Midas a miserly king who was granted the gift of being able to turn everything he touched into gold, with dire consequences

Milton John Milton (1608–74), poet, scholar and supporter of the Parliamentary side in the English Civil War; writer of *Paradise Lost* (1667)

Minerva the goddess of wisdom, celebrated for her chastity, who sprang fully formed from the head of Jupiter

Minos the judge of the Underworld

missal the book containing the Mass services, which in Papal Masses the Pope would kiss before proceeding to his throne

Mnemosyne one of the **Titans**; mother of the Muses by Jupiter; associated with memory

Momus the god of blame and mockery

Moneta another name for Mnemosyne, also associated by some sources with Minerva

Montmorenci the Falls of Montmerenci in Quebec, Canada

Morpheus the god of sleep and dreams

Mulciber see **Vulcan**

myrtle plant associated with Venus

naiad water nymph

Nais a sea nymph, in some versions Glaucus' mother

nantz brandy

Narcissus died of despairing love for his own reflection and was turned into a flower

Nemesis daughter of Nox, the goddess of vengeance

Neptune the Roman god of the sea

nereids sea deities

Nereus son of Oceanus, granted the gift of prophecy, resided in the Aegean

Niobe Her children were killed by the gods because of her arrogance, and she was turned into a stone.

Nox the god of night

numbers verses

nymphs female deities, the spirits of the fields, and of nature in general

Oberon the king of the fairies

Oceanus a Titan, god of the sea

Odysseus or **Ulysses** the hero of Homer's *Odyssey*

Ops see **Cybele**

orat'ries oratories, private side-chapels

Orion a giant huntsman turned into a constellation after an attack on Diana or one of her attendants, in some versions blinded as a result of other attempted seductions

Orpheus son of the Muse Calliope, a poet and musician whose music charmed the natural world; he lost his wife Eurydice when, rescuing her from the Underworld, he turned his head to look back

Osiris the chief Egyptian god, brother and husband of Isis

paean song of praise, especially to Apollo

palatine palatial, royal

Pallas see **Minerva**

palmer pilgrim

palsy the effects of illness and old age

Pan the god of shepherds, and more generally a nature god and poet

Paphos a town in Cyprus, a centre for the worship of Venus

pards leopards

parley speak, sound

passing bell the bell rung as a call to prayer for the soul of the recently dead

Pegasus the last of the winged horses, hence inspiration

Peona Endymion's sister, Keats's invention, probably based on Paeon, the physician to the gods

Peris good fairies

Petrarch (1304–74) Italian poet, originator of the Petrarchan sonnet

Philomel daughter of the King of Athens whom the gods turned into a nightingale for her own protection; the nightingale

Phoebe a daughter of Jove or Jupiter; see **Cynthia**

Phoebus the sun god Apollo

Phorcus son of Terra, a sea deity, sometimes identified as the father of Scylla

pight settled

pinions wings

Plato (*c*.428–347 BC) Greek philosopher

Pleiades the seven daughters of Atlas who became the constellation of the same name

Pluto god of the underworld

Polyphemus a one-eyed club-wielding giant

Pomona a nymph associated with gardens and fruit trees

pontiff priestly, relating to a high priest

pother a state of confusion

Prometheus the maker of the first humans, made with fire which he stole from the gods, for which he was punished

Proserpine daughter of Ceres and Jove who was abducted by Pluto to be queen of the Underworld

Proteus a god of the sea

prythee pray thee

Psyche a beautiful girl, seduced by Love (Cupid or Eros) and subsequently deified; also represents the soul; often represented by a butterfly

Pyrrha Deucalion's wife, who helped repopulate the world by throwing stones behind her

Python the giant snake which emerged from the slime after Deucalion's flood; killed by Apollo

quire choir

Raphael (1483–1520), painter particularly of religious subjects; exemplifies the ideals of the High Renaissance

raught reached

Red Cross Knight hero of Spenser's *The Faerie Queene*

Reynolds John Hamilton Reynolds (1794–1852), friend of Keats, minor writer

Rhadamanthus the judge of the Underworld

Salvator Salvator Rosa (1615–73), an Italian landscape painter popular in England in the eighteenth and early nineteenth centuries

Sappho Greek poetess born on Lesbos, *c*.612 BC

Saturn king of the gods before being deposed by his son Jove or Zeus; associated with contemplation and melancholy

satyr wood deity, often with animal body parts, associated with enjoyment and lust

scutcheon a coat of arms

Scylla the beautiful daughter of Typhon who had many suitors but rejected them all; in some versions she was turned into a sea monster by the jealous Circe

See place of abode, or region of responsibility

Semele wife of Jupiter, mother of Bacchus

shade shadow, ghost

shallop small boat

shent shamed, injured, marred

shrive confess

Silenus Bacchus' companion, usually depicted as a drunken old man on an ass

Sol the sun

Soother, soothest softer, softest

Southey Robert Southey (1774–1843), Romantic poet, friend of Wordsworth, became increasingly reactionary

Spenser, Edmund Spenser (1552–99) English Renaissance poet, writer of *The Faerie Queene*

spheres in Platonic tradition the earth was surrounded by spheres which carried the planets and the stars; these were held to make music which was audible to the inspired

sprite spirit

spumy foamy

swart black, dark

Sydney Algernon Sydney (1622–83), Whig hero of the Civil War, executed after the Restoration

sylph spirit of the air

sylvan of woodland

Syrens or **Sirens** sea demons whose singing lured sailors to their deaths

Syrinx a dryad pursued by Pan who turned herself into a reed, hence Panpipes

tambour frame embroidery frame

Tartarus Hell

Tasso Italian poet (1493–1569) born on the Bay of Naples

Tellus the earth goddess

Tempe a valley in Ancient Greece, celebrated for its beauty and the happiness of its inhabitants

Tethys wife of Oceanus

Thalia the muse of festivals and pastoral and comic poetry, one of the three **Graces**

Thea one of the **Titans**, Hyperion's sister and wife

Thetis   a sea deity, mother of Achilles

Tigh   Mary Tigh (1772–1810), poet whose *Psyche* (1805) was greatly admired by Keats

timbrels   tambourines

Titania   queen of the fairies

Titans   the children of Uranus, or Coelus, and Gaia, Terra, or Tellus, a race of gods displaced by the Olympians

Titian   Tiziano Vecellio (c.1488–1576), a painter of the Venetian School, famed for his use of vigorous colour

toils   nets, snares

Triton   a sea god, usually half-man, half-dolphin and blowing a shell

Troilus   a son of King Priam of Troy; the rejected lover of Cressida

Typhon   a rebellious giant who was imprisoned by Jupiter under Etna

Ulysses   see **Odysseus**

Urania   the muse of astronomy, also another name for Venus

vail   to lower, to submit

van   vanguard, front

vanward   leading

vassal   a protected underling in feudal societies

Venus   the Roman goddess of love

vermeil   a Spenserian word for crimson

Vertumnus   Roman god of the spring, at first rejected then accepted by the nymph Pomona

Vesper   the evening star
vespers   evening prayers

vintage   wine

visage   face

Vulcan   the god of fire and metal-work, often depicted with a hammer

ward   lock

wight   fellow

wox   waxed, grew, a Spenserianism

wroth   angered

Zephyrus   the (west) wind

zone   girdle or belt

Notes

Words or names that appear more than once are to be found in the Glossary.
Abbreviations:

FQ	Edmund Spenser's *The Faerie Queene*
Ovid	Ovid's *Metamorphosis*
PL	John Milton's *Paradise Lost*

I stood tiptoe

1 (p. 3) Motto from Leigh Hunt's *The Story of Rimini* 3:430. Many of Keats's early poems are influenced by Hunt's style and descriptive technique.
2 (p. 4) *sallows*   willows
3 (p. 6) *the moon*   Like many Romantic poets, Keats identifies the moon with the imagination – see *Endymion*.

Calidore

1 (p. 13) *The little chapel*   see *FQ* 6,5,35
2 (p. 13) *cat's eyes*   speedwell or forget-me-not
3 (p. 14) *Sir Clerimond*   an invented Spenserian name
4 (p. 15) *Sir Gondibert*   see Davenant's *Gondibert* (1651)

On Receiving a Curious Shell and a Copy of Verses from the Same Ladies

1 (p. 18) *Golconda*   the old name for Hyderabad, once famous for its diamonds
2 (p. 18) *Armida . . . and Rinaldo*   characters from Tasso's *Gerusalemme Libertata* (1581) which Keats read in translation

To —   [*Georgiana Augusta Wylie, afterwards Mrs George Keats*]

1 (p. 21) *alabaster*   white – see *FQ* 6, 8, 42

To Hope

1 (p. 22) *'mind's eye'*   quoted from Shakespeare's *Hamlet* 1,2,185

Imitation of Spenser

1 (p. 24) *Lear*   see Shakespeare's *King Lear*
2 (p. 24) *teen*   grief
3 (p. 24) *coerulean*   cerulean, sky blue

Three Sonnets on Woman

1 (p. 25) For Keats on women, see *Letters* 1:134, 404.

To George Felton Mathew

1 (p. 27) *the brother poets*   Beaumont and Fletcher – see Glossary

2 (p. 28) *Druid* common in the eighteenth century as a romanticisied poet-priest figure
3 (p. 28) *Helvetian Tell* William Tell, fourteenth-century Swiss patriot renowned as an archer
4 (p. 28) *William Wallace* thirteenth-century Scottish freedom fighter

To My Brother George

1 (p. 30) *sphery strains* a reference to the music of the spheres
2 (p. 31) *spell* enchant
3 (p. 33) *scarlet coats* soldiers, who often wore red uniforms at this time

To Charles Cowden Clarke

1 (p. 34) *Charles Cowden Clarke* the son of Keats's headmaster, and his friend
2 (p. 34) *Armidia* a character from Tasso's *Gerusalemme Libertata* (1581), which Keats read in translation
3 (p. 34) *Mulla's stream* the river near Spenser's home. *Belphoebe*, *Una*, *Archimago* are all characters from his *FQ*.
4 (p. 35) *Michael . . . Eve* the angel and Eve from *PL*
5 (p. 35) *Tell . . . Brutus* see *To George Felton Mathew*. Brutus was the Roman statesman who killed Julius Caesar.
6 (p. 36) *Mozart . . . Arne . . . Handel* eighteenth-century composers
7 (p. 36) *Erin* a poetical form for Ireland
8 (p. 36) *the music* the piano

Written on the Day that Mr Leigh Hunt Left Prison

1 (p. 39) Title: Hunt was released in February 1815 after serving a two-year prison sentence for attacking the Prince Regent in his journal *The Examiner*.

To a Friend who Sent Me Some Roses

1 (p. 40) *Wells* Thomas Wells (1800–79), a friend of Tom Keats and later Leigh Hunt
2 (p. 40) *spell'd* enchanted

To My Brothers

1 (p. 41) *household gods* gods of the home in Roman mythology

Keen, fitful gusts are whisp'ring here and there

1 (p. 42) *Laura* the subject of Petrarch's *Canzoniere*

To one who has been long in city pent

1 (p. 42) *debonair* pleasant, a common Spenserianism

On First Looking into Chapman's Homer

1 (p. 43) *realms of gold* the world of the imagination. Apollo, who as the sun god was related to gold, was also the god of poetry.

2 (p. 43) *Cortez*   Cortes was one of the first Europeans to see Mexico City; Keats confuses him here with Balboa, the first European to see the Pacific.

3 (p. 43) *Darien*   the neck of land joining North and South America

Addressed to Haydon

1 (p. 44) *'singleness of aim'*   quotation from Wordsworth's *Character of the happy warrior* (1807). Haydon won praise from Wordsworth for his part in securing the purchase of the Elgin Marbles for the nation in 1816.

Addressed to the Same

1 (p. 44) *Great spirits*   i.e. Wordsworth, Hunt and Haydon

2 (p. 44) *Helvellyn*   the third highest mountain in the Lake District

Sleep and Poetry

1 (p. 47) motto from *The Floure and the Lefe*, a poem believed in Keats's time to be by Chaucer, but now no longer attributed to him

2 (p. 48) *denizen*   an outsider granted citizenship

3 (p. 50) *the charioteer*   the sun god Apollo

4 (p. 50) *stalks*   trees

5 (p. 51) *ether*   the sky

6 (p. 51) *paragon*   surpass

7 (p. 51) *huge as a planet*   the poetry of the Elizabethans is seen as a planet which adds to the music of the spheres

8 (p. 51) *schism*   Keats, like many Romantics, attacked Augustan (or eighteenth-century) poetry, which was characterised by its use of the rhyming couplet, and its apparent adherence to the rigid rules of Neo-classicism.

9 (p. 52) *Jacob's wit*   the scheme by which Jacob increased his wealth at the expense of Laban – see Genesis 30:27–43

10 (p. 52) *the bright Lyricist*   Apollo

11 (p. 52) *Avon*   the river associated with Shakespeare

12 (p. 53) *swan's ebon bill*   a reference to Wordsworth

13 (p. 53) *a pipe*   probably a reference to Leigh Hunt's poetry

14 (p. 53) *Poets' Polyphemes*   the idea that many modern poets handle their material as roughly as the giant Polyphemus did his club

15 (p. 53) *Yeaned*   born or brought forth

16 (p. 55) *Dedalian wings*   Daedalus made wings for himself and his son to escape exile; but Icarus flew too close to the sun and the wax fixing on his wings melted – see Ovid 8, 183–235.

17 (p. 55) *assay*   attempt

18 (p. 56) *a poet's house*   Leigh Hunt's cottage in Hampstead, then a village on the edge of London

Endymion – Book I

1 (p. 64) *sated*   satisfied

2 (p. 64) *unmew*   set free

3 (p. 64) *white wicker*   basket

4 (p. 64) *younglings*   young plants

5 (p. 64) *vales of Thessaly*   Apollo's period of exile as a shepherd in Thessaly is recorded in Ovid 2, 677–82.

6 (p. 64) *Begirt with ministring looks*   surrounded by attentive onlookers

7 (p. 65) *poll*   the part of the head on which hair grows

8 (p. 65) *car*   chariot

9 (p. 65) *nervy*   muscular

10 (p. 66) *scrip, with needments*   a bag containing food

11 (p. 67) *pipy hemlock*   The poison hemlock has tall hollow stems.

12 (p. 67) *turtles*   turtle doves

13 (p. 68) *universal knowledge*   Keats is playing on the sense of *pan* meaning all here.

14 (p. 69) *Thermopylae*   defended by the Spartans in 480 BC

15 (p. 69) *genitors*   progenitors

16 (p. 70) *fire tailed exhalations*   comets

17 (p. 70) *feathery sails*   wings

18 (p. 71) *old tale Arabian*   see 'The History of the Young King of the Isles' in *The Arabian Nights*

19 (p. 72) *crystal mocking*   reflections in the water

20 (p. 72) *sere*   dry

21 (p. 74) *Delphic*   divinely inspired, after Delphi the location of Apollo's Oracle on mount Parnassus

22 (p. 75) *snorting four*   the four horses which drew Apollo's chariot – see Ovid 2, 153–5

23 (p. 75) *the zodiac-lion*   the star sign Leo, referring to the part of the sky occupied by Leo

24 (p. 75) *his rod*   Mercury's rod could lull mortals to sleep and even raise the dead.

25 (p. 76) *gordian'd*   knotted

26 (p. 78) *ouzel*   blackbird

27 (p. 79) *middle earth*   Earth is between Heaven and the Underworld in many mythologies.

28 (p. 80) *high-fronted*   of noble bearing, like so much of Keats's language an Elizabethanism.

29 (p. 81) *full alchemis'd*   Alchemy was the art of turning base metals into gold; in this famous passage Endymion considers kinds of imaginative transformation dependent upon love.

30 (p. 81) *lucid*   translucent, transparent

31 (p. 81) *bruit*   proclaim

32 (p. 82) *a pelican brood*   Keats is repeating the familiar myth that the pelican feeds its young on its own blood.

33 (p. 82) *commingling*   intermingling

34 (p. 82) *wilder'd*   bewildered

35 (p. 82) *atomies*   mites

36 (p. 83) *matron-temple*   see Latona in the Glossary

37 (p. 83) *the mirror*   the reflective surface of the well water

38 (p. 83) *character'd*   defined

39 (p. 84) *gnawing sloth*   Sloths are fruit-eating tree dwellers. Keats clearly intended a meat-eating predator.

40 (p. 84) *by hap*   by chance

41 (p. 85) *lave*   wash

42 (p. 85) *freaks*   caprices

Endymion – Book II

1 (p. 87) *What care . . . mast*   see Plutarch's *Life of Themistocles*

2 (p. 87) *Juliet*   see Shakespeare's *Romeo and Juliet*

3 (p. 87) *Imogen*   see Shakespeare's *Cymbeline*

4 (p. 87) *Pastorella in the bandit's den*   see FQ 6,11

5 (p. 89) *smutch*   smudge

6 (p. 89) *mealy gold*   the fine dust from a butterfly's wing – see Shakespeare's *Troilus and Cressida* 3, 3, 78–9

7 (p. 90) *burr*   confusion

8 (p. 92) *passion'd*   impassioned

9 (p. 92) *sparry*   rich in minerals

10 (p. 92) *antre*   cave

11 (p. 93) *descried*   saw

12 (p. 93) *fray*   frightened

13 (p. 93) *the mighty ones*   great poets, the only people who will be remembered after the end of the world

14 (p. 93) *quiver'd Dian*   Diana in her role as huntress is often depicted with a bow and a quiver of arrows.

15 (p. 94) *fog-born elf*   will-o'-the-wisp

16 (p. 94) *surcharg'd*   weighed down

17 (p. 94) *temple's chief*   the temple's upper end

18 (p. 94) *plain*   complain

19 (p. 94) *disparted*   separated, a form common in FQ; can also mean to open – see l. 407 below

20 (p. 95) *zephyr-boughs*   trees swayed by the wind

21 (p. 96) *Carian's ear*   Endymion's ear

22 (p. 96) *swart abysm*   black abyss

23 (p. 97) *a sleeping youth*   Adonis – see Glossary

24 (p. 97) *Ethiop*   black

25 (p. 97) *bugle blooms*   the bugle-shaped flowers of the woodbine

26 (p. 97) *virgin's bower*   a species of clematis also known as Old Man's Beard

27 (p. 97) *the pathos*   the pathetic sound

28 (p. 98) *all these things around us*   Keats's account is drawn from Shakespeare's *Venus and Adonis* and also *FQ* 3, 1 ,34–8 and Ovid 10, 519–52

29 (p. 98) *fond elf*   foolish individual. The word 'elf' is used commonly in *FQ* to refer to the knights.

30 (p. 101) *vexing Mars*   The love life of Venus and Mars is related in Ovid 4, 171–89.

31 (p. 101) *zoned*   surrounded

32 (p. 101) *minish*   diminish

33 (p. 101) *Aetnean throes*   the tremors caused by the volcanic Mount Etna

34 (p. 103) *Protean*   constantly changing

35 (p. 103) *a fathoming plummet*   a weighted rope used to measure depths at sea

36 (p. 104) *Hesperean*   western, after Hesperus – see Glossary

37 (p. 104) *starry seven*   the Pleiades – see Glossary

38 (p. 105) *the count/ Of mighty poets is made up*   Like many Romantic poets, Keats felt that the writing of poetry was now near impossible.

39 (p. 106) *Ida*   Ida was a mountain associated with Venus; here it suggests an invocation of the goddess.

40 (p. 107) *old hymns made nullity*   Cynthia fears that, if known, her love for Endymion would lose her the respect she gains as a goddess associated with chastity.

41 (p. 107) *ambrosial*   Ambrosia was the food of the gods.

42 (p. 107) *lispings empyrean*   heavenly or immortal speech

43 (p. 108) *sentinel*   watching

44 (p. 109) *Alecto*   one of the Furies – see Glossary

45 (p. 109) *arbour*   shelter

46 (p. 110) *The Olympian eagle's vision*   Jupiter is often depicted with an eagle.

47 (p. 110) *O Arethusa*   see Glossary. Keats reworks Ovid 5, 572–641 here.

48 (p. 111) *syren words*   see Glossary

49 (p. 111) *Oread-Queen*   Diana – see Glossary

50 (p. 111) *be a criminal*   break her vow of chastity

51 (p. 112) *mealy sweets*   nectar

52 (p. 112) *whelming*   overwhelmimg

Endymion – Book III

1 (p. 114) *Fire-branded foxes*   see Judges 15:4–5

2 (p. 114) *dight*   dressed

3 (p. 114) *empurpled vests*   the colour traditionally worn by cardinals, a reference to the Church as one of the corrupt powers listed here

4 (p. 114) *thunder clouds* a reference to the Babylonian god of storms and oracles, Rammon

5 (p. 114) *bourne* here in the sense of domain

6 (p. 115) *kine* cows

7 (p. 115) *spooming* foaming, from spume

8 (p. 116) *love-spangles* reflections of moon light playing on the water

9 (p. 116) *winged Chieftain* Cupid – see Glossary

10 (p. 117) *vast* the sea

11 (p. 117) *brazen beaks and targe* the bronze sterns of sunken warships and bronze shields

12 (p. 117) *behemoth and leviathan* monsters referred to in the Bible, which Keats may have recalled from his recent reading of *PL* – see *PL* 7, 471–2 and 412–4

13 (p. 118) *mesh* weave into garlands

14 (p. 118) *strange love* At this stage Endymion doesn't realise that the moon and his love are identical.

15 (p. 119) *conn'd* studied

16 (p. 119) *denizen* an outsider granted citizenship

17 (p. 119) *wilder'd* bewildered

18 (p. 120) *giant's arm* Typhon – see Glossary

19 (p. 120) *Sisters three* the Fates – see Glossary

20 (p. 121) *contumelious* insolent

21 (p. 122) *'My soul stands . . . '* Keats version of the story of Glaucus and Scylla is adapted from Ovid 8, 898–968 and 14, 1–74.

22 (p. 122) *thrall* slave

23 (p. 123) *distemper'd* deranged

24 (p. 124) *to the very white* absolutely

25 (p. 126) *umbrageous* shadowy, shady

26 (p. 126) *complain* complaint

27 (p. 126) *gordian* looped

28 (p. 127) *penny pelf* the fee paid to Charon – see Glossary

29 (p. 127) *Stygian* relating to the Styx, one of the rivers into the Underworld

30 (p. 127) *writhen* made to writhe

31 (p. 128) *phalanx* a formation of soldiers

32 (p. 128) *fate's gentle shears* The Fates would cut short someone's life by cutting a thread.

33 (p. 129) *thews* traits, qualities

34 (p. 129) *drave* drove

35 (p. 131) *aguish* fever causing

36 (p. 131) *Each Atlas-line* Each line bears a weight as heavy as that carried by Atlas.

37 (p. 133) *clue* nail

38 (p. 134) *corse* corpse

39 (p. 134) *All were re-animated*   Here, in restoring the dead, Endymion
performs the role of a kind of ideal doctor, reflecting Keats's own training.

40 (p. 134) *boundless emerald*   the sea

41 (p. 135) *Memphis, and Babylon, and Ninevah*   cities in antiquity celebrated
for their splendour

42 (p. 136) *Paphian army*   an army of lovers – see Paphos in the Glossary

43 (p. 136) *Beauty's paragon*   Venus

44 (p. 137) *The ooze-born Goddess*   Venus, who rose from the sea near
Cyprus

45 (p. 138) *pleach'd*   interwove

46 (p. 138) *co-inheritor*   Neptune inherited the sea, Jupiter the earth, and
Pluto the underworld.

47 (p. 138) *Gulphs*   rushes in

48 (p. 139) *Bright-winged Child*   Cupid – see Glossary

49 (p. 140) *Aegean seer*   Nereus – see Glossary

Endymion – Book IV

1 (p. 141) *Muse of my native land!*   an invocation of a muse which echoes
the opening of *PL* which Keats was reading at the time. What follows is a
history of the development of poetry.

2 (p. 141) *eastern*   Hebrew, a reference to the Bible

3 (p. 141) *the Nine*   the muses

4 (p. 141) *Ausonia*   Italy. The poets referred to are Virgil and Dante, whom
Keats began to read in 1818.

5 (p. 141) *Ganges*   the Ganges, a river in India

6 (p. 143) *both*   the goddess and the Indian Maid

7 (p. 144) *sith*   since

8 (p. 144) *weal*   a state of well-being

9 (p. 145) *sea-spry*   sea spray

10 (p. 146) *Bacchus and his kin*   For an account of Bacchanalia, see Ovid 4.

11 (p. 146) *To scare thee, Melancholy!*   As the god of wine, Bacchus was
believed to banish melancholy or sorrowful states.

12 (p. 147) *thorough*   through

13 (p. 147) *coil*   noisy bustle, an Elizabethanism – see *Hamlet* 3,1,67

14 (p. 147) *unicorn*   The fabulous horned horse was believed to be a native
of India, but is not usually associated with Bacchus.

15 (p. 147) *Abyssinia*   the old name for Ethiopia

16 (p. 148) *Tartary*   a kingdom in central Asia, home of the fierce Tartars

17 (p. 150) *in spleen*   in resolute mood

18 (p. 150) *Cimmerian*   cloudy, after Cimeria, an Asian town supposed to be
perpetually shrouded in cloud

19 (p. 151) *Skiddaw's top*   the top of a Lakeland mountain, known to Keats
through the poetry of Wordsworth

20 (p. 151) *proud birds* peacocks, traditionally associated with Juno – see Glossary

21 (p. 152) *kyrtled* skirted

22 (p. 152) *floating morris* airy dance

23 (p. 152) *he who died/ For soaring* refers to the story of Icarus – see *Sleep and Poetry*, n. 16

24 (p. 153) *daedale* cunning, derived from Daedalus a mythical inventor

25 (p. 153) *'haviour* behaviour

26 (p. 153) *witless* unaware

27 (p. 154) *death-watch tick* the sound of the death-watch beetle which is said to predict death

28 (p. 155) *mask* a musical entertainment; here celebrating Phoebe's wedding

29 (p. 155) *lucid* shining

30 (p. 155) *bibbers* drinkers

31 (p. 156) *the Bear* the constellation Ursa Major. The Lion here is the star sign Leo, and the Centaur represents Sagittarius.

32 (p. 156) *Danae's son* the hero Perseus; the constellation next to Andromeda

33 (p. 158) *silver lives* under the influence of the moon

34 (p. 158) *dew-claw'd* dappled with dew

35 (p. 158) *syrinx flag* a reed turned into a musical pipe

36 (p. 159) *barn* store

37 (p. 159) *light* alight

38 (p. 159) *my Delphos* my oracle, after Delphos, the Oracle of Apollo

39 (p. 160) *Young feather'd tyrant* Cupid – see Glossary

40 (p. 160) *not to my hunger* do not become too seductive an idea

41 (p. 161) *Ensky'd* Endymion has become part of mythology before the poem retells his story.

42 (p. 161) *lute-voic'd brother* Apollo

43 (p. 161) *amaranth* an imaginary unfading flower – see *PL* 3, 352–6

44 (p. 161) *fear'd* frightened

45 (p. 162) *ditties* songs

46 (p. 163) *betides* befits

47 (p. 164) *monitor* guide. Endymion intends to adopt a life of chastity at this point, following Diana.

48 (p. 164) *thing of yes and no* everyday thing

49 (p. 165) *serene father* Apollo, the sun – see Glossary

50 (p. 165) *Titan's foe* Jupiter overthrew the Titans – see Keats *Hyperion*

51 (p. 165) *seemlihed* seemliness

52 (p. 165) *Saturnus'* Saturn's – see Glossary

53 (p. 165) *lorn* forlorn

Lamia – Part I

1 (p. 171) *prosperous*   more widespread
2 (p. 171) *ever-smitten Hermes*   Hermes' pursuit of a nymph is recounted in Ovid 2, 708–832.
3 (p. 172) *cirque-couchant*   lying in coils
4 (p. 172) *gordian*   interwoven
5 (p. 172) *tiar*   tiara
6 (p. 173) *flakes*   clouds
7 (p. 173) *star of Lethe*   One of Hermes' tasks was to conduct the souls of the dead.
8 (p. 173) *weird*   bewitched
9 (p. 174) *damask*   red
10 (p. 174) *lythe Caducean charm*   Hermes rod, the source of his power, was called the caduceus; it was depicted entwined with snakes.
11 (p. 174) *to the lees*   completely
12 (p. 174) *besprent*   sprinkled over
13 (p. 175) *rubious-argent*   silver tinged with red
14 (p. 176) *sciential*   wise
15 (p. 176) *his vows*   Lycius would have been praying to Jove for a happy marriage.
16 (p. 177) *Platonic shades*   Lycius' thoughts are lost in philosophical speculation.
17 (p. 177) *his chain*   Lycius is snared by Lamia. Love is often described as a chain.
18 (p. 178) *the cruel lady*   see also *La Belle Dame sans Merci*
19 (p. 179) *lineal*   in the line of, descended from
20 (p. 179) *comprised*   absorbed
21 (p. 180) *temples lewd*   Corinth was renowned as a centre for the worship of Venus and for its prostitutes.

Lamia – Part II

1 (p. 182) *clench'd it quite*   proved it absolutely
2 (p. 182) *shafts*   columns
3 (p. 182) *a tithe*   a tenth, a fraction
4 (p. 182) *penetrant*   acute
5 (p. 182) *empery*   empire
6 (p. 184) *the serpent*   Python – see Glossary
7 (p. 184) *betray'd*   tricked
8 (p. 185) *subtle servitors*   invisible servants
9 (p. 185) *fretted*   carved
10 (p. 186) *daft*   resisted
11 (p. 186) *sophist*   a philosopher or reasoner, possibly with the sense of a false reasoner
12 (p. 187) *at meridian height*   at its peak

13 (p. 187) *osier'd* woven
14 (p. 187) *willow . . . adders tongue* plants associated with grief
15 (p. 187) *thyrsus* Bacchus' staff which was entwined with ivy and vine leaves
16 (p. 187) *cold philosophy* Much of Keats's writing was concerned with the detrimental effects of scientific thinking on imaginative views of the world. In particular, he blamed Newton and his followers for reducing the magic of the rainbow to a phenomenon which could be explained by the science of optics.
17 (p. 189) *deep-recessed vision* deep set eyes
18 (p. 189) *juggling* conjuring
19 (p. 189) *perceant* piercing

Isabella; or, The Pot of Basil

1 (p. 190) *palmer in Love's eye* pilgrim in search of love
2 (p. 193) *Thesues' spouse* Ariadne – see Glossary
3 (p. 193) *swelt* swelter, a Spenserianism – see *FQ* 1,7.6
4 (p. 193) *Ceylon* former name for Sri Lanka
5 (p. 194) *lazar stairs* the stairs in a lazar house which was occupied by the poor and the sick
6 (p. 194) *land inspired* Palestine
7 (p. 194) *ducats* gold coins
8 (p. 194) *Hot Egypt's pest* alludes to the plague of darkness visited upon the Egyptians – Exodus 10:21–3
9 (p. 194) *ghittern* a type of guitar
10 (p. 195) *stead* render
11 (p. 196) *Apennine* the Appenines, an Italian mountain range
12 (p. 196) *Arno's stream* The Arno is an Italian river which passes through Florence.
13 (p. 196) *freshets* floods, or currents of water
14 (p. 198) *Hinnom's vale* a place of human sacrifice in the Bible – see II Chronicles 28:3.
15 (p. 198) *feather'd pall* death
16 (p. 198) *waking an Indian* Keats had read about feats of endurance performed by Native Americans in William Robertson's *History of America* (1792).
17 (p. 198) *loamed* covered in loam, or soil
18 (p. 199) *sepulchral briars* briars growing in a graveyard
19 (p. 200) *atom* indivisible
20 (p. 200) *hie* go
21 (p. 200) *forest-hearse* place of burial within the forest
22 (p. 201) *dainities* breasts
23 (p. 202) *the old tale* Boccaccio's original version of the story

24 (p. 202) *the Persean sword*   Perseus cut off the head of the Gorgan with a sword.

25 (p. 202) *ancient harps*   referring to the tellers of old romances

26 (p. 203) *leafits*   leaves

27 (p. 204) *Baälites of pelf*   false worshippers of money, after the pagan god Baal

28 (p. 204) *chapel-shrift*   confession

29 (p. 205) *burthen*   refrain, chorus

The Eve of St Agnes

1 (p. 206) *Beadsman*   one who prays for the souls of others

2 (p. 206) *without a death*   His frosted breath resembles depictions of the soul leaving the dead, but he is alive.

3 (p. 206) *St Agnes Eve*   The folklore tradition that virgins could discover their future partners on St Agnes Eve was well known to Keats through his reading of Burton's *Anatomy of Melancholy* (1660), for example.

4 (p. 208) *all amort*   listless

5 (p. 208) *beldame*   nurse. Keats's figure, like much of the detail of the story as a whole, is modelled on the nurse in *Romeo and Juliet*.

6 (p. 209) *Gossip*   in the dual Elizabethan sense of a talkative woman and a female friend

7 (p. 209) *holy loom*   Traditionally, two lambs are sacrificed during the feast of St Agnes and their wool is woven by nuns into the pallium, or woollen band, worn by popes and archbishops.

8 (p. 210) *brook*   prevent

9 (p. 211) *weal or woe*   good or evil

10 (p. 211) *Merlin paid his Demon*   probably a reference to Merlin's perpetual imprisonment by his lover, the Lady of the Lake – see *FQ* 3, 3, 7–11

11 (p. 211) *dim espial*   any noise

12 (p. 212) *fray'd*   frightened

13 (p. 212) *No uttered syllable, or, woe betide!*   To speak would break the spell.

14 (p. 212) *emblazonings*   heraldic devices

15 (p. 212) *gules*   the heraldic term for red

16 (p. 213) *glory*   halo

17 (p. 213) *swart Paynims*   black pagans, possibly a reference to Muslims

18 (p. 214) *tinct*   tinged

19 (p. 214) *argosy*   a sailing boat

20 (p. 214) *Fez . . . Samarcand . . . Lebanon*   Fez is in Northern Morocco; Samarcand was an ancient Persian city, famed for its wealth and exotic markets. All three suggest exotic locations.

21 (p. 214) *unnerved*   weak

22 (p. 215) *woofed*   woven

23 (p. 215) *'La belle dame sans mercy'*   see notes to Keats's *La Belle Dame Sans Merci*

24 (p. 216) *Solution*   fusion

25 (p. 216) *flaw-blown*   wind-blown

26 (p. 216) *unprunned*   unpreaned

27 (p. 216) *haggard*   wild, fierce

28 (p. 216) *wassailers*   drinkers, revellers

29 (p. 217) *Rhenish*   wine from the Rhine region

30 (p. 217) *sagacious*   wise

31 (p. 217) *aves*   prayers

32 (p. 217) *aye*   yes, in the sense of an answer to his prayers

Ode to a Nightingale

1 (p. 218) *drains*   dregs

2 (p. 218) *warm South*   wine from the South

3 (p. 219) *viewless*   invisible

4 (p. 219) *embalmed darkness*   darkness steeped in scent, but also suggesting the concern with death in the following stanza

5 (p. 220) *Ruth*   In the Bible Ruth is forced by circumstance to work in foreign fields – see Ruth 2:3.

Ode on a Grecian Urn

1 (p. 221) *Sylvan*   of the woods

2 (p. 221) *sensual*   physical

3 (p. 222) *Cold Pastoral*   This paradoxical phrase captures the tension of the urn: it suggests the warmth of pastoral or idealised country scenes, and the coldness of static art.

4 (p. 222) *'Beauty is truth, truth beauty'*   There are a number of variants of these famous last lines. The first published version is in the *Annals of Fine Art* (January 1820) and has no inverted commas around the phrase. They do appear in *Poems* in 1820. This variation has added to the debate as to the meaning of the end of the poem.

Ode to Psyche

1 (p. 223) *soft-conched*   shell-like

2 (p. 223) *espied*   seen

3 (p. 223) *Tyrian*   crimson or purple

4 (p. 223) *eye-dawn or auroroean love*   Their love is renewed each time they open their eyes just as the day dawns.

5 (p. 223) *winged boy*   Cupid – see Glossary

6 (p. 223) *Olympus' faded hierarchy*   the Greek gods who were said to live on Mount Olympus

7 (p. 224) *fond*   carries the sense of devoted and also simple

8 (p. 224) *lucent fans*   shining wings

9 (p. 224) *feign*   invent

10 (p. 224) *Love*   Cupid – see Glossary

Ode to Fancy

1 (p. 225) *ingle*   fireplace
2 (p. 225) *shoon*   shoes
3 (p. 227) *Ceres' daughter*   Proserpine – see Glossary
4 (p. 227) *God of Torment*   Pluto – see Glossary
5 (p. 227) *kirtle*   short gown or tunic

Ode – Bards of Passion

1 (p. 227) *parle*   speech
2 (p. 228) *little week*   short lives

Lines on the Mermaid Tavern

1 (p. 229) *the Mermaid Tavern*   a London pub, traditionally the meeting
  place of Beaumont and Fletcher and other Elizabethan poets, which Keats
  may have visited
2 (p. 229) *Canary wine*   sweet wine from the Canary Islands similar to
  Madeira
3 (p. 229) *bowse*   drink, an Elizabethan word
4 (p. 229) *in the Zodiac*   in the sky

Robin Hood

1 (p. 230) *winter's shears . . . whispering fleeces*   The trees have lost their
  leaves to the winds just as sheep are shorn.
2 (p. 230) *ivory*   hunting horn
3 (p. 230) *polar ray*   Pole Star
4 (p. 230) *Thrumming*   strumming
5 (p. 230) *beguile*   while away
6 (p. 230) *pasture Trent*   the River Trent, in Nottinghamshire, which passes
  through pastureland
7 (p. 231) *morris din*   the music of Morris dancers
8 (p. 231) *Gamelyn*   the hero of *The Tale of Gamelyn* (*c.*1350), who becomes
  king of the outlaws
9 (p. 231) *'grene shawe'*   a quotation from Chaucer's *The Friar's Tale*, l. 88
10 (p. 231) *craze*   go mad
11 (p. 231) *tight*   skilful

To Autumn

1 (p. 232) *barred clouds bloom*   The clouds suggest both death and the
  'bloom' of life. Barred here means of varying colour.
2 (p. 233) *bourn*   stream

Ode on Melancholy

1 (p. 233) *Wolf's bane*   the poison, aconite

Hyperion – Book I

1 (p. 235) *Memphian sphinx*   Memphis was the capital of ancient Egypt.
2 (p. 236) *Rumbles reluctant*   The word order inversion here is typical of the Miltonic constructions to be found throughout *Hyperion*. 'Reluctant' carries both the current meaning and the earlier one of offering resistance.
3 (p. 237) *couchant*   lying, an heraldic term
4 (p. 237) *aspen-malady*   The aspen tree shakes in the softest breeze.
5 (p. 237) *nervous*   strong
6 (p. 238) *lorn of*   lacking in. Throughout, Keats's description of the cosmos is derived from Milton.
7 (p. 238) *sky-children*   the gods
8 (p. 238) *Druid locks*   long hair
9 (p. 238) *eyes to fever out*   to stare with a fevered expression
10 (p. 238) *The rebel three*   Saturn's sons, Jupiter, Neptune and Pluto, who divided his kingdom between themselves – see Glossary
11 (p. 239) *cleave*   pass through
12 (p. 239) *orbed fire*   the sun
13 (p. 239) *snuff'd*   sniffed – see *PL* 10, 272–3
14 (p. 239) *gloom-bird*   the owl
15 (p. 239) *portion'd to*   proportionate to
16 (p. 239) *angerly*   angrily
17 (p. 240) *slope*   in a sloping motion —*PL* 4, 591
18 (p. 240) *tubes*   pipes
19 (p. 240) *cupola*   a domed chamber
20 (p. 241) *lucent*   shining
21 (p. 242) *sable*   black, from heraldry
22 (p. 242) *colure*   in ancient astronomy, a circle passing through the equatorial poles – see *PL* 9, 66
23 (p. 242) *nadir . . . zenith*   the low and high points of the celestial sphere
24 (p. 242) *Two wings*   In Egyptian mythology the sun is depicted as a winged disc.
25 (p. 242) *a primeval God*   a Titan, or the first race of gods
26 (p. 243) *first-born*   Saturn – see Glossary
27 (p. 244) *region-whisper*   whisper from the sky

Hyperion – Book II

1 (p. 244) *uncertain where*   from an unidentified source, a Miltonic construction
2 (p. 244) *Coeus . . . Porphyrion*   names of minor Titans
3 (p. 244) *Dungeon'd in opaque element*   buried under the sea
4 (p. 245) *sanguine feverous boiling gurge of pulse*   violent and fevered action of the blood
5 (p. 245) *chancel*   the eastern part of a church
6 (p. 245) *Creus . . . Iapetus . . . Cottus*   the names of minor Titans

7 (p. 245) *Asia* The origins of Asia are invented by Keats. Kaf was a giant mountain often identified with the Caucasus.

8 (p. 245) *Oxus* a central Asian river, now known as the Amu Dar'ya

9 (p. 246) *Themis* a minor Titan

10 (p. 247) *spirit-leaved book* an imaginary book which contains the history of the universe from its beginnings

11 (p. 248) *engine our great wrath* transform our anger into instruments of war

12 (p. 248) *astonied* astonished

13 (p. 248) *cogitation* thought

14 (p. 248) *atom-universe* a reference to Saturn's searching in the elements of the universe

15 (p. 249) *intestine broil* civil war – see *PL* 2, 1001–2

16 (p. 250) *the young God of the Seas* Neptune – see Glossary

17 (p. 250) *pos'd* pretended

18 (p. 251) *mouthed shell* a shell with an opening against which the mouth can be placed

19 (p. 252) *winged thing,/ Victory* The goddess Victory is always depicted with wings.

20 (p. 253) *Mantled* clothed

21 (p. 253) *Numidian curl* like the mane of an African lion

22 (p. 253) *Memnon's image . . . harp* The Ancient Egyptian statue of the prince Memnon was supposed to utter melodious sounds when struck by the sun.

Hyperion – Book III

1 (p. 254) *Dorian flute* a flute from a part of Ancient Greece; music noted for its solemnity – see *PL* 1, 550–1

2 (p. 255) *Giant of the Sun* Hyperion – see Glossary

3 (p. 255) *osiers* willows

4 (p. 255) *unfooted* without a crossing

5 (p. 255) *antique mien* ancient form

6 (p. 256) *liegeless* owing no service

7 (p. 256) *step aspirant* aspiring step, a Miltonic construction

8 (p. 257) *elixir peerless* an unequalled drug granting immortal life

9 (p. 257) *enkindled* bright

10 (p. 257) *convulse* convulsion

Fill for me a brimming bowl

1 (p. 262) *'the joy of grief'* a quotation from Campbell's *The Pleasures of Hope* (1799), l. 182

Sonnet on Peace

1 (p. 262) *O Peace* The war with France ended in April 1815.

Sonnet – To Chatterton

1 (p. 263) *amate*   destroy
2 (p. 263) *ingrate*   ungrateful, unfriendly

Sonnet – To Spenser

1 (p. 264) *A jealous honourer*   The poem was inspired by Keats's friend Reynolds.
2 (p. 264) *Elfin Poet*   Spenser, the poet of fairy land – see Glossary
3 (p. 264) *quell*   the power to destroy

Ode – To Apollo

1 (p. 264) *western halls of gold*   the place where the sun sets and the gathering place for dead poets
2 (p. 264) *erst*   first, formerly
3 (p. 264) *adamantine*   diamond
4 (p. 264) *Maro*   the Roman poet Virgil
5 (p. 265) *terrific*   terrifying
6 (p. 265) *virgin chorus . . . Chastity*   a reference to the theme of *FQ*
7 (p. 265) *the Nine*   the nine muses

Sonnet – On Receiving a Laurel Crown from Leigh Hunt

1 (p. 266) *Minutes are flying*   Keats and others took part in Leigh Hunt's timed sonnet-writing competitions; the winner would be crowned with laurels.
2 (p. 266) *gain*   prize

Hymn To Apollo

1 (p. 267) *Thunderer*   Jupiter – see Glossary

Sonnet – As from the darkening gloom

1 (p. 268) *thy soul*   The poem was written to mark the death of Keats's grandmother in December 1814.
2 (p. 268) *bedight*   equipped

Stanzas to Miss Wylie

1 (p. 269) *Georgiana*   The poem was probably originally written to Emma Mathew, the sister of one of Keats's friends, the title and name being changed so that the poem could be used by George.

Sonnet – Oh! How I love

1 (p. 269) *wild*   wilderness

Sonnet – Before he went to feed with owls and bats

1 (p. 270) *Nebuchadnezzar*   The story of the King of Babylon whose dreams were interpreted by Daniel is contained in the Book of Daniel in the Bible.
2 (p. 270) *hus'if's*   housewife's

3 (p. 270) *naumachia*   any mock sea battle

4 (p. 270) *loggerheads and Chapmen*   fools and money grubbers

5 (p. 270) *'Ye are that head of gold'*   Daniel interpreted Nebuchadnezzar's dream: he was the idol with the feet of clay and the head of gold; here, a reference to materialistic values.

Sonnet – Written at the end of 'The Floure and the Lefe'

1 (p. 271) Title: 'The Floure and the Lefe' was a poem once, but no longer, attributed to Chaucer. The poem which follows contains many Chaucerian echoes.

2 (p. 271) *those whose sobbings*   a reference to the story of the Babes in the Wood, familiar in the eighteenth century in popular ballads

Two Sonnets

1 (p. 272) *upfollow'd thunderings*   poetry worthy of the Elgin Marbles

2 (p. 272) *freak*   feat

3 (p. 272) *star in the east*   In his adoration of the Marbles, Haydon is compared to the Three Wise Men or Magi.

4 (p. 272) *Elgin Marbles*   the frieze which was removed from the Parthenon in Greece by Lord Elgin, and acquired by the British Museum. Keats visited the Marbles in 1817.

5 (p. 272) *shadow of a magnitude*   part of something too great to be understood

Sonnet – On a Picture of Leander

1 (p. 273) *against*   in anticipation of

Sonnet – On the Sea

1 (p. 275) *the spell/ Of Hecate*   the effect of the moon on the tides

2 (p. 275) *quir'd*   sang

On Oxford

1 (p. 276) *trencher*   mortar-board

2 (p. 276) *chantry*   choir

3 (p. 276) *dominat*   bad Latin for 'he rules'

Modern Love

1 (p. 277) *weighty pearl . . . melted*   Cleopatra is supposed to have dissolved a pearl which she drank in a toast to her lover Anthony. Both are in the poem as representative exotic lovers.

The Castle Builder

1 (p. 278) *Convent Garden*   Covent Garden was, in Keats's time, an area in London famous for its market and theatre.

2 (p. 278) *chairmen … Hackney coaches*   Theatregoers would arrive in sedan chairs and coaches.

3 (p. 278) *imperial host*   Napoleon's army retreated from Moscow in 1812.

4 (p. 278) *in the pink*   perfect

5 (p. 278) *Turkish floor*   covered in Turkish carpet

6 (p. 279) *winding-sheet*   shroud

7 (p. 279) *'Mene . . . Upharsin'*   from Daniel 5:25 – see *Before he went to feed with owls and bats*

8 (p. 279) *Siamesian*   Siamese

9 (p. 279) *cinque-coloured*   of five different colours

10 (p. 279) *Jason's fleece*   The Golden Fleece was brought back from Colchis by the Argonauts.

11 (p. 279) *Numidian*   African

A Song of Opposites

1 (p. 280) *'under . . . atoms'*   a misquotation from *PL* 2, 898–903

Sonnet to a Cat

1 (p. 281) *grand climacteric*   old age

2 (p. 281) *the lists*   A soldier entered the lists when he joined-up. Here the cat is imagined as a kind of aged military hero.

Lines on Seeing a Lock of Milton's Hair

1 (p. 281) *organic*   organ-like

2 (p. 282) *Delian*   poetic, from Delos – see Glossary

Sonnet – On Sitting Down to Read King Lear Once Again

1 (p. 283) *impassion'd clay*   mankind. In *Genesis,* Adam was formed by God breathing life into a clay form.

2 (p. 283) *assay*   test

3 (p. 283) *Phoenix wings*   In myth, the Phoenix is a bird which is reborn in fire. Keats imagines his poetic development as one of rebirth through the reading of *King Lear*.

Sonnet – When I have fears

1 (p. 283) *charactery*   handwriting

2 (p. 283) *garners*   grain stores

A Draught of Sunshine

1 (p. 285) *rummer*   a large drinking glass

2 (p. 285) *Caius*   the pen name of Keats's friend Reynolds

Sonnet to the Nile

1 (p. 286) *moon-mountains*   The mountains from which the Nile rises are sometimes known as the Mountains of the Moon.

2 (p. 286) *Decan*   Deccan is a region of southern India.

Sonnet – To John Hamilton Reynolds

1 (p. 287) *Reynolds*   The poem is more correctly addressed to another of Keats's friends, James Rice.
2 (p. 287) *Levant*   the East

Sonnet – The Human Seasons

1 (p. 288) *threshold brook*   a river that passes by a cottage door
2 (p. 288) *misfeature*   haggardness

Extracts from an Opera

1 (p. 290) *abroach*   in a condition to let its contents out
2 (p. 290) *crumpt*   bent up

Faery Songs

1 (p. 292) *favonian*   gentle

Song – Written on a blank page

1 (p. 294) *Comus*   see the feast in Milton's *Comus*, lines 102–4

Teignmouth

1 (p. 294) *Bishop's teign . . . King's teign . . . Coomb*   settlements around the Teign estuary. Other names in the poem are places that Keats could have visited during his stay in Devon in 1818.
2 (p. 295) *plight*   attire
3 (p. 295) *spike*   ear of corn
4 (p. 295) *dack'd*   short
5 (p. 295) *Prickets*   deer

The Devon Maid

1 (p. 296) *junkets*   milk puddings

Epistle to John Hamilton Reynolds

1 (p. 297) *Voltaire*   pen name of French philosopher and writer François Marie Arouet (1694–1778), whose works are representative of the Age of Enlightenment
2 (p. 297) *casque . . . habergeon*   types of armour
3 (p. 297) *Miss Edgeworth*   Maria Edgeworth (1768–1849), a novelist enjoyed by Keats
4 (p. 297) *Junius Brutus . . . so so*   The imagination conjures the unlikely picture of the founder of the Roman Republic, renowned for his sobriety, drunk in Soho. It might also be a reference to the contemporary actor Junius Brutus Booth.
5 (p. 297) *tushes*   tusks
6 (p. 297) *Urganda's Sword*   The enchantress in the fifteenth-century romance *Amadis of Gaul* gave the hero a lance, not a sword.
7 (p. 298) *Santon of Chaldee*   a Muslim holy man

8 (p. 298) *Cuthbert de Saint Aldebrim*   an invented name
9 (p. 298) *Lapland witch*   such witches were associated with Black magic –
   see *PL* 2, 664–5
10 (p. 298) *lightening moment whiles*   intermittently reflecting light as they
   are lifted from the water
11 (p. 299) *my flag is not unfurl'd*   I lack sufficient experience
12 (p. 299) *lampit*   limpet
13 (p. 299) *Ounce*   lynx
14 (p. 299) *Kamschatkan*   Kamschatka was a bleak area in eastern Russia,
   whose inhabitants were late converts to Christianity.

Acrostic

1 (p. 301) *Anthropophagi*   cannibals – see *Othello* 1, 3, 143–4
2 (p. 301) *enchanted belt*   Ulysses possessed a magic veil which prevented
   him from drowning.
3 (p. 301) *felt/ Unbosom'd so*   Keats's verse is expressed with more feeling
   than that of Homer and Shakespeare.

Meg Merrilies

1 (p. 302) *Meg*   Meg Merrilies is a character in Walter Scott's novel *Guy
   Mannering* (1814).
2 (p. 303) *Margaret Queen*   perhaps Margaret, wife of James IV of Scotland
3 (p. 303) *chip hat*   a hat made from thin strips of wood

A Song about Myself

1 (p. 305) *postes*   posts or, possibly, masses of rock
2 (p. 306) *Miller's thumb*   a small freshwater fish

A Galloway Song

1 (p. 307) *oure*   over. The poem is written in a mixture of Scots, in
   imitation of Burns, and archaic English.
2 (p. 307) *yeve*   give
3 (p. 307) *Ane*   one
4 (p. 308) *Braw*   brave
5 (p. 308) *daffed*   daunted

Sonnet – To Ailsa Rock

1 (p. 308) *Ailsa Rock*   Ailsa Craig is a small rocky island at the mouth of the
   Firth of Clyde.

Sonnet – Written in the Cottage where Burns was Born

1 (p. 309) *budded bays*   poetic fame
2 (p. 309) *barley-bree*   ale

The Gadfly

1 (p. 311) *a Lawyer suit/ Of Seventeen-Forty-Three* Before reform, many legal cases could drag on for years.

2 (p. 311) *Lowther* William Lowther, Earl of Lonsdale (1787–1872), became Tory MP for Westmorland in 1818. Wordsworth's support for him, against the Liberal candidate, particularly affected Keats.

3 (p. 312) . . . Here Keats wrote 'upon thine a[rs]e'

4 (p. 312) *Mr D— . . . Mr V—* probably Robert Dundas and Nicholas Vansittart, Tory politicians of the day

5 (p. 312) *Mister Lovels* Lovel was the hero of Walter Scott's *The Antiquary* (1816).

6 (p. 312) *as King David pray'd* see Psalms 119:164

7 (p. 313) *summum bonum* the greatest

8 (p. 313) *'withouten wordes mo'* without another word, a Chaucerian tag

Sonnet – On Hearing the Bag-Pipe and Seeing 'The Stranger' Played at Inverary

1 (p. 313) *ninth sphere* The ninth was the most distant of the spheres.

2 (p. 313) *The Stranger* a play by the German dramatist Kotzebue, first performed in Britain in 1798

3 (p. 313) *Mum chance* dumb, or tongue-tied

Staffa

1 (p. 314) *Staffa* an islet in the West of Scotland

2 (p. 314) *wizard of the Dee* Merlin

3 (p. 314) *St John* St John the Divine is said to have experienced the visions which form *Revelations* on Patmos.

4 (p. 315) *Sacristan* an assisting priest in charge of ceremonial equipment

Ben Nevis – a Dialogue

1 (p. 316) *Mrs Cameron* Keats relates the story of Mrs Cameron's climb of Ben Nevis; she was reputed to be 'the fattest women in all [I]nvernesshire' (*Letters* 1: 354).

2 (p. 316) *bate* rest

3 (p. 316) *caudle* gruel

4 (p. 316) *Red-Crag* an imagined servant of the mountain

5 (p. 317) *gust* both taste and blast

6 (p. 317) *Block-head* another servant

Translation from a Sonnet of Ronsard

1 (p. 318) *Ronsard* sixteenth-century French poet

A Prophecy – To George Keats in America

1 (p. 318) *witching hour* midnight

2 (p. 319) *silly* simple

Stanzas – In a drear-nighted December

1 (p. 320) *frozen thawings* ice which has melted and refrozen
2 (p. 320) *petting* complaining

Spenserian Stanza

1 (p. 321) *Yclep'd* called, a Spenserianism
2 (p. 321) *Typographus* the power of the printed word
3 (p. 321) *the Giant* In *FQ* the Giant is defeated by Artegall (Justice) and his squire Talus.

The Eve of St Mark

1 (p. 321) *The Eve of St Mark* A popular superstition held that the ghosts of those who were to die in the following year could be seen on St Mark's Eve, if a vigil had been kept for three years. The feast of St Mark is 25 April.
2 (p. 322) *broideries* embroidery
3 (p. 322) *breastplate* priestly vestment
4 (p. 322) *seven/ Candlesticks* see Revelation 1:20
5 (p. 322) *winged Lion* the traditional symbol of St Mark
6 (p. 322) *golden mice* Five golden mice were sent by the Philistines as a peace offering when they returned the Ark of the Covenant to the Israelites.
7 (p. 323) *daws* jackdaws
8 (p. 323) *Avadavat* an Indian song-bird
9 (p. 323) *queen of spades* the card traditionally associated with death
10 (p. 323) *golden star, or dagger bright* marks on the page to indicate footnotes
11 (p. 323) *crow-quill* used for fine or small writing
12 (p. 323) *swevenis* dreams. Bertha's reading is presented in a language which owes something to Chaucer and to Keats's interest in the fake medieval poems of Chatterton.
13 (p. 324) *Somdel* something
14 (p. 324) *Sainte Cicilie* St Cecilia
15 (p. 324) *auctorethe* writes
16 (p. 324) *holy shrine* St Mark's, Venice

Ode to Fanny

1 (p. 325) *let . . . blood* Bloodletting was a common procedure for any number of medical conditions.
2 (p. 325) *Tripod* A three-legged vessel was used in the shrine to Apollo at Delphi.
3 (p. 325) *out* Some versions of the poem have the word 'not' here instead.
4 (p. 326) *blow-ball* the seed head of the dandelion

Ode on Indolence

1 (p. 328) *'They toil not, neither do they spin'* from Matthew 6:28

2 (p. 328) *Phidian lore*   Phidias was the sculptor of the Elgin Marbles, fourth century BC.

3 (p. 329) *demon*   here in the sense of an attendant spirit

4 (p. 330) *throstle's lay*   thrush's song

Sonnet – Why did I laugh

1 (p. 330) *ensigns*   banners

Sonnet – A Dream, After reading Dante's Episode of Paulo and Francesca

1 (p. 331) *Paulo and Francessca*   see Dante's *Inferno* 5

2 (p. 331) *Delphic reed . . . dragon-world*   Keats means that poetry took his mind off the harshness of the world.

3 (p. 331) *Ida*   a mountain near Troy

4 (p. 331) *Jove griev'd*   for the loss of Io – see Glossary

5 (p. 331) *second circle*   Dante's Hell was divided into circles or regions. Here, Keats conflates details from the second and third circles.

An Extempore

1 (p. 331) *Persian feathers*   a turban-like headdress decorated with feathers, fashionable in Regency England

2 (p. 331) *Ape . . . Dwarf . . . Fool*   Various critical attempts to provide identities for the figures here remain largely unconvincing.

3 (p. 331) *Otaheitan*   Tahitian

4 (p. 332) *quaver'd*   shook

5 (p. 333) *cup biddy*   probably a corruption of 'Come up Biddy', an instruction to the rain to stop

6 (p. 333) ' *Aye every inch a King*' . . . '*Fortune's fool*'   from Shakespeare's *King Lear* 4, 6, 108 and *Romeo and Juliet* 3, 1, 135

7 (p. 334) *filch*   steal

8 (p. 334) *trammels*   encumbrances

Spenserian Stanzas on Charles Armitage Brown

1 (p. 334) *Charles Armitage Brown*   a friend of Keats's in whose house he lodged

2 (p. 334) *weet*   know

3 (p. 334) *carle*   churl

4 (p. 334) *half-and-half*   a mixture of light and dark ale

5 (p. 334) *'sdeigned*   disdained

6 (p. 334) *wassail-bowl*   punch bowl

7 (p. 334) *Lemans*   lovers – see *FQ* 6, 8, 21

8 (p. 334) *Tom or ruin blue*   names for gin

Two or Three

1 (p. 335) *simples*   medicinal herbs
2 (p. 335) *Mrs* —   The missing word here is 'Abbeys', the wife of Keats's guardian.

La Belle Dame Sans Merci

1 (p. 336) *La Belle Dame sans Merci*   The title of the poem is borrowed from Alain Chartier's poem of the same name (1424). It means the beautiful lady without mercy.
2 (p. 337) *thrall*   a state of submission or enslavement – see *FQ* 2, 1, 54
3 (p. 337) *gloam*   twilight

Song of Four Faeries

1 (p. 338) *Salamander . . . Breama*   The salamander was a mythical creature associated with fire. The other fairies also each represent one of the elements – earth, air, fire and water; Dusketha (dusk) and Breama (bream, a freshwater fish) are names invented by Keats to represent two of the elements.
2 (p. 338) *live tapestries*   the shapes formed by the flames
3 (p. 339) *our Queen*   Titania
4 (p. 339) *unlucent*   dull
5 (p. 339) *aguish*   damp, chilly
6 (p. 339) *Adder-eyed*   dark eyed
7 (p. 340) *wist*   silent

Two Sonnets on Fame

1 (p. 331) *Nilus-born*   born around the Nile. Gypsies were believed to have originated in Egypt.
2 (p. 331) *Potiphar*   Potiphar was jealous of Joseph's interest in his wife – see Genesis 39.
3 (p. 331) *a fierce miscreed*   the worship of fame

Sonnet on the Sonnet

1 (p. 342) *bay wreath crown*   In the ancient world poets were rewarded with 'laurels' which were crowns often made with bay leaves.

Apollo and the Graces

1 (p. 342) *'Don Giovanni'*   The Don Giovanni or Don Juan story formed the subject of a pantomime performed at Drury Lane in 1817–18, which Keats reviewed.

You Say You Love

1 (p. 343) *weeks of Ember*   periods of fasting and abstinence

Otho the Great

1 (p. 344) *Otho the Great* Otho the Great (912–73) was King of Germany and later Holy Roman Emperor. The play, which Keats worked on with his friend Charles Brown, was an unsuccessful attempt to break into commercial theatre, capitalising on the current interest in German tragedy.

2 (p. 345) *petards* weapons used for launching missiles at fortifications

3 (p. 346) *To admiration* very well

4 (p. 346) *rifled* robbed

5 (p. 347) *baldric* a sword-carrying shoulder belt

6 (p. 347) *lackeying . . . beck* submissively following my advice

7 (p. 348) *amity* friendship

8 (p. 349) *(solus)* alone

9 (p. 351) *friendly Arab* Ludolph's Arab disguise has been seen through by Otho.

10 (p. 351) *lees* dregs

11 (p. 351) *rhomb* a diamond-shaped formation

12 (p. 351) *Saladin* Saladin (1138–93) was the Muslim leader who recaptured Jerusalem from the Christians.

13 (p. 354) *board* table

14 (p. 355) *basement* foundation

15 (p. 356) *Mussulman* Muslim

16 (p. 356) *warder* watchman

17 (p. 356) *Saracenic* Arab-like

18 (p. 356) *scymitar* A scimitar is a curved sword, commonly used by Arabs and Turks.

19 (p. 357) *cancel* repayment of debt

20 (p. 357) *Tartar* a member of Turkic-speaking groups of northern Russia and parts of Asia, held to be very aggressive

21 (p. 358) *housings* trappings

22 (p. 358) *thwart spleen* obstructing anger

23 (p. 359) *troublous* both troubled and causing trouble

24 (p. 362) *fever'd you* given you a fever

25 (p. 363) *By Peter's chair* by Papal authority. St Peter was the first Pope.

26 (p. 363) *mitigated into milk* turned into milk, indicating cowardice

27 (p. 365) *Nimrod's . . . clouds* refers to the building of the Tower of Babel – see Genesis 10 and 11

28 (p. 365) *in their cups* in a drunken state

29 (p. 367) *her Son* Eros – see Glossary

30 (p. 367) *Saint Maurice* an early Christian martyr celebrated in Germany, also known as St Moritz

31 (p. 368) *wen* wart

32 (p. 368) *corslet . . . helm* body armour and helmet

33 (p. 368) *vestal* virgin

34 (p. 369) *fledgy* feathery

35 (p. 369) *contumelies*   acts of rudeness
36 (p. 370) *husbandmen*   farmers
37 (p. 371) *Cain*   Cain and Abel were sons of Adam and Eve. Cain killed
    Abel from jealousy and attempted to hide from God.
38 (p. 371) *fast-limed . . . snare*   caught in a trap
39 (p. 371) *limbs of a wanton*   prison for an immoral person
40 (p. 371) *Henry the Fowler*   Henry I, Otho's father
41 (p. 371) *menial of Mars*   a soldier
42 (p. 372) *serge hangings*   coverings on the tavern walls
43 (p. 372) *the mitre*   a bishop's hat, but here meaning the bishop himself
44 (p. 373) *in fee*   given to you
45 (p. 373) *love philtres*   love potions
46 (p. 373) *Hyperborean*   of the far north
47 (p. 374) *sware*   swore
48 (p. 374) *lists*   a jousting area
49 (p. 374) *tourney*   (jousting) tournament
50 (p. 374) *senet*   sennet, the sound of a trumpet
51 (p. 375) *faggot*   a bundle of sticks used to start a fire
52 (p. 376) *yerk*   jolt, surprise
53 (p. 376) *zealous-pained*   very sensitive to pain
54 (p. 376) *devil's beads*   the monk's rosary
55 (p. 377) *chain up myself*   restrain myself, keep quiet
56 (p. 377) *matins*   morning prayer
57 (p. 378) *an attaint*   a sentence of guilt
58 (p. 379) *yeasting youth . . . crystal turn again*   The projected maturing
    process in Ludolph is compared here to the fermenting of beer until it
    reaches maturity.
59 (p. 379) *noon-day proof*   clear proof
60 (p. 379) *dolt*   fool
61 (p. 381) *court-Janus*   Janus was the Roman two-headed god of the old and
    new year. Here, Albert is being accused of being two-faced.
62 (p. 381) *minion*   obsequious follower (of Conrad)
63 (p. 384) *minute whiles*   this minute past
64 (p. 384) *cur*   dog
65 (p. 384) *sexton*   church official responsible for digging graves
66 (p. 385) *(sola)*   alone
67 (p. 385) *Hesperian tree*   see Hesperides in the Glossary
68 (p. 385) *weeds*   clothes
69 (p. 386) *stickle*   hesitate
70 (p. 387) *blazoning*   making public
71 (p. 388) *Good even*   good-evening
72 (p. 388) *Perforce*   due to the force of circumstances
73 (p. 389) *plaints*   expression of sorrow
74 (p. 390) *embassage*   message

75 (p. 390) *rubious* red

76 (p. 391) *rheumed* Rheum is the watery discharge from the eyes or nose often associated with the infirmities of age.

77 (p. 391) *battailous* ready for battle, a Spenserianism – see *FQ* 5, 12, 12

78 (p. 392) *wittol* a man who tolerates his wife's infidelities

79 (p. 395) *paramour* a lover, usually an adulterous one

80 (p. 396) *Cockatrice* a mythical snake with a stare which would kill

81 (p. 399) *gainsaid* disagreed with

82 (p. 399) *knell* a bell tolled at a funeral

83 (p. 400) *ghast* ghastly

84 (p. 401) *with me* in my opinion

85 (p. 402) *tilt* attack

86 (p. 403) *Margravines* the wife of a German nobleman roughly equivalent to a marquis

87 (p. 403) *bird-lim'd* Bird-lime was a sticky substance usually applied to branches of trees in order to catch small birds.

88 (p. 404) *Iberian juice* wine from Spain and Portugal

89 (p. 404) *pale Calabrian* wine from Southern Italy

90 (p. 404) *Aetna* Etna is an active volcano on Sicily.

91 (p. 405) *immolate* to offer up as a sacrifice

92 (p. 405) *steeled squares, and speared files* fighting formations in armour and armed with spears

King Stephen

1 (p. 407) *King Stephen* Stephen was King of England 1135–54. He gained the throne by usurpation, and his reign was marked by civil unrest. The poem deals with his defeat at Lincoln in 1141.

2 (p. 407) *plashy meads* marshy fields

3 (p. 407) *Glocester* Robert Earl of Gloucester defeated Stephen at Lincoln.

4 (p. 407) *Ply well the rowel* use your spurs

5 (p. 407) *flaunt* flaunted

6 (p. 407) *De Redvers . . . Baldwin* Baldwin de Redvers was an enemy of Stephen's. He is probably confused with Baldwin Fitz-Gilbert who fought on Stephen's side.

7 (p. 407) *Chester* Ranulf, Earl of Chester, fought with Gloucester against Stephen.

8 (p. 408) *Empress* Maud or Matilda (1102–69), who was married to Henry V, Emperor of Germany, fought Stephen for the English Crown.

9 (p. 409) *Duke of Bretagnes* Alan, Earl of Brittany, was a supporter of Stephen's.

10 (p. 409) *Welsh beagles* Gloucester's forces included Welsh troops.

11 (p. 409) *Pallas . . . Ilion* The goddess of wisdom aided the Greeks in the defeat of Troy.

12 (p. 409) *falchions* short broad swords

13 (p. 409) *morion*   a visorless helmet

14 (p. 410) *labourer Cain*   Cain killed Abel while they worked in the fields – see Genesis 4:8.

15 (p. 410) *truck*   exchange

16 (p. 410) *Pylos . . . Nestor's beard*   King Nestor survived the Trojan War and ruled in Pylos to old age.

17 (p. 410) *De Kaims*   William de Kahaines captured Stephen at Lincoln.

18 (p. 411) *presence-chamber*   the room in which a superior person, usually a monarch, receives an audience

19 (p. 411) *compass*   accomplish

20 (p. 412) *Boulogne*   one of Stephen's titles

21 (p. 412) *trenching*   encroaching

22 (p. 413) *To play the Alexander with Darius*   Alexander the Great was generous to his prisoners after defeating King Darius at Issus in 333 BC.

23 (p. 413) *late sovereign lord, your noble sire*   King Henry I secured the succession of his daughter, Maud, in 1127. On his death in 1135, his nephew, Stephen, seized the Crown.

A Party of Lovers

1 (p. 417) *a humane society*   The Royal Humane Society was founded in 1774 to aid those at risk of drowning.

2 (p. 417) *Mr Werter*   the sensitive Romantic hero of Goethe's novel *The Sorrows of Werther* (1773)

3 (p. 417) *cauliflower*   an untrimmed wick

4 (p. 417) *A winding sheet*   Wax collected on the side of a candle was said to resemble the sheet in which a body is wrapped, and so to be an omen of death.

5 (p. 417) *the circus gay*   Piccadilly Circus in London

6 (p. 417) *Wapping*   an area of East London

Sonnet – The day is gone

1 (p. 418) *woof*   some of the threads of a woven fabric

Lines to Fanny

1 (p. 418) *particolour'd*   here in the sense of being of varying quality

2 (p. 418) *throes*   is convulsed

3 (p. 419) *canon law*   the established rules of the Church

4 (p. 419) *most hateful land*   Keats is thinking here of the misfortunes and hardships his brother George experienced when first settling in America.

The Fall of Hyperion – Canto I

1 (p. 421) *Mother Eve*   The landscape and the details here owe much to Keats's reading of *PL* – see *PL* 5, 303–7, 326–8, 341–4, 377–9.

2 (p. 422) *fabled horn*   the mythical cornucopia or horn of plenty which is full of fruit and flowers or, in some myths, whatever its owner desires

3 (p. 422) *jealous Caliphat* In *The Arabian Nights* the Caliph's wife, Zobeide, attempts to poison Fetnah.

4 (p. 422) *the scarlet conclave* the College of Cardinals which elects a new Pope

5 (p. 422) *superannuations* obsolete remains

6 (p. 422) *faulture* weakness

7 (p. 423) *asbestos* any fire-proof material

8 (p. 423) *chafing-dish* a metal dish over a heater, used to keep food warm

9 (p. 423) *Maian incense* like the perfume of spring flowers – see Maia in the Glossary

10 (p. 424) *gummed leaves* the leaves of aromatic trees used in sacrificial ceremonies

11 (p. 424) *those streams that pulse beside the throat* arteries carrying blood to the neck

12 (p. 424) *angels . . . flew* a reference to Jacob's Ladder – see Genesis 28:12. Keats's idea of a climb, here, is influenced by the ascent of the Mount of Purgatory in Dante's *Purgatorio* 9.

13 (p. 424) *dated on* postponed

14 (p. 425) *suffer'd in* allowed to enter

15 (p. 425) *humanist* humanitarian

16 (p. 426) *antipodes* opposites

17 (p. 426) *Pythia's spleen* Pythia was Apollo's prophetess and mouthpiece, who often delivered prophecies in a heightened emotional state.

18 (p. 426) *misty pestilence* Apollo was held to be responsible for contagious diseases.

19 (p. 426) *a war* the war of the Titans against the Olympians which also forms the subject of *Hyperion*

20 (p. 427) *electral* electrical

21 (p. 428) *sullen* gloomy

22 (p. 428) *environed* contained

23 (p. 428) *the golden age* The reign of Saturn was held to be a time of peace and prosperity.

24 (p. 428) *Omega* the last (surviving member), from the last letter of the Greek alphabet

25 (p. 428) *Deep . . .* The first version of the poem, *Hyperion*, opens at this point.

26 (p. 428) *ken* knowledge, understanding

27 (p. 428) *pervade* perceive

28 (p. 428) *zoning* duration

29 (p. 429) *statuary* stature

30 (p. 430) *captious at* objecting to

31 (p. 430) *Rumbles reluctant* see *Hyperion*, Book I, note 2

32 (p. 430) *stay or prop* help or support

33 (p. 431) *pernicious Babes* the rebellious Olympians

34 (p. 432) *imps*   children, offspring
35 (p. 432) *erewhile*   previously
36 (p. 432) *grow pale from the waves*   rise like a ghost from the waves

The Fall of Hyperion – Canto II

1 (p. 433) *gloom-bird's*   see *Hyperion*, Book I, note 14
2 (p. 433) *portioned to*   see *Hyperion*, Book I, note 15

The Cap and Bells

1 (p. 435) *Hydaspes*   Indian streams – see *PL* 3, 436
2 (p. 435) *Elfinan*   a Spenserian fairy – see *FQ* 2,10,72. His character is also a satirical portrait of the Prince Regent, later George IV.
3 (p. 435) *Zendervester*   holy law, from Zenda-Avesta, the sacred writings of Zoroastrianism
4 (p. 435) *tart*   sharp
5 (p. 435) *espouse*   marry. The Prince Regent's arranged marriage to Caroline of Brunswick took place in April 1795.
6 (p. 436) *Imaus*   a mountain in Scythia
7 (p. 436) *Bellanaine*   an invented compound word, probably meaning beautiful dwarf; a reference to Caroline of Brunswick, though other figures have been suggested
8 (p. 436) *sapphir'd*   painted blue to look like the sky
9 (p. 436) *promener à l'aile*   to stretch her wings. The use of French here suggests affectation.
10 (p. 436) *somerset*   somersault
11 (p. 436) *Corallina*   The nurse's name comes from the coral traditionally given to teething infants.
12 (p. 436) *Crafticant*   a compound invention, crafty cant. Cant is hypocritical or empty language.
13 (p. 437) *beauteous mortal*   Bellanaine, like Elfinan, is in love with a mortal.
14 (p. 437) *lowland blood*   Bellanaine is from a mountainous region.
15 (p. 437) *Scarab Street . . . Head*   a fanciful name patterned on the publisher's name as it appeared in books. Books of scandalous memoirs were popular in the eighteenth century. Jubal, the father of music – see Genesis 4:21.
16 (p. 438) *tittle-tattle*   Most of the evidence for the divorce proceedings in 1820 was provided by servants of the Prince.
17 (p. 439) *damn'd his House of Commons*   The Prince Regent's relations with the government worsened partly as a result of his attempts to secure a divorce.
18 (p. 439) *chancellor*   Nicholas Vansittart, the Chancellor of the Exchequer (1812–22), was known for his support of Christian missionary societies.
19 (p. 439) *Palfior . . . Phalaric*   probably invented names

20 (p. 439) *upon tick* on credit

21 (p. 440) *garter* The Order of the Garter

22 (p. 440) *zany* fool

23 (p. 440) *Biancopany* a playful Italianised form of the name Whitbread, referring to Samuel Whitbread, a radical MP and supporter of Princess Caroline

24 (p. 440) *Eban* named to echo ebony

25 (p. 441) *Hum the soothsayer* A soothsayer is a fortune-teller; 'hum' was a common abbreviation for humbug or nonsense.

26 (p. 441) *bowstrung* strangled with a bowstring. Here and elsewhere Elfinian's behaviour resembles that of an Eastern despot in many of the oriental tales popular at the time, rather than that of the Prince Regent.

27 (p. 441) *neck'd* decapitated

28 (p. 441) *The gas* Gas lighting was first introduced in London around 1807.

29 (p. 442) *smelling-bottle* a bottle containing smelling salts or perfume as an antidote to bad smells

30 (p. 442) *Hurdy-gurdies* barrel organs

31 (p. 442) *the gallies* In some cultures it was the custom to sentence criminals to row on galleys, warships propelled by rows of oars.

32 (p. 442) *the string* the means by which a passenger told a coach driver to stop

33 (p. 442) *Jarvey* the popular term for the driver of a hackney carriage, here used to refer to both driver and carriage

34 (p. 442) *linsey-woolsey* a mixture of flax and wool

35 (p. 442) *litter* both a form of transport and rubbish

36 (p. 442) *all corn* horse food, more usually oats

37 (p. 442) *fiddle-faddle* a fuss or waste of time

38 (p. 442) *lazar-house* house for the poor or sick

39 (p. 442) *dowdies* poorly or badly dressed women

40 (p. 443) *Tilburies . . . Phaetons . . . Curricles* types of light fast coaches

41 (p. 444) *rout* party

42 (p. 444) *wis* believe

43 (p. 444) *cast a . . . figure* cast a horoscope

44 (p. 444) *aqua vitae* originally alcohol used in alchemy

45 (p. 444) *dentes sapientiae* wisdom teeth

46 (p. 444) *barber* At this time barbers commonly performed minor surgery, including the removal of teeth.

47 (p. 444) *nitre* a chemical used in the making of gunpowder

48 (p. 444) *grains of Paradise* the seeds of an aromatic plant used in medicine and as a spice

49 (p. 444) *doucer* sweetener, bribe

50 (p. 444) *a peg* an inch

51 (p. 444) *one shoe . . . my man John*   echoing the nursery rhyme 'Diddle, diddle, dumpling, my son John'

52 (p. 445) *Salpietro*   saltpetre, the main ingredient of gunpowder

53 (p. 445) *give you the rattan*   beat you with a stick

54 (p. 445) *Man-Tiger-Organ*   A mechanical Tiger, which would maul a model of an English soldier, was made for Tipu Sultan, an Indian leader defeated by the British in 1799. Parts of Elfinan's character may be derived from him.

55 (p. 446) *treen*   trees

56 (p. 447) *changeling*   a fairy child exchanged for a human one

57 (p. 447) *palanquin*   a one-person carriage or litter suspended on poles and carried by two people

58 (p. 447) *bam*   hoax

59 (p. 447) *son of Cham*   Cham, or Shem, Noah's youngest son, is said to have been the inventor of magic.

60 (p. 448) *Admiral de Witt*   John de Witt (1625–72) led the Dutch fleet against the English in 1667.

61 (p. 448) *Ottoman*   a cushioned seat

62 (p. 448) *lady's-fingers*   small cakes

63 (p. 448) *Candy wine*   sweet wine

64 (p. 449) *a sampler*   a piece of embroidery demonstrating the skill of its producer

65 (p. 449) *fay*   faith

66 (p. 450) *foolish matter mince*   be concerned with trivial things

67 (p. 450) *repeater*   a watch or a clock which marks the time by chiming out the hours and sometimes divisions of hours

68 (p. 450) *Almanack – Moore*   An almanac is an annual publication listing a range of information relating to dates, the weather, etc.; *Old Moore's Almanac* was first published in 1699.

69 (p. 451) *St Mark's Eve*   see note 1 to *Eve of St Mark*. Here, the superstition is altered slightly.

70 (p. 452) *extreme unction*   the Roman Catholic sacrament administered to the mortally ill

71 (p. 452) *cold pig*   to revive or awaken with cold water. The last rites involve the use of Holy Water.

72 (p. 452) *Zooks*   an abbreviation of gadzooks, a mild oath

73 (p. 452) *monster's*   monster meaning mob. The behaviour of the crowd and the following description of the city were probably inspired by the peace celebrations in London in 1815 to mark the end of the Napoleonic Wars, of which Keats was critical.

74 (p. 452) *pigsny*   a nonsense term of endearment

75 (p. 453) *snuff'd his mignonette*   sniffed his fragrant flower

76 (p. 453) *'scutcheon*   The mock coat of arms here is a mouse on a silver background.

77 (p. 453) *Gentlemen pensioners* gentlemen-at-arms, the monarch's personal military attendants at state occasions

78 (p. 453) *Janizaries* guards of the Turkish Sultan

79 (p. 454) *Angle-land* England

80 (p. 454) *Hocus* Hocus-pocus was used as a term for a magician in the eighteenth century.

81 (p. 454) *an invisible ring* a ring which makes its wearer invisible, a common element in fairy tales

82 (p. 454) *'Farewell . . . well'* a quotation from Byron's poem to his wife after their separation

83 (p. 454) *smoke me* find me out

84 (p. 454) *scrutoire* escritoire, writing desk

85 (p. 455) *glutted as a leech* drunk

86 (p. 455) *Boswell's* James Boswell (1740–95) wrote *The Life of Samuel Johnson*.

87 (p. 456) *Gobi* a dessert in Central Asia

88 (p. 456) *her hoop* her hooped skirt

89 (p. 456) *Balk* Baulkh, an important ancient Persian city

90 (p. 456) *Griffin* a mythical creature with the head and wings of an eagle and the body of a lion

91 (p. 456) *on their marrow-bones* on their knees

92 (p. 457) *Cinq-parted* in groups of five

93 (p. 457) *kettledrum* kettle drummer

94 (p. 457) *maugre* in spite of

95 (p. 458) *emulously* in a spirit of rivalry

96 (p. 458) *A plenty horn* see *The Fall of Hyperion* – Canto I, note 2

97 (p. 458) *Ionic* a type of classical Greek architecture

98 (p. 458) *Basilic* Basilica, originally a royal palace, then a building used for public assembly

99 (p. 459) *Congées and scape-graces* bowings and scrapings

100 (p. 459) *scullions* (menial) servants

101 (p. 459) *Powder'd bag-wigs and ruffy-tuffy heads* the well-to-do and the common. Bag wigs, with a bag in which the back hair was kept, were common in the eighteenth century among the wealthy. Ruffy-tuffy heads were those with unkempt hair.

102 (p. 459) *Prothalamion* a song in celebration of a marriage

Sonnet – Written on a Blank Page in Shakespeare's Poems

1 (p. 461) *pure ablution* a religious cleansing

Index of First Lines

Index of Poem Titles